EVERY LOVE STORY

IS A GHOST STORY

ALSO BY D. T. MAX

The Family That Couldn't Sleep: A Medical Mystery

EVERY LOVE STORY
IS A GHOST STORY

A LIFE OF DAVID FOSTER WALLACE

D. T. Max

VIKING

VIKING
Published by the Penguin Group
Penguin Group (USA) Inc., 375 Hudson Street,
New York, New York 10014, U.S.A.
Penguin Group (Canada), 90 Eglinton Avenue East, Suite 700,
Toronto, Ontario, Canada M4P 2Y3
(a division of Pearson Penguin Canada Inc.)
Penguin Books Ltd, 80 Strand, London WC2R 0RL, England
Penguin Ireland, 25 St. Stephen's Green, Dublin 2, Ireland
(a division of Penguin Books Ltd)
Penguin Books Australia Ltd, 250 Camberwell Road, Camberwell,
Victoria 3124, Australia
(a division of Pearson Australia Group Pty Ltd)
Penguin Books India Pvt Ltd, 11 Community Centre, Panchsheel Park,
New Delhi – 110 017, India
Penguin Group (NZ), 67 Apollo Drive, Rosedale, Auckland 0632,
New Zealand (a division of Pearson New Zealand Ltd)
Penguin Books (South Africa) (Pty) Ltd, 24 Sturdee Avenue,
Rosebank, Johannesburg 2196, South Africa

Penguin Books Ltd, Registered Offices:
80 Strand, London WC2R 0RL, England

First published in 2012 by Viking Penguin,
a member of Penguin Group (USA) Inc.

10   9   8   7   6   5   4   3   2   1

A portion of this book appeared in different form as "The Unfinished: David Foster Wallace's Struggle to Surpass *Infinite Jest*" in *The New Yorker*.

Grateful acknowledgment is made for permission to reprint excerpts from the unpublished writings of David Foster Wallace. Copyright © 2012 The David Foster Wallace Literary Trust. Used by permission of The David Foster Wallace Literary Trust.

Max, D. T. (Daniel T.)
    Every love story is a ghost story : a life of David Foster Wallace / D.T. Max.
       p. cm.
    Includes index.
    ISBN 978-0-670-02592-3 (hardback)
    1. Wallace, David Foster. 2. Novelists, American—20th century—Biography. I. Title.
    PS3573.A425635Z83 2012
    813'.54—dc23   [B]   2012008488

Printed in the United States of America
Set in Warnock Pro
Designed by Alissa Amell

For Flora and for Jules forever

What goes on inside is just too fast and huge and all interconnected for words to do more than barely sketch the outlines of at most one tiny little part of it at any given instant. —GOOD OLD NEON, 2001

CONTENTS

EVERY LOVE STORY

IS A GHOST STORY

CHAPTER 1

"Call Me Dave"

Every story has a beginning and this is David Wallace's. He was born in Ithaca, New York, on February 21, 1962. His father, James, was a graduate student in philosophy at Cornell, from a family of professionals. David's mother, Sally Foster, came from a more rural background, with family in Maine and New Brunswick, her father a potato farmer. Her grandfather was a Baptist minister who taught her to read with the Bible. She had gotten a scholarship to a boarding school and from there gone to Mount Holyoke College to study English. She became the student body president and the first member of her family to get a bachelor's degree.

Jim and Sally had their daughter, Amy, two years after David, by which time the family had moved to Champaign-Urbana, twin cities in central Illinois and the home of the state's most important public university. The family had not wanted to leave Cornell—Sally and Jim loved the rolling landscape of the region—but Wallace had been offered a job in the philosophy department in the university and felt he could not turn it down. The couple were amazed when they arrived to see how bleak their new city was, how flat and bare. But soon, happily, Jim's appointment turned into a tenure-track post, Sally went back to school to get her master's in English literature, and the family settled in, eventually, in 1969, buying a small yellow two-story house on a one-block-long street in Urbana, near the university. Just a few blocks beyond were fields of corn and soybeans, prairie farmland extending as far as the eye could see, endless horizons.

Here, Wallace and his sister grew up alongside others like themselves, in houses where learning was highly valued. But midwestern virtues of normality, kindness, and community also dominated. Showing off was discouraged, friendliness important. The Wallace house was modest in size and looked out at other modest-sized houses. You were always near your neighbors and kids in the neighborhood lived much of their lives, a friend remembers, on their bikes, in packs. Every other kid in that era, it seemed, was named David.

There was elementary school at Yankee Ridge and then homework. The Wallaces ate at 5:45 p.m. Afterward, Jim Wallace would read stories to Amy and David. And then every night the children would get fifteen minutes each in their beds to talk to Sally about anything that was on their minds. Lights-out was at 8:30 p.m., later as the years went on. After the children were asleep, the Wallace parents would talk, catch up with each other, watch the 10 p.m. evening news, and Jim would turn the lights out at 10:30 exactly. He came home every week from the library with an armful of books. Sally especially loved novels, from John Irving to college classics she'd reread. In David's eyes, the household was a perfect, smoothly running machine; he would later tell interviewers of his memory of his parents lying in bed, holding hands, reading *Ulysses* to each other.

For David, his mother was the center of the universe. She cooked his favorites, roast beef and macaroni and cheese, and baked his chocolate birthday cake and drove the children where they needed to go in her VW Bug. Later, after an accident, she replaced it with a Gremlin. She made beef bourguignonne on David's birthday and sewed labels into his clothes (some of which Wallace would still wear in college).

No one else listened to David as his mother did. She was smart and funny, easy to confide in, and included him in her love of words. Even in later years, and in the midst of his struggle with the legacy of his childhood, he would always speak with affection of the passion for words and grammar she had given him. If there was no word for a thing, Sally Wallace would invent it: "greebles" meant little bits of lint, especially those that feet brought into bed; "twanger" was the word for something whose name you didn't know or couldn't remember. She loved the word "fantods," meaning a feeling of deep fear or repulsion, and talked of "the howling fantods," this fear intensified. These words, like much of his childhood, would wind up in Wallace's work.

To outside eyes, Sally's enthusiasm for correct usage might seem extreme. When someone made a grammatical mistake at the Wallace dinner table, she would cough into her napkin repeatedly until the speaker saw the error. She protested to supermarkets whenever she saw the sign "Ten items or less" posted above their express checkout lines. (Wallace would later give this campaign in *Infinite Jest* to the predatory mother figure of Avril Incandenza, cofounder of "Militant Grammarians of Massachusetts.") For Sally, grammar was more than just a tool. It gave membership in the club of educated persons. The intimation that so much was at stake in each utterance thrilled David, and added to the excitement of having a gifted mother. As did her sensitivity—Sally hated to shout. If she was upset by something she would write a note. And if David or Amy had a response, they would slip it back under her door in turn. Even as a little boy, Wallace was attuned to the delicate drama of personality. He wrote when he was around five years old—and one hears in the words the sigh of the woman who prompted it:

> *My mother works so hard*
> *And for bread she needs some lard.*
> *She bakes the bread. And makes the bed.*
> *And when she's threw*
> *She feels she's dayd.*

The boy loved his father too, an affectionate if slightly abstracted figure, the firm, gentle man who read to him every night at the dinner table. "My father's got a beautiful reading voice," Wallace told an interviewer when he was in his mid-thirties,

> and I remember me being five and Amy being three, and Dad reading *Moby Dick* to us—the unexpurgated *Moby Dick*. Before—I think halfway through Mom pulled him aside and explained to him that, um, little kids were not apt to find, you know, cetology, all that interesting. Um, so they were—but I think by the end, Amy was exempted. And I did it just as this kind of "Dad I love you, I'm gonna sit here and listen."

The memory is exaggerated—Wallace's father says he knew enough not to read *Moby-Dick*, certainly not its duller parts, to small children—but it captures well the relationships in the family as David saw them: the kind, somewhat otherwordly father, the noncombatant younger sister, and David in the center, at once shielded by his mother and trying to break free of her dominion.

Wallace's childhood was happy and ordinary. He would emphasize this in later years. He was a skinny, gap-toothed kid with flaccid hair cut in bangs. He liked the Chicago Bears, loved their star linebacker Dick Butkus (he would make "a great sergeant in the war of Vietnam," he wrote in a school assignment), and wanted to be a football player too, or a brain surgeon, to help his mother's nerves. He thought of himself as normal—and was normal. But he was also identifiably from a talented family, one in love, not unlike Salinger's Glass family, with the ability to impose their notional world on the real one. "Behave," his mother once told him when he was three. "I am 'have,'" David responded. On a car trip when he was eight or nine, the family agreed to substitute "3.14159" for every mention of the word "pie" in their conversation. Wallace was verbal but he was not particularly literary; in fact he saw himself as at least as good at logic and puzzles. One childhood friend remembers going to a book signing of Wallace's and being amazed when his friend could still throw out a twenty-five-digit number they'd all memorized together as kids.

From Wallace's autobiographical sketch, written sometime around fourth grade:

> Dark, semi long hair dark brown eyes. . . . Likes underwater swim-ming football, T.V. reading. Height 55 inches weight 69 ½ pounds.

At the bottom of such short essays, Wallace liked to practice signing his name: Dave W. David W. "Hi," he introduced himself in a letter to his teacher when he was nine. "My name is David W. But just call me Dave." "David Foster Wallace," he put above another poem about Vikings when he was six or seven ("If you see a Viking today / it's best you go some other way"), trying on his middle name—his mother's family name—for size.

Wallace's writing as a child was ordinary too, mostly, though when he had the opportunity, his sense of humor came out. He had a fondness for parody. "Dougnu-Froots," he wrote in a grade school experiment in writing, are "inexpensive, colorful, tasty little angels of mercy to your hungry stomach," and Burpo Soda boasted "the taste of wetness—if you're not thirsty, you better change the channel." He had a mind that moved naturally to puns and satires, the obverse face of a thing.

The Wallace home was one where there was always room for an appeal. From the age of ten David would write memos to his parents detailing injustices, so it was natural for him to assume that the rest of the world would be as interested in his opinion. This approach led, predictably, to friction with many grown-ups. David's cries of "Why?" and "That doesn't make sense!" were familiar at Yankee Ridge Elementary, where he went from 1969 to 1974, and though teachers saw how smart he was, many found him a handful. One day at Crystal Lake Day Camp, where he and Amy went many summers, he grew tired of the counselors and their rules and simply walked several miles back to his house. (His mother drove back to the camp in a fury and asked them to produce her son. When they could not, she said, "Because he's at home!")

When David was ten, his mother began teaching English full-time at Parkland Community College. Their father might be home working on a book; other times a key was left under the mat. His hours were filled by reading. Wallace devoured the Hardy Boys and *The Wizard of Oz*, and Thornton Burgess's *Old Mother West Wind*. He liked adventure and fantasy and inhabited the typical imaginative life of a young boy, enjoying the tension in the journey from threat to triumph. He studied books about sharks and memorized dates and places of attack. A book called *Bertie Comes Through*, about an awkward teenager who perseveres ("'At least I'm in there trying,' says Bertie to himself"), he read over and over. In sixth grade, when he was twelve, he helped his elementary school get to the championships in the Battle of the Books—an "interschool range-of-reading-and-recall spelling-beeish competition," as he fictionalized it in *Infinite Jest*. Dave was in the local paper with a picture, hand up, pouncing on a question. His name appeared again that same year when a poem he wrote about Boneyard Creek, an old irrigation ditch that passed behind the local library, shared first prize:

Did you know that rats breed there?
That garbage is their favorite lair.

Wallace won $50 for it. He read *Dune*, the long science fantasy novel, P. G. Wodehouse's comedies, and went to a lot of movies, including *Jaws*, of course, which sealed his fear of sharks, and when he was older, *Being There*, starring Peter Sellers, which he saw over and over and which fascinated him with its portrait of a man who learns everything he knows from television. One Saturday afternoon a month Sally would drop her two children at the movie theaters in downtown Urbana or Champaign to see whatever they wanted. If there was an R-rated movie Sally would write them a note so they could get in.

And finally there was television itself. As a family, the Wallaces watched *Mary Tyler Moore*, *All in the Family*, and *M*A*S*H*. Jim and Sally believed in responsibility and autonomy, so when David was twelve he was given his own black-and-white set. Champaign-Urbana had only four stations— the three national networks and a public television one—but David would sit on the scratchy green couch in his bedroom for hours and watch and watch: reruns of *Hogan's Heroes*, *Star Trek*, *Night Gallery*, and *Kolchak: The Night Stalker*. The cartoons on Saturday morning he loved too, and Saturday night's *Creature Features*, which was so scary he'd take his little set into his closet. He even watched soap operas—*Guiding Light* was his favorite—and game shows, *The Price Is Right*. His TV watching was intense and extensive enough to worry his parents, and in later years he would acknowledge that television was a major influence in his childhood, the key factor in "this schizogenic experience I had growing up," as he called it to an interviewer in his early thirties, "being bookish and reading a lot, on the one hand, watching grotesque amounts of TV, on the other." He added, "Because I liked to read, I probably didn't watch quite as much TV as my friends, but I still got my daily megadose, believe me."[1]

Aggression was not welcome in the Wallace household—the only shows the parents restricted were violent ones—but David could be malicious. The preferred object of his anger was his sister. When she was three, he knocked out her front teeth in what was always known in the family as a tug-of-war accident. When he was in ninth grade, he got so mad at her after a slight dispute that he pushed her down and dragged her through the backyard through the excrement left by their dog. In exchange for her silence, Wallace traded her his beloved Motobécane, a bicycle that had taken him months of allowance and lawn mowing to buy.[2] He told his parents an elaborate cover story that they never believed. Even when they were teens, he would taunt Amy mercilessly, telling her she was ugly or fat, or would make exaggerated gestures of shrinking from her as she walked down the hall or wry faces when she would take a second helping.

This meanness stands out in the context of the rest of Wallace's life. His classmates remember him as cheerful, popular, funny, in the upper middle of the pack academically. But he saw himself as insignificant, unattractive, on the outside. Some of the things he wanted to be true weren't. In later years he would claim his athletic skills had been formidable—he was, he would say, "a really serious jock"—but in fact he was not good at sports. He didn't play football after school in the pickup games and was famously bad at basketball. He was graceless and used a hook shot to avoid contact. At night at home he would lie in bed and think of all the things that were wrong with his body. As he remembered in a later note:

Feet too thin and narrow and toes oddly shaped, ankles too thin, calves not muscular enough; thighs squnch out repulsively when you sit down; pecker too small or if not too small in terms of shortness too small in terms of circumference.

He called it his version of counting sheep. He sweated a lot and was embarrassed by it. But Wallace always had intense will—*David Comes Through*—and he managed to get on a Little League baseball team, the Meadow Gold Dairy squad, in fourth grade, a team widely remembered as terrible. He even got a toehold in the region's most prestigious sport when he was eleven or twelve, playing on a flag football team. Sports were an important currency, even at the rather sheltered Brookens Junior High School, where Wallace went after Yankee Ridge, for seventh grade. Socially, Wallace was becoming more of a clown, someone good at imitations, at times a teaser who would lash out with his wit, then retreat into the pack. He threw snowballs at a classmate on his paper route, then ran away when the boy confronted him, then came back out and threw them again. He mocked the boy's father's love of flowers. He was usually good at assessing power dynamics, but one time he sassed some larger kids, who hung him up by his underpants from a coat hook in the locker room. When he got down, Wallace gathered up his dignity and left. The image was not soon forgotten, neither by his friends nor by Wallace. (The cloying Leonard Stecyk suffers a similar wedgie in *The Pale King,* a novel Wallace would write more than twenty years later.)

There is another thread that weaves in and out of Wallace's childhood. He believed in later years that the mental disease that would in many ways define his life began at this time. "Summer, 71 or 72"—Wallace was nine or ten—"First occasion of 'Depressive, clinically anxious feelings,'" he wrote in a medical history summary toward the end of his life. He became excessively afraid of mosquitoes, especially of their buzzing. His parents say they did not notice problems this early, nor did his sister. "It's a lot easier to fix something if you can see it," a character comments in *Infinite Jest.* But in a family that prided itself on openness, Wallace never felt safe disclosing himself. He worried, then as he always would later, that to know him too well would be to dislike him. Or at least dislike him as much as he disliked himself. He felt a fake, a victim, as he would later write, of "imposter syndrome." He believed his parents expected great things from him and worried he was not capable. The one member of the family he felt truly comfortable with was Roger, the family dog. Roger lived year-round in a doghouse in the family's backyard, because David was allergic, and he would regularly go out to keep the dog company or to break the ice on his water bowl. He had, his sister remembers, "an incredibly keen sense of empathy" for the beagle-pointer-terrier mix.

Wallace made two important discoveries in his early teen years: tennis and marijuana. These were the twin helpers that carried him through high school. Because Brookens didn't offer tennis, Wallace took lessons at the local park. He was the first among his peers to play the sport. He immediately took to it and found that calculating angles and adjusting for wind velocity gave him an advantage over other players. He could excel at the game even though he was not strong for his age. It wasn't a cool sport; in fact for most midwesterners at the time, it existed only on television. "It wouldn't have been any stranger if he had been good at jai alai," one friend remembers. "No one else played tennis." But Wallace loved it and brought his focus to the game—the $50 he made from his Boneyard Creek essay went to a summer stint at John Newcombe's tennis camp in Texas. The Urbana high school had a team, and when Wallace was in ninth grade, he joined. The group was among the best in the public schools of the region. They fashioned an outsider image for themselves, in cutoff T-shirts, bandanas, and colored shoelaces in an era when tennis players were still expected to wear white—they were the tennis-playing toughs from a big public high school even if at that school they were the sissies who played tennis. Wallace, who was the best among his friends before high school, continued to be one of the top players.

But biology cannot be outrun forever. Wallace was late entering puberty, and the others began getting bigger than he was. His game peaked early in high school. His habit of rationalizing every hit had its downside; his teammates played more by instinct and so were faster. If no longer as good as his peers, Wallace remained very good—his boast in a memoir in *Harper's* more than a decade later that he was "near great" being only a slight overstatement. After senior year, he was still number eleven in the Middle Illinois Tennis Association, although his close friends John Flygare and Martin Maehr, who had started tennis after he did, were number five and number seven respectively. And he understood where things were headed. Flygare remembers their winning the finals of the eighteen-and-under doubles competition of the Central Illinois Open that summer of 1980 and Wallace's comment afterward that it was the last tournament he would ever win. And so it was.

The three friends taught tennis beginning in the summer of 1976, Wallace then fourteen, in the same Urbana public parks where they had learned. As an instructor, Wallace let his pleasure in words play out. Noticing that in tennis manuals overheads were usually abbreviated OH, he started calling them "hydroxides." And he would name his teams after sections of *Ulysses*: the Wandering Rocks and Oxen of the Sun. Another year he ran drills and any player who botched one had to listen to a section of Wallace's life story (made up).

The tennis team was Wallace's social life too. The sport drew a particular kind of kid, one for whom Wallace was more congenial than he was to many of the others in their large urban high school. He was odd to them but not unfathomable. When their children were freshmen, parents would drive the players to tournaments around the state, but soon the older kids got their licenses and the group could go anywhere they wanted. They drove the circuit of tournaments, staying in hotels, eating in hamburger joints, and killing time playing mini-golf. One time they went to a Van Halen concert; another time the others all ditched Wallace, who was in the hotel room taking one of the long showers he was famous for. They slept two to a motel bed and did "woody checks." Bonded into a team, no one was permanently in or out, blows were taken and given; if you weren't careful your bed would be peed in. Wallace, with his teasing sense of humor and energy, was always in the scrum. He was not the leader but he was not the last either. These boys—his pals from the place he called Shampoo-Banana—would stay Wallace's friends his whole life, able to approach him when he was famous the way few others could. His teammates were more successful with girls than Wallace, and, frustrated, he would try to solve the complexity of attraction the way he solved the trajectory of a tennis shot: "How do you know when you can ask a girl out?" "How do you know when you can kiss her?" His teammates told him not to think so hard; he would just know.

Marijuana—the other great find of his youth—helped Wallace with his self-consciousness and calmed a growing anxiety. Pot in the late 1970s was everywhere in the Midwest. Not quite legal, it was all the same barely hidden, a companion to beer as a recreational drug. One friend remembers the tennis team doing one-hitters in the back of the bus as they rode home from a match in Danville, the coach in the front pretending not to notice. Pot also deepened the consciousness of beauty—or at least they thought so. High, they listened to the stoner bands of the time:

> I remember KISS, REO Speedwagon, Cheap Trick, Styx, Jethro Tull, Rush, Deep Purple, and, of course, good old Pink Floyd.

The words are from Chris Fogle, a "wastoid" character in *The Pale King*, but they might as well be Wallace's. He liked to get high at home before he studied. His parents tolerated the behavior. All the same, Wallace preferred to smoke standing on a chair in an upstairs bathroom blowing the smoke out with an exhaust fan so no one would notice. He may have had himself in mind when he wrote of Hal in *Infinite Jest*, another pothead, that he was "as attached to the secrecy as he was to getting high." His sister remembers his father looking up from his newspaper to ask his son, who was on the way out the door, not to smoke marijuana in the car. A fellow high school student introduced him to acid, and he tried tripping one weekend when his parents were away. But he felt sick to his stomach and went to bed for the next twenty-four hours. Afterward he told his sister he thought he was going to die. Pot was what worked, allowing Wallace both calm and emotional privacy. But he also knew it could cause its own anxiety, marooning him in a private, claustrophobic consciousnesss. In such moments nothing was clear or stable and thoughts circled in on themselves in a way that called unassailable truths—the meaning of words, the structure of reality—into question. In a later essay, he would remember the problem with getting high, recalling how under the drug's influence one eats

> ChipsAhoy! and star[es] very intently at the television's network PGA event. . . . The adolescent pot-smoker is struck with the ghastly possibility that, e.g., what he sees as the color green and what other people call "the color green" may in fact not be the same color experiences at all. . . . [T]he whole line of thinking gets so vexed and exhausting that the a.p.-s ends up slumped crumb-strewn and paralyzed in his chair.

The beginning of high school was a good time academically for Wallace. The work was easy; he got all his reading and papers done within a few weeks of the start of classes, which left him time for hanging out and tennis. His intelligence stood out more with each year—one English teacher remembers him as the brightest student she ever had. Other kids tried to cheat off him and he developed a peculiar tiny uppercase script to foil them, or so he would later say. One day he asked his father to explain what philosophy was about. Jim Wallace had his son read the *Phaedo*, Plato's argument for an afterlife. Wallace grasped the philosophical reasoning of the dialogue immediately. It was the first time his father realized how brilliant his son was, his mind faster, his father remembers, than that "of any undergraduate I have ever taught." His mother remembers realizing around this time that David would just "hoover everything." His grades put him near the top of his class. He was also on the debate team and won a prize for best student writing.

But there was a brittleness to this surge too. Within, Wallace was growing less and less happy. His childhood anxiety was back. He could be obsessive, unwilling or unable to leave whatever impinged on his world unexplored. Mostly it seemed funny more than anything else to those who knew him, character rather than disease. "My particular neurological makeup [is] extremely sensitive: carsick, airsick, heightsick; my sister likes to say I'm 'lifesick,'" he wrote in a later essay. But by the end of high school his problems were hard to ignore. On his sister's fifteenth birthday, Wallace refused to go out with his family. "Why would I want to celebrate that?" he asked pointedly. The family was confused and chalked it up to his always simmering competitiveness with Amy, but in fact—as they realized years later—he was having an anxiety attack. They went without him. He talked about painting his bedroom walls black and added a newspaper picture of Kafka to the wall of tennis stars on the corkboard in his room with the caption: The disease was life itself. By the end of his junior year, remembers Amy, he was often too upset to go to class, and by senior year, with college nearing, the anxiety that had been shimmering just below the surface of his life grew into full-blown panic attacks. He was not sure what set them off, but he saw that they quickly became endless loops, where he worried that people would notice he was panicking, and that in turn would make him panic more. This was a crucial moment for Wallace's mental life and one he would never forget—he saw clearly the danger of a mind unhinged, of the danger of thinking responsive only to itself. From these experiences he would derive a lifelong fear of the consequences of mental and, eventually, emotional isolation.

To cover his attacks, Wallace walked around school with his tennis racket and a towel. He was sweating because he was just off the court—that was the idea he was trying to convey. He took extra showers. He was nauseated often before going to class. He thought maybe he was just upset. In a culture and a place still less than comfortable with mental illness, he likely tried to diagnose himself ("ruminative obsession, hyperhydrosis, and parasympathetic nervous system arousal loop" are some of the diagnoses the phobic David Cusk comes up with in *The Pale King*.) His mother thought of his anxiety, she would later tell an interviewer, as the "black hole with teeth,"[3] but neither she nor her husband knew what to do about it, beyond letting their son stay home from school when he had to. Perhaps they hoped the problem would go away when he went to college. Clearly biological changes were going on in Wallace—depression often first appears in puberty—but the young man may also have been responding to the environment he had grown up in, to the wide-open spaces and unstructured world of late-1970s midwestern America. If he was furtive or anxious, perhaps it was in part because he had a hard time figuring out what the rules were.

Though Wallace was growing sicker during the end of his high school years, no one saw it clearly, least of all Wallace. He was a top achiever and outwardly very functional. He got to school often enough. The intensity of his flashes of anger never quite called attention to themselves as symptoms. As a senior in high school, Wallace became interested in another Urbana High student, Susan Perkins. Perkins was dating another young man, Brian Spano, whom they were all friends with, but at a party that Wallace threw one night, Spano left early and something went on between Perkins and Wallace. He smashed his hand into the refrigerator. He appeared the next day in school with a cast on it.

Going to a prestigious private college was one of the ways the Wallaces differed from some of their midwestern peers. Wallace told friends he was expected to follow in his father's footsteps to Amherst, inventing a layer of pressure he hardly needed, but in fact, as Jim Wallace remembers, he thought Oberlin College might be a good match for his son and drove him east to Ohio to visit it first. Wallace dreaded interviews. Life for him had the quality of a performance, and being called on to perform within that performance was too much. At the admissions interview Wallace grew anxious. He would one day transform the scene into Hal's breakdown at the opening of *Infinite Jest*:

> My chest bumps like a dryer with shoes in it. I compose what I project will be seen as a smile. I turn this way and that, slightly, sort of directing the expression to everyone in the room . . . I hold tight to the sides of my chair.

When the interview was over, Wallace went back to his hotel and threw up in the ice bucket. Later in the fall, he traveled to his father's alma mater. The longtime head of admissions at Amherst ran the process himself. He liked to admit promising candidates right at the interview—it was how he kept the school competitive with Harvard and Yale. Wallace had tremendous grades, a good tennis game, and a family connection. He was in before he had to say anything. Back home, he told his parents, "If I agree to go, does that mean I don't have to go to another college interview?" Jim Wallace said yes. "Sold!" Wallace said.

During his last summer at home he taught tennis for the fifth summer in a row with Maehr and Flygare. What had gone on in the past year wasn't clear to him; mostly he must have hoped it wouldn't happen again, that he could leave his problems behind when he went east. He was eager to be a part of the larger intellectual world and equally eager to show that he was his father's equal academically. So, as the summer ended, he packed his suitcase, put in his favorite bathrobe, a suit and tie for dress-up occasions, and headed east. Before leaving, he spent the last couple of days wandering around the neighboring cornfields saying goodbye.

CHAPTER 2

"The Real 'Waller'"

At the opening convocation for the class of 1984, in Johnson Chapel, the president of Amherst urged the entering students to overcome ignorance and be tolerant of one another. He ended with a poem by Emily Dickinson, one of whose grandfathers had helped found the school:

> Speech is one symptom of affection
> And Silence one—
> The perfectest communication
> Is heard of None.
> Exists and its indorsement
> Is had within—
> Behold said the apostle
> Yet had not seen!

Wallace had been assigned to room with Raj Desai and Dan Javit, two young men who wanted to be doctors. Wallace had already marked himself as a bit of an oddball by writing a letter to Desai in the summer, suggesting, because his future roommate lived near Amherst, that he should, as Desai recalls, bring "some of the larger items—the refrigerator comes to mind." He ended by saying he looked forward to "a productive and inspiring year." It was the kind of formality that sometimes seized Wallace in unfamiliar situations, part of the reason that, smart as he was, the move from high school to college was bound to be challenging.

The three young men had a two-room suite in Stearns Hall on the main quad. The building was crowded and flimsy, built to house the flood of GIs enrolling after World War II, and so they could hear their neighbors through the wall.[1] The three young men slept in one room, Wallace in the upper level of a bunk bed (he called it the "vag"), Javit below. Desai was in a twin bed across from them. The second room was where they were supposed to study, but Desai had brought a tarantula. The spider unnerved Wallace, who had a fear of bugs. The arachnid would expose its huge fangs, as if trying to bite him through the glass. Wallace quickly came to prefer the library.

Wallace was by turns thrilled and terrified to be at Amherst, but mostly he was just disoriented. He was at a school a thousand miles away from home, nearly all male, and preppy. The first class of freshwomen had not yet graduated and one-quarter of the students were children of fathers who, like James Wallace, had gone to the school. The closest Wallace had come to this sort of world before were the frat houses at the University of Illinois, which could not have been further from his family's emphasis on the life of the mind. Wallace tended to dislike what he did not know and so he instinctively gave this culture a broad berth. (He would later nickname the Amherst of trust-fund children "Armrest.") At the same time he was excited—excited to be away from home, excited to be among top professors with other hand-selected members of his generation, excited to be fulfilling what he saw as a challenge to meet his parents' expectations for him. His self-image was still of a regular guy, a tennis player, a top student, and that was who he wanted to be at Amherst. The school was famous for its many singing organizations, and Wallace told his family he had joined the Glee Club, where another member was Prince Albert of Monaco.

But anxiety and the fear of anxiety were woven into his behavior by now too, and even as he tried to open himself up to the range of college experiences, he also protectively narrowed his life. He was happiest when things were predictable, when his work was under control and the people around him familiar. In Stearns he quickly developed routines. Every day he set his alarm for the same time to give himself the chance to climb down from the bunk and go to the hall bathroom to slick back his hair and then climb back in for a ten-minute catnap, stepping on the lower mattress twice—once coming and once going—and waking the sleeping Javit.

At first, he and his roommates ate together and socialized. They all joined the JV tennis team, whose practices were open to anyone interested. Wallace had lost his tennis ambitions—he told his old friend John Flygare the top players at Amherst were too good—and he never went out for the varsity. But against ordinary players he was still impressive. Desai and Javit were amazed at his big topspin strokes and the power he got out of his beaten-up racket. Otherwise Wallace made a slight impression as an extremely polite, strangely tentative, and very skinny classmate. His acne, which had first afflicted him late in high school, got suddenly much worse, and he treated it with a cream, the application of which involved a prolonged and careful examination of each pimple on his face. Behind his back he was sometimes called "mushface." His roommates, without knowing precisely what, suspected him to be under some sort of unusual stress. Javit remembers being surprised when Wallace, whom he usually found cerebral and low-key, would once in a while open the window of their room in the morning and scream out into the quad, "I love it here!" There was a loneliness to him, too, in their eyes. The other two boys had visits from family; they had friends. Wallace gave off the impression of having neither; his mother had dropped him there and left. The regular care packages she sent seemed not to satisfy whatever need Wallace had. He did not make friends the way Javit and Desai did. (The good-looking Desai, Wallace would later grouse, had girls lining up to do his laundry.) One day, the three took prank photos on the campus. In one, Wallace, straight shiny bangs, Chicago White Sox T-shirt over a black turtleneck, holds a cupped hand under his empty school mailbox, while he regards the camera with a look of hurt. If home did not seem to miss Wallace, Wallace missed home. He dreamed of the Illinois farmland and the small city he had grown up in. He wrote his family, they remember, that the mountains in Massachusetts were "pretty" but the terrain wasn't beautiful "the way Illinois is."

Over time, Desai and Javit, with their shared pre-med ambitions, separated from Wallace—he was the friendly but forlorn third roommate. They could not figure out what was going on in his head, though they suspected it was not what was going on in theirs. In fact, Wallace was probably not so sure what was going on either. No one had found out the things about himself he wished to keep private, but only because no one seemed to care enough to do so. He knew what he needed, what would make him feel better: great grades. It would be satisfying to show everyone what he could do; his shyness did not preclude competitiveness. Getting straight As, as he would later tell *Amherst* magazine, was "a way to hide from people, to try to earn—through 'achievement' or whatever—permission to be at Amherst that I was too self-centered to realize I'd already received when they accepted me."

Wallace had liked to study high when he was in high school. He reestablished the routine at Amherst, with two young men who lived down the hall from him. They would get together in their room most days in the late afternoon, do bong hits for forty-five minutes while listening to music, and then go to the dining hall as soon as it opened (they called themselves "the 5:01 brigade"). Wallace would eat his food quickly, with a tea bag dunked into a cup of coffee. At 5:45 he'd head for Frost Library, where he'd study for the next six hours until it closed. Over time he found study spaces on campus that stayed open all night—the Merrill Science Center, for instance, or Webster Library with its stuffed polar bears and botany books.

That first semester Wallace dug into introductory courses in English, history, and political science and one elective, Evolution and Revolution. Late at night he'd come back to Stearns with his books. Often he would then head off again to the room where the pot was. The discussion was light. Wallace was happy high, more like the Wallace of high school no one at Amherst had met. One member of the group remembers that the three friends would test each other's knowledge of TV jingles. "*Hazel*?" he remembers the discussion. "Now how did that one go?" Munchies were satisfied by the boxes of Freihofer's cookies in Sally Wallace's care packages. Afterward, Wallace would clamber back to his room, take his bathrobe, and march off to brush his teeth or have another shower before retiring to "the vag" for the night.

There was a moment in many of his fellow students' lives when they realized Wallace was not just smart but stunningly smart, as smart as anyone they had ever met. One friend remembers looking over his shoulder in a class on twentieth-century British poetry after the professor returned their essays on Philip Larkin and seeing on Wallace's, "A+—One of the finest pieces of writing I have ever read." In epistemology, he was dominant, peppering the professor with so many advanced questions he had to ask Wallace to keep them for his office hours. "I don't want to say he was scary but he made me work harder than any other student I ever had," remembers Willem DeVries.[2] For his freshman roommate Desai, the moment of awareness came one morning second semester around one a.m. when Wallace returned to their suite, likely stoned, and asked to borrow his paper on *Henry V.* Wallace, Desai remembers, had earlier glanced at the play for the freshman Shakespeare seminar they both were taking. Now he quickly scanned his roommate's paper, put it down, went away, and worked for several hours, producing an essay that would earn him an A in the class. "I thought I was smarter," Desai remembers thinking. "Now I was getting a glimpse of how much he could accomplish." So were others at Amherst. The first semester Wallace got two other As and an A-minus. Second semester he won the prize for the freshman with the best grade point average. "Un veritable bijou," his teacher wrote on reading his last paper for a class in the gothic.

Responses like these made Wallace happy, happier than he later felt they should have. And despite his shyness, over time he was piecing together the social puzzle and starting to make friends. Late first semester, he met another freshman, Mark Costello, a bright, mischievous boy who, like Wallace, lived in Stearns and spent every waking hour in the library. Both young men, from large public high schools, felt the gulf between their background and that of many undergraduates at a school that touted the well-rounded over the brilliant. (Costello had sent a photo of the star of his school track team to the freshman face-book in place of his own.) Neither was going to be invited to the DKE champagne party or the Psi U beach party, and both made it a point not to care. Costello had his own throwing-up-at-the-college-interview story: he had gotten sick on Route 9 on the way to the Amherst admission's director's office. Wallace responded by claiming he had thrown up in the bushes outside the Lord Jeff Inn en route to his own Amherst interview (and perhaps he had). There were differences, though. Wallace smoked pot; Costello didn't even drink. Costello, from a large Irish-Catholic family, was considering becoming a priest; Wallace was desperate to get laid. All the same, a close friendship developed. Soon Wallace was letting Costello in on the locations of secret places where he liked to study.

Wallace asked Costello to room with him the following year, and his new friend agreed.

When the summer came, Wallace was relieved. Paradoxically, the home that had made him anxious in high school now felt like the place he could go to decompress. It was off the stage that college was to him, safe from observation. Most of his old friends were still there, including Flygare and Maehr. He spent the summer teaching for a sixth time in Blair Park, reading, and getting high. One of his new freshman friends, Fred Brooke, an aspiring writer who had lived in Stearns too, visited him at home, and the two went out late at night to play tennis in the park. They hit balls back and forth amid the mosquitoes and drank beer in the Illinois heat.

Sophomore year Wallace and Costello were assigned one of the worst rooms on campus, a tiny double next to the TV pit in Moore Hall. Once a week at 3 a.m. a truck came and emptied the dining-hall Dumpster outside their window. All the same, Wallace found he was happier than as a freshman. He had his routines down and a growing sense of himself as competent. He no longer worried about disappointing his parents or wasting their money. To have Costello at his side—to have near him another person whose behavior he could rely on—was a huge help. A happier Wallace began to emerge. In the mornings he wore his tattered bathrobe from home—he worried that the smears from Clearasil looked like semen stains—a Parkland College Cobras hoodie, and untied boots to stomp off to shower. "Dave, why don't you ever tie the belt, walking around like this?" Costello would ask him. "You think I wanna look like a nerd or a jerk?" Wallace would answer. He always gargled and brushed for forty-five minutes, and then there came the microscopic examination and treatment of his acne. Back in the room, he would spread out his towels to dry, hanging them from shelves, chair backs, and bedposts. (Wallace's fear of germs was typical of his phobic mind. It was at once real and exaggerated, with an overlay of self-deprecating comedy to both underscore and hide the hurt.) His collection of stoner tapes came out: Pink Floyd, *Switched-On Bach*, REO Speedwagon, Frank Zappa's "Don't Eat the Yellow Snow." Wallace had watched little or no television his freshman year, but with the TV pit right next door he could time his indulgences for when it was empty. He enjoyed *Hawaii Five-O* reruns and a new show, *Hill Street Blues,* on Thursday nights. Soap operas, though—another favorite with their exaggerated plots and larger-than-life personalities—he was too embarrassed to turn on. In general he did not like being watched watching, and if others were there he'd pass by. Yet it was a welcome bit of routine, a nice refuge from the excess of interactions that communal living brought.

Costello and Wallace sat down at 5:15 at the same table most nights in the Valentine Dining Hall, united in their need to study. During exam periods, Wallace added a second tea bag to his cup of coffee. He'd down the caffeinated drink and go off to the library. (On Sundays he'd be waiting on the steps for the librarians to open after brunch.) Then after the library closed, he and Costello would calm down with a shot of scotch. "I think this is a two-shot night," Wallace would sometimes say. At various times, he gave up pot, saying it was bad for his lungs. He caught some of Costello's enthusiasm for political history. He already knew trivia about Illinois politics, about Big Jim Thompson and the Stevenson dynasty that produced the two-time presidential candidate Adlai. Now he set his eye on interning for his congressman, Ed Madigan. With Costello, another friend, Nat Larson, and a fifteen-year-old freshman name Corey Washington, he joined the school debate team. Wallace was afraid of public speaking—his voice was reedy and got stuttery when he was nervous—but he participated because being on the team would look good on his transcript if he applied to law school. They traveled up and down the East Coast competing. Chris Coons, another member of team, remembers Wallace as brilliant and funny in competition, with "literally the worst delivery I have ever heard—mumbling and awkward and turned away from the judges and audience." Wallace in turn denigrated him as the "Coonsgah" and amused his friends with a mean imitation of the future senator from Delaware.

The first semester Wallace again aced everything, with an A-plus in introduction to philosophy. He also got an A in his English class, his mother's field. He told friends he wanted to please both parents.

* * *

Wallace came back to school early in January. He had left with high hopes and a sense of growing happiness, but when he got back he told Costello that Christmas had been "bad." He would not be more specific. His banter, his roommate saw, had vanished. He seemed unresponsive. The impersonations were gone; Costello was surprised—he did not know that Wallace's clowning and showing off were, if more than a façade, not quite a self. He was amazed—but Wallace was amazed too. He was familiar with his anxiety and may even have associated it with depression, but this was a more intense version of whatever he had routinely dealt with in high school; it was as if some switch in him had been flipped. He felt despair and thought of killing himself. He held on for a few weeks, trying to white-knuckle his way back to being himself. But one day William Kennick, a professor of philosophy who had been his father's mentor, saw what was going on—he was familiar with depression from his own family—and took Wallace to see a therapist. Shortly after, Costello came into their room to find his roommate slumped over, his gray suitcase between his legs. Wallace was dressed in a Chicago Bears watch cap and tan parka. "I have to go home," he told Costello. "What's wrong?" Costello asked. "I don't know. Something's wrong with me," he said. He was hugely apologetic and told Costello he was worried the college would slot someone awful into the room once he left. "I've let you down," he told his roommate. Costello thought it was strange that Wallace kept focusing on him. Wasn't Wallace the one in distress? In silence he walked his roommate to the bus to Springfield, which would take Wallace to the airport.

Wallace's parents took their son in and put him back in his bedroom on the second floor. After his difficult senior year in high school, they could hardly have been surprised by such an outcome, but if they felt this, they did not say it. They were not unfamiliar with suicidal depression: Sally's sister and uncle had both taken their own lives. The family let Wallace come and go as he pleased. "We didn't press him," his mother says. "We figured if he wanted to talk about it he'd talk about it." But he began to confide in his sister, Amy, whom up until then he had mostly looked on as a nuisance. He told her how frightened and uncomfortable the world felt to him and how nothing seemed meaningful anymore. He wondered who he really was—the star Amherst student or a young man who would never make it out of the home on his own?—and his sister quietly worried the same thing. Yet over time he began to heal, and by the spring he got a job driving a school bus. It was good to be back in the Midwest, experiencing the comforting flatness of the prairie. But when the kids mouthed off at him, he quit, left the bus behind, and walked home. In semi-mock outrage, he wrote Costello how appalled he was that Urbana would permit someone with a known history of mental disease to handle a motor vehicle with children on board. Never liking the phone, he instead established a lively correspondence with Costello, who was kept informed of his travails.

He also wrote some fiction. Wallace had written occasional comic stories in high school but any interest had dropped away when he got to Amherst.[3] Fiction on campus was the province of, as he would later describe them, "foppish aesthetes" who "went around in berets stroking their chins." They were sensitive, and his sensitivity was not something he wanted to emphasize. The cast of mind he thought it took to be a writer was scary to him. But home on his own he gave it another try. One story he worked on, according to Costello, was called "The Clang Birds," about a fictional bird that flies in ever decreasing circles until it disappears up its own ass. In Wallace's story, God ran an existential game show where contestants were asked impossible or paradoxical questions. God wielded the buzzer and no one could stop playing. He also tried writing in a more delicate vein. He started a prose poem about the cornfields of Illinois, which he sent to Costello to read, and also a story about a pretty girl whose drunk boyfriend kills her in a car crash. There may have been bigger efforts—certainly he conceived his goals ambitiously. Costello remembers getting a letter from Wallace announcing that he wanted to write fiction that would still be read "100 years from now." He was impressed—he had no inkling either that his roommate wanted to write or could write fiction.[4]

There had been problems in the Wallace parents' marriage for some time. In early summer Sally Wallace discussed them with her daughter and told her she was moving out. She asked Amy to tell David in turn. The blow to her son was enormous. He refused to visit her in her new home. Her brother, Amy realized, "felt personally betrayed. He really thought that in a family everybody is expected to tell the truth by word or by deed."

Years later, he would write a girlfriend that what had devastated him about the moment was his mother's "not trusting me with reality, fearing it would pain me." Yet at the time these events did not derail Wallace's recovery. The relationship between event and crisis for Wallace was not always a direct one. It may have helped cushion the blow that as the summer wore on, he started hanging out with Susie Perkins. Perkins was now a psychology major at Indiana University. They became involved. Wallace was deeply drawn to her, seeking a caregiver to replace his mother. To Costello, her affect toward his friend reminded him of a girl looking after a wounded bird.

Wallace came back to Amherst in the fall of 1982. He was extremely embarrassed: the myth of his capability had been shattered. He was elusive about what had happened—among his close friends only Costello knew the truth. The two friends had agreed to live together again, adding Nat Larson to their group. Just before the start of school, they went on a camping trip to Maine and Nova Scotia. "We stuffed ourselves with fresh seafood from buffets and lay around on the beach," remembers Fred Brooke, who also went along. For Wallace, all-male dynamics were often the most comfortable, but he was also so agitated by the bugs, he chose to sleep in the car. The rest were amused by the slapping noises they heard through the night, though to Costello, who knew him best, Wallace's behavior was as frightening as it was funny. He knew that Wallace when he was under stress or fragile acted out his full complement of phobias.

In the housing lottery the group was awarded a room in Stone, one of the "social dorms," as they were called. The social dorms were designed with bedrooms radiating off a common room and were much more pleasant than the rooms in Stearns or Moore. Wallace, his friends noticed, looked different now. He no longer wore the generic clothes—the corduroys and White Sox and Bears T-shirts of the Midwest—choosing instead worn thrift-shop T-shirts and torn shorts, often with his beloved hoodie. He liked untied Timberland boots and double socks. The sartorial change was representative of an interior one. He was beginning to distance himself from the culture of the Midwest that had formed him, where one could be radical but never rude. Adopting the "dirt bomb" look, as it was called, was one small way of saying he was done trying to be Joe College. His inchoate political hopes were gone too. "No one's going to vote for someone who's been in a nuthouse," he told Costello, and mentioned Thomas Eagleton, the senator and Amherst graduate who had briefly been a vice presidential candidate before the news that he'd had electroconvulsive therapy for depression forced him to withdraw in 1972.

Wallace took no chances with his classes on his return. His first semester back he enrolled in logic, Christian ethics, and ancient and medieval philosophy with Kennick. The only nonphilosophy course he took was French, which was necessary if he wanted to get a degree in the department. He aced all four classes, taking particular pleasure in logic. The course description promised to cover "the categorical, hypothetical, alternative and subjunctive syllogism," as well as the "concepts of consistency, completeness and decidability." In logic, you were either right or you were wrong, and the things that could keep you from always being right— lassitude, sloppy thinking—with Wallace's enormous focus he could always overcome. He would later talk about the "special sort of buzz" logic gave him, how after "a gorgeously simple solution to a problem you suddenly see after half a notebook with gnarly attempted solutions," you almost heard a "click." In no time he was a self-described "hard-core syntax wienie."

Wallace's father thought little of the discipline, objecting that logicians tended to replace important questions—free will, beauty—with technical discussions about the language behind those questions, but this was work of the sort that made Wallace's mind hum. It replaced the ambiguity of actual life with clarity. And as he would later tell an interviewer, highly abstract philosophy gave Wallace both the pleasure of being in his father's field with the "required thumbing-the-nose-at-the-father thing." (Another interpretation is that he was still trying to please both parents—grammar is another logical system, after all.)

Kennick's ancient and medieval philosophy was a class that gave Wallace pleasure for a different reason. His father had taken the course some thirty years before, and much as he wanted to escape his father's shadow, he also wanted to be protected by it. The ancients were part one of Kennick's three-part introduction to the field he loved. Kennick required a paper every two weeks. The student was supposed to encounter the material fresh, using only original research and thinking, without consulting secondary sources. "I want you to be writers of prose, not processors of words," Kennick would explain. Wallace met this rigorous timetable with a routine of his own. He would write a draft, then revise it twice longhand, then revise that revision twice on his Smith-Corona, pecking away with two fingers.

Kennick restricted papers to five pages, because he thought that compression made for better thinking. Wallace, in thrall to his galloping mind, could not write short. One time Kennick had Wallace count the words in one of his papers and found he had squeezed five hundred onto each page, nearly double the norm. He gave Wallace an A-plus in the class anyway. Wallace for his part basked in Kennick's affection.

Wallace liked comedy, and comic writing had come easily to him from childhood. So that semester he and Costello revived the campus humor magazine, *Sabrina*. From an office in the basement in Frost Library they put out several issues a year modeled on the *Harvard Lampoon*. The headquarters also served as an informal social club to gossip and postulate, an extension of their table in Valentine Dining Hall. The atmosphere was, appropriately, sophomoric. One member of the editorial team remembers a long discussion on whether women farted, with Wallace insisting they did not. The magazine itself was likewise often juvenile, but in its pages Wallace could satisfy his passion for parody, mimicry, and farce. In *Sabrina*, he wrote an advice column called "Ask Bill," in which readers were invited to bring their questions to Professor Kennick. Bertrand Russell wrote in to reveal his crush on Alfred North Whitehead and ask what he should do. "Any relationship that depends for its security on the proposition that monistic atomism has **any** relevance to post-Enlightenment conceptions of phenomenological reality is not worth saving," the *Sabrina* Kennick sternly replied. Most stories were collaborations, but Wallace revived his childhood love of Hardy Boys mysteries to write "The Sabrina Brothers in the Case of the Hung Hamster" himself:

> Suddenly a sinister, twin-engined airplane came into view, sputtering and back-firing. It lost power and began spinning in toward the hill. It was heading right for the Sabrina brothers!
> Luckily at the last minute the plane ceased to exist.

"Crikey!" exclaimed Joe. "It's a good thing we're characters in a highly implausible children's book or we'd be goners!"[5]

By spring semester Wallace and Costello were becoming well known on campus because of the magazine. Their table in Valentine began drawing a small but intense group of adherents. Nicknames had been a staple of his friendships in Urbana, and Wallace reveled in them here. He was "the Daver" and also "the Waller." Costello was "Marcus Aurelius" for his first name, philosophical air, and high forehead; Nat Larson was "the Bumpster," via the name "Natty Bumppo." Corey Washington, Wallace's friend from the debate team, was "Apple" or "the Reactor," a play on "core reactor." Eventually they were joined by Washington's roommate Miller Maley, a wunderkind who had entered the school at twelve, Amherst's youngest student in decades. Self-conscious about his iffy entry into puberty, Wallace liked having the younger Washington and Maley around. Washington was African American too, a distinct minority at the school, adding to the flavor of a table of refuseniks amid the mostly hail-fellow-well-met atmosphere of Amherst. In their undertrafficked corner of the dining hall, the conversation among the group bounced between social and sexual frustration, intellectual enthusiasm, and nerdy inquiry. Washington remembers the roving subjects as "Wittgenstein, the New Deal, Cantor, current politics, mathematical logic, Descartes, hot girls, Kant, etc." They'd talk about classes, imaginary or hoped-for girlfriends, and weekend parties at the University of Massachusetts or Mount Holyoke College, where Amy Wallace now went.

Costello and Wallace were the twin centers of the group. Costello had authority, gravitas, and a boundless interest in the New Deal. Wallace was intense, with a brain that seemed to whirr faster than he could speak, and he was funny, shooting off clever comments and entertaining with his impressions. He had been in an economics course that semester. Did anyone want to see Friedrich Hayek hit on by a girl from Wilton, Connecticut? He could do his grandparents, his neighbors in Urbana, or Costello (when he wasn't at the table). But his affection for his roommate was evident to all. Many people never saw the one without the other. To young Washington, their relationship was "like a marriage."

His new popularity didn't prevent Wallace from bearing down even harder in his studies. John Drew, another member of the circle, remembers an undercurrent of competitiveness in the group, of "a whole lot of score keeping and who's the smartest." That spring Wallace took the next installment of Kennick's class, on early modern philosophy. This second unit began with Hobbes, continued through Locke, Berkeley, Hume, and finished with Kant. Wallace thrilled to (and had fun imitating) the announcement Kennick made when he got to the German idealist: "Fasten your seat belts. We're going up!" He also took French again, metaphysics, and economics. In economics, Wallace had to try. He was good at theory, not calculation. But with his grade point average at risk, he worked ceaselessly at the subject and even won a prize for best undergraduate work in the discipline. Costello, also in the class, now had *his* moment of realization about the gifts of his roommate. Wallace got straight A-pluses that semester, spring 1983, his grades perfect. The depression of early 1982 was in the past, forgotten almost, even perhaps by him. When people would ask about why he had left school, he would not answer, or say vaguely that a friend had died and he had needed time away to get over it.

In May, Wallace returned home. He signed up for a summer logic class and another in calculus at the University of Illinois. He would study right through the summer break. But soon he was sorry. He wrote Washington that he just couldn't focus while "the smell of flowers is in the air and the birds are singing and the pop of frosty Old Mil cans can be heard from the classroom window. I rose one day and said 'No.' That's what I said." In fact the reason may have been Susie Perkins—Wallace told friends the two were growing more deeply involved. He dropped calculus and contented himself with more logic classes, which he preferred to math anyway—in math he didn't hear the "click."

Home was not the place it had been. His father had spent the year alone, keeping a radio on for company. But nothing could tarnish Wallace's exuberance. He was on a high and cocky, the smartest kid at Amherst. He felt raised up and vindicated. Early in the summer, he warned Washington, who was going to work at the particle accelerator at Stanford University, that he needed to get used to "dealing with, yes, living with, dull, unappealing people." This brotherly advice was a sign of how far Wallace's confidence had come back since his breakdown.

Though they lived apart, Wallace's parents had not given up on their marriage and continued going to therapy. They now wanted the family to attend as a group. Wallace and Amy reluctantly agreed. Seeking to get to the root of the Wallace family's dynamic, the therapist asked Amy to position the different members of the family in the room as she perceived them. She refused, drawing instead a schema of interlocking gears on the blackboard.

Afterward, Wallace was no less sour about the experience than he had been going in: "Marriage therapy degenerated into family therapy," he would later write in *The Broom of the System*. "God knows what all went on." He fictionalized the marriage therapist's attempt to get Amy to draw images of how she saw her family into a scene in the novel in which Lenore's sister's family put on masks in a ritualized attempt to express their emotions, to the applause of a LaserDisc audience. Perhaps Wallace was angry because the therapy did not avert the formal dissolution of the family. Soon, Jim and Sally told the children they were getting divorced. But one day a month later, their mother was back in the house she had not been in for a year. The children didn't ask what happened and the parents didn't offer, Amy remembers.

During the summer Wallace was also beginning to think about fiction differently. He had always liked and read novels; he found them absorbing and relaxing and mined them for the information they provided. He had hoovered everything on his parents' shelves, from a compilation of the underground nineteenth-century porn magazine *The Pearl*, a favorite, he once told a therapist, of his high school masturbations, and *Fanny Hill*, to popular crime novelists like Ed McBain and John D. MacDonald, to creators of literature—Updike and Kafka. Friends and relatives often tried to suggest books to him that combined his parents' two interests. This usually meant recommending the big popular philosophical titles that were a mainstay of the era, like *Zen and the Art of Motorcycle Maintenance*, which, Wallace noted in a letter to Washington that summer, his mother "practically rammed . . . up my ass."[6] But this wasn't the reading he was after. Instead, the first story that, as he later put it, "rang his cherries" was Donald Barthelme's "The Balloon." Barthelme didn't tell straightforward stories. He sought to fracture the surface of fiction to show the underpinnings on which its illusions depended. As with other postmodernists, the point was not to make the reader forget the conventions of the charade but to see them more clearly. A truly fulfilled reader was one who always re-membered he was just reading a story.

"The Balloon" is typical of Barthelme's work. In the story, a large bal-loon appears over Manhattan. While it hangs above the city, various char-acters approach and consider it, each from his own point of view. Children jump up and down on it for fun, while adults grouse that it serves no pur-pose or talk about how looking at the balloon makes them feel. The police worry about the threat to public order. In the end the narrator reveals that the balloon is an artifact, something he just felt like inflating because he was lonely. This was writing that a self-described "hard-core syntax wie-nie" like Wallace could appreciate. It peeled back the skin of literature just as logic peeled back the skin of language. Wallace told an interviewer years later that Barthelme was the first time he heard the "click" in literature. He added that Barthelme's sort of writing appealed to him far more than the fiction he had enjoyed in high school, writing that contented itself with telling a story. "Pretty" as Updike's prose was, Wallace acknowledged to the interviewer, "I don't hear the click."

Soon another postmodern work came his way. That book was Thomas Pynchon's *The Crying of Lot 49*. Charlie McLagan, a fellow student, had turned him on to Pynchon the semester before. McLagan, who was a year behind Wallace, was different from the rest of their circle. He came from a wealthy suburban Chicago family who belonged to a country club. At Amherst he kept himself apart, rooming alone in Tyler House, a distant dorm, in a room he nicknamed "the Womb" with madras prints on the wall. His two cats were named Crime and Punishment. McLagan read widely and imaginatively, and let everyone know he had sex with his girl-friend. When Wallace and Costello would go to his dorm, the three would drink gin and tonics and eat Nutter Butter cookies and listen to U2. (Wallace was delighted to find his roommate looked like the band's gui-tarist, The Edge.) But when Wallace came alone, the atmosphere was more intense: despite Wallace's effort to stop smoking pot, he and McLa-gan would get high together. "God damn Charlie and his damn drug-allure," he wrote Washington that summer. The two would sometimes even drop acid, but Wallace found he preferred mushrooms. "Don't do LSD, and don't do coke, because they're both dangerous and expensive in that order," Wallace advised Washington, but "mushrooms are fun and giggly and they make you think you're smarter than you are . . . which is fun for a while." While they tripped, Wallace and McLagan would listen over and over to "The Big Ship" by Brian Eno on McLagan's expensive stereo. McLagan heard birth in it; Wallace thought it captured the earth in the time of the dinosaurs.

One day McLagan had run into Wallace and Costello discussing *One Hundred Years of Solitude* and tossed them his copy of *Lot 49*, which they promptly read. The novel is the story of Oedipa Maas, a young woman trying to uncover a centuries-old conspiracy involving a secret postal organization known as Trystero. Maas travels around California encountering people who give her clues to the puzzle—or the whole action of the novel may be a hallucination or a hoax set in motion by an ex-boyfriend; the reader is left uncertain. One thing that caught Wallace's eye about the book was the idea that to live in America was to live in a world of confusion, where meaning was refracted and distorted, especially by the media that engulf and reconfigure every gesture. As one character announces, pointing at a television, "It comes into your dreams, you know. Filthy machine."

Lot 49 was an agile and ironic metacommentary, and the effect on Wallace cannot be overstated (so much so that in a later letter to one of his editors Wallace, ever nervous of his debt to the other writer, would lie and say he had not read the book). Wallace reading Pynchon was, remembers Costello, "like Bob Dylan finding Woody Guthrie." One postmodernist made way for another. Barthelme was hermetic, Pynchon expansive. He tried to take in the enormity of America in a way that Barthelme did not. And he showed you that the tone and sensibility of mainstream culture—*Lot 49* drew its energy from pop songs, TV shows, and thrillers—could sit alongside serious issues in fiction. At the very least, the book was funny, and Wallace already knew how to be funny. The irony of the writing was a more directed version of what he and Costello had been turning out at *Sabrina*.

Wallace had been free of depression since the beginning of 1982, but now, twenty months later, the black hole with teeth got hold of him again. Toward the end of an otherwise happy summer, he began to have acute anxiety attacks, perhaps brought on by a feeling of letdown after his perfect semester. His life had had the quality in the past year of using one click to drown out another. He himself in later interviews would—not entirely credibly—blame the breakdown on a sudden realization that he did not want to be a professor of logic, that he had "a kind of midlife crisis at twenty, which probably doesn't augur real well for my longevity," as he told an interviewer. The discipline suddenly seemed lifeless and pedantic to him; and his amazing grade point average was just an evasion, a reflection of his fear of dealing with living people as opposed to dry equations. "The same obsessive studying that helped me come alive," he would later explain to an interviewer, "also kept me dead." Whatever the onset of the attack, things got worse when a psychiatrist prescribed Tofranil, a tricyclic antidepressant, to help ease the anxiety.

Wallace hated the drug, which made him feel apathetic. He was preparing for the third leg of Kennick's history of philosophy course, but now when he tried to read Wittgenstein's *Philosophical Investigations*—"Uncle Ludwig" in his formulation—he couldn't focus. Wittgenstein was a core interest of Wallace's. His father had studied with a disciple of the Austrian philosopher, as had Kennick. For a while Wallace tried to ignore the side effects. He played tennis, went to the gym, swam "a teenyweeny bit," "farting off," as he wrote Washington, to whom he did not at first mention the crisis. The upset was augmented by the fact that Wittgenstein seemed to be saying what he was thinking and Pynchon writing: that experience was like a game, that people were all and ever radically disconnected. Still hopeful, he went to rejoin his classmates, only to find himself falling into deeper agony.

Back at school for the fall, he found himself in an uncongenial housing situation. He and Costello, now a senior, had joined a large rooming group, some eight people divided into two suites. Wallace could not find a way to be comfortable among so many young men. The group included preppy students, who on principle rubbed Wallace the wrong way (Wallace had ended a friendship with one of his freshman stoner friends when he had joined a fraternity). His brittle balance shattered, Wallace began to withdraw into himself. He would sit quietly at the Valentine dining table in the midst of his friends' chatter and say nothing. They would urge him to do his impersonations but he wouldn't respond. Just as Costello had the year before, they were learning that there was another side to their friend.

Quietly, Wallace again thought about hurting himself. McLagan was on his mind. During their hours in the "womb," Wallace had debated suicide with McLagan. Music playing, they kicked around the fate of Ian Curtis of Joy Division, who hanged himself at the age of twenty-three. In high school McLagan himself had once stood on the edge of an overpass with a bottle of champagne in his hand, contemplating throwing himself onto the Illinois Tollway. For McLagan, killing yourself could be the fitting—maybe even necessary—exit for the sensitive artist from the brutal world. Wallace, though he'd known a despair deeper than his friends could imagine, wasn't so sure. Suicide looked to him like an escape rather than a solution. He knew depression too well to see it as glamorous. He looked around for ways to harm himself but decided instead to withdraw from school again and find a psychiatrist.

Leaving school a second time for Wallace was even more humiliating. No one had known him sophomore year; no one cared if he came or went. But by the fall of 1983 he was one of the school's champion students. He had just won a scholarship for most promising philosophy student and would have to give the money back. The scene from sophomore year repeated itself with variations. Costello drove Wallace to Bradley Airport outside Hartford for the flight home. (The car, an AMC Pacer, would later surface, with Wallace's mother's Gremlin, in *The Pale King*.) The first time Wallace had left, a year and a half before, he had fought back tears; this time he showed little emotion. He kept telling Costello he had thought he'd had a strategy and now it was clear he had been deluding himself. For the last twenty miles he was silent and wouldn't let Costello park the car to see him to his gate.

Wallace had told none of his other friends that he was leaving. He did not give his trust easily but felt he could bring Corey Washington into his confidence by now. So, shortly after he got home, he explained his departure in a letter: "I came very close to doing something stupid and irrevocable at Amherst but finally opted, sensibly or wimpishly, depending on whether your point of view is that of my parents or that of Charlie

M[cLagan], to try to get better so that I could exist." He added that he now found himself in the hands of a doctor he trusted. He made light of some of the revelations to his friend: "One hideous symptom of severe depression is that it is impossible both to do anything and to do nothing; as a devotee of Jumping Joe's [their logic professor's] Celebrated Excluded Middle I am sure you can assess that this is an Intolerable Situation." More seriously the psychiatrist, whom Wallace nicknamed "Dr. Tetemaigrir" (French for Head Shrinker), had, he wrote Washington, "real valid and non-sterile things to say" about depression. The doctor took him off Tofranil and likely put him on a different antidepressant. Wallace was beginning to understand things that had either never been told to him before or that he was only now ready to hear: that he had a biological condition that was with him for the rest of his life. He couldn't just ignore it. Though he shared his family's worry that, as Amy says, "his potential as an autonomous adult was pretty much vaporizing," Wallace began healing, the "festering pus-swollen c[h]ancre at the center of my brain" diminishing, as he wrote to Washington. He apologized for the façade he had been putting up, adding in another note, "You now see before you, indirectly at least, the real 'Waller': an obscurely defective commodity that has also been somewhat damaged in transit."

Even in the midst of his depression and treatment, Wallace continued to read widely. He picked up Pynchon's *Gravity's Rainbow* and finished it in eight nights, or so he told McLagan. He wrote as well, focusing as he had not before. The work Wallace undertook now was at a different level. His hope that he could lose himself in the rigors of logical philosophy shredded, he may have felt he had no other choice. He had nowhere left to hide. In the event, he was now able to achieve things he had not before. One result was "The Planet Trillaphon as It Stands in Relation to the Bad Thing," the story of a young man who withdraws from college with psychiatric problems. Though it was not pure autobiography, the authorial "I" and the "I" of the narrator parallel each other in the story in a way they never would again in Wallace's fiction; the sense of dismay at being mentally ill is fresh. The layers of asserting and then hedging those assertions to assert slightly more emphatically and imaginatively that would constitute Wallace's style are beginning to form. For much of his story, Wallace drew on his memories of his recent traumatic breakdowns. His nameless narrator is also suffering from "the Bad Thing"—his phrase for depression. He has tried to commit suicide in his parents' house—"a really highly ridiculous incident involving electrical appliances in the bathtub about which I really don't wish to say a whole lot"—and at story's beginning he finds himself in a psychiatric hospital. In the ward, Dr. Kablumbus gives the narrator a choice between electroconvulsive therapy and a course of antidepressants. The narrator chooses the latter, but the drug he is given, Tofranil, makes him feel tired and affectless, just as it had Wallace the previous summer. Still the narrator—earnest in the style of Wallace when he first entered Amherst—assures us that being medicated is not so bad. "They're fine, really," he claims of antidepressants, "but they're fine in the same way that, say, living on another planet that was warm and comfortable and had food and fresh water would be fine: it would be fine, but it wouldn't be good old Earth, obviously."

A fellow patient may come to the rescue, though. In the ward the narrator meets May Aculpa, a young woman likely recycled from the story Wallace had shown Costello the year before. May Aculpa and the narrator chat and flirt, but just as a human connection is being made, the pretty young depressive is discharged, only to die in a car accident shortly after. "I tried to call May's parents," the narrator tells us at story's end, "just to say that I was incredibly sorry," but he gets the parents' answering service.[7]

"Planet Trillaphon," which Wallace would publish in the *Amherst Review* when he got back to college, is more original in subject than in style.[8] Its structure and pacing are those of well-made student fiction; Wallace was still deconstructing existing stories trying to find what held them together. He boasted to the interviewer David Lipsky years later that his gift in college was to be "a weird kind of forger. I can sound kind of like anybody." Here he was rifling Pynchon for names and J. D. Salinger for tone, but the Salingerian faux naïveté becomes magnified with a lens worthy of Gogol as Wallace reimagines his nightly battles with acne as something surreal:

> I began to suffer from what I guess now was a hallucination. I thought that a huge wound, a really huge and deep wound, had opened on my face, on my cheek near my nose.... Right before graduation—or maybe a month before, maybe—it got really bad,

such that when I'd pull my hand away from my face I'd see blood on my fingers, and bits of tissue and stuff, and I'd be able to smell the blood, too. . . . So one night when my parents were out somewhere I took a needle and some thread and tried to sew up the wound myself.

A literary sensibility is emerging too. The prose feels fraught and necessary. The writing conveys a sense that consciousness tricks and torments us, helps us build a wall to hide from who we are, yet at the same time the pleasure-giving power of words eases the despair of the story, along with a hope that love can rescue, a wispy hint that is quickly obliterated and will not appear in Wallace's work again for many years.[8]

What is most original and distinctive in "Trillaphon," though, is the precision with which the narrator captures what it is like to be deeply depressed, his skillful evocation of a state of mind he wants us urgently to understand. One would hardly mistake this for ordinary student fiction about depression, the kind the narrator dismisses as "just sort of really intense sadness, like what you feel when your very good dog dies . . . and in a couple days it's gone altogether." Real depression, the narrator insists, is different:

To me it's like being completely, totally, utterly sick. I will try to explain what I mean. Imagine feeling really sick to your stomach. . . . [Now] imagine your whole body being sick like that. . . . Imagine that every cell in your body, every single cell in our body is as sick as that nauseated stomach. Not just your own cells, even, but the e. coli and lactobacilli too, the mitochondria, basal bodies, all sick and boiling and hot like maggots in your neck, your brain, all over, everywhere, in everything. All just *sick* as hell. Now imagine that every single *atom* in every single cell in your body is sick like that, sick, intolerably sick. And every proton and neutron in every atom . . . swollen and throbbing, off-color, sick, with just no chance of throwing up to relieve the feeling. Every electron is sick, here, twirling off balance and all erratic in these funhouse orbitals that are just thick and swirling with mottled yellow and purple poison gases, everything off balance and woozy.

But even this doesn't capture the overwhelming experience of depression for the narrator. "The Bad Thing is you," he concludes, echoing the caption under the Kafka picture he had on his bulletin board at home (the disease was life itself),

> nothing else . . . you are the sickness yourself. . . . You realize all this, here. And that, I guess, is . . . when you look at the black hole and it's wearing your face. That's when the Bad Thing just absolutely eats you up, or rather when you just eat yourself up. When you kill yourself. All this business about people committing suicide when they're "severely depressed"; we say, "Holy cow, we must do something to stop them from killing themselves!" That's wrong. Because all these people have, you see, by this time *already* killed themselves, where it really counts. . . . When they "commit suicide," they're just being orderly.[9]

Wallace wrote Washington a bit of doggerel to herald his return for the second semester of the 1983–84 school year:

> *Roses are Red.*
> *Violets are Blue;*
> *I am well*
> *And hope you are too.*
> *Wittgenstein,*
> *Was a raving fairy;*
> *I'll be in Amherst*
> *In January.*

Charlie McLagan, leaving his parents' house in suburban Chicago, picked him up in Urbana and drove him east in the family's station wagon. They listened to Joy Division and Brian Eno as they sped along the interstate. McLagan was himself taking a year off, and Wallace stayed with him and his roommate for a week in Boston. McLagan thought Wallace seemed different now—fragile, tentative, apologizing for everything he did, whether it was playing the TV too loud or using up the soap in the shower (he washed his hair with soap, not wanting to waste his friend's shampoo). McLagan's roommate joked to him that Wallace seemed on the point of apologizing for using the oxygen in the air. On New Year's Eve, the three went to a nudie bar in the Combat Zone. Wallace said he found it depressing. McLagan told him he needed to toughen up. "This is reality," he pronounced.

When the semester started, Wallace showed his new commitment to fiction. He believed that if he was going to write better, he had to study it, just as he had philosophy. So during the next two semesters he took classes in the American novel and modern British poetry, finding himself particularly drawn to Frank Norris's ungainly naturalist novel *McTeague* in the former and to T. S. Eliot's cryptic "The Waste Land" in the latter. He took a course in literary approaches and theory and reveled in Jacques Derrida's essays, "The Double Session" and "Plato's Pharmacy." Norris's novel showed how much room there was for the bizarre in fiction, even in supposedly realist works; Eliot, whose poem has dozens of famously ambiguous endnotes, suggested a place for self-consciousness in literary creativity. (Wallace would one day say that he loved endnotes because they were "almost like having a second voice in your head.") Derrida would be the longest-lasting influence of the three. Wallace told his professor, Andrew Parker, that he was happy to find a philosopher who cared about literature.

The biggest innovation in Wallace's life was a class in creative writing he signed up for. For him, this was an extraordinary departure. He still did not like the literary environment at school. It seemed effeminate and sensitive and self-absorbed. And then, too, he was a young man from the Midwest, and midwestern boys might teach or read or make ironic fun of novels, but they did not go to college to learn how to write them; fiction wasn't quite school and it wasn't quite work. Wallace's attitude might be summed up by a comment the narrator makes in "Planet Trillaphon" about May: "She wanted to write made-up stories for a living. I said I didn't know that could be done."

Amherst was similarly skeptical of creative writing. The school offered only one class, under the sponsorship of the English department. That year its teacher was Alan Lelchuk, the school's visiting writer. The veteran novelist immediately noticed the skinny boy in the back with the backward baseball cap and strong opinions. Wallace submitted a story; Lelchuk told him the writing was shallow and tricky, "philosophy with zingers." The young man would have, Lelchuk remembers, a clever thought and then "three wise-ass sentences around it." Lelchuk called Wallace in to discuss it with him, expecting the student might get angry and quit the class. He told Wallace that he could be a philosopher or a writer, and if he wanted to be a writer, Lelchuk could be of use; he should take the week to think about it. To his surprise, Wallace was back the next day asking for help. Lelchuk was pleased; he thought Wallace was acknowledging how much he had to learn. But privately, Wallace was seething. He was probably Amherst's best student and expected the respect that came with that rank. He did not like to be criticized. But then Lelchuk, a realist in the style of Philip Roth, gave a reading of a portion of his new novel, *Miriam in Her Forties*, and Wallace relaxed. At one point an inmate has his first meal after getting out of jail and exclaims, "A mite better than prison fare." A new punch line was born among Wallace and his friends, as Costello remembers. Looking at the weather: "A mite rainy, no?" And on the way to Valentine: "Care to get some breakfast fare?" To Wallace, Lelchuk's effort embodied the clumsiness of mainstream realist fiction. He thought he could do better.

Lelchuk was never thrilled with Wallace's writing, but he recognized his unusual talent and gave him an A-minus. This was the lowest grade Wallace had gotten since the first semester of his freshman year. (He would claim in a later interview that he had to write his stories once, then rewrite them more conventionally to get the grade.) Elsewhere that semester, he got A-pluses in the literary theory class, epistemology, and ethical theories, and an A in American fiction after the Civil War. He was admitted to Phi Beta Kappa and won three academic awards, one for having the highest grades for his first three years.

Back at Amherst in the fall of 1984 for his senior year, Wallace found himself with a new challenge. Costello was gone, having graduated with a double summa, said to be the first student to do so in forty years. He had written two theses, one a novel, the other a study of the New Deal. Ever competitive, Wallace decided he would match his friend. In philosophy he remained interested in the structures of language. Though fiction had taken over his enthusiasms, this highly technical subject still intrigued him and he was aware that once he graduated it would be easier to make a living in a philosophy department than writing fiction. In school he had encountered the work of Richard Taylor, a professor of philosophy at Brown University, who in 1962 had written an elegantly spare paper that argued that the future is predestined. The assertions in Taylor's "Fatalism" weren't philosophical in the commonly understood sense but really assertions about the implications of the logic behind language. In their contentions Wallace saw room for a thesis-length response.

Taylor's argument went like this: Since every statement is by definition either true or false, all statements about the future are also currently either true or false. But if that's so, then how can our actions have any causal influence over how things turn out? Aren't we merely acting in accordance with a future that is already set in stone? One example Wallace gave in his paper was of a bomb going off at Amherst. If a terrorist were to set off a nuclear explosion at the school, then there would be a high amount of radiation on campus. So if it is true now that there will be that amount of radiation, then it must follow that a nuclear explosion will go off. Contrarily, if it is false now, then an explosion won't go off. But since that proposition is right now either true or false, then one or the other result is already fated to occur.

Taylor's elegant formulation seemed airtight, and if it were correct, then vast, unappealing implications followed. But perhaps even more important to Wallace was that such a simple-seeming line of reasoning—he called it "the famous and infamous Taylor argument" in his thesis—with its suggestion that free will was an illusion, constituted a sort of wormhole in the logic of the universe, and Wallace himself, always struggling with the world as it was, did not like the idea of another wormhole.

He was not the first to try to counter Taylor's argument. He was impressed with how well it had withstood determined opposition; it would not be easy to overturn. "It's really ulcer-city," he wrote Professor Kennick. He chose to combat Taylor on his own linguistic and formal grounds. He asserted that Taylor had confused two slightly different forms of futurity in his paper. There is a difference, Wallace pointed out, between a future that (paradoxically) shapes the present and a future that (commonsensically) is shaped by the present. When, looking back at the past, you say either, "It was the case that X could not happen" or "It cannot be the case that X did happen," you are actually saying slightly different things. In the first case, you are arguing controversially that events in the future constrained what happened in the past; in the second case, you are merely noting that events in the future were consistent with the past. Taylor, he believed, could only assert that the future was determined by the present, not the other way around.

Wallace wrote his philosophy papers in an informal, conversational tone, almost like offshoots of the bull sessions at Valentine. But analytic philosophy also required formal mathlike notations. Wallace, for all his gifts of mimicry, didn't know how to do them. He had avoided straight math classes at Amherst, afraid they might lower his grade point average. He was aware how odd this looked: being good at the theory of math without being able to solve math problems. "It seems sort of cheaty," he had written Washington his junior year, "something like throwing a girl's skirts over her head and kissing her on the bare stomach before you've even introduced yourself or taken her for a malted or anything." An undergraduate acquaintance, Jamie Rucker, helped him on some of the notations. A junior professor at Hampshire College, Jay Garfield, who was an adviser to the thesis, worked with him on the others. Wallace ended his thesis with a scold that almost sounded out of the mouth of his father: "If Taylor and the fatalists want to force upon us a metaphysical conclusion, they must do metaphysics, not semantics. And this seems entirely appropriate." The philosophy panel awarded him a summa. He spent the remainder of the semester helping other students with their work. "It was a great year for theses," Willem DeVries remembers.

That same fall he began his second thesis, a novel, and saw immediately that he preferred it to debunking Taylor. (He would later say that fiction took 97 percent of his brain, philosophy only 50 percent.) He already had a slight reputation on campus as a writer. He had, after consulting with his friends, published "The Planet Trillaphon" in the college literary magazine, the *Amherst Review*, the semester before. "As far as we know," the editors wrote for Wallace's author note, "he has never left this planet." But some of the undergraduates who read the story wondered. They rightly took its portrait of a boy with depression for the autobiography it partially was. Students would see Wallace and tell their friends there was the guy who had had electroshock treatment. They showed one another an oak crossbeam in the former fraternity house for Chi Phi—the fraternities were banned from campus Wallace's senior year—and confided knowledgeably that Wallace had tried to hang himself from it. For the first time in his life he was becoming a person of note, his reputation consisting in equal parts of his huge appetite for work and the penumbra of mental illness that hung about him.

Amherst women were becoming interested in him in particular. They admired his nonconformity and his extraordinary intelligence, and they admired how he admired them. Given purpose or courage by being a writer—"Fiction writers as a species tend to be oglers," he would write in a later essay—he began appraising them in a way he had not dared before. One, he told his friends, "applied make-up skillfully." Another—pretty to him—had "puke-white skin." His comment about the pale blue-green eyes of Washington's first girlfriend was that they "needed some food coloring." His extreme self-consciousness about his own body was turning outward, into sustained erotic—a favorite word of his—focus. He remembered that his sister's best friend in high school was a pretty girl with really ugly feet and made the observation into a truth universally acknowledged in the novel he was starting for his thesis. He had relationships, avidly and with guilt. He began what he called his "body count." "Smell that, Core?" he said to his friend one day in April as they walked on the green in front of the Valentine Dining Hall. "It's springtime. The smell of cunt in the air." He took up clove cigarettes, got headaches, took Advil, quit the cigarettes, and the headaches went away. He joked that he was responsible for most of Bayer's profits. He would try to quit pot, then start it again, never quite admitting that he had. After getting high, he would dig up Washington and persuade him to go to the convenience store to calm his munchies. "Core," he'd ask his friend, "don't you want chips?" and get him to buy them for him. He had a work-study job as a telephone operator, working the 1970s-era contraption with its big square buttons. He enjoyed the jumble of voices pouring in, callers asking for directions, the campus police, or information they should already have had—he refused to give out the delivery number for the most popular pizzeria. During quiet times, he would write scenes from the novel.

Wallace also watched TV in Moore, in a common room that he told

Washington smelled of the women students who worked out in it each morning. He watched his usual programs and added *Late Night with David Letterman* and religious programs on weekends, the latter useful for sections of the novel he had started. Mostly, though, with Costello gone and the novel moving fast, he wrote. As a senior, he was entitled to his own room and the privacy he had little of since high school. The towels came out to be spread over everything. On the wall over the desk of his single, he put the famous photograph of Thomas Pynchon as a buck-toothed undergraduate at Cornell. Most evenings Wallace could be found either at his desk or in Frost Library writing. He had gotten to know Dale Peterson, an English professor who taught a class on the literature of madness.[10] Peterson—Wallace nicknamed him "Whale"—was gentle and supportive. He understood Wallace's enormous gifts and wanted to encourage them. He became Wallace's thesis adviser and simply let Wallace do as he wished. Wallace could feel the words pouring out, and superstitiously he tried to follow the same routines day after day to keep them coming. He had bought a motorcycle jacket from Charlie McLagan and wore it whenever he was working on the thesis, listening at one point, for example, to U2's "MLK" and Bruce Springsteen's "Born in the USA" over and over as he worked. He composed with cheap Bic pens. If he lost one that he had written well with, he would retrace his steps until he found it, then keep using it until it ran out of ink. He referred to these luck-filled pens as his "orgasm pens."

After he had finished his first draft, he'd type it up on his Smith-Corona, making changes as he went, into the early morning. His typing was so relentless that the student in the next-door dorm room in Moore moved his bed away from their shared wall. Wallace asked Professor Kennick if he could borrow his office, to spare his neighbor the noise of his "Blob-like" and "out of control" English thesis. When McLagan asked him how things were going, Wallace told him the book was coming so fast it was like a scroll unwinding in his head; he wasn't the author so much as the transcriber. He told Washington that during one three-hour session he had written twenty-four pages. He was so excited that when he wasn't writing he would go to the gym and do sit-ups until he puked.

Word of his gargantuan project got out—most undergraduate English theses were fifty pages—and stoked his celebrity. He wasn't above using his renown as a buffer for his long-standing insecurity. After one class-mate beat him at tennis, Wallace invited him back to his library cubicle. "I'm writing this five-hundred-page-novel," he bragged, and showed him his transcript for good measure.

The premise of the novel that became *The Broom of the System* began, he would later tell his editor, with a chance comment from a girlfriend. She had told him that she would rather be a character in a novel than a real person. "I got to wondering just what the difference was," Wallace wrote. In addition, he had been mulling over the hoary literary advice given by Lelchuk: "Show, don't tell." What did that mean, really, since all writing was telling? But if words were pictures of the things they represented, wasn't all writing also by definition showing? This last was an extension of the thinking of Ludwig Wittgenstein ("Uncle Ludwig"), whose explorations of the relationship between language and reality were becoming more and more interesting to Wallace. His enthusiasm for technical philosophy was declining, and Wittgenstein was filling the gap. The Viennese philosopher had written two very different treatises on language. In one, as a young man, he wrote that language mirrors reality, that the concept of an abstract thought is meaningless—words correspond to reality in the same way that a photograph corresponds to the thing photographed. The concomitant of this idea, in Wittgenstein's idiosyncratic vision, is that you can with certainty know nothing outside of yourself. This identification—"the loss of the whole external world," as Wallace put it to a later interviewer—frightened him but also intrigued him deeply. He considered the opening statement of the *Tractatus Logico-Philosophicus*, in which Wittgenstein laid out this thesis, one of the two "most beautiful opening lines in Western Lit": "The world is everything that is the case."[11] Language—and by extension thought—only had dominion over things of which we can have direct sensual knowledge. The *Tractatus*'s preface begins, "This book will perhaps be understood only by those who have themselves already thought the thoughts which are expressed in it—or similar thoughts." If the *Tractatus* wasn't calling out for him, nothing was.

But he also knew that Wittgenstein had gone on to reverse his early thinking and come later to the idea that language was communal, a Ponzi scheme based on shared acceptance; language, in Wittgenstein's later appraisal, was like a game. This point of view also spoke to Wallace, with its invitation to unleash his sense of humor and verbal playfulness. Later, Wallace would make the issues Wittgenstein raised in him seem trite and funny. To an interviewer he would describe *Broom* as banal, a covert autobiography, "the sensitive tale of a sensitive young WASP who's just had this midlife crisis that's moved him from coldly cerebral analytic math to a coldly cerebral take on fiction . . . which also shifted his existential dread from a fear that he was just a 98.6°F calculating machine to a fear that he was nothing but a linguistic construct." But at the time the implications of Wittgenstein's theories were very alive for him. After all, late Wittgenstein was Wallace well; early Wittgenstein, the author depressed.

Wallace's fictional manuscript and the philosophy thesis were also of a piece: both asked whether language depicted the world or in some deeper way defined it and even altered it. Does our understanding of what we experience derive from objective reality or from cognitive limitations within us? Is language a window or a cage? Of course, Wallace, with his mental travails, wanted a real and truthful view, or at least a benign and playful illusion. There was a favorite example of the vibrant bond between language and objects that Wallace and his friends kicked around in Valentine. Which was the more important part of a broom, the brush or the handle? Most people would say the brush, but it really depended on what you needed the broom for. If you wanted to sweep, then indeed the bristles were the important part; but if you had to break a window, then it was the handle.

Wallace set his story in the near future, 1990, and to give these sorts of philosophical questions an airing, he created twenty-four-year-old Lenore Stonecipher Beadsman, a recent graduate of Oberlin College (though all her female relatives went to Mount Holyoke and all her male ones to Amherst). Like Wallace in college, Lenore is a switchboard operator. And like women in general to Wallace, she is a mystery, a cipher, an erotic object for the male eye. Dressed in a "uniform of white cotton dress and black Converse hightop sneakers," she is "an unanalyzable and troubling constant," an uncomfortable soul who "works in neurosis like a whaler in scrimshaw." At root what worries her is whether she is real or made up. As her boyfriend, Rick Vigorous (Amherst, class of '69), comments:

> She simply felt—at times, mind you, not all the time, but at sharp and distinct intuitive moments—as if she had no real existence, except for what she said and did and perceived and et cetera, and that these were, it seemed at such times, not really under her control.

Lenore comes by this anxiety through her genes: her great-grandmother and namesake, Lenore Beadsman, now in her nineties and in a local nursing home, studied with Wittgenstein, from whom she adopted his radically potent idea of the independence of language.[12] Says Rick:

> She has, from what little I can gather, convinced Lenore that she is in possession of some words of tremendous power. No, really, Not things, or concepts. Words. The woman is apparently obsessed with words. I neither am nor wish to be entirely clear on the matter, but apparently she was some sort of phenomenon in college and won a place in graduate study at Cambridge. . . . There she studied classics and philosophy and who knows what else under a mad crackpot genius named Wittgenstein, who believed that everything was words. Really. If your car would not start, it was apparently to be understood as a language problem. If you were unable to love, you were lost in language. Being constipated equaled being clogged with linguistic sediment. To me, the whole thing smacks strongly of bullshit.

He adds, "Words and a book and a belief that the world is words and Lenore's conviction that her own intimate personal world is only of, neither by nor for, her. Something is not right."

At novel's beginning, the older Lenore has disappeared from her nursing home, taking with her many of the other residents. She has left behind a clue, a drawing of a head bursting, as a guide to her whereabouts. Lenore pursues her forebear, Oedipa Maas–like, as she tries to figure out where her great-grandmother went and how this relates to her ontological unease. To accompany Lenore, Wallace gave her a parrot based on his thesis adviser Dale Peterson's cockatiel, now reimagined as the horrible bird

Vlad the Impaler, who quotes scripture and bits of dirty conversation he overhears.

There is another character of importance to Wallace, LaVache Stonecipher. Lenore's brother, LaVache is a depressive and brilliant Amherst undergraduate, who helps other students with their schoolwork in return for drugs that he hides in his artificial leg. (Wallace claimed that he traded thesis help for pot in school.) LaVache is the cleverest character in the book, smart enough to put Wittgenstein to his own uses. He, for instance, calls his phone "a lymph node," so that when his father, whom he wishes to avoid, asks if he has a phone, he can honestly say no. Unlike his sister, Lenore, LaVache is protected by his irony and his distance, but simultaneously he is trapped, marginal, without a center: he literally barely has a leg to stand on. He exudes what Wallace would later call "the 'moral clarity' of the immature." "No one expects me to be anything other than what I am," LaVache says, "which is a waste-product, slaving endlessly to support his leg." It is hard not to see in him a foreshadowing of Wallace's soon to be deepening problems. The novel's title came from a phrase Sally Wallace remembered from her grandmother, who when she would encourage her children to eat an apple would say, "Come on, it's the broom of the system." With its overtones of Wittgenstein, the image delighted Wallace.

If Wittgenstein was the obvious philosophical point of departure for Wallace's book, the literary influences were even clearer. Wallace had a technical mind, and in *Broom* he reverse-engineers the postmodern novels he was enjoying. The overwhelming influence is Pynchon: from him come the names, the ambience of low-level paranoia, and the sense of America as a toxic, media- and entertainment-saturated land. He took the flat, echoing tone of his dialogue from Don DeLillo, whose novels he had been reading while working on the book. (One night a friend who did part-time work as an Amherst security guard bumped into him at his switchboard working his way through *Ratner's Star*.)[13] The minute, flirtatious appraisal of women seems borrowed from Nabokov, himself a teacher of Pynchon. The farrago of forms—stories within stories, transcripts of meetings, duty logs, rock medleys, and madcap set pieces—comes from Pynchon too, as well as from other postmodernists like Barthelme and John Barth. When Lenore points out that East Corinth, the suburb of

Cleveland she lives in, is meant to look like the outline of Jayne Mansfield seen from the air, it is hard not to think of Oedipa Maas getting her first look at San Narciso, the imaginary city near Los Angeles, which, she muses, resembles a transistor radio circuit board with its "intent to communicate."[14]

Pynchon saturates the book's DNA: he is in the atmosphere of not quite serious corporate intrigue, in the meetings in obscure bars, and the psychiatrists more in need of help than their patients (Dr. Jay shares *Lot 49's* Dr. Hilarius's "delightful lapses from orthodoxy"), so much so that when Wallace gave his manuscript to McLagan, he read a few pages and returned it; he did not have time for a Pynchon rip-off. And yet McLagan was too dismissive. The book is original. It differs from Pynchon in delicate but pervasive ways. Pynchon's Oedipa Maas is emotionless, surfing above dysfunctional America with a light 1960s sense of indestructibility. By contrast Wallace's Lenore—"a beautiful, bright, witty, largely joyful albeit troubled and anyway interestingly troubled" girl, as Dr. Jay describes her—strives for contact.[15] There is an ache in *Broom*. If on the surface even lighter than the Pynchon novel, just a bit below it exudes discomfort and yearning. Wallace's anxiety, his fear of a world in which nothing is rooted, and his intense attempts to understand what women want and how to form a relationship with them ("How do you know when you can kiss her?") are apparent. The borderline between the self and the other preoccupies: Rick Vigorous's penis is too small to have sex with Lenore; another character, Norman Bombardini, is so vast he literally tries to eat her, while Lenore herself almost seems as incorporeal as her great-grandmother. The bizarre up-and-down of Wallace's Amherst life is there too, the school that for Wallace, as for Vigorous, was "a devourer of the emotional middle, a maker of psychic canyons, a whacker of the pendulum of mood with the paddle of Immoderation." Wallace would in future years dismiss the book as written by "a very smart fourteen-year-old," but that is unfair: this adolescent is not just smart; he is attempting to communicate.

In the late spring of 1985 Dale Peterson and the other members of Wallace's thesis panel gave *Broom* an A-plus, and Wallace matched Costello double summa for double summa. But he had also discovered something more important about himself—he knew now what he wanted to do. Fiction held him as no other effort had; it took him out of time and released him from some of the pain of being himself. He told his roommate that when he was writing, "I can't feel my ass in the chair." On a visit to campus the spring of Wallace's senior year, Costello bumped into Kennick walking across the college green. "Costello? Wallace's friend, right?" The professor commanded, "Tell him he must study philosophy." Costello passed on the message to Wallace, who shrugged it off.

CHAPTER 3

"Westward!"

During his senior year Wallace applied to creative writing programs. It never occurred to him that he could just go somewhere and write: he came from academia and believed in the classroom. Moreover, he knew with his shaky mental state that he needed health insurance, and to get health insurance you needed a job, and the only job a writer could do was to teach, and to teach you needed an MFA.

He sent out a chapter from *Broom* along with his stellar transcript and his long list of prizes. He was accepted at several programs, among them the University of Iowa Writers' Workshop and the writing program at the University of Arizona. Iowa was the most prestigious school in the country—Wallace was keenly alert to this, telling Costello it was the "Harvard Law of MFAs"—but it was also the center of the sort of realist fiction that interested him least.[1] In contrast, Arizona sent him a tempting letter. "Instead of the 'guru' system (which tends to foster a 'school' of writing, and a tendency of the student to write for or like one master)," the director, Mary Carter, wrote, "we encourage diversity." In other words, at Arizona Wallace wouldn't have to come out writing like John Cheever, as he would almost anywhere else; he could follow his own voice. The program, though small, had a national reputation and the offer of admission came with an $8,000 scholarship. When the Iowa Workshop told Wallace he would have to pay full tuition, the deal was done. He wrote the Workshop with the news. "I don't have any money and need to go where I can get some financial aid," he reminded them pointedly. McLagan told him he was lucky to be heading west. The desert was beautiful, the girls extraordinary. At his Amherst graduation Wallace received several more academic prizes, bringing his total awards to ten, likely an Amherst record.

Wallace arrived in Tucson in mid-August. Arizona's beauty was revelatory to him. The light was different, the dunelike mountains "lunar." "They," he told his college friends in an audio letter they sent to one another that fall, "catch the sun in really pretty ways, really interesting ways." "Accidents in Tucson," he continued, "are basically people hypnotized by the sun, looking out through the screen." He thought he could be happy there, amid the browned-out lawns and the cactus-dotted foothills.

He was ready for a fresh start. Earlier that year, he and Perkins had finally ended their relationship. At first Wallace found the breakup a relief, but then waves of guilt followed. He saw that his behavior at Amherst had ruined the relationship with the woman who had stuck by him at his lowest point.

In early summer, he decided to drive back to Amherst from Urbana and pick up Corey Washington, who was planning a visit, and by the time he did he was in a quiet crisis. Like Rick Vigorous in *Broom*, his imagination had begun to run away with him. Perkins was in Urbana too and the nearness tormented him. What was she doing? he would ask, Washington remembers. Whose car was now in her driveway? Wallace imagined her sleeping with other men. The predicament he was thrown into was not unlike the one brought about by his mother after his first breakdown at Amherst: it came from the same sense, justified or not, that someone on whom he had deeply relied, had betrayed him. They had committed the crime of remaking his reality. Wallace held so fast to his sparse emotional certainties that when they proved unstable, the impact was crushing. Then unleashed feelings of hurt and confusion would go round and round, bending in on themselves, mixing with guilt, until his brain reached a point of exhaustion.

Washington saw his friend withdraw. Wallace spoke softly and soberly, without humor. They watched hours of television together, Wallace seeming to gain comfort from the TV; his friend held his hand and tried to maintain contact with him. Offstage there were conversations between Wallace's parents about what to do. To Washington they seemed surprisingly unsurprised, but then they had been down this road twice before in the past few years. After two days, they took their son to a local hospital, apologizing deeply to Washington, who took a bus home to Amherst.

Wallace stayed at the psychiatric unit at Carle Hospital for several weeks. The doctors likely considered the possibility that he suffered from bipolar disorder, manic depression. That he was crashing after an enormously productive spring would lend credence to that diagnosis, but they decided instead to give him Nardil, a MAO inhibitor often used to treat atypical depression. Atypical depression—its key characteristics are unusual sensitivity to social rejection and a quick return to mental health when circumstances improve—was a more welcome diagnosis in Wallace's eyes. It seemed less a sentence of insanity than the medical acknowledgment of a condition he was already dealing with. But Nardil—Wallace described the pills in a story he wrote in Arizona as "look[ing] just like the tiny round Red Hots we'd all eaten as children"—was an older antidepressant, a 1960s and '70s staple that came with many dietary prohibitions. He would no longer be able to eat chocolate or drink coffee, nor should he drink alcohol or take drugs. Smoky cheeses and hot dogs were also out, and he was supposed to avoid aged or fermented food in general, as well as liver. If he slipped up, the result would be fierce headaches and potentially dangerous spikes in blood pressure.

The Nardil helped Wallace quickly. By August he was out of the hospital and on a kind of high. On his way to his new school he stopped in Los Angeles to see a young woman he'd been close to at Amherst. Back in college, Wallace had begun a relationship with Andrea Justus, a fine arts major. Justus admired Wallace, by then a storied figure at the college. (In her circle he bore the nickname "the smart guy.") She had approached him to help her with the language in her thesis, which was about gesture in art. Quickly they became friends. When Justus was given a B-plus by the art history department, Wallace marched into her professor's office to ask why she hadn't gotten an A. With Perkins far away, Wallace got more deeply involved with Justus. She loved his talk and his intense gaze—he commented on an eyelash she had pointing off to the side that no one had ever noticed before. The story he told of how he had taken a semester off to cope with the suicide of his best friend particularly moved her. When Justus invited Wallace to stop in California on his way to Tucson, Wallace accepted. In August he came to Los Angeles. Soon after he got to her home in Fullerton, a town in Orange County, Sally Wallace called to tell his friend's mother that her son was on a powerful antidepressant and had to be careful around certain foods.

What Wallace knew about Southern California came mostly from books, including *The Crying of Lot 49*, where the fictional city of San Narciso is described as "a vast sprawl of houses which had grown up all together, like a well-tended crop, from the dull brown earth." But Wallace was in an upbeat mood and loved the area. "A real blast," he wrote Washington. Even better was the coastal city of Newport Beach, a "revoltingly tacky and ritzy Venice-like town." In his gloomier moments, this was the sort of environment he couldn't tolerate, but the world appeared cheerful and well to him now. The couple went to a party where a small boat took them out and putt-putted around the bay past John Wayne's house. They spent a night at the Hotel Laguna in Laguna Beach too, and Wallace overcame his fear of sharks enough to go in the ocean for only the second time in his life. This again may have been a tribute to the confidence and the sense of wellness the successful drug treatment was giving him. Justus's mother was generous and indulgent, not unlike his own. When he did not want to be sociable, he passed the time in his friend's bedroom, the lights off and the shades down, listening to Squeeze and INXS. He was still adjusting to the antidepressant, which tended to bring him morning highs and afternoon tiredness. (Justus's father, a physician, was unsurprised to find Wallace asleep in the car while they were touring Los Angeles.) That summer wildfires burned in the region, sending up huge plumes of smoke, and Wallace wrote to Costello how amazed he was to see rich Angelenos walking on the beach admiring the sunset, as the world burned.

After his visit, Wallace drove the eight hours to Tucson with Justus, ready to move into his graduate housing. She had friends in the city and they were having so much fun she thought about moving there too, a proposition that set off warning bells for Wallace. "I'm not ready or able for anything as serious as a Susie situation," he wrote Washington, "and couldn't have the obligation of [Andrea's] being in town because of me." There were other considerations too. "Most of the girls here are just incredibly beautiful, like a 10,000 member class of '88," he wrote. Happily, it turned out Justus was no more serious than he was. "She's breathtakingly level-headed (Salingerian trope)," Wallace reported, "and so having her here on the sort of level we've established would be terrific for me."

Justus was intrigued by her friend's impracticality. She helped him to take the money he routinely kept in his sock drawer and open a bank account with it. They visited his future apartment, which he was supposed to share with a student in optical sciences, and found the walls painted "a kind of urine-yellow" and the whole smelling, as Wallace told his friends in his audio letter, of, "in descending order, Lysol, another kind of air freshener, very, very, very old semen and again, urine." Justus urged him to find someplace else, reminding him he was an adult now. (Wallace to Washington: "Perhaps only half true.") With the deposit he got back, the two went house hunting. Soon Wallace found a small apartment on North Cherry Avenue, a shabby district a few blocks from the campus. The complex looked like an overgrown Motel-6 and was mostly parking lot, an unattractive part of an unattractive city, "replete with poisonous spiders and dead grass, gravel, violent crime," as he later wrote Professor Kennick at Amherst.

But Wallace was content. He had a young woman near but not too near and a place to write. His apartment consisted of two rooms and a kitchen and, as when he lived with Costello sophomore year, a view of a Dumpster. "It's a good dumpster," he reported to his friends. "It's painted white. It's about as large as a small truck. It gives off a fairly powerful odor when the wind is from the north."[2] He set himself up, Smith-Corona on the desk, towels spread out everywhere. Outside was a pool and lots of palm trees. "Their trunks," he told his friends, "tend to be kind of meaty. And their fronds—they're not called leaves; if you call them leaves people cock their eyebrows at you—the fronds tend to occupy angles that are sort of Lovecraftian. They don't quite match up to any known laws." The black widow spiders everywhere in Tucson excited his imagination too. "You use a propane torch to fry them in their webs and hope their grieving mates don't fall on your head from the palm trees above," he claimed.[3]

What made the room best of all was that he was soon writing in it. He could work hours without breaks, smoking heavily—he began the habit senior year of college—writing longhand on sheets of yellow paper or in notebooks. The notebooks also functioned, as he wrote in a story from

that period, for "trapping little inspirations before they could get away."
He found that he could write not just in his little apartment but anywhere—
in the smoking room of the library, on a bench, in a café. And he did not
need fiction workshops or input from teachers to get him going; he was
just exploding with words. One story he focused on was "Forever Overhead," the tale of a thirteen-year-old boy who stands atop a high-dive
board on his birthday and contemplates his imminent leap into maturity.
The boy wants both to turn back and to get in the pool. Frozen atop the
tower, he certainly experiences anxieties familiar to Wallace. "You have
decided being scared is caused mostly by thinking," the narrator notes.
Wallace uses the boy's moment of doubt to encapsulate the ambivalence
he felt about his own passage from childhood to his teen years (or perhaps the perils of writing). In the end the boy will dive, as he must. "The
board will nod and you will go," the narrator intones, "and eyes of skin
can cross blind into a cloud-botched sky that is forever, punctured light
emptying behind sharp skin that is forever. Step into the skin and disappear." The story was not typical of the writing Wallace was becoming interested in—it would soon seem to him sentimental and overblown—but
in his early days in Arizona he was happy with how easily everything
came to him.[4]

School began soon after he arrived. Among the seven thousand graduate
enrollees at the University of Arizona, the students in the writing program
were a miniscule contingent, comparable to Wallace's small band of
friends at Amherst. They rented houses together, ate together, drank together, dated each other, and read and commented on one another's stories. The symbolic hub of their world was a pretty adobe building called
the Poetry Center, but most of the work was done in the ugly, newish
Modern Languages Building. The program was run by Carter, a novelist of
uncertain age.[5] She had been famous for standing at her office desk, writing and smoking, but by the time Wallace arrived she had given up
smoking—and so stopped writing. Competitiveness and not a little jealousy laced the air of the program, though Wallace at first either did not
notice or did not care. "I love it here, Corey," he wrote his friend Washing-

ton shortly after arriving. "The place, the weather, the school, the girls, the students in the program, the girls, the professors, etc. I will be here for the next three years at least."

Most MFA students looked on writing as a calling unto itself. They took a few literature classes to satisfy the requirement for their degree. But Wallace was still interested in the ideas behind fiction, so he signed up his first semester for a class on the history of the English language, which prompted an attempt to write a story in Old English, and another class on literary theory that focused on Derrida's *Of Grammatology*. The course was a cinch for Wallace, who was familiar with much of the reading list from Amherst, if not from before. He wrote his old theory professor and friend Andrew Parker about how much he enjoyed grappling with difficult texts again and asked his Arizona literary theory professor if he should reread Hans-Georg Gadamer's *Truth and Method*, a book that criticized attempts to turn the study of literature into a science. The professor assured him once was enough. He wasn't sure if the question had been serious or not or a bit of both. All he knew for sure was that Wallace was far and away his best student.

The fiction survey was taught by a visiting professor, Richard Elman, a veteran novelist, essayist and teacher. One time he invited students in his class to read their stories and then fell asleep in his chair, snoring loudly. But he was intelligent, well-read, and closer than anyone else Wallace knew to New York and publishers, so of interest to the ambitious young Wallace. They would gossip, play tennis, and in his class Wallace read for the first time Gilbert Sorrentino, whose precise, almost analytic evocations of childhood in *Aberration of Starlight* felt like something he might like to try.

Wallace was not a tentative freshman anymore. He had matured, if not emotionally, then at least socially, and graduate programs, familiar to him from his childhood, were easier for him to navigate than undergraduate life at a preppy school. He knew where the levers of academic control were and how to work them. But he still he had no gift when it came to human interactions. His default mode was to show off in a way that struck others as less than nice. "How well do you know Pynchon's work?" he would ask when he met a fellow student. "Excuse me," he said, overhearing a fellow student say "nauseous" when she meant "nauseated." "My mother's an English teacher and I have to tell you the way you're using that word is wrong." (He would tell an interviewer in 1999 about this time, "I was a prick.")

Yet his cockiness was always muted by politeness and even gracious-ness. All teachers were "Professor"; anyone even slightly older than he was "Mr." or "Ms." His decorousness bordered at times on parody. "What I came to believe over time," remembers the novelist Robert Boswell, who was teaching as an adjunct in the program when Wallace arrived, "was that it was both affected and genuine in some way." And Wallace was gen-tler on paper, where he was more secure, than verbally. In workshops his written comments on his fellow students' papers were as generous as his spoken comments could be spiky. He had a way of seeing the promise in stories. "Don't get me wrong: I like this," he wrote on the last page of one fellow student's story, "too much to have you put it away as 'perfect.'" He drew a large happy face below his signature, a huge pair of eyes, a long descending line for the nose. With his friends, he would often tell them to ignore the negative comments by their teachers and go with what they thought was right.

Wallace made most of his friendships with other students from the Midwest. They tended to be simpler to read and embodied the culture of forthrightness he'd grown up with. In Elman's class, he grew close to Heather Aronson, who was from Iowa, and Forrest Ashby, from St. Louis. Wallace tried to make friends with them in his usual way by asking how they could call themselves fiction writers without having read Derrida, but they got past this. Ashby, who was athletic, played tennis with Wallace and was astounded by his skills. One day when Aronson was frightened by black widows in her house, Wallace came to the rescue with goggles and a blowtorch. When they all got together, the other two loved Wallace's talk and were saddened by his story about the suicide of a friend in college that had led to his taking a year off.

He mined them for material, as he did everyone. Ashby told him a story about having kissed the feet of his newborn sister because he had mumps. Soon it appeared in "Forever Overhead," along with the "very soft yellow blanket" of Ashby's childhood.[6] The same night, as the three were watch-ing Kansas City and St. Louis clinch spots in the World Series, Wallace quietly stiffened their gin and tonics. How had they lost their virginity? he asked them. He claimed to have excellent "gaydar"; then was astonished to learn Ashby was gay.

Wallace had by now realized that the "perfectly symmetrical" under-graduate beauties at Arizona were not going to be interested in him. In his grandfather's old long-sleeved T-shirts, lace-up Timberland boots, and McLagan's beloved leather jacket, he hardly fit the relaxed and sunny Arizona mold. So he turned his attention to the women in the MFA program. "The girls in the writing program are erotic in a different way," he reported to his Amherst friends. "There's a propensity towards sandals. Long hair. Armpits make the acquaintance of shavers not quite as often as I'd prefer." He allowed, though, that "there's a kind of mystical, dreamy, spacey eroticism about them."

At a "Fuck Art. Let's Dance" party that fall, Wallace met Gale Walden, a young poet. She came from the Chicago area and embodied everything his parents in their house of reason were skeptical of. Her thinking was elliptical and imaginative and seemed to hold the promise of a less anxious relationship to reality. She consulted the horoscope, drew tarot cards, and wore vintage beaded sweaters in the Arizona heat.

Walden's independence and disheveled appeal attracted Wallace. ("Sloppy sexiness pulls Erdedy in like a well-groomed moth to a lit window," Wallace writes of one of his characters in *Infinite Jest*.) Walden also knew a great deal of poetry of the sort he had never considered, not Eliot's poetry of ideas, but of sensibility. She called him "David" instead of "Dave." He helped with her grammar and taught her history.

Walden wasn't sure about getting involved with Wallace. Four years older, she found him immature, "almost as if he chirped rather than talked," she remembered. She would go around asking her friends, "Shall I date this boy?" Wallace tried to help her make up her mind. He peppered her with letters, popped out of bushes to surprise her, and wrote her a condolence note when her dog died. The note persuaded her to go to a movie with him, and when that turned out to be sold out, they went to a coffee shop, where Wallace was able to persuade her with his brilliant mind.

Soon they were a couple, well known in the program—he the left-brained genius, she the right-brained beauty. They agreed she wouldn't have to play tennis and he wouldn't have to dance. They split their age difference: he would say he was two years older; she would be two years younger. That way when they talked of the future, Walden remembers, they could say, "When we are thirty..." He went along to her poetry classes. One evening Wallace dropped by his old friend Andrea Justus's house to borrow her car and wound up taking her to a favorite spot in the mountains, where, as they sat on the hood looking at the twinkling city below, he put her levelheadedness to the test by telling her about the remarkable, beautiful, and talented woman he was now dating. (Justus was annoyed.) For Wallace, Walden was a new kind of girlfriend: he had until now gravitated toward women who could ground him, save him, if necessary. Now he had found a muse, a spur to his creativity. He let Costello know he had met an epochal beauty.

Wallace had been able to be himself with Susie Perkins, a hometown girl, but with Walden he felt the need to pretend, not hard given his natural bent for mystery and secrecy. She liked musicians, so he played her an album by the esteemed Amherst a cappella group the Zumbyes, and claimed he was one of the voices on the recording. Then he had to get his Amherst friends to cover for him.[7] There was a mythopoeic, volatile quality to their relationship. One time Walden demanded he find her a bun with no burger. Wallace disappeared and came back two hours later with a story about having had a fight with a McDonald's counterman.

But mostly, once again, Wallace was writing. He was starting new stories and reworking old ones. The work was coming quickly and easily. He would look up and hours would have passed. He was evolving into a different kind of writer. The change was gradual and never involved entirely abandoning his interest in words and play and how we know what we know about the world, the material of *Broom*, but it took a new direction. Spurred by his readings in literary theory, he was trying to grow beyond such self-referential questions, to answer the question of how to write in a new way.

Trying to write in a new way was not a goal unique to Wallace; it is the exemplary act of each new literary generation. For writers from the 1920s to the 1950s the main route had been modernism, with its emphasis on psychological subjectivity and its retreat from assertions of objective knowledge. Many writers in the 1960s and '70s, faced with the ugliness of the American landscape and its saturation by the culture of mass media, turned to highlighting the artificiality of the literary act itself. Wallace of course had a great fondness for many of the writers of this postmodernist movement, primarily Barthelme (who, as he would say, had "rung his cherries" in college) and Pynchon, whom he had all but engulfed Bombardini-like in *The Broom of the System.*

But the path the writers who had come just before Wallace's generation chose was very different. They sought to pare down their prose, to purvey an exhausted realism. Life weighed heavily; existence carried few possibilities of pleasure or redemption. In minimalism, simple sentences carried great meanings and a waitress's trip to the K-Mart telegraphed misery and blighted opportunity. It was the world according to Raymond Carver, as interpreted by his thousands of descendants.[8]

As Wallace entered Arizona, MFA students all over America were writing stories in the minimalist style, affecting ennui and disappointment toward a world they knew mostly from other minimalists. Wallace accepted the minimalists' attitude toward the landscape of America and its debilitating effect on its inhabitants, but he disliked how formally and verbally claustrophobic their writing was. Minimalist stories gave the reader little experience of what it was like to be assaulted the way in real life their characters would be. They were effectively unease recollected in tranquillity. While Wallace certainly knew what it felt like to be overwhelmed by the stimuli of modern life—indeed his response to them when under stress was more extreme than anyone knew—this was not his stance when he recreated experience. As a writer, he was a folder-in and includer, a maximalist, someone who wanted to capture the *everything* of America.

Most of the teachers at Arizona were not fans of postmodernism, which they associated with a different era and condition and a preciousness that stories in the true American grain should not possess, but they also did not like minimalism, which smelled trendy to them. They particularly disliked one thing the minimalists did that Wallace admired. In his class Elman assigned both Jay McInerney's *Bright Lights, Big City* and Bret Easton Ellis's *Less Than Zero.* Ellis and McInerney were minimalists with attitude, bored with being bored. Dubbed "the brat pack," by the mid-1980s they had become required reading among the affluent and college-educated young. Predictably, then, the students in Elman's class tore apart their easy plots and heartstring-plucking narratives. Wallace, though, did not go along entirely. He was interested in the way their simple narratives swept up and held the reader and, in the case of Ellis, how he used brand names as shorthand for cultural information like status and even to stand in for emotional states. "What should we be writing about?" he demanded to know, "Horses and buggies?"[9]

What the teachers at Arizona did like was the well-made realist short story. The well-made story was teachable, annotatable, and suitable for differing levels of talent. The professors were themselves mostly trained at the Iowa Writers' Workshop, where such stories were the orthodoxy. They believed stories should be character-driven; they should have arcs, with moments of crisis ending in epiphanies. Most of all, for a story to succeed the reader had to know who he was reading about and why the events of the story mattered so much to him or her. "Show us what's at stake for the character," was a constant request from the faculty, as was, "Why is this person telling us the story?"

Wallace probably did not know much about any of the faculty when he applied to the school. Mary Carter's welcome letter suggested the opposite of a program bias toward realism. But it did not take long for him to learn that the teachers in Arizona wanted one thing, and he wanted another. He was at a point where he was more interested in experimentation in form and voice than in conventional narratives. He felt he had entertained readers once in *Broom*; what else, he wondered now, could he do with them? And once he grasped these were not the questions on the table at Arizona, he may even have enjoyed the consequent head-butting—Lelchuk had shown him that opposition could energize him. He perhaps even baited the teachers to bring it out.

His first-semester workshop was with Jonathan Penner, an Iowa Workshop graduate and a writer principally of well-honed, closely observed realist novels. Penner, then in his forties, had supported Wallace's application for admission, thrilled by his submission of a chapter from *Broom* in which two Amherst fraternity pledges barge into Lenore's sister's dorm room and try and get her and her roommate to sign their rear ends. A flashback to 1981, it does not sound like anything else in the book. Someone familiar with only these pages might have thought Wallace had written a ribald tour de force, in the bravura style of early Roth or an update on Terry

Southern—maybe even something by Lelchuk.[10] When Penner began reading Wallace's new efforts in class he was surprised to find that a very different writer had apparently come to Tucson. The comic energy and verbal
dexterity had been replaced by something experimental, self-referential,
and deliberately graceless. Wallace was beginning to play around with the
props of narrative, rearranging them to see what might catch his attention. He was also going through the various tools in the postmodern tool
kit, trying each one out. Part of his goal was to erect a wall between his
writing and the pleasure it could give. A passage at the beginning of the
first story Wallace submitted, "Here and There," is a parody of minimalist
openings: "I kiss her bitter photo. It's cloudy from kisses. I know the outline of my mouth from her image. She continues to teach me without
knowing."

The story goes on in the same arch vein. Bruce, a Wallace stand-in, is
reeling after his girlfriend, a Susie Perkins–like nurse/lover figure—"a certain cool, tight, waistless, etcetera. Indiana University graduate student"—
has ended their relationship. In an exaggerated variant on the typical
college breakup story, he reflects on what went wrong as he flees toward
elderly relatives in the mythic Maine town of Prosopopoeia (literally,
"mask-making," but also a literary trope for the voice of an absent
speaker).[11] The ex-lovers and their therapist converse in the space the
rhythms of the highway open in Bruce's brain, the story told as a flashback, a memory dance in three voices.

Part of what ended the lovers' relationship—we learn—was Bruce's desire to be "the first really great poet of technology." To which the therapist
(who seems to have something of Lelchuk or Penner in him) chimes in:

> Bruce[,] here I feel compelled to remind you that fiction therapy in
> order to be at all effective must locate itself and operate in a strenu-
> ously yes some might even say harshly limited defined structured
> space. It must be confronted as text which is to say fiction which is
> to say project.

Bruce, unrepentant, answers, "This kind of fiction doesn't interest me,"
and lays out his manifesto for a different sort of writing (and a new sort of
relationship):

No more uni-object concepts, contemplations, arm clover breath, heaving bosoms, histories as symbol, colossi; no more man, fist to brow or palm to décolletage, understood in terms of a thumping, thudding, heated Nature, itself conceived as colored, shaped, invested with odor, lending meaning in virtue of qualities. No more qualities. No more metaphors. Gödel numbers, context-free grammars, finite automata, correlation functions and spectra. Not sensuously here, but causally, efficaciously here. Here in the most intimate way. . . . I admit to seeing myself as an aesthetician of the cold, the new, the right, the truly and spotlessly *here*.

As the miles roll by, Bruce struggles to hold on to his vision of a fiction whose "meaning will be clean" between the harangues of his ex and his writing teacher. The story finishes in a more traditional mode, when Bruce tries to rewire his relatives' broken stove, only to discover that, despite his degree in engineering from MIT, he has no idea how the device works. But at this point the reader suspects another parody, a subversion of the MFA-perfect trope of the stove as symbol of hearth and family, of the tidy ending.

When Wallace presented "Here and There" for comment in Penner's workshop, the students were impressed. They were struggling to fit themselves within the boundaries of the well-made story; he was struggling to get out of them. But Penner considered the story "talky, slow and boring."[12] Wallace next presented "Love," a story within a story from *Broom*, about a conversation between characters named Donald and Evelyn Slotnik and their neighbor Fieldbinder about another neighbor who may have been stalking the Slotniks' son. The third story was "Solomon Silverfish," the tale of a lawyer whose wife is dying of cancer. For most of its nearly thirty pages, the story adheres closely—even mockingly—to the rules of narrative. Points of view alternate obediently among the characters; each one speaks in an identifiable voice: "Sophie is Solomon's life and vice-versa, Mrs. Solomon thinks, Thirty-two years of such luck and happiness she did not even know how to begin thanking God on her knees." But the last scene erupts into a Malamud-like moment of magic, a rapturous love-making in a cemetery as witnessed by Too Pretty, a pimp, high on heroin, who happens to drive by:

I be sittin up straight in my ride, and she be doin my man standin up, they be doin each other like children, too clean, too happy, my mans ass on marble, and theres no noise I can hear but my breathin and . . . this high thin whine of the burnin gate and the stones that be flashin a fire of they own light in the sun.

"There's a fine and moving story here, David," Penner wrote his student in response. "It's about half this long."[13] A conservative Jew himself, Penner found Wallace's idea of Jews as targets of comedy "mildly offensive" and remembers wondering why Wallace kept submitting stories about people of his own religion to him. Other students assumed it was Wallace's attempt to get under the skin of a professor who was not giving him the praise he expected. If so, it may have worked. Penner saw the talent that Wallace possessed and felt he was misusing it. At one point, he took Wallace aside and told him that if he continued to write the way he was writing "we'd hate to lose you."[14]

Penner thought he was giving Wallace just the sort of help he had come to Arizona for, but Wallace was flabbergasted and furious, and also excited. As often when goaded, he fought back with humor. He liked to sit around with friends, imitating Penner's mannerisms; the hemorrhoid pillow the teacher brought to class was fair game. He joined Penner's Sunday basketball games. Wallace no longer threw a timid hook shot. He enjoyed battling his professor in the pebbleless paint. (Penner was famous for scrupulously sweeping the court before a game.)

In December, when a small studio opened in a row of bungalows on East Adams Street where several of the other writing students lived, Wallace moved. He brought his books and towels to the "casita." The rent was cheap and Walden's new puppy, Jonson, could spend the night with them there. (The North Cherry Avenue apartment building had prohibited pets.) The bungalow had only a swamp cooler, and Wallace, who sweated heavily even when he wasn't in the grip of anxiety, took to wearing his tennis bandana off the court. As the months passed at Arizona, he let his hair grow; the bandana became useful to hold it back. The look felt right—part of his rejection of midwestern conformity, a light shock to the bourgeoisie that also kept the sweat off his face—and he began trying out various headscarves to see others' reaction. Sometimes he borrowed Walden's.

One day he poached a turquoise sash from Heather Aronson and wore it around his head. Her sister Jaci, who also lived in town, told him he looked like a member of Kajagoogoo.

Wallace thought he was doing new and stimulating work at Arizona. *The Broom of the System* belonged to his creative past, but he understood the importance of getting it into print. He did not want to wait any longer to make his mark. He asked around for a teacher who would be willing to read it and make some suggestions for how to improve it, but no one offered. The prospect of spending time on a large undergraduate project of postmodernist tendencies did not appeal to the faculty. So, soon after arriving, Wallace asked Boswell to help. Boswell, who had been a star student in the program, made suggestions for the novel and also told Wallace he should get an agent. He suggested his friend send fifteen pages of the work to fifteen different literary agencies and see who responded first. A little more than a month after getting to Tucson, Wallace had a draft of the novel ready to submit. His cover note was coy:

> I've been advised by people who seem to be in a position to know that *The Broom of the System* is not only entertaining and salable but genuinely good, especially for its being the first major project of a very young writer (though no younger than some—Ellis, Leavitt— whose fiction has done well partly because of readers' understandable interest in new, young writing).

He enclosed a chapter from the middle of the book, explaining that to send the beginning would only confuse the reader, "since the novel itself isn't really constructed in an entirely linear, diachronic way." Perhaps he had also learned from his experience with Penner that certain chapters might not prepare readers for the medley of parody, philosophy, and Wittgensteinian teases that followed. One of the agencies the package went to was Frederick Hill Associates in San Francisco, where Bonnie Nadell, a new associate who had worked in the subsidiary rights department at Simon & Schuster when *Less Than Zero* was published, opened it. Nadell liked the cocky tone of the letter and was impressed by the term "diachronic," which she did not know. She read the chapter and responded to its energetic comic voice. It reminded her of Pynchon, whom she had studied in college. Nadell asked for more pages. Wallace sent her the balance, and soon afterward she took the novel on. When the two first spoke by phone, Wallace called her "Ms. Nadell," until he found out she was only a year older than he. He had so little cash he asked her to make a copy of the manuscript for him. "I defy you to picture a boy living on Ritz crackers and grape Kool-Aid . . . and be unmoved." Nadell had no money either and instead got a friend at a publisher to photocopy it.

There was already a well-known nature writer named David Rains Wallace, so Fred Hill, Nadell's boss, who had once worked for Sierra Club Books, suggested he use his full name. Wallace was to claim in later years that the change in his byline to David Foster Wallace had been against his will—"I would have called myself Seymour Butts if he'd told me to," he wrote to Don DeLillo nearly two decades later—but Nadell remembers Wallace as happy with his new triple-barreled moniker. He had been experimenting with various names since he was a little boy and the homage to his literary mother was fitting.

After Thanksgiving, Nadell sent the novel out to a group of editors, including one at Viking Penguin, Gerry Howard, who responded at once. Howard had an affection for postmodernism and nostalgia for the literary culture it came out of. He loved words and word games and writing that exposed the artificiality of narrative. He was steeped in the works of Pynchon and had edited an anthology of prose from the 1960s as well. But he also thought *Broom* was different, that it used postmodernism in new ways. He remembers reading the manuscript and thinking he was reading something truly new, "a portent for the future of American fiction," as he remembered it: "It wasn't just a style but a feeling he was expressing, one of playful exuberance . . . tinged with a self-conscious self-consciousness." For him—and for many others who would read the book—Wallace held the hope of an alternative to minimalism and to Ellis-type fiction, a way out of the etiolated mind-set of the moment. There was optimism in *Broom*'s despair, elation in its loneliness. Words tumbling over words might, it suggested, overwhelm the depressing anomie of American life. Howard offered a $20,000 advance to Nadell, quite large under the circumstances, as a minimum bid in return for the right to top any other publisher's subsequent offer. As it turned out, no one else bid on the book. Howard decided he would publish the book primarily as a paperback original.[15] This strategy had worked for *Bright Lights, Big City*, the publication of which was the industry's model for how to reach younger fiction readers.

Wallace was thrilled. Finding a publisher had happened so fast it seemed unreal. He waited two hours on Walden's stoop to tell her the news. Soon he flew to New York, where Nadell had found him an apartment to borrow on the Upper West Side. He met Howard and, separately, Nadell, who had grown up in the city. At the Hungarian Pastry Shop near Columbia University, they hung out with some of her college friends. They talked about favorite authors, including Pynchon, but they worried, one of her friends remembers, that the discussion was making Wallace uncomfortable so they changed the subject. The same friend said that his favorite word was "moist" and that it gave him particular pleasure to hear it used in conjunction with "loincloth." (The phrase would turn up in a later story of Wallace's out of the mouth of *Jeopardy!* host Alex Trebek.)

At the Viking Penguin offices on 23rd Street, Wallace, wearing a U2 T-shirt, sat down with his editor, who was amazed at how young he looked. Howard worried that Wallace would trip over the untied laces of his huge sneakers and found it funny that his new author insisted on calling him— he was only in his mid-thirties—"Mr. Howard." He wondered at his diffidence and what seemed to him his tenuous connection to the larger world, thinking of the twenty-three-year-old Wallace, he would later tell an interviewer, "as a newly-hatched chick."

Wallace went home intoxicated with excitement, so much so that he was carried away, reporting back to Costello that Howard had been the editor for *Gravity's Rainbow* (not quite true, though Howard had gotten Pynchon to write an introduction to a reissue of Pynchon's friend Richard Fariña's novel). Once back in Urbana, he joined Walden in Chicago to see *Fool for Love*, the movie version of Sam Shephard's play about battling lovers, and ate at a restaurant called Printers Row. Wallace, the ambitious part of his psyche coming to the fore, asked Washington to plant the good news with their class agent for the Amherst newsletter, "not, of course, letting her know that I requested or even endorsed your doing so."

Howard felt he had a prodigy of a novel on his hands, a book that was brilliant, intuitive, obeying no rules. He settled down to edit the long manuscript, accompanied by a reference book on Wittgenstein. Early in the New Year he sent Wallace a note with four pages of suggestions, focusing on passages he found self-indulgent and on problems of chronology. He thought his edit quite light, given the length of the manuscript.

Wallace was just now settling in for the spring semester. Howard's letter knocked him off stride. Fragile in his confidence, even mild criticism hurt him, and since negative comments could plunge him into effulgences of self-doubt, he responded immediately, hitting the ball right back over the net. "If this seems fast," he assured his editor, "be aware that I have done nothing ELSE besides eat and smoke since I got your letter and suggestions," adding sneakily, "Don't think because I've sent this back to you so quickly I'm not ready and willing to go over it again if you decide it's necessary . . . I'll just pull another all-weeker."

Wallace had promised Howard he would find him reasonable when it came to editing, "neurotic and obsessive" but "not too intransigent or defensive about my stuff." Generally, he was true to his word. If Howard adduced publishing wisdom or reader response, Wallace stepped quickly out of the way. Wallace had made a pun on the names of Raymond Carver and Max Apple, a comic novelist. "This Carver/Apple joke is too cute and you'll be picked on for it. Drop it," Howard wrote; Wallace did. Howard thought Wallace overdid the use of ellipses in quotes in dialogue as a way of indicating a lack of verbal response, dead air. Wallace trimmed them back. Howard found Dr. Jay, the bizarre psychiatrist whom both Rick Vigorous and Lenore see, tedious. "The more you condense or even eliminate his palaver, the better for the book," he insisted. Specifically, he found Dr. Jay's "membrane theory" of personal relations "disgusting and far too strange for the book's good—and it is *very* tenuously related (I think) to whatever Lenore's plans for Lenore B might be."

This was pushing too hard. Accusations that he was careless or meandered set Wallace on edge. It mattered enormously to him that the power of his mind be acknowledged. The membrane theory was one of his favorite moments of the book. It was the unbalanced Dr. Jay's assertion that human relations could be entirely understood with regard to the struggle over the boundary between the self and the other. Physical limits were mental limits too: "Hygiene anxiety," the therapist points out, "is identity anxiety." The membrane around us kept us safe and clean but also carried the risk of isolating us. It sounded Freudian, came out of Wallace's reading of literary theory, and struck a chord with the hygiene-obsessed Wallace. It played off of Vigorous's sexual problems with Lenore as well—her own boundaries frustrate his small penis. In response to Howard's letter, Wallace gave his editor a bit of the razzle-dazzle methodology he was riddling his Arizona writing teachers with. The membrane theory, he wrote,

> while potentially disgusting . . . is deeply important to what I perceive as a big subplot of the book, which is essentially a dialogue between Hegel and Wittgenstein on one hand and Heidegger and a contemporary French thinker-duo named Paul DeMan and Jacques Derrida on the other, said debate having its root in an essential self-other distinction that is perceived by both camps as less ontological/metaphysical than essentially (for Hegel and Witt) historical and cultural or (for Heidegger and DeMan and Derrida) linguistic, literary, aesthetic, and fundamentally super or metacultural.

This long sentence was Howard's first glimpse of how thoroughly his young author had worked out the philosophical thinking behind the book—or perhaps of the rigid will behind a hyperverbal façade—and he backed off. Howard's more concrete problem was with the ending: the book didn't have one. In the last pages, Lenore appears to be closing in on her great-grandmother, but we never find out for sure. Nadell had raised the issue even before she sold the book to Viking Penguin. The story, she felt, just seemed to stop. She suggested Wallace think about a more traditional last scene. Wallace had dug in—*The Crying of Lot 49* famously ends in mid-scene.

Howard too thought the text called for some sort of resolution. He urged his author to keep in mind "the physics of reading." The physics of reading were, as Wallace came to understand the phrase, "a whole set of readers' values and tolerances and capacities and patience-levels to take into account when the gritty business of writing stuff for others to read is undertaken." In other words, a reader who got through a long novel like

Broom deserved to know what had happened. "You cheat yourself as well of the opportunity to write a brilliantly theatrical close to the book," the editor chided his young author.

Phrases like "the physics of reading" were seductive to the theoretician in Wallace. His clumsiness in the world of emotions also led to odd mixtures of gratitude and indifference. Over the years many editors would wonder whether Wallace was making fun of them with his excessive-seeming deference. The answer is he both was and wasn't. To Wallace's mind now, Howard had hazarded everything on his youthful work and no amount of gratitude could repay the gesture. At the same time he was not without diffuse cunning. He already had in mind to publish a follow-up volume of short stories; it would not be prudent to alienate his editor—or his readers, before he even had any.[16] So, sincerely or not—or sort of—he wrote Howard that the idea of the physics of reading had "made an enormous, haunting impression on me." He assured him that he didn't want his novel to be like "Kafka's 'Investigations of a Dog' . . . Ayn Rand or late Günter Grass, or Pynchon at his rare worst." To him these were writings that gave pleasure only to their authors. All the same, he simply could not rewrite the ending. To do so would risk turning the book into a realist novel and betray his deepest belief about the relationship between reader and character (and by extension between life and reader):

> I admit to a potentially irritating penchant for anti-climax, one that may come out of Pynchon, but a dictum of his that I buy all the way is that, if a book in which the reader is supposed to be put, in some sort of metaphysical-literary way, in something like the predicament of the character, ends without a satisfactory resolution for the character, then it's not only unfair but deeply inappropriate to expect the book itself to give the reader the sort of satisfaction-at-end the character is denied—the clear example is *Lot 49.*

He'd tried, he said, to write a proper conclusion, in which, he told Howard, "geriatrics emerge, revelations revelationize, things are cleared up." But the scene, never sent (if it ever existed), felt too pat to him. The issue was a serious one for him. "I am young and confused and obsessed with certain problems that I think right now distill the experience of being human in a human community," he begged Howard. "Can you help me with this?" What he meant was he knew reality to be fragmented, oblique, unbalanced, and his book had to capture that fragmentation if that experience was to count for anything—that was *why* he wrote the way he did. In the end, he insisted on keeping the ending he had written, breaking the novel off in midsentence, with Rick Vigorous, Lenore's ex-boyfriend, attempting to pierce the physical boundaries of Mindy Metalman, assuring her, "I'm a man of my"—the missing word being, elegantly and self-referentially, the word "word."[17]

Howard was satisfied; he had tried. He was still in awe of the book he held in his hands and felt, with or without a conventional ending, it was, as he remembered, full of "the sheer joy of a talent realizing itself." He wrote to Nadell, even before he had finished editing Wallace's book, "It is a great joy to be in at the start of his brilliant career."[18] The title of the book was open to discussion. It had begun, at Amherst, as The *Great Ohio Desert*, a reference to a fictive human-engineered pile of sand near Cleveland with its suggestive acronym that figures in the story; to *Three Deserts* ("Rick, Lenore, and the G.O.D.," Wallace noted to Howard); to *The Broom of the System,* the name it was submitted to Howard under. Amy Wallace now suggested *Family Theater,* a reference to the therapy that the Wallaces had undergone as a group in summer 1982, but in the end *Broom* won out.

Wallace's life began to go on two tracks. His book was soon to be the first original novel in a fiction line from an important New York publishing house, but he was still a first-year MFA student, facing a faculty less than enchanted by his success. Personal dislike, professional jealousy, and opposition to postmodernism made anything good that happened to Wallace dubious in the eyes of his teachers—at least that was how he read the situation.

Wallace had grown close to a fellow student named JT. "Jate"—no one knew what the initials stood for—was a former marine, who wore a hat and leather bomber jacket in the heat of Tucson. He called his apartment on 9th Street "the lair." It featured a Soloflex machine in the living room and a stack of Diet Coke cases reaching almost to the ceiling in the kitchen.

For Wallace 9th Street became a replacement for the lost "womb" at Amherst. He would go there to relax, hide out from Gale Walden, get high, discuss their fiction, and engage in what he called in a story he wrote of the time "macrocosmic speculations." JT was the sort of friend Wallace was increasingly drawn to, the sort to whom he could be at once a pal and still somewhat mysterious to. They had a routine together. "How'd you get to be so smart?" JT would ask. "'Cause I did the reading," Wallace would respond. They called first novels "big shits" because everything you knew got poured out into them. Together with an undergraduate friend they put out a parody issue of the writing program newsletter, a publication of the "University of Aridzona Piety Center":

How many Jonathan Penners does it take to screw in a lightbulb?
One. Having more than one Jonathan Penner violates basic point-of-view considerations.

How Many Robert Boswells does it take to screw in a lightbulb?
Two: One to screw in the bulb, and one to accept the award.

JT created a joke for Wallace, but the latter cut the entry when he sat at the printing shop alone with the manuscript. The parody offended many of its targets, not entirely a surprise to Wallace, who as they finished up the issue began to downplay his involvement.

JT helped Wallace in crucial ways. Wallace was a child of academia with little knowledge of the larger world. That world frightened him easily and often overwhelmed him, but he saw that without broader experience he was going to have a hard time growing as a writer. Fantasizing about his future biography, Wallace joked with JT one day, "'Dave sat in the smoking lounge of the library, pensively taking a drag from a cigarette and trying to think of the next line.'" He added, "Who wants to read *that*?" JT's stories held a partial solution. He told him he had been in a severe accident involving an International Harvester truck in the 1970s that had left him in a coma; Wallace put the accident in a story. Another day, early in the semester, as JT remembers, Wallace put on a recording by Keith Jarrett. While they listened to the improvisation, JT told Wallace, who was high, a story about a road trip he took to see the Grateful Dead with his brother, a bouncer nicknamed Big. Just before, Wallace had been flipping through a collection of records put out by Placebo Records, a punk rock label. Many of the Placebo musicians and their associates were friends of JT, and two of their names came up in the road trip story too: Big and Mr. Wonderful. Wallace ran off to his bungalow and a few days later came back with a story narrated by a rampaging young Republican named Sick Puppy who delights in burning women while they fellate him.[19] The story starts:

> Gimlet dreamed that if she did not see a concert last night she would become a type of liquid, therefore my friends Mr. Wonderful, Big, Gimlet and I went to see Keith Jarrett play a piano concert at the Irvine Concert Hall in Irvine last night.

The story, "Girl with Curious Hair," was in the same key as *Less Than Zero*. Wallace felt that employing bored, vapid characters to capture boredom was poor writing, but as a natural mimic he admired the strong voice Ellis had found; he saw its potential. So he pushed the voice past where Ellis had taken it, moving it from the stylish into the gothic or repulsive.[20] When Costello came to visit, Wallace recited the opening of *A Clockwork Orange*, and Costello realized that the Anthony Burgess novel had also been a model for the story his friend had just written. Wallace told his friend that Burgess's novel showed how to use hyperbolic language to convey deadened emotional states. (The debt to Bret Easton Ellis was one Wallace would never acknowledge. When Howard asked after reading the story whether Wallace had read *Less Than Zero*, Wallace told him no.)

When Wallace was not with JT, he was with Walden. During the return from Christmas 1985 break, they each had car trouble, so they agreed that it would be romantic to join up and drive in a convoy back to Tucson, Wallace from Urbana, Walden from the South Side of Chicago. The only problem was that Wallace had already agreed to make the trip back to Tucson with his sister, Amy, who was coming to visit him, and his friends Heather from Iowa and Forrest from St. Louis. So when Wallace, Amy, Heather, and Forrest, traveling in two cars, got to Oklahoma, he called Walden, to discover she needed his company while she waited for a mechanic to fix her car. Then he drove off with barely another word, his change of plans pulled off so quickly that his sister's suitcase was still in his trunk. When he and Gale finally got to Tucson—"two broken cars limping across the desert," as Walden would remember it in a later poem— they found Amy hurt and bewildered, her feet bleeding from Heather's borrowed shoes.

On the trip, Wallace listened to the southwestern accents. He had long wanted to write a variation on William Gass's novel *Omensetter's Luck*. The laconic hillbilly voice of the story appealed to him. As a "weird kind of forger," imitating it would be a fun challenge. "He started to talk out 'John Billy' at rest stops," Walden remembers. "He was trying to get the cadence of the dialogue down." When he got home, he wrote a draft. "Was me supposed to tell Simple Ranger how Chuck Nunn Junior done wronged the man that wronged him and fleen to parts unguessed," the eponymous narrator states. There was, as ever, an element of parody in the homage. The goal was to push the original author out of sight. That the story was not easy to read mattered not at all to Wallace; all he cared about was the sentences.

Back at school for the spring 1986 semester, Wallace decided to try to finish his MFA more quickly. From his original boast to Washington that he would stay for "the next three years at least," he now wanted to try to wrap up his graduate work in two. He may have wanted to be done at the same time as Walden, who was planning to graduate the next June, or to save tuition. He signed up for a workshop with program director Mary Carter, in which he would write extra stories for double credit, as well as a seminar on literary theory and an independent study on the theory and practice of poetry. In the last, when another participant called Derrida a waste of time, Wallace got so mad that everyone thought there would be a fight. He was still convinced that theory was what separated the serious novelist from the others, that without it writers were just entertainers. His interest in theory, like his fondness for stories with strong voices, also had a compensatory element. It served to satisfy energies that would have been frustrated had they gone into aspects of fiction writing he did not naturally excel at, like character development. It was a handy refuge for a writer who was still an odd combination of a mimic and engineer.

The workshop with Carter was Wallace's happiest time at Arizona. The program director was supportive in the same way Dale Peterson had been at Amherst. She herself was an entirely conventional writer and not even a very good one, but she understood that her protégé's work was special and encouraged him to write what he wanted. "He is going to make us all very proud," she would tell the other students. Her support for him was evident to all. At a publishing conference Carter convened, she squired Wallace around to meet important fiction agents and editors. Wallace rallied to the challenge, surprising his fellow students who thought of him as shy. They had not realized that he could play the game when he wanted to.[21]

The double credit in Carter's workshop required Wallace to supply six new stories in a semester, a rigorous pace. But he continued to write well and fast and anywhere he wanted, caught up in gusts of inspiration. One weekend that spring he disappeared. Walden grew worried, called him, went by and rang the doorbell of the casita but got no response. The next Monday at the offices of the program's literary magazine, the *Sonora Review*, he presented her with the story "Little Expressionless Animals," a tale about a young woman who is a champion *Jeopardy!* player. It was thirty pages long. "I wrote straight through," he told Walden, who had been sure he had run away with another woman.

"Little Expressionless Animals" was Wallace's first attempt to treat seriously issues that had mostly been played for laughs in *Broom*. Its central preoccupation is the relationship between people and the images they appropriate from media to shape and infuse their thoughts. The narrative tells the story of Julie Smith, the winner of the last seven hundred episodes of the game show. She is a smart, twentyish square peg of a young woman, a descendant of Lenore Beadsman, herself a descendant of Oedipa Maas (and of Amy Wallace). The question at hand for the show's executives, Merv Griffin and Alex Trebek, is whether to let her continue her *Jeopardy!* streak. "Rules, though," points out one of their staff. "Five slots, retire undefeated, come back for Champion's Tourney in April. . . . Fairness to whole contestant pool. An ethics type of thing." Griffin, though, prizes the ratings and the advertising income, and, more complexly, the ineluctability of a great image. He sees that Julie Smith is different. "She's," he says, "like some lens, a filter for that great unorganized force that some in the industry have spent their whole lives trying to locate and focus." That filter operates only when she is on television. This girl, who is almost affectless off camera, comes alive on the set. As the narrator points out:

Something happens to Julie Smith when the red lights light. Just a something. . . . Every concavity . . . now looks to have come convex. The camera lingers on her. It seems to ogle. . . . Her face, on-screen, gives off an odd lambent UHF flicker; her expression, brightly serene, radiates a sort of oneness with the board's data.

Julie, TV's natural spawn, seems to be assuming some of its properties, to be acquiring, like Pynchon's San Narciso, a sort of "intent to communicate." In the end Griffin decides to have Julie play against her autistic brother—"Great P.R.," as one staffer points out—and the story, full of mirrors and characters' glimpsing themselves in the glass, ends appropriately with the most important mirror moment of all: "Julie and the audience look at each other."[22]

Wallace was maturing as a writer. The preoccupation with media now went deeper than just a statement of purpose. The voice of the story was diffuse, hovering, omnipresent without being omniscient. As the critic Sven Birkerts noted in a later essay in *Wigwag*, "Wallace does not, in fact, tell the story. Instead he inhabits for extended moments the airspace around his characters." This charged airspace is where the artistic activity of the story resides. The story ably frustrates the MFA ukase, the order to "hook" the reader fast. What is at stake for the main character? Everything, and also nothing, the story's tension residing, with the narrator, in the ether above her.

The story received a favorable reception in Carter's workshop. (It would continue to be one of Wallace's best known. He would read it publicly for years.) At one point in the story, Alex Trebek says, "My favorite word is *moist*, . . . especially when used in combination with my second favorite word, which is *loincloth*." Later when Wallace saw the young man who had supplied the phrase at the Hungarian Pastry Shop waiting in line at one of his signings, he called out, "You're the moist loincloth guy!"

At semester's end, Wallace decided to stay in Tucson. Walden would be there, and he could get credit for attending a teacher-training workshop at the Southern Arizona Writing Project. Wallace was used to going home in the summer and staying away turned out to be an unpleasant experience. He found the desert heat oppressive and the relationship with Walden developed problems: they had begun talking about the future, marriage and children; Wallace was not ready. They went to Nogales, just over the Mexican border—"kind of a depressing place," as Walden remembers—and stayed for a few days, listening to the mariachis play all night long. They broke up, if temporarily. "It's hot, here. Over 100° and climbing," Wallace wrote Washington in July. "I have no job, no girlfriend, no friends." He was "getting high too much, and moping."

The early part of the summer was taken up by the page proofs of *Broom*, which was to be published the next January, but the work felt old and stale to him. He told JT he wished he could pull a Norman Mailer and rewrite the book from scratch. He also soon entered into what would come to be a familiar struggle with copy editors. They wanted to standardize his prose, not understanding how thoroughly thought through were his departures from standard grammar. If he used a comma in an unusual place or chose to indicate direct speech with single quotes rather than the usual double ones, there was a reason. He was going, he had written Nadell in April, to have to "copy-edit the copy-editor." The process exhausted him. When the final proofs came in July, he sent them back to Howard with a typically confused sign-off: "Hoping Very Much I'll Never Have To Look At That Particular Confoguration Of Words Again, Yet Eager To Do So If It Will Help Viking One Little Bit."

Meanwhile, Howard was soliciting prepublication quotes for the novel. "No autobiography, no cocaine, no rock clubs, lots of ambition and inventiveness," he promised Don DeLillo, who passed, as did dozens of others. Most, if they even leafed through it, likely saw the book as derivative of Pynchon, or of DeLillo himself. Elman was one of the few to offer praise— sort of. At Wallace's request, he read the manuscript and wrote to Howard, in part, "As wild elk produce many elkins, so the American heartland produces its own Menippean satirists. David Wallace's young genius is undimmed. The magnitude of his borrowings he pays back with interest." When he shared the quote with Wallace, Wallace asked his old teacher what he meant. "You must not confuse the modesty of hype for lack of admiration of your talent," the teacher replied evasively. To Howard, he was less disingenuous. "I would be hard put to defend David's writing, for all its charm, as original, in most of the standard senses of the word." He added, half joking, "If you want to publish really good writing you should publish mine."

Shortly after sending off the page proofs in July, Wallace drove up to see Costello, who was now a summer associate at a law firm in Denver. They planned a weekend road trip, but at the last minute Costello was called in to work. Wallace came along to get a little experience of what it was like to be in an office. They parked in the underground garage of the nearly sixty-story building and took the elevator up to Costello's office. Wallace, wide-eyed, settled in an empty conference room. While his old roommate took a long call from another lawyer, Wallace wrote the first draft of "Luckily the Account Representative Knew CPR" in a notebook. It is the story of two executives whom chance throws together in a huge office building, the building itself "empty and bright, dispossessed, autonomous and autonomic." The older one has a heart attack in the building's garage and falls slowly, inexorably to the ground:

> The Account Representative watched as the Vice President in Charge of Overseas Production pirouetted, raked a raw clean streak in a cement pillar's soot and clipped a WRONG WAY sign's weighted concrete doughnut with a roundabout heel as he pirouetted, reached out at air, hunched, crumpled, and fell.

The younger of the two men then tries to come to his rescue. It is unclear whether he succeeds in saving the other's life with CPR. "They shared pain, though of course neither knew," the narrator of the story asserts.

The effort was an early example of the paradoxical approach that would come to dominate Wallace's later fiction: a passionate need for encounter telegraphed by sentences that seem ostentatiously to prohibit it, as if only by passing through all the stages of bureaucratic deformation can we touch each other as human beings. This would prove one day to be the stance of much of the writing in the story collection *Oblivion* and, finally and problematically, in *The Pale King*, but in its earliest incarnations it came easily to Wallace.[23]

The next day he and Costello took to the road. They planned on going to St. Francis, Kansas, about two hundred miles to the east. There was a well-known NPR station there. Wallace wanted, Costello remembers, Oedipa Maas–like, "to get to the source of the signal." On the way they stayed overnight in a cheap motel in eastern Colorado. Wallace realized the next morning en route that he had left behind the notebook with the "CPR" story in it, so the two turned around and drove back the twenty miles to the motel to get it; Wallace mentioned to Costello that it also contained "a big thing"—Costello assumed a new novel was being started. They turned around one more time and got to St. Francis, where they sat in the parking lot for a few minutes. That month, a friend of Walden's took a photo of Wallace for his book jacket. He chose to wear the leather jacket he'd bought from McLagan, the one that always brought him luck.

The fall 1986 school term came with two big changes. Mary Carter was gone, forced out by the faculty. She did not go quietly. Soon, as Wallace wrote to Nadell, she was "going through both a lawsuit and a nervous breakdown in London." Carter's departure was awkward for Wallace. He was her favorite; indeed, some people assumed that they were involved, not least because she had some years before published a novel about an older woman and a younger man. Fueling the rumor was that he moved into her apartment after her departure. Some guessed it was a present of some sort (in fact she charged him rent and told him not to smoke inside). He enjoyed the condo, which was much more pleasant than the swamp-cooled bungalow he'd lived in for the past year. It had color-coordinated furniture and wall hangings, not to mention access to a pool. "I got darned little work done," he complained to Washington about the summer when September finally came around, "just took one gutty class and sat around smoking pot in airconditioning."

His scholarship having ended, that fall Wallace had to teach. The prospect did not delight him. In his audio letter to his Amherst friends on arriving, he had declared the undergraduates at UA to be "roughly of an intelligence level of a fairly damaged person." More important, he was aware that the teacher-student relationship was one of performer and spectator. The teacher was under constant pressure to *entertain* if he wanted to be liked—and no one wanted to be liked more than Wallace did. The bind was not just that he did not think he could do it, but that if he did do it, was he actually doing something he would admire himself for having done?

The first morning of classes found him lying on the floor of the *Sonora Review* offices in the Modern Languages Building, unable to move. "Give him space. He's nervous," Walden whispered to everyone. The others were shocked. Wallace to them was by now the epitome of confidence.

But once he had decided to become good at something, Wallace usually succeeded. It was the decision to dive, not the entry into the water that was hard. Quickly, he became a top instructor, charismatic and popular. He scoured every piece of undergraduate writing, striving to overwhelm the students with the volume and sincerity of his comments. It did not matter that much of what they wrote was indifferent, nor that he was teaching ordinary undergraduate expository writing classes, classes, in other words, for people who by and large only wanted to be done with the class to move on to other things. The vitalizing—he would have said "erotic"—power of his mind made what they did interesting. What he wrote of Julie Smith in "Little Expressionless Animals" applied equally to him:

> This girl not only kicks facts in the ass. This girl informs trivia with import. She makes it human, something with the power to emote, evoke, induce, cathart.

And as with Julie Smith, there was at once an out-of-proportion commitment and a hint of irony to his behavior. When the university sent an examiner to evaluate his teaching, Wallace had every student in the class bring an apple to present to him. Whether his mockery was appreciated or went unnoticed, that year he won the prize for best teaching assistant in the department.

Teaching taught him a hard lesson, though: he had only a limited amount of energy. If he taught, that drew down the tank with which he wrote. "I leave at dawn and get home at night," he wrote Washington as the semester began, "promptly get drunk and fall into a sweaty half-sleep." Two months later, he was back to Washington with more complaints: "I mostly sit around smoking pot, cigarettes, worrying about not working, worrying about the tension between the worry and the absence of and action fuelled by that worry."

*   *   *

The page from Penguin's winter 1987 catalog promised "an ambitious, irreverent novel that speaks to the anxieties and concerns of a new generation," but trade magazine reviews of *Broom* failed to spot what was special about Wallace. *Kirkus Reviews*, for instance, dismissed the author as "a puerile Pynchon, a discount Don DeLillo," though conceding he was "even a bit of an original." Walden read the review to Wallace over the phone, sending her boyfriend into a tailspin. "The guy seemed downright angry at having been made to read the thing," an upset Wallace complained to Howard afterward. He took particular issue with the reviewer's characterization of the ellipses in quotes to denote a non-response that Howard had warned him against overusing as "pseudo-Wittgensteinian" pauses. "If the technique is a rip-off of anyone it's of Manuel Puig," he noted. The book was officially published on January 6, 1987, and came with a nasty surprise. Viking Penguin sent Wallace a bill for $324.51 for his reversal of some of the copyedits. He was incensed. "Maybe," he wrote Howard, "they never found out that the copy editor had a wild hair up every orifice of his/her body? I can't see any way that I made 300 bucks worth of my own whimsical corrections in galleys."

Post-publication book reviewers were kinder than *Kirkus*. If they didn't exactly see *Broom* as a portent, they at least tended to appreciate that a writer in his mid-twenties was reviving some of the energies of postmodern fiction in the midst of the entropic wasteland of minimalism. The *Washington Post Book World* put its review of *Broom* on its front page, declaring it "a hot book . . . a terrific novel." The *New York Times Book Review* proclaimed the book

> an enormous surprise, emerging straight from the excessive tradition of Stanley Elkin's "Franchiser," Thomas Pynchon's "V," John Irving's "World According to Garp." As in those novels, the charm and flaws of David Foster Wallace's book are due to its exuberance— cartoonish characters, stories within stories, impossible coincidences, a hip but true fondness for pop culture and above all the spirit of playfulness that has slipped away from so much recent fiction.

But the review's author, Caryn James, didn't like the ending of the book, in which a "tortured running joke turns into a contrived explanation and characters we expect to appear never show up." Other reviewers filed in in similar fashion: exuberant versus sloppy, homage versus theft. Wallace was particularly hurt by the review in the daily *New York Times* by Michiko Kakutani. Many first-time authors would have been excited to be written up by a critic known for spotting young talent. Her praise of Wallace's "rich reserves of ambition and imagination" was flattering, to be sure, but Wallace told a friend he hid in his room for two days and cried after reading yet another paragraph devoted to parallels between his first book and Pynchon's most popular novel. "I didn't think the review was all that favorable," Wallace wrote Howard afterward. "But if you and Bonnie think it's nice, I'm more than happy to see it that way." To Howard he noted in general that the reviews had him "kind of down."

A film company, Alliance Entertainment, optioned the book for $10,000. There was talk that Terry Gilliam, famous for the near-future satire *Brazil*, a movie Wallace had loved, might want to direct it. Wallace took a try at writing a treatment in the winter of 1987, simplifying the plot and minimizing the philosophical underpinnings. The story, he wrote in the précis, "is one not only about coming of age, but also about romantic love, and familial love, and the reconciliation of the heroine's present with her past, and how these three sub-elements relate to the process of 'growing up' in particular and being a person in general." "Bonnie," he wrote, "I've never had more difficulty and less fun working on anything in my life. This project is dead to me, and my head is full of fiction." He joked that if she would write the screenplay she could have the money.

For all the misgivings and the mixed reviews, *Broom* made its mark. A consensus among critics emerged that Wallace was a writer worth paying attention to, if for no other reason than as a corrective to the literary brat pack of Bret Easton Ellis, Jay McInerney, as well as the short-story writer Tama Janowitz. Some readers may even have seen the "portent" Howard did, the emergence of a new, youthful self-questioning sensibility. Penguin printed fourteen thousand copies of the paperback and went back to press for more. One indication of the book's standing was that the *Wall Street Journal* ran a short profile of Wallace entitled "A Whiz Kid and His Wacky First Novel." "You would think that a brilliant young man who had produced his first novel before commencement would forgo more classes, but this one is not only well-educated, he is smart," the writer began. Wallace responded to Nadell, "Nice, in a condescending way. I kept getting the impression that my hair was being affectionately ruffled by an elderly relative."

Another sign of the growing interest in Wallace's writing that spring was an invitation to participate in a reading at the West Side Y in Manhattan. Other authors reading that night would be T. C. Boyle, Laurie Colwin, and Frank Conroy. Wallace had never performed at such a large or important gathering, and thinking about it terrified him. "I'm so nervous about the reading," he wrote Nadell just beforehand, "I can hardly breathe." The night of the event he went to a dinner with the other authors at a Chinese restaurant in the west 60s. He quietly excused himself several times to throw up in the bathroom.

At the theater, the writers read in alphabetical order, so Wallace's nervousness had time to swell, as Gerry Howard looked on with worry. Finally Wallace's turn came. Howard introduced him, Wallace stood up on the stage, very slowly poured himself a glass of water, took a sip, put it down, and, smacking his lips, said, "Aaaah." "You know," he told the audience, "I always wanted to do that." Peals of laughter. Wallace opened the book and read one of the stories within a story that Rick Vigorous tells to Lenore, in which a child's crying unleashes a chain of improbable, catastrophic events. The audience loved the bravura homage to and parody of John Irving and sensed the young writer's charisma, participating in the pleasure he took in having surmounted his own anxiety. Howard thought the performance was "maybe the best reading I've ever seen." A Penguin publicist wrote Nadell a few days afterward to assure her she had nothing to worry about. For his part, Wallace wondered what had gone on. "The reading went really well," he reported to Nadell, "and I had a marvelous time on stage (a bit disturbing)."[24]

As Wallace began his last semester at Arizona, things between him and Gale Walden reached a breaking point. School would end soon and what was ahead was blank. Wallace wasn't clear on what he wanted, unless it was to be left alone—except when he didn't. He drank and got high a lot, which was helpful in keeping Walden at a distance. They decided to get married— Walden says Wallace wanted to elope—but by late spring it was clear no wedding was going to take place. "I guess the engagement is more or less off," he wrote to Nadell in mid-April, whatever relief he felt buried under a sense of being wronged; "it's hard to be engaged to someone who won't speak to you."

Weighing Wallace down was the growing certainty that he would soon be a professional writing teacher. Income from *Broom*, he knew, would not support even his modest needs. "Writing means teaching," he told anyone who would listen. But if he needed to teach, the past year had also taught him to be careful how much. Dale Peterson at Amherst held out the prospect of a part-time engagement. Wallace was interested; he had turned down a tenure-track job offer from Northwestern (or so he wrote Peterson, though the school has no record of it and it seems unlikely). The prospect of being back where *Broom* had unscrolled held special appeal. "Could you give me a general idea about the whole thing's modal status?" he followed up in the spring. Peterson said to be patient; it would take time to get his protégé the appointment.

In April Wallace was the subject of a profile in *Arrival*, a small glossy magazine based in Berkeley. The article, written by a friend of Nadell's, carried a photo of Wallace in a saguaro cactus–dotted desert, dressed in jeans and a checked button shirt. His arms dangled loosely, as if ready to grab his gun. "Hang 'Im High" was the title. Clearly, there was a new sheriff in FictionTown, USA. In the article, Wallace made evident his disdain for the workshop writing he had spent the past two years battling. "I'm not interested in fiction that's only worried about capturing reality in an artful way," he asserted. "What pisses me off about so much fiction these days is that it's just boring."

Alongside the profile, *Arrival* published a sample of Wallace's work, the story "Lyndon," a fictionalized biography of the thirty-sixth American president in the style of Robert Coover's 1977 novel *The Public Burning*, which Wallace had read shortly before. Wallace fabricated an aide to LBJ named David Boyd and gave him a male lover, anachronistically dying of AIDS, and indeed the challenges of love—theirs for each other, Lady Bird's for LBJ, strangers' for a public figure—form the creative core of the story. "I never saw a man with a deeper need to be loved than LBJ," an aide comments.

"Lyndon" was noteworthy for its tight control of tone and careful observation, some of it gleaned from books and another portion borrowed from JT, whose mother had had a friend in the administration. What was also noticeable was that Wallace's characteristic manic quality was again tamped down. As with "Little Expressionless Animals," it was as if a newer, more serious writer had entered the room. Pynchon as model was being replaced or at least added to. In a later interview, Wallace would credit the movie *Blue Velvet*, the offbeat noir film by David Lynch, for this new poise. He had seen the film several times and found it revelatory, so much so that he brought it up in an interview he gave nearly a decade later:

> It was my first hint that being a surrealist, or being a weird writer, didn't exempt you from certain responsibilities. But in fact it obligated, it upped them. . . . That whatever the project of surrealism is works way better if 99.9 percent of it is absolutely real. . . . I mean, most of the word surrealism is realism, you know? It's extra-realism, it's something on top of realism. It's that one thing in a Lynch frame that's off, that, if everything else weren't picture-perfect and totally structured, wouldn't hit.

Around this time Wallace was also finishing a new short story about a guest on *Late Night with David Letterman*. Wallace told Costello he had gotten the idea for it from a show he'd seen several years before. The singer Billy Idol had bragged to the talk show host that his songs were so popular that dealers named street drugs after them: cocaine was "White Wedding," Quaaludes were "Rebel Yells," and marijuana was "Dancing with Myself." Letterman, after a beat, responded, "You must be a very proud young man."

This was the general inspiration; the direct source was that Wallace had watched the actress Susan Saint James on a recent Letterman show and taken extensive notes—"w/r/t [with respect to] the fact that the idea of having a television actress who's agreed to represent Oreos face questioning by Letterman on why she would do such a thing and what the potential implications for her career might be seemed fascinating," as Wallace would later write in response to a publishing lawyer's inquiry when the story raised legal issues.

In the story that resulted, "My Appearance,"[25] Wallace wanted again to show the way media colonized everything from history to our private thoughts. But in the Letterman story, Wallace narrowed his concern, focusing on what he saw as television's elevation of a rising attitude of knowingness in the culture. "My Appearance," set, like *Broom*, slightly in the future, begins with a straightforward statement of fact: "I am a woman who appeared in public on Late Night with David Letterman on March 22, 1989." The story then goes on to recount how her media-savvy husband, Rudy, and his friend Ron prepare the actress for a segment in front of the talk show star. At first the actress resists the idea that to be on Letterman is any different than, say, to be on the talk show hosted by Johnny Carson. "I don't see this dark fearful thing you seem to see in David Letterman," she objects. Her handlers patiently explain that their coaching is about more than Letterman; it's about understanding that the definition of what is admirable or acceptable behavior has changed. We no longer esteem those who know or care; we esteem those who affect not to know or care. There is no arguing with this cultural change, of which Letterman is just a symptom.

> "Act as if you knew from birth that everything is clichéd and hyped and empty and absurd," Ron says, "and that that's just where the fun is."
>
> "But that's not the way I am at all."
>
> The cat yawned.
>
> "That's not even the way I act when I'm acting," I said.
>
> "Yes, Ron said, leaning toward me and pouring a very small splash of liquor on my glass's ice cubes, furred with frozen cola.

Ron and Rudy continue to talk, explaining that irony has become the language of the elite. "I think being seen as being *aware* is the big thing, here," the actress's husband stresses. The actress goes on the show, mocks herself lightly, and succeeds with her host—the fictional Letterman pronounces it "grotesquely nice to have her on"—but she feels somehow depleted afterward. This isn't, after all, the way she is.

Wallace had already proposed to follow *Broom* with a collection of stories. Howard, after some hesitation—story collections didn't sell as well as novels—came around to the idea and paid an advance of $25,000. This was great news to Wallace, confirmation that *Broom* had done what it had to—made him a writer with a publisher and a career. The new book, tentatively titled *Long and Short of It*, would give him, he wrote Nadell with delight in April 1987, a chance to "try . . . to fuck a bit with the fiction current on the scene."

But if he was going to publish Wallace's stories as a book, Howard said, he needed someone else to publish some of them first; Wallace had no reputation as a short story writer and he had had very little success with magazines so far. This had not been for lack of trying. "I am working on a lot of short fiction, and actually have a few stories together that I think are pretty good," he had written to Dale Peterson the year before. He had asked Nadell to start sending them out: "I think they're good—though somewhat off the beaten path." He saw them for *Esquire,* the *Atlantic,* and the *New Yorker.* Nadell gently suggested that such mainstream publications would find them too avant-garde. The dominant genre in these magazines remained realism and minimalism—taut stories with bald denouements. That was not what Wallace was offering. Even Nadell found some of Wallace's stories hard to like. "Not a nice noise, Bonnie," he wrote after she had an unflattering reaction to "John Billy." Nadell's instincts were right. *Playboy* found the Letterman story "too smart for its own good." The *Atlantic* wanted it cut down, as did *Esquire,* which turned down "Luckily the Account Executive" too. Said the *Atlantic* editor, "Wallace clearly is the talent Mary Carter has insisted he is," but "Little Expressionless Animals" was "too long, too idiosyncratic, and too loosely constructed for our purposes."

Wallace minded these dismissals less than one might have expected. The vagaries of magazine publishing barely touched his sense of what he should be doing. Instead he saw submitting stories as sort of a game, publishing-tennis, and offered to take over from Nadell when it was time to approach smaller magazines. He put a bulletin board on his wall where he pinned rejection notes. But in the meantime, the future was bearing down on him. He decided to try to get out of Arizona still faster. He had planned to return briefly in the fall of 1987 to finish his MFA but instead arranged to leave in May. Any leftover work could be done from home and the manuscript mailed.

But he still had no idea where he was going next. Dale Peterson continued to work on getting him a part-time job at Amherst. He thought about
doing a road trip on a motorcyle *à la* Charlie McLagan or even going to
Los Angeles to write television shows. In the meantime, he rewrote and
organized his stories for his thesis committee. He was coming to the end
of his complicated, unsatisfactory life at Arizona. When a presentation
copy of *Broom* he had given one of his professors surfaced at a nearby used
bookstore, he was appalled. In late spring, he left Carter's condo, taking a
print he liked from the wall with him, headed home, and set up in his old
bedroom again to work. Quickly, his energy was focused on what he was
writing. He was now busy with a new story that was meant to show the
failings of metafiction. The story got longer and longer, Wallace's old gi-
gantism bursting the bounds of his newfound discipline. His new story, he
wrote JT in June, now was "cruising . . . at a wildly disordered 150pp."
Wallace had only one certain engagement. He had applied and been accepted to Yaddo, the artists' colony in Saratoga Springs, for late July,[26] but
after that, what? "Maybe to Breadloaf," he wrote JT, "maybe to Boston,
maybe to Albany, maybe to L.A. Nothing is sure in the dry burg that is
this boy's future."

CHAPTER 4

Into the Funhouse

Wallace drove east to Saratoga Springs in July 1987. In Urbana, before leaving, he had spent his evenings relaxing with pot and bourbon and videos. Amy was also there. "God I feel lucky to have a sister who's also a prized friend," he wrote JT. But he'd also pushed forward quietly with his new story. One day Amy came downstairs to find her brother in the kitchen frying a rose in a pan and he said it was for something he was working on. At Yaddo he was taken, as so many writers had been before him, with the gothic main hall in the mansion, the smaller houses on the four hundred acres of grounds, the grand expanse devoted to literature and art. Roughly a dozen writers were in residence, alongside composers and other artists. Wallace felt proud to be among them. This was creative life as he had never experienced it, and, ever competitive, it excited him to be among the best.

Wallace had brought along his story-in-progress to work on. He quickly took it up again. The story takes as its point of departure John Barth's long story "Lost in the Funhouse," a touchstone of postmodern fiction written in 1967 that Wallace had long loved. "Funhouse" tells the story of two brothers, Ambrose and Peter, whose parents drive them to an amusement park in Ocean City, Maryland, on a summer weekend during World War II. The two boys are competing for the attention of a young family friend, Magda, who has also come along—and at story's end we find Ambrose, the younger of the two, lost in the amusement park funhouse, literally and metaphorically left behind by Peter and the girl.

This is all conventional enough storytelling. As Wallace would promise in "Westward" of a similar plot in his own story: each character will expe-

rience "numerous insights, revelations and epiphanies; and will, ultimately, at the end of the time confront his future." But within his
conventional matrix, Barth consistently breaks through the narrative wall
to remind the reader what he or she is experiencing as real is an artifact,
words on paper. So the narrator keeps track of how long it takes his characters to get to the amusement park. He can be didactic, noting after a
string of deftly turned images their function in fiction: "It is . . . important
to 'keep the senses operating'; when a detail from one of the five senses,
say visual, is 'crossed' with a detail from another, say auditory, the reader's
imagination is oriented to the scene, perhaps unconsciously." And when
the three teenagers are horsing around a pool, he interrupts to note, "The
diving would make a suitable literary symbol." He interferes with the se-
ductions of fiction by unmasking them.

It is easy to see why this sort of performance had for so long resonated
with Wallace. Metafiction was the sort of technique that had first formed
the bridge for him from philosophy to fiction when he was at Amherst. It
contained that second level of meaning that made Wallace confident that
what he was reading was intellectually richer than just entertainment
("meatfiction," the narrator of his new story calls it), and it was clever and
sardonic, just as Wallace was. Indeed, Barth had been one of the original
stars in Wallace's firmament, along with Barthelme. And in "Lost in the
Funhouse," he shows himself to be just the sort of fiction teacher Arizona lacked—Wallace's own story featuring diving, "Forever Overhead,"
had won great praise in Tucson, even as he saw how thin it was. Barth,
then, was the teacher Wallace deserved, "Lost in the Funhouse" the wise,
self-aware text his own teachers could never produce to help him on his
own way.

And that had been Wallace's whole response for a time. But as he finished his work at Arizona, he also had come to feel that there was something irritating about "Lost in the Funhouse," condescending, and, if you
were a recursive cast of mind, false about the way Barth kept breaking into
the narrative to show readers falsity. Didn't such an intrusion, in the end,
just create more of a performance? Wasn't it seduction pretending to be
renunciation? How in the end did Barth really propose to challenge or re-
ward the reader? Preparing to rebut Barth in his own story, Wallace scribbled notes in the margins of his paperback of the *Lost in the Funhouse*

story collection, contesting sentences and penning criticisms like "Talmudic—obsessed w/its own interpretation" alongside Barth's words. It was clear that metafiction no longer satisifed Wallace as it once had. But just after his last semester at Arizona, when he probably began his new story, he himself likely couldn't tell whether he was writing an homage, a parody, a eulogy, or an act of patricide. The desire to get out what he had to say was made more intense by his sense that his old life was ending: this was the time for last things, for summings up, for boiling the whole of the fictive act, at least as practiced in MFA programs, down to, as he would later tell an interviewer, "this tiny, infinitely dense thing." To strike down metafiction was also to show what was next, to point the way forward; it was also, in a way, a promise to go beyond what Wallace had been able to achieve in the stories he'd written at Arizona in their farrago of post-modern styles. As the poem by Bishop Berkeley from which the novella title derives concludes:

> *Westward the course of empire takes its way;*
> *The first four Acts already past,*
> *A fifth shall close the Drama with the day;*
> *Time's noblest offspring is the last.*[1]

Like "Funhouse," "Westward the Course of Empire Takes Its Way" is the story of a group of young people on a car trip. But instead of Barth's ordinary American teenagers, Wallace gives us MFA students. And rather than go to a beach, they are on a more typically postmodern errand. They are on the way to the town of Collision, Illinois, for a reunion of the forty-four thousand "former actors, actresses, puppeteers, unemployed clowns" who have ever taken part in a McDonald's commercial. At the same time there will be a ribbon-cutting for a "flagship discotheque" of a new company, whose goal is to "build a Funhouse in every major market." Running this effort to add "a whole new dimension in alone fun" are two people: Leo Burnett, the advertising guru, and none other than John Barth, the metafictionist called her Professor Ambrose (for legal reasons Burnett's name is changed to J.D. Steelritter in the published version of the book). Wallace's suggestion is clear: advertising and metafiction share the same goal, to lull by pleasing, to fatten without nourishing. A third intoxicant is present in the story as well: a marijuana-like product derived from frying roses, which Steelritter has discovered and expects to serve the actors who participate in his great final commercial to some unspecified apocalyptic end.[2]

This two-sided slash at advertising and metafiction was where Wallace's story began, but as he worked on it, it kept outgrowing its original shape, lengthening, if not deepening.[3] Most notably, it came to annex the tempestous story of Wallace and Walden. Wallace felt their relationship was ending and their connection needed telling before, like his life in Arizona, it was gone forever. Wallace himself appears, altered, in two places in "Westward": he bears a resemblance to one of the students in the car, Mark Nechtr, a competitive archer, fried rose addict, and MFA student at Ambrose's East Chesapeake Tradeschool (note the initials), "a boy hotly cocky enough to think he might someday inherit Ambrose's bald crown and ballpoint scepter, to wish to try and sing to the next generation of the very same sad kids." For Nechtr, as for Wallace, metafiction is an addiction, exerting "a kind of gravitylike force" on him at the same time as he tries to fight its malign influence, "feel[ing] about Allusion the way Ambrose seems to feel about Illusion." Nechtr is also Wallace's inverse—full of promise but too blocked to write a word. At Nechtr's side is Drew-Lynn Eberhardt, another student in the program. D.L. is at once alluring and off-putting. She has some of Walden's affect, "reads painted Elkesaite cards, knows her own rising sign, and consults media." She is also working on a long poem consisting only of punctuation. The couple are married but in a sexless relationship, D.L. pretending—or perhaps believing herself to be—pregnant.

As in "Lost in the Funhouse," "Westward" alternates the seductive rhythm of realist narrative with authorial interruptions meant to remind the reader that the story is a fabrication. But Wallace then takes his writing to the next metalevel, striving to outdo "the locutionally muscular and forever *terrible enfant*" Barth. Thus one intrusion, billed as "A Really Blatant and Intrusive Interruption," reads:

> If this were a piece of metafiction, which it's NOT, the exact number
> of typeset lines between this reference and the prenominate refer-
> ent would very probably be mentioned, which would be a princely

pain in the ass, not to mention cocky, since it would assume that a straightforward and anti-embellished account of a slow and hot and sleep-deprived and basically clotted and frustrating day in the lives of three kids, none of whom are all that sympathetic, could actually get published, which these days good luck, but in metafiction it would, nay *needs* be mentioned.

And he adds one last trill at the end. In the final pages, Nechtr himself becomes a writer of the story of two characters named Dave and Gale. Gale—changed to L in the published version—"is self-conscious, neaurasthenic, insecure, moody, diffracted," the narrator notes. "Dave is introverted, self-counseled and tends to be about as expressive as processed cheese." They love each other but battle constantly:

When the hottest darkest mood in L—s weather collides with his cold white quiet, they have violent arguments that seem utterly to transform them. . . . They scream and fight and carry on like things possessed.

But in the climactic fight, the Gale figure stabs not Dave, but herself, "which makes her climactic lover's thrust at him sort of perfect in both directions." It is the ultimate metafictional act, not homicide but suicide. (Wallace would say that one of the problems of metafiction is that there is no difference.) For good measure, it is a death the David figure watches not directly but in the "dead green eye" of his TV.

L— dead, "Westward" ends with a proffer of peace to the reader:

See this thing. See inside what spins without purchase. Close your eye. Absolutely no salesmen will call. Relax. Lie back. I want nothing from you. Lie back. Relax. Quality soil washes right out. Lie back. Open. Face directions. Look. Listen. Use ears I'd be proud to call our own. Listen to the silence behind the engines' noise. Jesus, Sweets, *listen.* Hear it? It's a love song.

For whom?
You are loved.

Few readers have taken Wallace up on this offer, and with reason. "Westward" feels like watching a family fight, worse because it is only the son who wants the combat and it may be himself he really wants to wound. The story is as much an attack on the work Wallace had done at Arizona with its mix of postmodern styles as it is on Barth. Wallace's quintessentially metafictional mind is searching for something to move on to—but nothing is yet present. In its absence the story careers along like the car its MFA students ride in, endlessly, fitfully, and compulsively, battling the readers' needs. But the story is also evidence of how readily at the time Wallace was seeing connections around him—between love and addiction, and storytelling and advertising, for instance—beginning to put together a worldview that would be fundamental when he turned his attention to *Infinite Jest* a few years later. Foremost is the idea he debuted in his Arizona stories that our passions are no longer our own. In the age of media, we are nothing but minds waiting to be filled, emotions waiting to be manipulated. There is a sense—again brought to full boil in *Infinite Jest*—that our obsession with being entertained has deadened our affect, that we are not, as a character warns in that book, choosing carefully enough what to love. And "Westward" suggests for the first time in Wallace's fiction that not just he but his whole generation share this difficulty. He begins to take the key step of universalizing his neurosis. This is a tricky pass—Wallace hardly had a normal relationship with television, let alone life—but it is the very intensity of his engagement that seems to permit it. The potential payoff artistically was huge, and Wallace was beginning to organize his brief. The characters, the narrator tells us, are members of "*this awkwardest of post-Imperial decades*, an age suspended between exhaustion and replenishment, between input too ordinary to process and input too intense to bear."[4] "Westward" also represented how seriously Wallace had come to take fiction, how much he believed that in the wrong hands it could demoralize and passify the unwary.

At Yaddo Wallace was under considerable pressure to be done with his story collection—from his publisher, and from himself. He was working all the time and with a passion others noticed. Most writers spent the mornings in their rooms writing, and the afternoons lounging by the pool or going on outings. Wallace wrote always and everywhere: stretched out on the floor or wedged into an alcove or late at night. "I've never been in a work environment this powerful before," he explained to JT in a postcard. An older writer warned him that his working so hard was unsightly—or so he told Mark Costello.

At the same time, he was aware of the opportunity Yaddo offered to meet other writers and networked enthusiastically. To this new group of colleagues, he brought his odd blend of arrogance and politeness, calling everyone "Mr." or "Ms." until told to do otherwise. Some of the other writers thought he was being ironic; the more prescient spotted him as midwestern, or just socially challenged. He was voluble at dinner and active on the tennis courts, where he beat Jay McInerney and lost to Stephen Dunn, a poet who had once been a semiprofessional basketball player. He met an editor from the *Paris Review*, Jeanne McCulloch, and offered to improve her serve if she would consider his story "Little Expressionless Animals," which larger magazines kept turning down. He grew infatuated with a young woman composer who was writing a piece using the "devil's interval"—the augmented fourth musical interval considered so seductive that the church forbade it. In general, he gyrated between wanting to impress and disliking himself for having such impulses, between making his mark as the genius in the room and getting his work done. One day he suggested to another resident, the composer Michael Torke, that they leave behind the chatter of the communal dining room and go for a silent dinner off the grounds to clear their heads, only then to surprise his new friend by bringing along a young woman.

During his stay, Wallace fell under the wing of the thirty-two-year-old McInerney. They would drink together in the evenings and read each other's manuscripts. McInerney was writing his novel *Story of My Life*, the memoir of a twenty-year-old socialite and addict named Alison Poole. Wallace admired the older novelist's control of voice, and also how he could work after a long night of drinking. Wallace liked pot, not alcohol, but he could find none at the retreat so he had to learn to deal with hangovers. The older McInerney was surprised to find Wallace so obsessed with postmodernism; for him and his peers it had largely ceased to matter. "All that tormented stuff about . . . whether fiction was the world or the word," he remembers, "it seemed to my generation that Carver and Mary

Robison and Tobias Wolff just pushed that question off to the side of the road." "Forever Overhead" was in second person, and Wallace quizzed McInerney, who had used it memorably in *Bright Lights*. He made a trip to the Bennington Writers Conference to read at the invitation of Alice Turner, the fiction editor at *Playboy*, who had been impressed by his stories. They fell to intense talking in the common room—about his writing, her work, other writers. Wallace in the same breath said he was on an MAO inhibitor and refreshed their drinks. Eventually, the two went into a bedroom. Their noise disturbed the other writers, themselves hardly early-to-bed types. In retaliation the novelist George Garrett took Wallace's boots and socks and hid them under the sink. The next morning Wallace had to read in his bare feet. Deeply embarrassed, he told Garrett, whom he did not suspect, "I hope you don't think I'm a hippie."

Yaddo turned Wallace's head. In Arizona he had been the top student, his success the object of envy, even among some of the teachers. Now he would go by the mail table in the main hall and see messages from famous agents urging their writers to call them back about movie deals and foreign rights. McInerney had a Porsche and a girlfriend who was a model. While Wallace was at Yaddo, a feature from *Esquire* came out, "Who's Who in the Cosmos," an update of a graphic the magazine had first published in the mid-1970s, a map of the literary universe. Wallace was both pleased and disappointed to find he was among the writers "on the horizon"; better than being left out entirely, but not in the "media showers" section with McInerney, let alone in the "Red-Hot Center" with John Updike, Norman Mailer, and Saul Bellow. At the same time, he was mad at himself for caring about such trivialities—indeed caring about them obsessively, as he was discovering.

This seductive overload came at a delicate time for Wallace. He was still trying to come to terms with the fact that writers of interesting and challenging fiction had to teach. He had never met one who could make a living just on his or her writing until now. Writers like McInerney and Mona Simpson, who was also at the retreat, seemed to him to have found a solution, and their success suggested to him that he was maybe on his way to being famous enough that he might be able to avoid his fate. But what did you have to do to be a famous, rich writer? Wallace wanted to know. Could you still be *serious*? Or did success inevitably corrupt the artist? By concidence, he was about to answer that question for himself. *Us* magazine had approached Wallace to take part in a fashion spread at El Morocco, the reborn New York supper club. The shoot was to center around Tama Janowitz, whose story collection *Slaves of New York* had followed McInerney's and Ellis's books onto the bestseller lists. *Us*'s article was meant to convey—or if necessary invent—the excitement of New York literary life and put forward a cohort of hot young writers. In the middle of his stay at Yaddo, Wallace drove down to New York. The four authors other than Janowitz met in a trailer outside the club to choose their clothes. The others reached for loud checks and glistening sequins. Wallace somehow found an old T-shirt and ripped jeans, emerging even more himself than he had gone in. Exchanging pleasantries with the others, he bragged that he had just been at Yaddo, shooting pool with Jay McInerney.

The group gathered in the salon of the nightclub. Janowitz entered, her hair teased out into a mountainous coif, wearing a leopardprint dress. "You look beautiful," Wallace told her quietly. The photographer began barking directions. He choreographed the other writers in attitudes of adulation toward Janowitz. "Look like you're having fun!" he ordered. Wallace quickly walked out. He told Walden later it was the look of his fellow writers, their eyes as they stared at the camera, that made him flee.

He went to see his editor, Howard, who took him to lunch. Wallace was very shaken. He was confused by what he had seen; yes, this lust for fame, for recognition, he certainly had it too, especially if it could get him out of teaching. But where did it lead? To what he had just witnessed? What if he fired Nadell and hired a powerful New York agent? Might he then have the life he wanted? Of course he wanted bigger advances, more fame, a more powerful agent, but to have these things one had to write to please and was he really willing to do that? He did not even know how to do that—or maybe he knew it too well. If he was going to fight the devil would he have to spend his life teaching? His mind was stuck in a loop and he cried in anguish. He talked on and on. Howard was now getting a first glimpse of the "obscurely defective" Wallace, the one having so much trouble being "human in a human community." He talked the twenty-five-year-old Wallace down, he remembers, as if he were on "a bad acid trip." Finally Wallace calmed down and went off to Alice Turner's house near Washington Square to spend the night.

An already hard visit to New York became harder. That night a bag with the manuscript of "Westward" was stolen from the trunk of Wallace's beat-up Nissan. He found the bag in a nearby Dumpster but not the manuscript. He was devastated, but this turned out to be a break in a way, because he then had reason to race back to Yaddo, where he wrote a draft of the entire story from scratch in, he would claim, "like, a week." He took cold baths every evening to stop his brain from whirring. He finished it just in time for the short-story manuscript Viking Penguin was planning to publish in 1988.

Wallace was proud of what he had achieved at Yaddo. He left with a feeling he had never had before of having done what he set out to do. "I'm sure page for page, it's a better book than TBOTS," he wrote Nadell of the collection, "maybe not as fun to read, but it's smarter, and there's a lot less deadwood." He added that he hoped Viking Penguin wouldn't see it as some sort of detour until "the kid can get back on track writing gags." His unsual enthusiasm may have been more of a response to the stress he was under—withdrawal from pot made him highly agitated—than from what he had achieved on the page, but he was certain he had done remarkable work. He told Howard that with the story "Westward" he had "broken through." Even two years after, he would write, in a letter to Jonathan Franzen, who had become a friend and, like nearly all Wallace's friends, wondered why Wallace held "Westward" in such special regard, that the novella was

> in my view far and away the best piece of sustained fiction I've ever written. It is exactly what I wanted it to be [and is] also truly about everything I either had to write about or die in '87. . . . My hope is that it succeeds on about 12 different levels, depending on whether you're more interested in advertising or 80's fiction or 60's metafiction or the revelations of John—disciple not Barth or etc.

The story served such a personal need that he did not care what anyone thought about it—or him. When Franzen told him that the effect of the story was as if the reader had walked into a party full of "asshole[s]," Wallace responded, "If the story seems pretentious maybe it is," and went on:

I have met assholes, and if "Westward" strikes you as the work of an asshole I'll smile and apologize and say I appreciate your letter.

If proud of his fiction, though, Wallace was ashamed of his behavior. He did not like to expose his fragility. "I actually cried in front of [Howard] at lunch in some 23rd St. Bistro—*gak*," he wrote Nadell in September, still worried a month later. But she, he felt, deserved an even bigger apology: if he had offended her, it would give him "the howling fantods." For the "dark time" in New York, he blamed the stress induced by writing "Westward" ("I sort of *had* to get myself in a *State* to finish that thing," he explained), as well as

> a very strange social, hierarchical Yaddo atmosphere, affecting the above Dark Time most directly as a bunch of advice from Older Writers that was, I'm sure, meant as helpful but turned out to be sort of misguided. Many of these Older Writers seem to have the equipment both to try to write OK fiction and to concern themselves aggressively with issues like money, representation, etc. I simply cannot.

He added, hopefully, "You and I have good enough communication lines that I don't worry about irreparable offense to you." He was right: Nadell knew Wallace better than he knew himself, and she knew he now knew how much he needed her.[5]

Fortunately, by now Dale Peterson had gotten Wallace the teaching position at his *alma mater*, a development that for Wallace held the hope of calm after the perturbations of Yaddo and New York. If he was going to have to teach, this seemed the way to do it. He would get $6,500 for just one weekly two-hour fiction workshop in the fall, considerably more than he'd been paid for an entire year of teaching at Arizona. The rest of the time was his for writing. And he could begin by staying at Peterson's home, where he had housesat in his college years. He could have a bedroom— "like a real person," Peterson offered in a letter—or sleep in the family room if he preferred, with Lolita, the parrot he had transfigured into Vlad the Impaler in *Broom*, until he found, he wrote, "less seedstrewn accommodations." Wallace was superstitious. He thought if he could recreate some of the ambience by which that novel had coalesced like magic, a similar inspiration might strike again. He sensed that he was at a crossroads; it had been a long time since he had tried to write without teachers and workshops.

So by late August he was back at Amherst, slightly more than two years after he had left it. He moved temporarily into the Peterson home. It was perhaps a bad omen that Lolita had just died—"Her little ticker didn't quite hold out long enough to meet her re-maker," Peterson wrote. But he was happy to find that Andrew Parker, his favorite literature theory teacher, was willing to share an office. Peterson was lending him his cubicle in Frost too. Even so, immediately Wallace sensed that he'd made a mistake. Amherst in 1987 wasn't his Amherst. Nearly everyone he knew was gone; he was alone. Walden and Wallace had left their relationship on hold over the summer, and now he reached out to her, suggesting marriage for the second time. Wallace told his friends they'd chosen a date in the late fall at a church in Cicero, outside of Chicago; Walden's father, a minister, would preside. Wallace asked Costello to be best man. His friend suggested he make sure he was going in with his eyes open. "They're saucers," Wallace replied. But Walden was wary, understandably. She came east to be near Wallace, moving in with a friend in Belchertown, a few miles from Amherst, and she and Wallace made efforts to reestablish their relationship. But his drinking and depressiveness worried her and she kept her distance.

At the core the problem for Wallace was what to write next. He had said what he had to say in "Westward." It was what he had been born to write, and having done so, as he would later explain to an interviewer, he had "killed this huge part of myself doing it." Much like an addict looking back on a final binge, Wallace would later shudder at its memory, calling the effort "a horror show . . . a permanent migraine . . . crude and naïve and pretentious." To Franzen he would reflect, "I wanted something utterly open," like "the bleeding guts of a patient who should die on the table, aetherized, but won't." Since finishing the novella, he hadn't written a word; the story, he realized, as he would tell a later interviewer, was also "a

kind of suicide note"—if he wasn't precisely a metafictionist, he was certainly someone for whom pulling off the façade of realism was congenial.
The arrow he had killed the fictional Gale with had pierced him too.

At Yaddo he had drunk heavily as a replacement for pot, and because
McInerney did, and a part of him wanted to be McInerney. But here at
Amherst, still without pot, the alcohol itself became an issue. He wrote JT
that he had "picked up a bit of a drinking problem and am currently grappling." The blithe note belied his upset that what had begun as a place-
holder was now a new addiction and thus a new source of disgust with
himself. He might not have drunk if he had had some work to do, but his
days seemed empty and pointless.[6] When he got the news that the *Paris
Review* had taken "Little Expressionless Animals," he told JT that the sale
made "Viking pretty happy," but "at this point I don't really care." On arriving in Amherst, he had worked his way through Peterson's liquor cabinet and then quietly replaced the bottles, only to work his way through
them again. Soon he got an apartment in North Amherst—"not really all
that nice, plus expensive," he wrote Washington, and for a moment he was
able to summon some joy at the sight of a New England fall again—at least
from behind the scrim of his letter-writing. "I'm squatting amid boxes," he
wrote Nadell in early September, "offering prayers of thanks for some un-
furnished privacy. The leaves are threatening to get pretty already." But his
good mood did not last long. "Please *please* get me out of here," he pled to
Nadell a few weeks later. He said he was listening to "sad Springsteen and
Neil Young. I wander around Rick [Vigorous]-like, remembering disas-
ters." He wrote Forrest Ashby that he was thinking of moving to Canada
to be a high school teacher.

Wallace was on the verge of falling into a new depression. The struts
that held up his life—classes, his work, his relationships, his drug use—
had all been removed. He turned to television now, his drug of last resort,
soothing himself with hours of sitcoms, soap operas, and sporting events.
He drank still more.[7] "Do Not Send Any Bob, Please," he wrote a connection in Tucson, knowing that marijuana was the last thing he needed. But
then, later: "Bob's presence urgently requested."

Class began. *Broom* had done well for a first novel, but Wallace was far
from famous.[8] To the Amherst undergraduates, he was just a name on the
syllabus. In fact, because he was a last-minute addition meant to fill a

teaching hole, they knew less about him than about most of their instruc-
tors. The students who showed up for his class were surprised to find a
man barely older than themselves, carrying a pink Care Bears folder and
a tennis racket. Before the first seminar meeting, Wallace had asked for
writing samples—admission to seminars at Amherst was selective.
When one girl asked why she had to provide a sample of how well she
wrote in order to get into a class to learn how to become a better writer,
Wallace acknowledged the tautology—and perhaps her anxiety—and
told her she could just submit a grocery list. In the end, he taught thirteen students.

Wallace knew that if he taught hard he wouldn't be able to write, but he
also knew that he wasn't writing anyway, so he went at teaching with fer-
vor, covering the students' papers with pages of annotations, throwing
himself into their work. Teaching brought focus and a sense of accomplishment and the knowledge that he was honoring his parents, and Wallace needed all that. The students were astonished at his intensity.

Feeling he had endured the scorn of the Arizona professors, Wallace
made sure his comments were supportive and the tone of the class positive. He did not want to replicate the discouraging classroom atmosphere
he had just left. He cautioned the students, as one remembers, not to "tap
dance in cleats" on one another's stories. His syllabus was conventional,
meant to teach the basic tools of writing: character, dialogue, and plot. He
gave his students Eudora Welty's "Why I Live at the P.O." to illustrate the
unreliable narrator and Lee K. Abbott's "Living Alone in Iota" to showcase
voice. "Just because it really happened, doesn't make it good fiction," he
would remind them. He had the ability to shift gears in this way—to go
from the pyrotechnics of writing "Westward" to teaching the rudiments
of fiction; in fact, the simpler the teaching, the happier it made him. He
did not go to class for challenges, personal or intellectual, he went to find
certainties of the sort that eluded him in his own writing. Every meeting
started with a grammar lesson—the difference between "between" and
"among" or "further" and "farther." "I'm a grammar Nazi," he liked to tell
his students. One day he put the words "pulchritudinous," "miniscule,"
"big," and "misspelled" on the blackboard. He asked his students what the
four words had in common, and, when no one knew, happily pointed out
that the appearance of each was the opposite of its meaning: "pulchritudi-

nous" was ugly, "miniscule" was big, "big" was small, and "misspelled" was spelled correctly. The students had rarely seen him so happy.[9]

To their eyes, the twenty-five-year-old Wallace was a mystery. He came to class in his Arizona bandana (some thought it was to keep his hair from falling out), Timberland boots, and plaid shirts, cursed, and took frequent smoking breaks. He was trying to quit smoking and so had begun chewing tobacco.[10] He was happy to extend office hours for as long as students wanted, but if he bumped into them on the street he hardly acknowledged them. One student was reminded of Dostoevksy's Underground Man. Costello came for a visit and found his old roommate strangely diminished. He remembers "everything happening in very slow motion—getting dressed to go out, finding car keys, finding dip, notebook, working pen, writing a phone message." There were only blondies and mustard in the fridge. Wallace told his college roommate he worried that pot smoking had ruined his brain permanently and he would never be able to write again.

Depressed, he was still not without romantic appeal. Two undergraduate women in his class set off one day to see where he lived and were excited to find his apartment above a sandwich shop in a run-down part of Amherst. When two students in his class asked if he wanted to go hear an Irish band play in Springfield, forty minutes south on the interstate, he surprised them by agreeing. On the way home the car, which Wallace was driving, spun out, leaving them all scared by the side of the road before they climbed back in and returned to the college. They did not repeat the adventure. To them, he looked spooked, hollowed out, adult.

Toward the end of the semester, Wallace occasionally dropped hints of a different life. When he gave his class an excerpt from *Story of My Life* to read, he mentioned he had been with the author at Yaddo when he was writing it. That fall he went to New York to receive a Whiting Award, and afterward told the class he had met Eudora Welty. At semester's end, Wallace gave his students his *Jeopardy!* story, "Little Expressionless Animals," to read and critique. "I've spent all semester reading your stuff and now you can read something of mine," he told them.

Wallace's only obligations were his once-a-week class and office hours. "I'm basically on my own," he wrote Ashby. He turned out to miss structure, writing in a letter later in the semester, "The view from my apartment, where I spend staggering amounts of time, always seems accessed through dirty windows, no matter how vigorously Windex is applied." Andrew Parker, with whom he was supposed to be sharing an office, was surprised how little he saw of his former student. And when he was around, there was something about Wallace's behavior that discouraged questions.

No one in his orbit guessed the intensity of Wallace's suffering—the television he watched (six to eight hours a day, he told one of his students), the drinking, drugs, and loneliness. It was not that he was not trying to write; it was that he was not succeeding. He may have picked up some older stories at this time and reworked them, especially "Church Not Made with Hands," an intricate story about an art therapist and a man coping with his daughter's brain injury that he had first submitted in Mary Carter's workshop at Arizona. He started two novellas sometime around this time, of which he would later say that they were "just so *unbelievably* bad. . . . Hopelessly confused. Hopelessly bending in on themselves." (They have never surfaced.) The feeling he had said all he had to say in "West-ward" still lingered. The story pointed backward but not forward; metafiction was done, but what was to come? He had no experience writing without inspiration—creativity was tied in to the manic part of his personality. *Esquire* was interested now in publishing his Letterman story, but he would have to cut ten to fifteen pages. Wallace dutifully tried but in the end the magazine turned it down.

Predictably, the planned late November wedding began to come apart. Walden had returned to her family in Chicago, worried about her fiancé's drinking, and in mid-October he visited her there. They fought. One issue was that Wallace had invited Alice Turner to their ceremony, and Walden, when she discovered what had gone on at Bennington, refused to have her at the celebration. Wallace strove to explain, but Walden could not be convinced—at least this was the version Wallace gave Turner in a letter; Wallace may have been exaggerating or simply inventing. One way or another, the relationship appeared truly finished. Wallace went on a new bender, considering suicide. "I've hurt not just me but her and her family," he wrote a friend three weeks later, saying the new break with Walden left him "feeling dead."

But though breakups were often the prompts for Wallace's collapses, they never quite seemed the cause. Indeed, the decision to force things

with Walden may have been a deliberate whack of the Paddle of Immoderation, an attempt to shock himself into writing again. Whatever the motive, the break with Walden felt final.

Becalmed back in Amherst, Wallace began to yearn for Tucson. He had
not particularly liked the city, but he had written well there. As the fall
wore on, he asked JT to confirm the rumor of "gorgeous new poetesses" in
the MFA program, and when the faculty invited him back to give a reading at the Poetry Center in January 1988, he went. He flew west and met
up with old friends, many still in the writing program. He and Ashby went
climbing in the Tucson Mountains west of the city. A new graduate student, Martha Ostheimer, whom Forrest was friends with, came along.
Wallace strove to impress her by running up the mountain before the
other two, but he was out of shape and wound up vomiting in some bushes
near the summit. That evening there was a party, and afterward, he and
Ostheimer talked for hours in her car about literature, particularly Pynchon. He wound up in her apartment, where they spent the next several
days. A relationship no sooner begun, Wallace fled it. Quickly he flew off
to San Francisco, where, he told Ostheimer, he had to see Nadell. He came
back to Tucson for the reading and impressed his old pals by crumpling
and tossing the pages of "Westward" as he read it. "It was," remembers
Ostheimer, "as if they no longer existed after he'd read them." When Ostheimer went around to see him at JT's, the former marine told him Wallace was not available. Afterward, Wallace sent JT a note thanking him for
his help, but to Ashby he admitted, "I think I've again fucked up girl-wise."
He apologized to Corey Washington, who was at Stanford, saying he'd
been "too hung over" to visit. One last note he sent was to Rich C., a friend
from the writing program with whom he used to get drunk. Rich C.[11] had
recently entered an alcohol abuse program. "Let me know how it's going,"
Wallace wrote. He saw that things couldn't continue this way indefinitely.

Wallace had returned home to Urbana by January 1988, his semester appointment over. He had tried to find a job after Amherst but failed. One
place he approached was the MFA program at the University of Arizona.
"I asked the fiction faculty," remembered Steve Orlen, then the director.
"They didn't want him." Frank Conroy, with whom he had read at the West

Side Y in spring 1987, was a fan but told him that the Iowa Writers' Work-shop had no positions open right now. The Provincetown Fine Arts Center said he was "over-qualified" for a residency. Wallace had no choice but to turn to his parents, resubscribing to what he later called "the Mr. and Mrs. Wallace Fund for Aimless Children."

Six months had passed since he had received his MFA. Little had gone right in that time and nothing had gotten written. He finally recognized that he had a drug and alcohol problem. In February, he began going to weekly sobriety meetings. Wallace would later tell friends he enjoyed them and also that he could see that what they were asking him to do was ex-tremely hard. He had smoked pot heavily for most of the past decade. Pot had opened the door for him as a writer. Now he was targeting it in the hopes his life, haunted by anxiety, failed relationships, and a feeling that he could no longer write well, would improve.[12] One comfort was that his story collection would be out in the fall. Alice Turner had bought the Let-terman story for *Playboy* and *Conjunctions*, a literary journal, had even taken "John Billy," the Gass homage. All seemed aligned for *Girl with Cu-rious Hair* to appear, a second book from this promising young author.[13]

Instead, things were about to get worse. Shortly before the Letterman story went to press, a different editor at *Playboy* had happened to watch a rerun of a Letterman show and been amazed to hear some of the dialogue from the story spoken by the actress Susan Saint James. He passed the news on to Turner, who, astonished, reported the lift to the magazine's lawyers. For Wallace to take dialogue from a living person was a legal problem on many levels, not least because the character, also called Susan in the story, has an addiction to Xanax. (Wallace would later explain to the lawyers that the detail came from his own addiction at the time.)

The lawyers at *Playboy* told everyone to just stay quiet and hope for the best—it was too late to make changes in the story and likely no one would notice. All that happened on the *Playboy* side was Turner sent Wallace a furious letter. "Much fiction," she wrote him, "is based on fact; as an expe-rienced editor, I know how to deal with that." She warned him that his reputation was at severe risk; that writers who committed plagiarism were never forgiven. "I hope this letter scares you," she concluded. "It's meant to scare you."

The June 1988 issue of *Playboy* came out, the story ran, was well received, and nobody representing Saint James ever contacted the magazine.

But *Playboy* had also passed on the news to Viking Penguin that Wallace had not told them about lifting the material. Gerry Howard defended his author. (He suggested, for instance, to Turner that the whole thing was a "postmodernist prank.") But Viking Penguin had recently suffered two expensive lawsuits and was not eager to take any chances. The publishers' lawyers asked Howard to ask Wallace about the real-life models for stories in the collection. They wanted the source of every fact and assertion, paragraph by paragraph. Howard remembers it as "the literary equivalent of a strip search. . . . 'Spread 'em.'"

From his parents' house, Wallace became a writer in reverse, laying bare sources of fiction some of which he'd written two years before. He whipped off an eighteen-page response to Howard.[14] He was still not sure how much trouble he was in. In his letter he tried at times to be coy:

> p. 148 David Letterman has never to my knowledge said "Some fun now, boy"—at various intervals or not. It is, though, weirdly just the sort of thing he'd say.

Other places he was apologetic. He admitted he'd seen Saint James on Letterman in late 1986 or early 1987 and had thought her appearance might be

> a neat device for exploring both the way Letterman's program's humor and interaction worked and the feelings a mildly famous person who must confront, publicly, the fact that her fame is and is deservedly mild must be experiencing.

While admitting that the essence of the story had been taken from real life, Wallace was disingenuous about the implications:

> While the main character is in no way supposed to represent the person Susan St. James, her interview with Letterman, their discussion of the Oreo subject, and her way of insisting to Letterman (with

much more sarcasm than is in the story) that she did the commercials for fun is truly both a subject of the story and a purloined piece of actual public data. That this might suggest to people that the story is "about" Ms. St. James the person never crossed my mind.

He remembered Turner's asking him where he'd gotten the dialogue for the story from but said it just "did not occur to me as a thing to tell about." Nor had he thought to mention the source of the protagonist's name, Susan—"a colossal boner." There was, he admitted, giving up, "at least a line a page that's either lifted or I just don't remember."

"My Appearance," he knew, was a lost cause: "In terms of legality and fairness to editors, it's a fucked piece of work," he wrote Howard. But he continued to fight for the other stories in the collection, where he felt less indebted to real-life models. He annotated "Little Expressionless Animals" for Howard:

> p. 11—John Updike is the name of a real writer whom the character Julie dislikes a lot.
> p. 20—Some of the tics mentioned here, i.e. antipathy toward digital watches and caffeine, fear of flickering fluorescence, are tics of girls I've gone out with.

And when he came to his beloved "Westward," his wit revived:

> p. 260—Kierkegaard is long dead, and I think his ideas are public domain—either that or a lot of professors everywhere are doing actionable stuff.

Behind the snark there was also a germ of true confusion, of mystification. If you were exploring the nature of reality, especially media reality, didn't you have to enfold that reality in your work? Since he was a boy, Wallace had expected to know the reason behind the rules. Why could you use the names of characters from "Lost in the Funhouse" in one story, he asked Howard now, but not incidents from a Letterman show in another? "Maybe I'm stupid; I don't see the difference." Howard passed on the long letter to the lawyers for Viking Penguin. The stories were riddled with legal issues; Wallace had proven anything but reliable; short stories were not moneymakers. Though galleys had already been printed, they decided not to go ahead with publication, to its editor's and author's horror. "They didn't even think they were gonna lose, they just thought they'd get sued," Wallace complained to an interviewer almost a decade later, still appalled:

> They invoked the principle of what they called the right of publicity. Not right to privacy, but a right to publicity, such that publishing the *Jeopardy!* story would be the equivalent of my capitalizing on a physical resemblance to Pat Sajak—like running around at mall openings *as* Pat Sajak, and receiving income that was rightfully his. Which seemed to me so utterly bizarre.

He had a point. What had he done besides what a writer must do? He had taken several entertainments most Americans were so familiar with that they could not see how important they were and showed why they mattered. He had pointed out toxins in the culture and warned readers against them. He had been enormously but not falsely entertaining. Far from trying to make money off Pat Sajak's or David Letterman's reputations, he had showed how they made money off of us, off of our flaccid idea of humor and our corrupted sense of self. And for this he had received an unceremonious dumping.

The turn of events would be a terrible blow to any writer, but to Wallace, who felt he had traveled so far in his work from *Broom*, it was particularly devastating. The demise of "Westward" was especially upsetting, as it had found no magazine publisher. He had written a suicide note that no one would ever read. But even as this debacle was unfolding, Wallace was pushing forward with his career. While he had been teaching at Amherst, he had gotten a request from the *Review of Contemporary Fiction*, a small avant-garde journal, to contribute a piece to their "Novelist as Critic" issue. Other participants included Gilbert Sorrentino and Barth himself. Wallace was to represent the younger generation, his pay $250. He found the company "daunting . . . but that obviously makes the whole thing an honor," as he wrote to the editor, Steven Moore.

Wallace responded with a long essay, "Fictional Futures and the Conspicuously Young." For those who had read only the soufflé-light *Broom*, the intensity with which he explicated the current malaise writers found themselves in might well have come as a surprise. "Our generation," Wallace began, "is lucky enough to have been born into an artistic climate as stormy and exciting as anything since Pound and Co. turned the world-before-last on its head." In his view, the key force in this unstable environment was the ubiquity of television, which creative writers and their teachers had not yet grasped fully:

> The American generation born after, say, 1955 is the first for whom television is something to be *lived with*, not just looked at. Our parents regard the set rather as the Flapper did the automobile: a curiosity turned treat turned seduction. For us, their children, TV's as much a part of reality as Toyotas and gridlock. We quite literally cannot "imagine" life without it.

There was more than a bit of self-reference in this point: if anyone couldn't imagine life without TV, it was Wallace. But the personal was becoming the societal for Wallace, and in his cosmology, TV was an enormous force. It had already remade narrative by breaking stories up into short, palatable, and reassuring segments. Everything from our myths to our relationships was succumbing to this great dispenser of pabulum.

Wallace believed the "three dreary camps" of current fiction writers corresponded to three different responses to this insidious force. One camp consisted of the young hip brat pack writers like McInerney and Ellis, whom he defined as practicing "Neiman-Marcus Nihilism, declaimed via six-figure Uppies and their salon-tanned, morally vacant offspring." A second camp were the minimalists. He characterized their style as "Catatonic Realism, a.k.a. Ultraminimalism, a.k.a. Bad Carver." And the third was just about every other writer he'd ever read, especially those favored by his teachers at Arizona. These writers practiced

> Workshop Hermeticism, fiction for which the highest praise involves the words "competent," "finished," "problem-free": no character without Freudian trauma in accessible past, without near-diagnostic physical description; no image undissolved into regulation Up-

dikean metaphor; no overture without a dramatized scene to "show" what's "told"; no denouement prior to an epiphany whose approach can be charted by any Freitag [sic] on any Macintosh.[15]

Wallace allowed that some critics might see minimalism or postmodernism as attempts to escape the prison of modern television-shaped reality, but he argued forcefully that they were each too limited to solve the problem:

> Both these forms strike me as simple engines of self-reference (Metafiction overtly so, Minimalism a bit sneakier); they are primitive, crude, and seem already to have reached the Clang-Bird-esque horizon of their own possibility.

For Wallace, the great flaw of most fiction was that it was content to display the symptoms of the current malaise rather than to solve it. Wallace wasn't even sure exactly what fiction that surmounted television-mediated reality would look like, but he believed that any writer who figured it out would sound different from one who didn't:

> If one can stomach a good dose of simplification . . . there can be seen one deep feature shared by all the cutting-edge fiction that resonates with the post-Hiroshima revolution. That is its fall into time, a loss of innocence about the language that is its breath and bread. Its unblinking recognition of the fact that the relations between literary artist, literary language, and literary artifact are vastly more complex and powerful than has been realized hitherto. And the insight that is courage's reward—that it is precisely in those tangled relations that a forward-looking, fertile literary value may well reside.[16]

Of course readers who knew his recent work from magazines would realize that this wasn't a bad description of the stories Wallace had collected in *Girl with Curious Hair*, but Wallace could hardly put himself forward as an ideal anymore: he wasn't writing and even worse, just as the article was appearing, it was becoming clear the volume of stories his essay was meant to gloss were not going to come out. His prolegomenon would have no follow-up.

As the spring of 1988 passed, Wallace's thoughts turned again to Arizona. If he could get back there, he became increasingly hopeful, he could return to the work and the pleasure in the work he had known during his previous stay. Even if the creative writing professors at the university there did not want him, the undergraduate writing program staff still remembered his extraordinary teaching and the award he'd gotten. They were happy to have him back as an instructor, to start in the fall. Wallace decided to go west in May, rather than spend the summer months as an overgrown child in his parents' house. "I miss the heat and the plethora of feminine pulchritude," he wrote Corey Washington, acknowledging that "I return less than triumphant to Tucson."

In Tucson, Wallace first stayed with Heather Aronson's sister Jaci, in a house with a swamp cooler. He slept in the living room, where there was a stereo, so he could listen to meditation tapes he had brought. He ate all the Pop-Tarts in the house and tried to give his hostess money for them and never unpacked his computer, saying he was worried about the humidity.

With Heather's help, Monica's, a local bakery, hired him. His job was to come in early and prepare the sourdough bread for baking. The proprietors loved his company, Aronson remembers—Wallace could turn on his "jus' folks" quality when he wanted to. And he found relief in the physical labor—it requires a lot of upper body strength to stir sourdough mixture. "I mark time by the number of headbands I soak and have to put in the sink," he wrote Nadell in July, with some satisfaction. But within he was unhappy, nervous, and felt now like whatever could go wrong would. He wanted to know what had happened to the *Jeopardy!* story that the *Paris Review* had taken almost a year before. It had been awarded the John Train humor prize and $1,500, money he could use. "Do you suppose," he asked his agent, "they decided I was playing a joke on them with the story and decided to play an even crueler one on me?" He did not realize or had forgotten that the story had come out in the spring, while he was explaining himself to the Viking Penguin lawyers.

He spent time with Rich C. It was he who had sent Wallace the tapes, actually testimonials by Bob Earl, an alcoholic whose talks on faith and recovery had inspired many addicts. Rich C. was a member of a more focused recovery group than the Urbana one Wallace had attended. They derided the therapy-like techniques of such chapters as, he recalls, "tissues and issues." The members of the Tucson chapter, were, by contrast, "Big Book fundamentalists" who emphasized a careful adherence to the twelve steps to sobriety that the founding text of alcohol recovery prescribed.

Rich C. became Wallace's sponsor in the Tucson chapter, the more experienced recovering addict to whom he could turn for practical and spiritual help. One step in the program required the alcoholic to make "a searching and fearless moral inventory" of his life and all the decisions that had gotten him to this point—this Wallace did in a ten-hour-long monologue in which he recounted to Rich C. everything from his childhood anxieties to the troubles in his parents' marriage to his worries about not being able to write. Another step required the alcoholic to apologize to people he had harmed. Wallace went to see Ostheimer and said he was sorry, explaining that there had been another woman waiting in San Francisco the weekend he had left her and that he suffered from a sex addiction. He wrote to Professor Kennick at Amherst and admitted that, against the rules, he had consulted secondary sources for papers he'd written in his class. He sent Dale Peterson money for the alcohol drunk from his cabinet. "I'm enclosing a small but I think accurate sum to reimburse you for liquor-losses," he wrote, saying it would be "a personal favor" if Peterson took the money. "This stuff is no fun," he added, "but I absolutely ran out of rope last winter, and I simply have got to find a different way to live." He said the group he had joined "has an incredibl[e] success rate for people even more f—ed up than I, and I am just doing what they tell me."

Wallace moved out of Jaci's house and in with Rich C. Part of the time sobriety left him so confused that he just lay on the couch and watched TV, but slowly he regained his footing and began to participate in the recovery group. He apologized to Heather Aronson for exaggerating his SAT scores (in fact it was to Forrest Ashby he had claimed they were perfect) and to Amy for his cruelty when she was younger. He asked his sponsor whether it might be possible to smoke pot if he dropped the drinking; after all, that had been his routine for almost a decade. "Why not just shoot heroin to avoid alcohol?" Rich C. replied, unconvinced. His sponsor taught him the Saint Francis prayer—"*Lord, make me a channel of thy peace*"—and he recited it often. A key part of the recovery program is to surrender to "a power higher than ourselves." This was the hardest part for Wallace. He came from a family of skeptics. He claimed that his parents refused to let him or his sister go to church because it would contaminate the rigor of their thought; believers were little better than dupes.[17] Yet Wallace was also a habitual top student; when he took a class he wanted to ace it. He invoked thinkers from Aristotle to Wittgenstein in an attempt to understand just what or whom he would be surrendering to. Rich C. sought to simplify the challenge: "All this step says is are you willing to make a decision."

For the first time in his life, Wallace found his outsized intelligence a liability. To do well in recovery required modesty rather than brilliance. It was not easy for him to accept humbling adages like "Your best thinking got you here." But then how smart could he be, the other program members would remind him at their meetings, if here he was in a room in the basement of a church with a dozen other people talking about how he couldn't stop drinking? Wallace looked for other ways to excel. Some recovery fundamentalists insist that a true return to health means abstaining from all substances, including prescription drugs. So despite the reminders Wallace was getting to "Just do what's in front of you to do," as another of the program's slogans goes, he quickly found himself with a new goal. To do without the Nardil, on which he'd relied for the past four years, would mark him as an exceptional recovery member. He hoped for an additional benefit—it was always possible that getting completely clean would jump-start his writing. His concentration was often poor, though whether it was the pot and alcohol or the Nardil and Xanax and other prescription drugs he sometimes took he did not know. When he bruited getting off the Nardil to his sponsor, Rich C. gave him an organization pamphlet emphasizing that meetings were not a substitute for a medical opinion. Wallace may have gone to talk to a psychiatrist (he noted on a medical history years later that he had consulted a doctor "only slightly if at all"), but whatever it was he heard or didn't hear, he emerged ready to be completely drug-free.

He stopped taking the Nardil in mid-August and for a while seemed fine. Earlier in the summer he had moved to a cabin in the foothills to the west of the city, far from the campus and his past. He was determined to avoid his drinking and drug buddies, most of whom were still in Tucson. They worried about him and asked him if he was okay. "I'm lonely but I don't want to come out of my house," he told Jaci when she called him. "The effort is really hard for me." From his kitchen he had a view of saguaro cactuses and sandy hills.

While he was in the cabin, a publisher sent him a galley of a novel by a writer he had barely heard of, one that impressed him deeply and seemed to embody all the literary qualities he had called for in his "Fictional Futures" essay. The book was Franzen's *The Twenty-Seventh City*. Set in St. Louis, it mixed postmodernism and traditional storytelling and showed a familiarity with its chosen city that Wallace could only marvel at. It decanted a Pynchonesque conspiracy in media-mediated language; it was about the word *and* the world, realism for an era when there was no real. Wallace responded with enthusiasm to its editor, Jonathan Galassi:

> I'm having a lot of trouble with my own stuff right now, and this book, a freaking first novel, seems so much more sophisticated than anything I could do plot-wise, so precocious in its marriage of theme and character and verisimilitude and phantasm, so simultaneously wild and *controlled*, that I found myself hugging criticisms of it to myself in unabashed self-defense (a subspecies of envy).

The novel was so good, Wallace concluded, that it "depressed" him. Later, he saw a copy of Franzen's novel in an Arizona bookstore and was disappointed to see that the blurb he had given wasn't used.

The semester started. Nardil leaves the body slowly, over weeks, and Wallace was by now feeling what it was like to be in an unmedicated depression, as he had not since his breakdown the summer after graduating from Amherst. His friends in recovery told him they were worried. He looked haggard, withdrawn, with slumped "barstool shoulders," as Rich C. remembered it.

He began teaching a fiction writing class. He gave his students Updike's "A&P" to read, and also the first paragraph of Flannery O'Connor's "Good Country People," to show the different ways you could describe a woman's expression. He also threw in more innovative writing, such as Sorrentino's *Aberration of Starlight*, the book he'd fallen in love with his first year in the MFA program, and a story by his friend Forrest Ashby. But within a few weeks he knew he was not going to make it through the semester. When Franzen asked where to write him—the two had struck up a correspondence after Wallace's note to Galassi—he replied that by mid-October the chances of his still being in Tucson were "remote." And in fact in late September, only weeks after the start of school and about a month after stopping the Nardil, he called his mother and asked her to come and get him. Amy Wallace called Heather Aronson, who with her sister Jaci went and looked after Wallace while they waited for Sally to arrive. They found their friend lying on his couch under blankets. His eyes were glued to the TV and he refused to drink or eat. A pot of weeks-old chili sat on the stove, and the computer that he had brought to Arizona was still in its boxes. He said he'd befriended a tarantula on his back porch.

A few days later, his mother came. The two rented a U-Haul, piled his stuff in the back, and took turns reading a Dean Koontz novel on the sixteen-hundred-mile trip back to Urbana. At twenty-six, Wallace was home for the fourth time after a breakdown. He was bitter and humiliated and felt as if his life was over. The same psychiatrist who had prescribed Nardil for him the first time put him back on the drug, but it did not have the same effect. For Wallace, life without any protection from depression was unlivable. His agony deepened. The Bad Thing was taking over again, eating him up. One night he took an overdose of Restoril, a sedative he'd been given for insomnia. His father found him the next morning, and an ambulance rushed him to the hospital, where he was put briefly on life support and had his stomach pumped.

Despite this near-tragedy, Wallace continued to write letters—the need to express himself in words never flagged. He wrote to Nadell on October 23 from the intensive care ward:

> By now I expect maybe you've heard . . . I finally did something stupid last Wednesday simply because it hurt so bad I was willing to kill myself to have it end. A lot of the trouble has to do with writing, but none of it with having stuff to send you or publications or careers, nothing to do, really, with anything exterior to me.

He explained how hard the past few months had been on him: "I just seemed to lose my will to work as well as the ability to organize myself or my thoughts. . . . So far these haven't come back and my confidence as a writer has left too . . . , confidence in being . . . a minimally functional human being. My ambitions at this point are modest and mostly surround staying alive." He promised he would not try to kill himself again for the sake of his family, instead swore he would "try . . . to find a way to live and find a way of writing even if it's not for publication. It's what I really love to do. I'm figuring now, though, better an alive janitor than a dead whatever."

The Nardil didn't stabilize Wallace and his psychiatrists recommended electro-convulsive therapy. Wallace felt he had no choice but to try it. His sister came and sat with him the day before the treatment. She tried to distract him, but she could see how terrified he was. He had six courses of ECT, and afterward Wallace's mother remembers that he emerged as delicate as a child. "He would ask, 'How do you make small talk?' 'How can you know which frying pan to pick out of the cupboard?'"

His friends who came to visit him then were upset to see his short-term memory gone, but time passed and the depression eased and Wallace thought the treatments had been worth it. "They were unpleasant," he wrote to his former sponsor in Arizona a month or so later, "but they helped quite a bit." The Bad Thing had been beaten back. He also finally got some encouraging news about his writing. Gerry Howard had changed jobs, presented the same legal problems to the lawyers for his new employer, W. W. Norton, and gotten an answer opposite to the one Viking Penguin had given. At the end of November Wallace signed a letter consenting to the transfer of publishing rights to Norton, who then paid Viking Penguin the $25,000 it had advanced and became Wallace's publisher. With a few changes, Norton felt they could publish *Girl with Curious Hair.* "Isn't it a marvelous feeling to see the light at the end of the tunnel—and not just another tunnel?" Howard wrote Wallace in late December, with a list of proposed legal alterations. Among the few changes was that the words "moist loincloth" out of Alex Trebek's mouth had to go. "Please find another 'favorite word' besides 'loincloth,' one without homoerotic associations," Howard wrote. Wallace agreed to the changes—"loincloth" became "induce."

"My favorite word," says Alex Trebek, "is *moist*. It is my favorite word, especially when used in combination with my second-favorite word, which is *induce*." He looks at the doctor. "I'm just associating. Is it OK if I just associate?"

At last the book would be published, small consolation for what was, Wallace wrote his sponsor, "far and away the worst year of my life." He added: "I think I got the idea that if one got clean & sober and worked very hard" on the program, "life couldn't help but get better. Well for me it's not been true."

Amazingly, the beginning of 1989 found Wallace at work. He had begun something, he wrote the editor of *Conjunctions*, Brad Morrow, in mid-January, "that's shaping up to be very long and very strange." And to Steven Moore, at the *Review of Contemporary Fiction*, he added the same day, "I have only very recently been able, emotionally and time-wise, to start on a new project." He began sending out his work and collecting rejections just as he had at Arizona. He wrote to Brad Morrow in an upbeat mood three weeks later:

Personally I love sending stuff out—the careful Xeroxing, the cover letter that talks the thin line between unctious [sic] and arrogant, the SASE, the plumpness of the envelope . . . I'm the only Aspiring person I know who actually kind of likes (the first few) rejections, because that means I get to send it out again. I'd love to send you something out of the hopper, but as I said all I've got is a hundred or so pages of something that's shaping up to be very long, possibly incoherent, and almost completely unexcerptable."

What Wallace was working on is unclear—it may have been the pages that frustrated him at Amherst pulled out again or a reworking of the short story "Order and Flux in Northampton," which he would shortly offer to *Conjunctions*.[18] And his rediscovered élan seemed slightly forced—even to him.[19] In his heart he was aware that something had to change. He could not go on this way forever. He was about to turn twenty-seven and he was still dependent on his parents for food and housing. His encounters with the mental health system had cost his insurance company a lot of money, and when the insurance ran out, his family had had to foot the bill, filling Wallace with guilt. To Morrow he wrote, "I figure if I ever want a mate and kids with straight teeth and command of the language I'm going to have to figure out a way to ensure income. The stuff I'm working on now is almost incoherent, and it would be at least two years before it was either done or any good or both."

Remembering his early years at Amherst, he thought perhaps he might turn back to a professional career in philosophy. There was a literary precedent for such a decision—William Gass taught philosophy at Washington University—and he would have both structure and health insurance. Wallace applied to the graduate programs at the University of Pittsburgh, Princeton, and Harvard. One advantage of this last was that Mark Costello lived in nearby Boston, working as a legal associate. All three schools admitted Wallace and offered aid: he still had his remarkable college transcript, as well as stellar recommendations, a well-reviewed novel, and a second book on the way. What was troubling him was hidden. He chose Harvard. It had prestige, Costello, and three renowned philosophers, Hilary Putnam, John Rawls, and Stanley Cavell. To be admitted alone was an obvious honor, one his father would appreciate. He wrote a friend that he thought he could get a doctorate in two or so years. The average student took almost a decade.

By the time Wallace arrived in Boston in April 1989, Costello had already found them a two-bedroom apartment on the second floor of a clapboard house in Somerville, near the Cambridge line. The neighborhood was known as Little Lisbon, described by Wallace in a letter to Franzen as "95% Portuguese and Brazilian aside from the young paleface refugees from the prices of H[arvard] Square and Back Bay." On his way east Wallace's car broke down in Ohio in front of a bar with a cigarette machine, which prompted him to take up smoking again (he had likely already started with pot and alcohol when he began to write again). He and Costello built cinderblock bookshelves and bought a futon and two thrift shop easy chairs. One smelled so bad that Wallace took it out to the curb and bought a new silver velour recliner instead. He took the front bedroom, Costello the back.

Costello would leave every morning in his suit and tie for his work as a lawyer, while Wallace stayed behind in the same Clearasil-stained bathrobe he'd worn since college, his shower towels spread out to dry. Wallace was writing, Costello saw, and filling notebooks—he came with a maroon spiral-bound one—though Costello did not know with what and Wallace did not tell him. Costello would come home and find his friend where he had left him, in his recliner, many hours and several showers later, a pen in his mouth and the notebook on his lap. "How was your day, honey?" Wallace would call out. For Wallace it was fun being back with his old roommate in the Northeast, and he was riding a high, not unlike the one after he had begun Nardil just before graduate school. Everything must have looked like it once had. "It's lovely and crowded and ethnic and a far cry from flat black land straight to the world's curve," he wrote Steven Moore in mid-April.

Professionally Wallace was in a holding pattern combined with a juggling act. He was waiting for the Norton publication of *Girl with Curious Hair* in August and the start of graduate school a month later. Most of his time was taken up with nonfiction pieces, one a review of David Markson's *Wittgenstein's Mistress*, a book he'd bought because he found the advertisement in the *Review of Contemporary Fiction* irresistible. "I may well be," he acknowledged to Moore, "the world's most kindly predisposed reader" of the novel.

But he found out the hard way that not everyone admired the book as much as he. Downstairs from Wallace and Costello was a freelance intellectual and part-time furniture mover, who called himself "the World's #1 David Foster Wallace fan." "Not that *Broom of the System* isn't a piece of shit, mind you," he would tell Wallace. "It's just less of a piece of shit than anything else being published." Wallace was drawn to this "failed english grad student," as he called him in a letter to Moore. The two would watch police shows—the mover called such viewing "monitoring the popular culture," a congenial phrase for Wallace. The mover's girlfriend was a beautiful heiress from Texas, whom he had nicknamed "the Lizard." Wallace began a relationship with the young woman, and he and her boyfriend wound up fighting—though not over the Lizard. It was over Markson's novel, which Wallace had recommended to him.

Thinking and writing about the novel was an enormous gift and time-snare to Wallace. The book narrates the thoughts of Kate, a woman who is either the last person on earth or else deluded that she is. The novel dramatizes the Wittgensteinian stance that the world is nothing but observed facts, a proposition that leads, as Wallace would write in "The Empty Plenum," his essay on the book, to the belief that "one's head is, in some sense, the whole world." Kate's affectless thoughts thus could be a record of Wallace's mind at its most depressed:

> There is nobody at the window in the painting of the house, by the way.
>
> I have now concluded that what I believed to be a person is a shadow.
>
> If it is not a shadow, it is perhaps a curtain.
>
> As a matter of fact it could actually be nothing more than an attempt to imply depths, within the room.
>
> Although in a manner of speaking all that is really in the window is burnt sienna pigment. And some yellow ochre.
>
> In fact there is no window either, in that same manner of speaking, but only shape.
>
> So that any few speculations I may have made about the person at the window would therefore now appear to be rendered meaningless, obviously.
>
> Unless of course I subsequently become convinced that there is somebody at the window all over again.

This was not a book that spoke to most readers—Kate does not, cannot, find a way out of her prison, and the book ends where it begins, with her isolation—but it spoke to Wallace. His downstairs friend was not convinced. He felt that Markson's novel was finally conventional and found Kate's voice "inauthentic." Wallace, having written a novel from a woman's point of view, considered himself the authority here. In any event, he loved the book—in his essay he would declare it "one of the U.S. decade's best"— and wasn't going to see anyone tap-dance in cleats on it. The dispute turned into a fight—at least according to an account Wallace wrote Moore. His downstairs neighbor swung, Wallace swung back, the mover swung a second time and broke Wallace's nose—"the exact part of my nose that was already x'rayed and covered with a useless bandage" from a basketball injury, Wallace wrote with pride in a letter to his editor.[20]

Wallace's other big project was a long piece on rap music. In Somerville, *Psychotic Reactions and Carburetor Dung*, by the late rock critic Lester Bangs, was required reading. Wallace admired Bangs's exultant prose, which probably came closer to the way Wallace talked than any other writing. Bangs's phrase "an erection of the heart" became one of Wallace's favorites, leading to the definition of great fiction in his essay on *Wittgenstein's Mistress* as "making heads throb heartlike."[21] Greil Marcus's *Mystery Train* was another book the roommates handed back and forth, in part an exploration of Elvis Presley's musical roots. Bangs and Marcus had found their subject in the music of earlier eras, but Wallace became increasingly interested in whether a parallel effort might be able to extract some larger meaning from current popular music. Early in the spring, a slacker friend of Costello's from New York brought up a cassette of *It Takes a Nation of Millions to Hold Us Back* by Public Enemy, and the roommates were intrigued. Rap was just entering the mainstream, a mixture of verbal innovation and societal defiance. N.W.A.'s *Straight Outta Compton* had just come out, and Tone Lōc's "Funky Cold Medina" was one of the fastest-selling singles ever. Rap was on its way to becoming gangsta rap, nihilism replacing hedonism, but at the moment the claims that could be made for it as serious art were enticing. One night, at a diner near their house, the two young men took stock of the situation. They read, as Costello remembers, in the *Boston Globe* that cars were being stopped just for playing N.W.A.'s "Fuck tha Police." Wallace admired the energy in rap, its careless creativity while he felt so burdened. He found the way the singers played with their own fame in their lyrics intriguingly postmodernist. There was also the irony to be explored that rap musicians were able to lift from others without fear to create their own art, just the transgression for which Viking Penguin had punished him.

Wallace's passion for rap was theoretical, verbal, abstract. The music never touched him as did the stoner songs of high school or the moody tripping songs of Amherst. His interest had the quality of a very smart kid slumming it. But he was drawn to its defiance, its opposition to the authority and decorum by which he had lived his difficult life. There was an element of self-hatred to his stance. If his world had collapsed, let art collapse with it. One day the two young men went to a concert of Slick Rick and Gang Starr at a Roxbury high school, but the sound system failed and the gym grew hot. Wallace, as often happened at concerts, had an attack of claustrophobia, and Costello drove him home.

Wallace no longer felt he was writing well—the lift post–shock therapy had dissipated—and even nonfiction was bringing problems. He was, remembers Costello, writing seventy-five-word sentences, all the information in his head pouring out at once. "No one writes nonfiction like this," he told his roommate. Sometimes he would write twenty-five thousand words in a day, Costello remembers, then cut them the next. Wallace's relationship with the page was now so confused and volatile that he felt he needed a collaborator to face what in his *Wittgenstein's Mistress* review he calls "typing paper's blankness." He began to leave the portions he'd drafted for Costello to comment on when he got home. Soon the roommates were alternating writing sections of the essay, Wallace by day, Costello by night. ("Chess by mail," is how Costello describes the collaboration.) Wallace's gesture to include his roommate was at once generous— he knew Costello still held literary aspirations—and defensive, even desperate.[22] He lived on Pop-Tarts and cigarettes and listened to Brian Eno's "The Big Ship" over and over. When Gale Walden came by, he told her he was in bad shape and she should stay away.

Still he had escaped the Wallace Fund for Aimless Children and was having at least the semblance of a good time. He invited Bonnie Nadell to come and visit in June. "Boston is *fun*," he wrote her. "We'll have laughs, listen to rap and James Brown." Whatever warnings he had gotten in his Arizona recovery group if he returned to substances, as drugs and alcohol were called, had not come to pass—at least not yet. He would get high or drunk most nights and, as he later told an interviewer, "fuck strangers." Another nonconformist industry now caught his eye: the pornography business. Pornography fit well into Wallace's ongoing areas of inquiry: it linked to advertising—the thing really being sold was the idea that we are all entitled to sexual pleasure, which in turn feeds the secondhand desire that Wallace saw at the root of the American malaise, our lives lived, he wrote in his *Wittgenstein's Mistress* essay, in "an Information Age where received image & enforced eros replace active countenance or sacral mystery as ends, value, meaning. Etc."

Wallace began his investigation as a novel. He immediately ran into difficulties. "I'm bogged down in research for something that's scaring me a lot," he wrote Franzen in May. "It's so big and complicated and requires a voice I don't seem to have in the old quiver." He told his friend he was lucky to be enjoying his talent and wondered where his own voice for fiction had gone, putting his writing at "3.5 on a 10 scale."[23] He pushed forward and the pornography project gyrated between fiction and nonfiction. In a later essay in the *Review of Contemporary Fiction*, Costello remembered Wallace's frenetic and intensive research method this way:

> Wallace set timetables for his work, intricate as the Croton-on-Hudson local. Get up. Talk on phone with porn actress famous for giving screen blow jobs. Hang up. Ask: is the porn queen an actress? Look up actress in the OED. Actress: a female actor. Look up actor: one who acts in a drama. Surely a blow job is an act. OK then: is a blow job drama?

At some point, Wallace thought some actual on-set knowledge might help. He explained to Nadell, "You'd be surprised, or maybe not at the paucity of material on the actual nuts and bolts (no pun) of the adult film business." He went on:

> I just need access to sort of mundane facts that I think only hanging quietly out in the background of the real thing would afford: Questions of scripting, average time of shooting, average time of production from purchase of treatment through casting through rehearsals (are there rehearsals? I'd guess rarely) and choreography (obvious) and straight shooting and position-shooting (money shots, come shots, facial reactions, etc.) to editing, printing, distribution negotiations.

Always interested in how media changed the reality it was meant only to record, he focused on porn movie conventions: why the lesbian love scene, the masturbation scene?

Why do many of the movies have a kind of shadowy, dramatically superfluous character who seems to stand for the man watching film (truck driver in Debbie Does Dallas II, obnoxious airplane passenger in Mile-High Girls) and whose final access to female lead(s) effects film's closure?

Nadell promised to try to help, as did Alice Turner at *Playboy*. Hurt feelings had healed between them; the two met again in New York when Wallace visited there. "Alice has been marvelous and generous as usual," he wrote Nadell in late May, "and looks to have ways to pretty much grease the skids." Turner told him he could use *Playboy*'s name in his research. She had hopes he might write a novelist-visits-a-porn-set piece.

Nadell came to Somerville in June. Wallace moved to the futon and Nadell slept in his bed. She found her writer writing every morning. In the evening she would go with the two young men for cheap falafel or hamburgers or stay in and listen to music. Soon afterward in New York, she met Lee Smith, an editor at Antaeus who had been in touch with Wallace and Costello. She suggested that their rap collaboration would make a book and he agreed. Smith paid $2,000 as an advance. Wallace was pleased but scared; he wasn't confident the world needed his nonfiction. *Signifying Rappers*, as the book was called after a song by Schoolly D, he wrote Steven Moore, "was not meant to carry a cardboard-bordered burden all by itself; it wasn't meant to."

In early July, Wallace started a long second visit to Yaddo. Just before, he flew to Los Angeles to research his porn novel and decided definitively while there that his approach to the subject ought to be through nonfiction. He was intrigued by how the women seemed to boss around the men, despite the latter's large sex organs, and admired the veteran actresses in porn who handled desire with the cool of businesswomen. He watched dozens of sex scenes and interviewed some of the actors. He asked Joey Silvera, a porn actor in his thirties and the star of *Slick Honey*, how he could have so many erections in a day: "Is it natural glandular horniness or is it a professional thing? Are you all trained to be that way?" He was impressed, he told Tori Welles, the star of *Torrid Without a Cause*, by how much nicer porn actors were to one another than writers. While in Los Angeles, he also finished up another pass on his rap book and went to Compton to hear some rappers but got so scared he had to leave before he could find the concert—or so he told a friend. He signed a note to Nadell just after returning, "Stay Fly, and Shit . . . DF Fresh W."

All this made it hard for him to settle down in Saratoga Springs afterward. The retreat felt different two years after he had last been in residence. The trendy writers whose camp follower he had at times wanted to be were gone and he himself was less impressionable. He believed he knew the limits on his audience and accepted them. "The thing I like about my own prison," he wrote Moore shortly before arriving, "is I have *tenure* in my prison." He had a room in the old main house, on the top floor, and he set up fans facing out of the windows (writers were not allowed to smoke in the building). He had brought along an impossible amount of work: William Gaddis's *The Recognitions*, a postmodern novel he had always meant to read, his pornography manuscript, and his research material for his article on *Wittgenstein's Mistress*. He assured Steven Moore that he would "carve out two days at Yaddo to reread the book, reread the Tractatus (gulp), and do the piece." While there he also went quickly through Russell's *Foundations of Logical Atomism*, to which Wittgenstein had been responding in the *Tractatus*. "Fine prep. For the innumerable times I'll be having to do this sort of instant-mnemonic-pretense shit during the upcoming year," he told his editor.

He was a dominant figure this time at Yaddo, one of the best-known writers there, with a book published and another soon to come out. Intriguing packages came for him at the mail table. "Let's move on to the next vector," he liked to say, when he meant: Let's get out of here. He would play tapes of his interviews with porn stars for the curious in the common areas, but if you wanted to hear Tami Monroe, you had to come to his room. The others were amazed to learn he was giving up a career in fiction for one in philosophy. He told them it was to free himself from publishers and editors and their demands but at the same time opined that writers were tired of freedom and experimentation and looking for something to believe in. He said he was less worried that the *New York Times Book Review* would ignore *Girl with Curious Hair* than that they would put it in their "Briefly Noted" section. He met and became involved with Kathe Burkhart, a conceptual artist. Just as Gale Walden was less conventional than the young women he grew up with in Urbana, Burkhart was less conventional than Walden—he was curious about bondage, so one time she tied him up, using a jump rope he'd brought to exercise with.

Wallace had learned from past mistakes. This time he made sure he had pot at the retreat, and when he ran out, Burkhart flew to New York and got more. When her stay was over and she returned to New York for good, he took up with the novelist Ann Patchett. He wrote Nadell, astonished at the complexity of his dating life, that he was "looking into celibatee orders'." One day, on a visit to his father's family in Troy, New York, he drank most of a bottle of Glenlivet and threw up in his sleep: "Thank God I don't pass out on my back; what a dumb way to die," he wrote Burkhart, imagining the headline: "SENSITIVE AESTHETE DROWNS IN OWN PUKE! ARTISTE'S ASPIRATIONS ASPIRATED!" He added in another note, "You seem doomed to be involved with addicts."

Yaddo the second time was a hurried-up parody of the first. He worked late into the night—Burkhart guessed he was taking speed to stay up—but he had no satisfying project to commit to. He worked mostly on the pornography manuscript, struggling to separate what was interesting from what was not and always feeling he had failed. He came to think that what was needed was a reported piece on how the industry had changed as the so-called golden age of porn gave way to the era of inexpensive and inartistic video.[24] Inevitably, he returned to Somerville dissatisfied, nothing finished, the time nearing when he would have to, as he wrote Franzen, "toddle off with my Get Smart lunchbox for the first day of grad school." He had ambitions beyond the rational at this point. He wanted to write full-time, fulfill his first-year graduate philosophy student requirements, plus "intro german plus intro library science plus a seminar on Cowper, Collins and Smart in the English Dept., plus probably a part-time job," he had written to Moore in the spring, adding without irony, "I'm leery of committing myself to more." Having no center to his work, Wallace seemed to have no limits either.

The final weeks of the summer were hectic. He was often drunk or stoned, but also snuck off to recovery meetings, at least fitfully. Costello would come home from his office and find that Wallace had turned on the fan in his room to disperse the smoke. Since Costello did not care if his roommate got high, he concluded that the only person Wallace could have been hiding his habit from was himself. One night the two went to a party; Costello came home first and Wallace appeared in the early morning with a bloody hand. Remembering that part of recovery was the obligation to make amends, he went back to the grocery whose window he had busted and shoved $200 into the surprised cashier's hand. "There was no shortage of chaos around 35 Houghton Street, apartment 2," Costello wrote in summary in his memoir of his time there with Wallace. "Lost bills went unpaid. The phone rang at 3:00 A.M. and women banged on the back door two hours later."

Everything was coming to a head as Wallace got ready for school. The piece on Wittgenstein remained unwritten, and the porn essay was a mess. He had written an unsuccessful "short journalistic version . . . a waste of 2 Yaddo weeks," as he wrote Nadell. He'd thrown that away and now it was again, he added, "horribly long. . . . I've got about 200 pages and am only half done ('*NOT* a nice noise, Bonnie')." Yaddo seemed a complete washout. When he looked for comfort he realized his relationship with Walden was past repair.

Even Alice Turner was furious with him again. She had thought he was researching a novel, but it had turned out he wanted her to publish his insights on the pornography industry. "This magazine is way beyond you," she lectured him. "We already know the things that you are offering as new discoveries." Wallace hemmed and hawed, apologized for the "confusion, misunderstanding, deception, whatever," explained he was trying to get out of the "rut of 'self-conscious meta-shit' you seem to think is my only interest and forward gear." "I must say," Turner wrote back, "you're like one of those Bozo bags that bounces back every time you take a shot at it."

In August 1989, *Girl with Curious Hair* came out at last. "The stories in his first collection," Norton's catalog stated, "could possibly represent the first flowering of post-postmodernism: visions of the world that re-imagine reality as more realistic than we can imagine." These words perfectly captured Wallace's hope for the book. *Kirkus Reviews*, though, found the writer "too much impressed with his own gifts and with some current critical theory." It was, Wallace wrote to Morrow, "a real brown helmet. . . . I've told Gerry I'm just not going to read fucking reviews, good or bad, this time." On the plus side, the *New York Times Book Review* gave the book a full review. Written by Jenifer Levin, a young novelist, hers was the most positive notice his fiction would ever get in that paper. It praised Wallace as "a dynamic writer of extraordinary talent" and singled out not just "Lyndon" but the little-loved "John Billy," his Gass homage. An even brighter spot was an essay by Sven Birkerts in *Wigwag*. Birkerts was Wallace's natural reader, because he too was keenly interested in how writers adapt to a changing world. To the question "What is the fiction writer—the writer who would try to catch us undistorted in our moment—to do? What prose will raise a mirror to our dispersed condition?" he put forward Wallace:

> We sense immediately that Wallace is beyond the calculated fiddle of the postmodernist. He's not announcing as news the irreparable fragmentation of our cultural life; he is not fastening upon TV and punk culture and airport lounges as if for the first time ever. Wallace comes toward us as a citizen of that new place, the place that the minimalists have only been able to point toward. The rhythms, disjunctions, and surreally beautiful—if terrifying—meldings of our present-day surround are fully his. Wallace is, for better or worse, the savvy and watchful voice of the *now*—and he is unburdened by any nostalgia for the old order.

Few other critics felt as Levin and Birkerts did. Most newspaper reviewers skipped the book entirely, and those who wrote about it mostly evaluated the individual stories. Wallace felt that missed the point—who cared if one story was better than another? The point was that the collection *as a whole* was meant to open the door to a new kind of fiction. "A lot of it is like being told your soup needs less salt," he complained to Moore.

Not that Wallace himself didn't have clear favorites in the collection. These are evident in an exchange of letters with Franzen. Wallace had never had close literary friends; he was too competitive, judgmental, and self-absorbed. Most literary fiction he did not care about, and what few books were worth reading were worth writing, which meant in turn that he wished he'd written them. The no-writer-friends rule was not conscious but grew out of his personality, and like most of Wallace's behavior, had a refractory edge: he also felt guilty that he felt this way, which made him all the more want to avoid the whole issue.

But the past few years had been humbling ones for Wallace, and the humiliation had made him more open to other writers' writing. In fact, in such moments some aspect of his self-anger made him overestimate the work of others in order to diminish his own. Thus, during his time in Somerville two authors had earned his intense admiration. One was William Vollmann, whose collection *The Rainbow Stories* Wallace had read three times that spring in galleys and thought evidence, as he wrote to Moore, of "the best young writer going." In that collection, the novella "The Blue Yonder," half expressionist nightmare, half reportage, "simply separates sock from pod," he reported to Franzen. Vollmann reminded Wallace of Pynchon, Coover, and William Burroughs but was "remarkably unselfconscious" in his debts, a writer whose every word satisfied Wallace's call for fiction that subtly parried the media that saturated it in creating a new kind of art.[25]

In person, though, Vollmann was too odd for the fundamentally bourgeois Wallace. The two had had dinner that spring in New York with Brad Morrow, and afterward Wallace reported to Moore that his counterpart was "more than a bubble off plumb—prefers bloody venison and chocolate cake washed down with Stout for supper, speaks easily of blow-jobs and cooze while we're eating." Franzen, the more conventional of the two and a midwesterner, was the better match for Wallace. For one thing he was hungry for the company of other writers. A friendship for him consisted in equal parts of affection and challenge, a dynamic Wallace knew well from his days on his high school tennis team.

Wallace had been exuberant in his praise of *The Twenty-Seventh City*. Now Franzen wrote Wallace after reading the galleys of *Girl with Curious Hair* to tell him that he thought he'd written *half* of a great book. He particularly loved, he wrote the author, "Here and There," the story of the young man who begins by trying to reinvent literature and ends up failing to fix his uncle and aunt's old stove; and he particularly hated "Westward," which he felt provided none of the nourishment of good fiction. For him the heart of the story was the coda, the part with the David and L.—'s relationship that climaxes in L.—'s suicide-by-arrow:

> By merely abstracting this story, aren't you showing pretty much the opposite of what you're telling? That you're too impatient and too proud to do the stoop-work of creating character, suspense and emotional involvement? For something that's "NOT metafiction,"

the piece, as it stands, is awfully short on these commodities. I think
it should have been mailed to Barth, not Norton.

Franzen felt he'd gone too far and crossed out the last line before he
mailed it, but even so Wallace, opening the envelope at Yaddo, was
stunned to read that Franzen had liked only "stories 1,2,6,7, and 8" in the
collection, leaving out "Westward," "Lyndon," "John Billy," and "Girl with
Curious Hair" among others. Wallace had never been written to in this
way before. "This Jonathan Franzen guy," he wrote to Moore in mystification a month later, "keeps sending me these 15-page missives describing
how I've violated every precept of 'fiction as a moral exercise, an affirma-
tion of life'." His own favorites in the book were nearly the reverse of
Franzen's: only the Letterman story, the *Jeopardy!* story, "Lyndon," "John
Billy," and of course "Westward" deserved to be in the collection. The
other tales, he wrote Moore, had been part of the trade-offs he had had to
make with Howard to get "Westward" into the book. "Here and There,"
he wrote his new friend, was nothing but "sentimental pretentious pseudo-
autobiographical crap."

Yet he was happy to be attacked in this way; just beneath his self-
confidence was always plenty of doubt, and the attention was flattering.
He thanked Franzen for his critique, adding that he found his "extensively
explained dislike for Westward fascinating." It was "in its violence im-
mensely gratifying." He hoped they could meet in Boston soon to "drink
or eat or whatever." Franzen in turn suggested a Red Sox game. Wallace
agreed to write a recommendation for his new friend's Guggenheim Fellowship application.[26]

Meanwhile, Wallace was facing the reality that few readers cared as
much as Franzen about his attempt to remake literature. He hoped for a
tour to go with the publication of *Girl with Curious Hair*, but there wasn't
much of one. He gave a reading at the Cambridge Public Library with a
handful of people in attendance, including a schizophrenic woman who
kept shrieking. He went down to New York and appeared with Vollmann
at Dixon Place, a performance space. At the reading, Vollmann accompanied a story with a starter pistol shot into the air, Wallace covering his
ears in pain. Afterward, he and Gerry Howard and a few others went to

Café Pig, a restaurant on Houston Street. Howard was unsettled to see Wallace drink three bourbons "in dismayingly quick order" and then disappear downstairs into a bathroom for a half hour with a "proto-Goth girl with black lipstick"—Kathe Burkhart. He realized that the innocent boy in the U2 T-shirt was gone.

Girl could barely be found in bookstores, Wallace observing the increasingly unpromising situation. "The book is not yet out anywhere in New York or Boston," he complained to Nadell in early November, "and apparently likewise in the Midwest. Curioser and curioser." The nonreception of *Girl* was making its author more and more upset—after all, he had no new fiction with which to follow it. He saw the publication, he later told an interviewer, as "a kind of shrill jagged laugh from the universe. About, you know, I'm done, and now this *thing*, what was it like? This thing sort of lingers behind me like a really nasty fart." He had risked a psychotic breakdown to create really serious work and hadn't even gotten a review in the daily *Times*. He inscribed a copy to Rich C., praising the "pretty jacket" but adding, "This book is dying. You probably have the only copy in Tucson."

Improbably, come September, the twenty-seven-year-old Wallace became a student again. The philosophy department at Harvard was located in Emerson Hall, a turn-of-the-century redbrick building in the Yard with a quotation from the Psalms inscribed on its façade. Wallace was among only six students admitted from hundreds of applicants. Nearly all had been graduate students in philosophy before. Yet within the department the students were considered beginners, neophytes. "There is no fathoming the subdoctoral mind," was a phrase one professor liked to invoke, quoting the famous retired departmental head W. V. O. Quine.

As often happened with Wallace, the realization he'd made a mistake was nearly immediate. He went to a seminar taught by Stanley Cavell, a philosopher who held a special place in Wallace's esteem. Cavell's lively, learned, but friendly approach to philosophical investigations in books like *Must We Mean What We Say?* was the closest Wallace knew to his own; indeed Cavell may have been one of his literary models. But in person Cavell seemed to be talking only to himself and his initiates, who circled him like acolytes. Wallace, one student remembers, interrupted the professor and asked him to "make himself intelligible please," a snarl on his face. Shortly afterward, he stopped going.[27]

There were other problems. He took a first-year colloquium with John Rawls and found the reading, an anthology called *Free Will*, impossibly dense. He realized he was too old to go back to school; his classmates in the program seemed academic and sheltered to him. One time he went out with two of them to the Hong Kong, a Chinese restaurant near Harvard Square that specialized in heavily alcoholic drinks, and in the midst of a conversation between the two on semantic externalism, he interrupted to ask, "Have you ever tried LSD?"

His fellow students in turn regarded Wallace as a curiosity, a mystery, almost a primitive type, with his interest in porn and rap. One remembers thinking he'd gone back to school as "an anthropologist." It was clear to most that he did not have the focus to keep up with the pitiless workload. He was still trying to finish his various freelance projects, and he looked tired and wrung out when he came to class. Gerry Howard visited Wallace around this time and found him in an apartment "messier than any I had been in since college." He remembered philosophy and mathematics textbooks so abstruse he "could not even understand their titles," and his author "shaky and unhappy." Toward the end of Wallace's brief stint at Harvard, one student came upon him fast asleep under one of the old wooden desks in the library on the second floor of the philosophy building.

Wallace wrote on the dedication page of the copy of *Girl with Curious Hair* he sent to Rich C. that he was "fucking up." He added that he still attended two recovery meetings a week, but often hungover, and now had the shakes.[28] Faced with the possibility that he would fail at the second of his chosen careers, the one his father had pursued so admirably, Wallace found his stunning energy collapsing in on itself again. It was, he later told an interviewer,

as though the entire, every axiom of your life turned out to be false, and there was actually nothing, and *you* were nothing, and it was all a delusion. And that you were better than everyone else because you saw that it was a delusion, and yet you were worse because you couldn't function.

Wallace went to a doctor who told him he needed to quit drinking and go to a rehab facility. But Wallace was worried that Harvard would fail him if he took a month off. In late October he forced the issue. He called Costello from the Harvard Health Services and said that he had told the school he was thinking of hurting himself. Once you did that, he explained, the university had no choice but to put you on suicide watch. He asked Costello to bring his bathrobe, his cigarettes, his notebook, and a small TV and meet him at McLean Hospital, the psychiatric institute in Belmont affiliated with the university. "The lovely medical staff at Harvard is putting me in an alcohol rehab and detox center on 11/2," he wrote Brad Morrow. "Apparently I have liver problems. No joy in mudville."

CHAPTER 5

"Please Don't Give Up on Me"

The four weeks Wallace spent at McLean in November 1989 changed his life. This was not his first or most serious crisis, but he felt now as if he had hit a new bottom or a different kind of bottom. For all that he had thought of "Westward" as an "Armageddon," as he would later tell an interviewer, he had really expected it to be a phoenix. From the ashes to which he had reduced postmodernism a new sort of fiction was meant to arise, as laid out in "Fictional Futures and the Conspicuously Young." How else to understand the love note to the reader at the end of "Westward"? But instead of rebirth, a prolonged dying had followed, and for the past year the corpse had moldered. Wallace hadn't even been able to finish a nonfiction piece without help since 1987. Never before had he worked so hard with so little to show for it.

Wallace was placed in Appleton House. Outside, the building was attractive—colonial revival *à la* Harvard. Inside it had the look of a faded country hotel, with tattered wine-colored carpets, old brass lamps, and a deep smell of tobacco. Appleton was where the addicts went, with a large room for substance abuse recovery meetings. The medical staff interviewed the twenty-seven-year-old Wallace and told him that he was a hard-core alcohol and drug user and that if he didn't stop abusing both he would be dead by thirty. Wallace in turn reported the news to Costello, who came the next day. "I'm a depressive, and guess what?" Wallace said. "Alcohol is a depressant!" He smiled through his tears, as if, Costello remembers, he "was unveiling a fun surprise to a five-year-old." It was of course information Wallace knew already.

The program was meant to shake up the addict, and, with Wallace, it succeeded. Pulling him out of his old life and keeping him away from its temptations and habits helped. In the end, though, what mattered most was probably that the intoxicated Wallace was no longer writing success-fully, which left open the hope that a sober one might. Wallace saw a ther-apist and went to substance abuse meetings every day. He detoxed from the alcohol. Nadell, back in the Northeast to be with her family for Thanksgiving, came by to see her author a few weeks after his admission. Wallace was already calmer by then. He met them in a brightly lit room full of other patients, all smoking and drinking black coffee and meeting with friends and family. Wallace looked so ragged that Nadell borrowed a pair of scissors from the staff and cut his hair. But she was happy to see he was writing in a notebook. His doctors gave Wallace a pass, and he and his friends walked in the woods at the foot of the campuslike property. McLean was the storied holding tank for many literary depressives, from Sylvia Plath to Robert Lowell, and it occurred to Wallace's friends that this gave him at least some comfort, that he thought of himself as at a mental health Yaddo. Wallace's cheerfulness, Nadell felt, kept breaking out.

It was Wallace's expectation that he would go back to Harvard after his stay at McLean. He was, after all, still enrolled in the graduate program. But the psychiatric staff kept advising him against it. They told him that without continuing support he would just go back to his old habits. Re-turning to Somerville would be a catalyst for that mistake. Wallace was at first resistant—he did not recognize himself in their phrase "hard-core recidivist," but as the weeks went by he felt farther and farther away from his old self and must have begun, amid his anxiety about writing, to con-cede the point that survival had to come first. In any event, he chose to go to a halfway house in Brighton run by a woman who had worked in a psy-chology lab funded by NASA before she herself went into rehab. He hoped she would understand what he saw as the particular problems of a person as intelligent and educated as himself and provide support. It would be the next best thing to McLean, which Wallace was—Costello noted—sorry to have to leave. He had gotten used to the routines—the meetings, the ther-apy, the order, the prepared meals—not entirely unlike home. Brighton was a world away from Cambridge, and he did not know what to expect. Despite having written a book on rap, his knowledge of anything other than middle-class academic life was minimal. He wrote Nadell at the end of November, "I am getting booted out of here and transferred to a half-way house. . . . It is a grim place, and I am grimly resolved to go there."

Granada House was on the grounds of the Brighton Marine hospital near the Massachusetts Turnpike.[1] Wallace gives a good picture of its fictional counterpart in *Infinite Jest*, the novel it would help inspire:

> Unit #6, right up against the ravine on the end of the rutted road's east side, is Ennet House Drug and Alcohol Recovery House, three stories of whitewashed New England brick with the brick showing in patches through the whitewash, a mansard roof that sheds green shingles, a scabrous fire escape at each upper window and a back door no resident is allowed to use and a front office around on the south side with huge protruding bay windows that yield a view of ravine-weeds and the unpleasant stretch of Commonwealth Ave.

The compound consisted of seven buildings—"seven moons orbiting a dead planet," as it is described in *Infinite Jest*—all leased to various substance abuse and mental health assistance groups. Wallace met Deb Larson, the director, at his new temporary home. Tall and blonde, she walked with a limp: drunk, she had fallen down in her kitchen, hitting her head, causing a partial paralysis. Even then she hadn't stopped drinking. Wallace respected her. She was pretty and smart and gave him a link to an old life that was still his present—you could almost see Harvard from the top floor of the building.[2] Recovery facilities tried to control the stress levels of their participants, and one activity they generally prohibited was school. Wallace had no choice but to call the philosophy department at Harvard and ask for a leave of absence. He was too humiliated to go back to get the vegetable juicer, a gift from his mother, that he had left behind in the graduate office.

As a new arrival, Wallace was not allowed out of the building on his own for the first ten days. For the next twenty he could go out only to substance abuse meetings. Then he was expected to find low-level work. Wallace, whose only real skill was teaching and writing, cast around and was able—probably thanks to the presence on his résumé of the head of Amherst College security as a reference—to get hired as a guard at Lotus Development, a large software company. Granada House rules stipulated a forty-hour workweek, so Wallace got up at 4:30 in the morning to take the Green Line subway and worked until 2 p.m., walking a vast disk packaging plant in Lechmere, clocking in his whereabouts every ten minutes and twirling his baton (or so he later said). He would tear pages out of his notebook and send letters to his friends, maintaining contact with the small group of editors and writers who were vital to him. The Lotus experience, he recalled in a later interview, reminded him of "every bad '60s novel about meaningless authority," but at the time he bore it well. "Give me a little time to get used to no recreational materials and wearing a polyester uniform and living with 4 tatooed ex-cons and I'll be right as rain," he wrote Moore with ironic brio shortly after starting. Even inside Granada House, he managed to attend to the business of being a writer—following up on submissions to magazines and reading pages of stories he had coming out. He could see the strange side of his situation. When the galleys of "Order and Flux in Northampton" arrived from *Conjunctions* with a page missing, he told Morrow he could send it at his convenience. "I'm not going anywhere for Xmas," he wrote.

But in his heart he was stunned with what had happened to him. "I am," he wrote Dale Peterson, "OK, though very humiliated and confused." He was sharing a barracks-like room in Granada House with four men, one of whom, he wrote Rich C., had had a stroke while on cocaine and had a withered right side. "Mr. Howard," he told his Norton editor, "everyone here has a tattoo or a criminal record or both!" To Peterson he reported, "Most of the guys in the house are inmates on release, and while they're basically decent folk it's just not a crowd I'm much at home with—heavy metal music, black t-shirts & Harleys, vivid tattoos, discussion of hard- vs. soft-time, parole boards, gunshot wounds and Walpole—" Massachusett's toughest prison. Wallace continued at his security job for more than two months, and then, unable to bear getting up so early, he quit. He went to work as a front desk attendant at the Mount Auburn Club, a health club in Watertown. His job was to check members in—he called himself a glorified towel boy—but one day Michael Ryan, a poet who had received a Whiting Award alongside him two years before, came to exercise. Wallace dove below the reception desk and quit that day.

Wallace's friends were accustomed to his exaggerations and inventions over the years—they came with his clownish, hyperbolic persona—but when they visited him at the halfway house, they found that what he said was true: he had stepped through the looking glass. His friend Debra Spark, a fiction writer, remembers sitting in on a group therapy session with Wallace one day and being amazed to hear someone recount killing someone while drunk. All the same, Wallace found his place; order, no matter how foreign the context, was always easier for him than the un-structured world. He met with a counselor, as required, and nearly every evening he drove to different parts of the city with other Granada House members for substance abuse meetings. His sponsor was named Jimmy, "a motorhead from the South Shore," as he called him to David Markson, with whom he had begun a correspondence. Wallace read the Big Book and enjoyed making fun of its cheesy 1930s adman vocabulary to his friends: "tosspot," "Dave Sheen heels," "boiled as an owl." "He laughed at them, but he also knew he needed them or he would die," Mark Costello, who visited him at Granada House, remembers.

If Wallace found himself in unfamiliar territory, the residents didn't know what to make of him either. One remembers wondering, "This guy can go probably go to Betty Ford. Why's he here with us welfare babies?" No one really cared for his cleverness. He was to them a type they'd seen before, someone who, like the character Geoffrey Day in *Infinite Jest*, tries to "erect Denial-type fortifications with some kind of intellectualish showing-off." Wallace was back in high school, trying to figure out his place in the pack. "It's a rough crowd," he wrote his old Arizona sponsor, "and sometimes I'm scared or feel superior or both."

Yet a piece of him was beginning to adjust to the new situation. He re-membered his last failed attempt to get sober and how he was no longer writing and asked himself what he had to lose. He came to understand that the key this time was modesty. "My best thinking got me here" was a recovery adage that hit home, or, as he translated it in *Infinite Jest*, "logical validity is not a guarantee of truth." He knew it was imperative to abandon the sense of himself as the smartest person in the room, a person too smart to be like one of the people in the room, because he *was* one of the people in the room. "I try hard to listen and do what [they say]," he wrote Rich C., "I'm trying to do it easy . . . this time," not "get an A+. . . . I just don't have enough gas right now to do anything fast or well. I'm trying to accept this."

Not that things came easily. The simple aphorisms of the program seemed ridiculous to him. And if he objected to them, someone inevitably told him to do what was in front of him to do, driving him even crazier. The logical tautology behind recovery bothered him too: that recovery defined an alcoholic as anyone who drank heavily and denied he was an alcoholic, which made believing you weren't an alcoholic a symptom of the disease, whether you were or not. He was astonished to find people talking about "a higher power" without any evidence beyond their wish that there were one. They got down on their knees and said the Thankfulness prayer. Wallace tried once at Granada House, he told Costello, but it felt hypocritical.[3]

There were many times when he was sure he would start drinking again. "I'm scared," he wrote Rich C. "I still don't know what's going to happen." He asked his friend for some words of encouragement, and just when he thought he would give up, a letter arrived in which his former sponsor recounted the last time he had been in detox. "They gave me Librium," he wrote Wallace, "and I threw them over my left shoulder for luck, and I've had good luck ever since." The image, Wallace told his sponsor years later, was just the "good MFA-caliber trope" he'd needed.

Required to do chores in the house, Wallace helped out in the office. This gave him access to a typewriter. Stunned as he was, he understood from the beginning that his fall from grace was a literary opportunity. He had been hypothesizing beforehand about a nation in thrall to its appetites, and here he was living among its casualties. So in the midst of his misery, he was alive to the new information he was getting. The communal house, he would later write, "reeks of passing time. It is the humidity of early sobriety, hanging and palpable." Wallace was known for sitting quietly, listening as residents talked for hours about their lives and their addictions. (Later, residents would often be surprised to find that though he had heard their stories they had not heard his.) The explanations people gave for their behavior startled him with their simplicity, but their voices—always his way in to composition—were unforgettable, and their stories had a clarity his lacked. This was the sort of access to interior lives a novelist could not get elsewhere. He was finding, as he later told an interviewer, that "nobody is as gregarious as someone who has recently stopped using drugs." Where else could a writer find, as Wallace wrote in *Infinite Jest*, in a passage that sounds as if Lester Bangs had written it,

> twenty-one other newly detoxed housebreakers, hoods, whores, fired execs, Avon ladies, subway musicians, beer-bloated construction workers, vagrants, indignant car salesmen, bulimic trauma-mamas, bunko artists, mincing pillow-biters, North End hard guys, pimply kids with electric nose-rings, denial-ridden housewives and etc., all jonesing and head-gaming and mokus and grieving and basically whacked out and producing nonstopping output 24-7-365.[4]

Wallace and his notebook were a familiar sight in the communal rooms and recovery meetings, trapping little inspirations before they could get away.

Within a few months of arriving, Wallace had already drafted a scene centered on one of the most intriguing residents at Granada House, Big Craig. Big Craig—Don Gately in the novel—was one of the Granada House supervisors and sometimes the house cook. He had first met Wallace when he found the new resident's stuff on his bunk and threw Wallace's bag on the ground. Craig was in his mid-twenties, "sober and just huge," as Wallace would later write in *Infinite Jest*, looking "less built than poured, the smooth immovability of an Easter Island statue." Wallace quickly chose a different bed. Craig had grown up on the North Shore and been a burglar and Demerol addict. Friends closed elevator doors on his head for fun when he was a teenager, a detail Wallace would put into *Infinite Jest* too.[5]

But he turned out not only to come from a different world but also to be quite sensitive. And it did not take Wallace long to see the possibilities in a lug with an interior life. There was a sort of Dostoevskian gloss to him, the redeemed criminal, and Dostoevsky was on Wallace's mind. He wrote to Dale Peterson shortly after arriving that "going from Harvard to here" was like "House of the Dead . . . with my weeks in drug treatment composing the staged execution and last minute reprieve from same." The reprieve, he hoped, would spur the same creative surge it did in the Russian.[6] But his sense that he could write fiction came and went. Fortunately, Wallace had nonfiction left over from before his intake. He had given up on the pornography essay, but he still owed his piece on *Wittgenstein's Mistress* to the *Review of Contemporary Fiction*. "I think part of why WM is so hard for me right now is that I'm feeling very Kate-ish," Wallace wrote Steve Moore a month after arriving at Granada House, meaning he was still battling to make a movie when snapshots were all his newly-sobered mind was offering. At Yaddo and in Somerville, he explained, he had also had a great deal of trouble with the project, giving it two tries, "one a vapid gushy book-review thing and the other—not yet typed—a 70-page screed that's like Harold Bloom on acid." All the same, he trundled his *Tractatus* and David Markson's novel now to the nearby library and in a matter of a month produced a work several times the length of a typical essay.

A new clarity was beginning to emerge in his attempt to wrest such central concerns as self-consciousness and loneliness into controllable form. The prose style that would later separate Wallace's nonfiction writing from that of his peers was taking form. The approach owed something to Cavell's plainspokenness and to Bangs's hipster idiom and yet it was distinctive. It combined informal diction—"way" as an adjective, "weird" and "sort of" where most would write "strange" and "to some extent"— with recondite polysyllabic nouns, a mixture that hinted at the way high and low culture were jumbled in his mind. "And but so" became a way to begin his sentences, an apt phrase to kick off his hurrying, zigzagging thoughts. Wallace was beginning to find the meeting place between a brain in overdrive and a language that had been invented for more leisurely use. It helped that the issues *Wittgenstein's Mistress* raised were slightly behind him now. He could look back from his new position of sobriety when he wrote of Kate's "continual struggle against the slipping sand of English & the drowning-pool of self-consciousness" or asserted that "the empty diffraction of Kate's world can map or picture the desacralized & paradoxical solipsism of U.S. persons in a cattle-herd culture." When Moore had editorial questions, he'd call the halfway house, and Wallace, at the front desk, would pick up.

Wallace also began to write book reviews for newspapers and magazines. Though he took them for money, these too helped him organize his thinking. Since his teenage years he'd had a taste for thrillers—they answered the need in his brain for instantly recognizable structures and cartoonish characters—so he was well suited to review Clive Barker's *The Great and Secret Show* for the *Washington Post*, criticizing the writer as "one of those dreaded commercial successes who've become so impressed with themselves they no longer think they have to work at being interesting."

Fiction was, of course, what Wallace really wanted to write, but here he was having less luck. Some piece of him still felt too fragile to attempt an effort so key to his well-being. The problem, he felt, was not really the words on the page; he had lost confidence not in his ability to write so much as the need to have written. Franzen offered to get together that April when he was in Boston, despite Wallace's changed circumstances. Wallace said fine but stood him up after they made plans. But because one tenet of recovery is to make amends to those you have wronged, he sent a quick note to his friend explaining his behavior. "The bald fact is that I'm a little afraid of you right now," he wrote. He begged to be allowed to bow out of their embryonic competition, to declare a truce against this writer who was so "irked by my stuff," because Wallace was no longer "a worthy opponent in some kind of theoretical chess-by-mail game from which we can both profit by combat."

He went on:

All I can tell you is that I may have been that for you a couple/three years ago, and maybe 16 months or two or 5 or 10 years hence, but right now I am a pathetic and very confused young man, a failed writer at 28, who is so jealous, so sickly searingly envious of you and Vollmann and Mark Leyner and even David Fuckwad Leavitt and any young man who is right now producing pages with which he can live and even approving them off some base-clause of conviction about the enterprise's meaning and end that I consider suicide a reasonable—if not at this point a desirable—option with respect to the whole wretched problem.

His avoidance of his only literary friend made him mad at himself, as his anger looped, but to be sitting at a table discussing how to create art would be an inherently false gesture, he felt, because, as he explained to Franzen, he was no longer really an artist:

> The problem's details are at once shameful to me and boring to anyone else. I always had great contempt for people who bitched and moaned about how "hard" writing was, and how "blockage" was a constant and looming threat. When I discovered writing in 1983 I discovered a thing that gave me a combination of fulfillment (moral/ aesthetic/existential/etc.) and near-genital pleasure I'd not dared hope for from anything.

He added, "I have in the last two years been struck dumb. . . . Not dumb, actually, or even aphasic. It's more like, w/r/t things I used to believe and let inform me, my thoughts now have the urgent but impeded quality of speechlessness in dreams."

Franzen quickly wrote to reassure him there were no hard feelings. He had only been hoping for "some laffs and companionship from a late afternoon with you in Cambridge." He too had felt "joyless" in his writing lately. Wallace, though, like a cancer patient having to explain himself to a headache sufferer, did not think their discomfort was equivalent. Two weeks later, hiding out in the Brighton library instead of working on a rulebook for Granada House, he read a popular adventure novel—"a kind of a ripping good read"—and wrote his friend again to try to explain his problem: "I think back with much saliva to times in 1984, 5, 6, 7 when I'd sit down and look up and it would be hours later and there'd be this mess of filled-up notebook paper and I just felt wrung out and well-fucked and, well, blessed." His anguish, he wrote, had multiple sources, from a fear of fame to a fear of failure. Behind the ordinary fears lurked the fear of being ordinary.

Even as Wallace was complaining that he had lost his old reason for writing, Franzen in his letters was quietly suggesting a replacement. He would remind Wallace of the pleasure Franzen took in creating characters he loved and how the stories he had liked in *Girl with Curious Hair* had given him the same satisfaction; both were part of "the humble, unpaid work an author does in the service of emotion and the human image." A year before when Franzen had suggested something similar, Wallace had dismissed it as twaddle. Back then, in the same letter in which he said readers were welcome to think he was an asshole, he had made clear that

> [f]iction for me is a conversation for me between me and something that May Not Be Named—God, the Cosmos, the Unified Field, my own psychoanalitic cathexes, Roqoq'oqu, whomever. I do not feel even the hint of an obligation to an entity called READER—do not regard it as his favor, rather as his choice, that, duly warned, he is expended capital/time/retinal energy on what I've done.

But now he wondered if his resistance toward a more supportive idea of the writer's relationship with the reader wasn't the cause of his blockage. He responded to Franzen:

> I'd love to hear more on what "humble, unpaid work an author does in the service of emotion and human image" is. . . . And how, as a vastly overselfconscious writer, might one still go on having faith and hope in literature and some kind of pleasure. . . ? I admit it: I want to know. I have no clue. I'm a blank slate right now. Tabula rasa or whatever.

He reluctantly acknowledged that he might suffer from "a basically vapid urge to be avant-garde and poststructural and linguistically calisthenic— this is why I get very spiny when I think someone's suggesting this may be my root motive and character; because I'm afraid it might be."[7]

Wallace's stay at Granada House finished in June. Where he chose to go next, he knew, would be important. He had not drunk alcohol or gotten high for seven months. He considered Somerville, Urbana, and Arizona, but instead moved into a transitional facility on Foster Street, just a few blocks away, with Big Craig and two other men from Granada House. The "sober house," as it was called, was split into men's and women's sections. The residents spent most of their time at work and the building had an empty feel compared to Granada House—Amy Wallace visited and found it remarkably clean, considering more than a dozen adults lived there.

When the other residents went off to their jobs, Wallace would head for the library in bandana with knapsack to spend the day trying to write. He still did not feel well. He wrote David Markson that he was "so blank and depressed and befogged" that he couldn't even tell if he liked what he was *reading*. He and Costello went around Harvard Yard, Wallace showing his friend all the places he had tried to study when he was a graduate student and failed. When he got to Emerson he said he often thought of throwing himself down the stairs. With his friend Debra Spark he went to his Somerville apartment and emptied his things out. He threw out books and piles of manuscripts and drove his computer to the Costello family house in Winchester, Massachusetts. Spark urged him not to throw the material out, saying he'd want it later. "I cannot sit still," he wrote Markson, "can barely read, and have thoughts that don't race so much as intertwine in a boily and clotted and altogether nauseous way. Fiction-wise I'm dead in the water." How he yearned, he said, for "just one tall cool frosted bar-glass of Wild Turkey." For his nine-month anniversary of sobriety, in July, Wallace's sponsor gave him a Jolly Pecker, "a squat little fireplug of a phallus, with feet, which when you wind it up hops up and down in a plaintive eager way that just breaks hearts. It seems to capture my state . . . so aptly I can't even be bothered to think the guy's a dork."[8]

Wallace had paid $20 a week in rent at Granada House. He had had few other costs as he worked to kick his addiction. But now he was facing the ordinary expenses of a Boston-area resident. Book reviews paid a trifle; he had no grant money left. He was back against the old problem that if he taught he might not write but if he didn't teach he would not eat. It was the one thing he knew he knew how to do, the only thing he thought he could do. Determined to stay in Boston, where he had made a new beginning, he applied to Tufts and Harvard as a creative writing instructor.

Someone new came into his life now, as if to counter this disappointment: Mary Karr, a poet. The Texan-born Karr was in her mid-thirties, seven years older than Wallace. She lived in Belmont with her husband and young son, drove a station wagon, and had the stability and the grit that Wallace felt he lacked. They had in fact met once at a party before he'd gone to McLean and he'd been very taken with her; she was witty and had a raunchy vocabulary. Soon after he moved out of McLean, he saw her at a meeting in Harvard Square. That she was a recovering alcoholic too seemed like serendipity. He quickly grew infatuated. When his friend Mark Costello came up to visit him, the two waited in the back of a meeting hall in the hope that this extraordinary woman would come by. (She did and seemed pleasant but harried to Costello, who was used to his friend's exaggerations.)[9] There were warnings Wallace was well aware of against pursuing another person newly in recovery. (Ignoring the prohibition is derided by members as "thirteenth stepping.")[10] It did not matter to him: here was a kindred spirit, another writer struggling to surrender to a greater power but for whom phrases like "One day at a time" and "Do what's in front of you to do" hurt the brain.

Deb Larson counseled Karr and Karr also volunteered at Granada House, so Wallace often had occasion to see her. Immediately, he wanted to be involved, but Karr, who was in a shaky marriage and trying to protect her son, says she had no interest. She sensed instability and trouble. "We were both just shocking wrecks," she remembers; he bragged that he had perfect SATs, and called her Miss Karr "in this obsequious, Charlie Chanish fawning kind of way." He saw her, she realized, as some sort of mother/redeemer figure.

Wallace did not hear subtle variations in no; he knew only one way to seduce: overwhelm. He would show up at Karr's family home near McLean to shovel her driveway after a snowfall, or come unannounced to her recovery meetings. Karr called Deb Larson and asked her to let Wallace know his attentions were not welcome. Wallace besieged her with notes anyway. He called himself Sorrowful Werther. She was "Sainte Nitouche," the saint who cannot be touched, a reference to her favorite book, *Anna Karenina*. She felt an affinity for him, considered him brilliant but also unsound. One day, she remembers, he arrived at a pool party she was at with her family with bandages on his left shoulder. She thought maybe he had been cutting himself and wouldn't show her what was underneath—a tattoo with her name and a heart. He called Walden, with whom he was not much in contact anymore, to tell her what he had done. He clearly felt he had made a commitment there was no retreating from. The details of the relationship were not clear to others though: Wallace told friends they were involved, Karr says no.

Karr did not admire Wallace's writing. She read *Girl with Curious Hair* and "told him it was not a great book," she remembers, praising only "Here and There": "His interest in cleverness was preventing him from saying things." She advocated more direct prose.[11] But Karr was not impervious to his restless mind and contacted a friend who ran the writing program at Emerson College, DeWitt Henry, to recommend Wallace for a job there and assure him that if he proved too unstable to teach the class, she would step in. Henry agreed to take Wallace on as an adjunct professor in the fall of 1990.

In that month he began his reluctant return to academia. He took the Green Line subway to Emerson, "a hip kids' college in the Back Bay," as he described it to Markson. The combined rejection of the stories he most admired by the two people whose opinions he admired most—Franzen and Karr—was beginning to tell. When DeWitt Henry put up an advertisement for *Girl with Curious Hair* on a bulletin board, Wallace pulled it down, saying he was embarrassed by the book. A few weeks into the semester Wallace checked in with Franzen. "Teaching is going OK," he wrote his friend. "I'd forgotten how young college students are. They're infants, though: you can see the veins in their little eyelids, you almost have to cradle their heads to help their necks support the skull's weight." He found he was popular, known for a loose style and an appealing willingness to digress. "We spend most of our time talking about Twin Peaks and The Simpsons so they think I am an okay caballero," he told Markson. This was clearly a very different approach than the one he had taken at Arizona and Amherst, where his commitment to his students was preternatural and even a little maniacal, but Wallace was tired and confused: the stage didn't feel like a stage without drugs and alcohol; it felt like a classroom.

Wallace did have one literary project in which he was putting his energy. *Harper's* had asked him to write a 1000 word piece on television for a forum. It had of course sprung to larger-than-life dimensions, consuming his untapped energy. TV remained a subject of paramount interest to him. When he had accepted the assignment, he had joked to Markson, who had been a friend of Malcolm Lowry, that having him write about television was "rather like asking the Consul in his late stages to write a haiku on the history of distillation." He found interesting tidbits in Widener Library at

Harvard to suggest he might be an outlier but he wasn't a singleton. In recent years, he learned, for instance, educated viewers had come to watch as much TV as uneducated ones; six hours a day was now the national average. He wrote page after page as he tried to wrestle the filthy machine to the mat. He had little hopes of the work being published, so what he was doing was memorandizing himself, though, as he told Markson, even the kill fee—around $1,000—would be "sumptuous."

The assertion that television promoted passivity was not new—it was standard in the works of cultural critics like Todd Gitlin and Mark Crispin Miller—but for Wallace the charge wasn't theoretical; it was personal, crucial. TV's treacly predictability held him in strange thrall, and during periods of collapse he seemed almost literally attached to it. The students he was teaching made him feel the problem was worse than he had known. They were the Letterman generation he had imagined in "My Appearance," proud of their knowingness. "They're all 'television' majors, whatever that means," he complained to Markson, adding that he'd had his wrist slapped by his department for "'frustrating' the students" with a De-Lillo novel (he does not say which) by which he meant to wake them up: "Most . . . desire to read nothing harder than news headlines off TV cue cards."

Wallace knew he did not want to stay at Emerson long. He thought about applying for a fellowship but realized he had nothing to propose to fund. "I want to start trying some creative writing again," he wrote Moore in November 1990, "but I find now that I am terrified to start, have forgotten most of what I (thought I had) learned, and feel like the little reptile section of my brain that used to be in charge of really good writing is now either dead or playing possum in protest." But whereas a few years before his frustrations would have sent him on a pot binge, his daily recovery sessions taught him how to wait it out. He had just finished his first year of sobriety, a significant event for him. There were still meetings, time with his sponsor, and he also eventually saw a private therapist at Karr's urging. Predictably, he found therapy both appealingly and apprehensively absorbing. But it gave him another tool to deal with moments of frustration such as this one. "There is absolutely nothing I can do except accept the situation as it is and wait patiently for some fullness-of-time-type change," he wrote Moore. "The alternative to patience is going back to the way I used to live, which Drs. and non-hysterics at the rehab told me would have killed me, and in a most gnarly and inglorious way, before I was 30."

Still, acceptance wasn't a lesson that he took in evenly in all aspects of his life. Where the alcohol and pot had held sway there was now an enormous amount of anger that was not easily acknowledged. Big Craig happened to watch a car cut off Wallace one day when the latter was driving near Foster Street. In fury Wallace rammed his car into the other person's. "He got out of the car, scratching his head," Big Craig remembers. "'Oh Gee, what happened?'"

Signifying Rappers: Rap and Race in the Urban Present, Wallace's collaboration with Mark Costello, who was now an assistant district attorney in Manhattan, came out in November 1990, a volley from the past. "*Signifying Rappers* is the first serious consideration of rap and its position as a vital force in American cultural consciousness," an ad for the book in the *Voice Literary Supplement* declared. But Wallace cautioned in the book's pages, "If you're reading this in print it's already dated." And he was right. By the time the book was published, rap had ceased to be a revelation, though it was still in the news. Its threat to be, as Wallace put it in the book, the "prolegomena to any future uprising," had been contained. Tipper Gore and George Will had denounced it, the noted professor Henry Louis Gates supported it, and a Florida prosecutor was bringing charges against 2 Live Crew for obscenity. The publisher's press release offered, "The Authors—white, educated, middle class—occupy a peculiar position, at once marginal and crucial to rap's us and them equations." Few reviewers or readers seemed to know what to make of the joint effort. The authors' stance that rap was "quite possibly the most important stuff happening in American poetry today" felt at once too clever and obvious. The way their alternating short takes on rap resembled rap's own samplings went unappreciated. At the least, Wallace got to set out his new awareness of the power of addiction. He might have been looking around the Granada House common area when he wrote of a centerless pop-culture country full of marginalized subnations that are themselves postmodern, looped, self-referential, self-obsessed, voyeuristic, passive, slack-jawed, debased.[12]

Or it may have been his idea of the student body at Emerson.

Though the book attracted little notice, Wallace welcomed its appearance. He was happy to have it in his hands at a moment when he had so little else to show for his work. "I've gone from thinking it slight and silly to something I want to send to friends," he wrote Moore, who arranged a review of the book in the *Review of Contemporary Fiction*. Wallace was so poor that Moore gave him a free subscription so he could read the piece. Wallace asked him whether he might help him find a way out of teaching. "I am the best copyeditor I've ever seen," he bragged, wondering if he could make enough at the trade to "move to the midwest and live in a hovel." Moore responded that the Dalkey Archive at Illinois State University was looking for a publicity director. Wallace begged off, saying he "couldn't even take prom-rejection in high school."

The relationship with Karr was not moving forward, becoming another source of anger. Karr and her husband were still living together. She says she had cut off all contact. Still, Wallace thought if he could have Karr, his life would come together. His time in the house of the dead would be over. She worried about his tendency to what he called "black-eyed red-outs." She took a fellowship at Radcliffe. He went to the Harvard Law Library and wrote her a note explaining how she could divorce her husband and still keep custody of their son and a share of their assets. She showed it to her spouse. One day she looked out her office window to find Wallace cursing her and demanding the return of a Walkman he'd lent her. When she threw it down to him, he took it, stomped off, and put his fist through a car window.

Several months later, in April 1991, he wrote to Markson that he had torn the ligaments in his ankle playing softball and refused the painkillers the doctors offered him, a decision that took "every shred of will I've got." "What's unendurable is what his own head could make of it all," Don Gately thinks in an important scene in *Infinite Jest*, as he lies in the hospital with a gunshot wound, refusing any drugs. "But he could choose not to listen." Real life was not so heroic: "I am not taking it well," Wallace remarked to Markson. "I have substituted chronic complaining for analgesic, and so far it's worked OK."[13] He walked with crutches but could not sit up, which meant he could not type, which in turn excused him from book reviewing, a relief. He read for pleasure instead, enjoying James Baldwin a lot and Thomas McGuane much less. Walker Percy gave him "the creeps." He started *The Armies of the Night* by Norman Mailer and hated it, admitting in a letter to Markson that he found the writer "unutterably repulsive. I guess part of his whole charm is his knack for arousing strong reactions. Hitler had the same gift." He read *Vineland* and discovered his love for Thomas Pynchon was gone, whether because he had changed or his hero had. He wrote Franzen that he found Pynchon's first novel in nearly two decades "flat and strained and heartbreakingly inferior to his other 3 novels. I get the strong sense he's spent 20 years smoking pot and watching TV—though I tend to get paranoid about this point, for obvious reasons." Franzen and he were continuing their bumpy version of bonding. He scolded Franzen for moving back to New York City. "The people I've known there who've led real lives there never seem quite to escape," he wrote. In response Franzen sought to cheer his friend with a gentle cuff: "I think that eventually you're going to start doing fiction again and that it will be even better than what you've done so far—as funny, as smart, but with some clearer connection to the soul." He quoted Wallace a poem by Emily Dickinson to underscore his point:

Mirth is the Mail of Anguish
In which it cautious arm
Lest anybody spy the Blood
And "you're hurt!" exclaim.

Wallace finished up the academic year amid disappointment. He told people he and Karr were growing closer but she had decided to move with her family to Syracuse, where she had been offered a teaching job. In a postcard to Franzen Wallace recorded his amazement at her departure. "I finally told Mary I'd marry her," he complained, "and within 3 weeks she'd decided she couldn't divorce her husband. She's moving away with him in August. I am not pleased, but there is literally nothing I can do. I am sad." (She says they were not in contact.) He spent a confused summer in Boston, pining for Karr. "Nothing is new," he wrote to a college friend, "I go to . . . meetings, volunteer on their phone lines, read a lot, write a little."

In late September Wallace moved out of the "sober house" on Foster Street and into a double-decker clapboard one on an anonymous stretch of Massachusetts Avenue in Arlington. He shared the apartment with another recovering substance abuser, probably a pairing Granada House had arranged. The man had a large collection of Tito Puente records, which Wallace called "crime jazz." (He would work the witticism into *Infinite Jest*.) "The apartment is strange," he wrote Franzen in October. "Most everything is still in boxes. I have a mattress on the floor and wake up with dust on my tongue." Franzen visited and found his friend in a messy bachelor pad, cold and dimly lit, a place to pass through. Wallace bumped into Gale Walden on the T—she had a research associate position at Harvard—and when she came by, she saw draft pages of a novel spread everywhere.

When a second year at Emerson began, Wallace undertook his work without pleasure. He had increased his load to three classes to make more money, teaching "back to back in the afternoon three days a week." "All I do is work," he complained to Franzen in October, threatening to sell his computer for cash. He still did not like the students and sedulously kept apart from his colleagues. Some of the other teachers in turn found Wallace standoffish, odd. One thought he seemed like he had Asperger's syndrome and remembers him as theatrical in his isolation, taking up "some position from which the staff could view him, and from his small corner of the room stage he would pose as if in deep contemplation, or emotional pain or genius." Wallace wrote Franzen, "I've had to educate myself about people like Stephen Crane and Edith Wharton. Actually that's been a blast. I had no idea they were so good. I remember reading them a little in high school and mostly wondering when they were going to get done so I could go eat something sugary and then masturbate." Liking "the canon" was one way of signaling to Franzen his aesthetic voyage. If he could read realist fiction, maybe he could write it. "The last thin patina of rebelliousness has fallen off," he reported proudly to his friend in the same letter. "I am frightfully and thoroughly conventional."

For nearly two years, Wallace had been living a hectic, unbalanced life. If he was no longer a substance abuser, he was still a drama junkie, a man afraid to be alone with his own thoughts. But Karr, around whom his every emotion orbited, was gone for good—or appeared to be so—and in early November 1991, Wallace suddenly collapsed again. It was his first breakdown since quitting drinking, and it devastated him. He was admitted to the Newton-Wellesley Hospital psychiatric unit with a diagnosis of suicidal depression. He lay in a locked ward for several days. Afterward, Debra Spark brought him student papers, because he wanted to keep up with his grading. "The people here are crazy," he told her. She found the ward he was in scarier than McLean, where she had also visited him, and Wallace more frightened and depressed. The doctors at Newton-Wellesley increased the dose of Nardil he was on and he began to improve. After two weeks, he was released. He would write in a later medical history that depression and desperation came and went in the ensuing months, but over time the Nardil coursing through his blood relieved his condition and gave him back hope. Immediately, he was making plans. He had called Karr just before he was admitted to the hospital to tell her he loved her; now, as Karr remembers, he called her mother to say he was going to marry her daughter. "Didn't you just get out of someplace?" she responded.

Wallace had not forgotten his literary hopes. Throughout 1990 and into 1991 he had fought off the worry that, sober, book reviewing and essays were all he was capable of. He wrote Nadell in the spring of 1991, as much to reassure himself as his agent, that things would change:

> Please don't give up on me. I want to be a writer now way more than in 1985. I think I can be better than I was but it's going to take time— and believe me, I know that quite a bit of time has elapsed already. . . . Do not assume, please, that I am being slothful or distracted because I have not sent you any fiction to publish. Do not assume I've given up in despair, or that I've burned out. I haven't, I swear. It may be a couple more years before I finish anything both long and respectable, but I will. Please don't forget me, and please don't let Gerry forget me either. . . . I write daily, on a schedule, am at least publishing hackwork and I will be a fiction writer again or die trying.

The *Review of Contemporary Fiction* had decided to devote an issue to Wallace and Vollmann and another young writer, Susan Daitch. In a long interview for the magazine that Wallace gave to Larry McCaffery that April, he hinted how much trouble he was having writing. "It seems like the big distinction between good art and so-so art lies . . . in be[ing] willing to sort of die in order to move the reader, somehow. Even now I'm scared about how sappy this'll look in print, saying this. And the effort to actually do it, not just talk about it, requires a kind of courage I don't seem to have yet." But by August 1991, four months later, the courage was mysteriously back. In that month he wrote Forrest Ashby that he was "slowly trying some fictional stuff, which so far is not very good, and almost completely unrecognizable vis a vis the stuff I was doing before I well, whatever," and to his old professor Dale Peterson he spoke of "writing quite a bit and enjoying it for the first time in years." What had helped him break through? Part of the credit should go to the *Harper's* essay Wallace had been writing. The subject of the essay had expanded from how television changes our perception of reality to the crisis in the generation of which Wallace was a part, the two being, of course, to him, closely related. Since Arizona, Wallace had been calling for a fiction that captured how thoroughly television had altered the minds of its watchers. But since McLean and recovery, he had begun to realize that portraying such a world in fiction might be just as harmful as TV itself. There was no reason to think that limning a hopeless condition would show a way out; it might just make imprisonment more pleasant. Now Wallace reformulated his goal: American fiction was not in just an aesthetic crisis, but a moral one. Exhibit A was a writer he had once lavished a great deal of affection on, Mark Leyner, whose novel *My Cousin, My Gastroenterologist* he had touted when he lived in Somerville. The novel, really seventeen linked stories, is clever and almost schizophrenically scattered, embodying less a plot than an attitude toward modernity. One story—it might almost have been a set piece in *Broom*—features a character named Big Squirrel, who is, in Wallace's words, "a TV kiddie-show host and kung fu mercenary." In another story a father lives in his basement centrifuging mouse hybridoma. One section is entitled "lines composed after inhaling paint thinner." When Wallace first read the book, he had reveled in its aggressive, postrealist stance, its avant-pop insistence that the overwhelming incoherence of modern culture was a joyride for the brain. But the new Wallace, in his television essay, would call the book "a methedrine compound of pop pastiche, offhand high tech, and dazzling televisual parody," and quote the jacket copy's claim that the book was "a fiction analogue of the best drug you ever took," a description that anyone aware of Wallace's situation would have recognized as far from an endorsement on his part. America was, Wallace now knew, a nation of addicts, unable to see that what looked like love freely given was really need neurotically and chronically unsatisfied. The effect of Leyner's fictional approach to life—mutated, roving, uncommitted—like that of *Letterman* and *Saturday Night Live*—was to make our addiction seem clever, deliberate, entered into voluntarily. Wallace knew better.

And now he was far clearer on why we were all so hooked. It was not TV as a medium that had rendered us addicts, powerful though it was. It was, far more dangerously, an attitude toward life that TV had learned from fiction, especially from postmodern fiction, and then had reinforced among its viewers, and that attitude was irony. Irony, as Wallace defined it, was not in and of itself bad. Indeed, irony was the traditional stance of the weak against the strong; there was power in implying what was too dangerous to say. Postmodern fiction's original ironists—writers like Pynchon and sometimes Barth—were telling important truths that could only be told obliquely, he felt. But irony got dangerous when it became a habit. Wallace quoted Lewis Hyde, whose pamphlet on John Berryman and alcohol he had read in his early months at Granada House: "Irony has only emergency use. Carried over time, it is the voice of the trapped who have come to enjoy the cage." Then he continued:

> This is because irony, entertaining as it is, serves an almost exclusively negative function. It's critical and destructive, a ground-clearing. . . . [I]rony's singularly unuseful when it comes to constructing anything to replace the hypocrisies it debunks.

That was it exactly—irony was defeatist, timid, the telltale of a generation too afraid to say what it meant, and so in danger of forgetting it had anything to say. For Wallace, perhaps irony's most frightening implication was that it was user-neutral: with viewers everywhere conditioned by media to expect it, anyone could employ it to any end. What really upset him was when Burger King used irony to sell hamburgers, or Joe Isuzu, cars.[14]

What was really behind this objection, which gathered strength with the years? The stance was a nearly complete turnaround for a young writer who had made his identity as a clown and then a parodist and whose gifts as a "weird kind of forger" hardly depended on clarity of intent. Suddenly, in his eyes, sincerity was a virtue and saying what you meant a calling. Nostalgia seemed to play a part, as well as discontent with the person he had grown up to be, the two intertwined. Wallace was signaling that cultural health lay in a return to the earnestness he'd grown up with. Back then in his midwestern boyhood, a person said what he or she meant. It did not matter that he had never really been that person nor that his mental health issues had walled him off from ever becoming that person; it was reassuring for him to imagine it.

This led Wallace to conjure—easy enough since he was simultaneously already working on it—a new kind of fiction that might one day displace the Leyners of the world:

> The next real literary "rebels" in this country might well emerge as some weird bunch of "anti-rebels," born oglers who dare somehow to back away from ironic watching, who have the childish gall actually to endorse single-entrendre principles. Who treat of plain old untrendy human troubles and emotions in U.S. life with reverence and conviction. Who eschew self-consciousness and hip fatigue.

He continued:

> The old postmodern insurgents risked the gasp and squeal: shock, disgust, outrage, censorship, accusations of socialism, anarchism, nihilism. The new rebels might be the ones willing to risk the yawn, the rolled eyes, the cool smile, the nudged ribs, the parody of gifted ironists, the "how *banal*."

Wallace knew whose thinking had influenced his own. He sent Franzen a draft of the piece, "mostly just to see what you think about all the anti-irony stuff. You'll see I've adopted a Franzenian view of Leyner, too."

And he dedicated the article to M. M. Karr, his other fount of sincerity. Crucially, Wallace was confident that his malaise was not just a personal issue but a societal condition. He sensed that there were others like himself. He mentioned to an interviewer after the publication of *Infinite Jest* that it was in Boston that he had

> decided that maybe being really sad, and really sort of directionless, wasn't just that I was fucked up. Maybe it was, maybe I was, maybe it was *interesting* in a way. . . . I just had *so many* friends who went through terrible times exactly when I did. In so many various different ways. And so many of them seemed to have so much going for 'em. . . . We're talking lawyers, stockbrokers, young promising academics, poets.

His new commitment to single-entendre writing, writing that meant what it said, brought with it a surge in confidence that Wallace hadn't felt in years, not since his 1987 visit to Yaddo. Not even his breakdown in November could stop it. And Karr's departure for Syracuse didn't hinder it: in fact it may even have been the spur for it, leaving Wallace with the need to prove he deserved her love. At any rate, he later wrote about the following year in the margin of a book, "The key to '92 is that MMK was most important; IJ was just a means to her end (as it were)." "The writing is going surprisingly well," he wrote Karr, probably in the spring of that year. "I'm scared, and physically I write very slowly, rather like a small child. It's a long thing I want to do, and I'd started it before, so right now I divide my time between writing new stuff, which is a little disjointed . . . and looking back through two Hammermill boxes worth of notebooks and notecards and incredibly pretty laser print from my computer, which is now with Mark."

He had been eyeing his old drafts for a long time without knowing what to make of them. He hadn't known what the right or wrong track was because he didn't know where he was going. That explained his fitful efforts since Yaddo. He told Karr, "I'd remembered the old stuff, a couple years old, as being just awful, but it turns out it isn't; it just doesn't go much of anywhere and is way too concerned with presenting itself as witty arty writing instead of effecting any kind of emotional communication with people. I feel like I have changed, learned so much about what good writing ought to be."

*   *   *

There is no clear start date for *Infinite Jest*. Pieces of the novel date back to 1986, when Wallace may have written them originally as stand-alone stories.[15] The work contains all three of Wallace's literary styles, beginning with the playful, comic voice of his Amherst years, passing through his infatuation with postmodernism at Arizona, and ending with the conversion to single-entendre principles of his days in Boston. These three approaches correspond roughly to the three main plot strands of the book: the first, the portrait of the witty, dysfunctional Incandenza family; the second, the near-future dystopian backdrop of the book, in which the United States has united with Canada and Mexico to form the Organization of North American Nations ("O.N.A.N.," its symbol an eagle crowned by a sombrero, maple leaf in claw), spawning a Quebecois separatist movement; and the third, the passion of Don Gately, set in the thinly fictionalized version of Granada House. Some parts of the book had already been with Wallace for five years by the breakthrough of 1991–92. In the fall of 1986, in Arizona, for instance, Gale Walden noticed a draft of some pages with her sister Joelle's name under Wallace's bed. She asked what he was working on and Wallace said it was fiction about a terrorist organization in Canada. "At which point," she remembers, "my eyes glazed over and I didn't ask any more." This is at least the beginning of the dialogue between the two secret agents, Marathe, of Québec, and Steeply, of the U.S., which takes place on a mountain not unlike the ones Walden and Wallace liked to hike outside of Tucson, where the desert had, as Wallace writes in *Infinite Jest*, "the appearance of [a] mirage. . . . The sun of A.M. had no radial knives of light. It appeared brutal and businesslike and harmful to look upon."[16]

On his first application for Yaddo, filled out in September 1986, Wallace wrote that along with "Westward" he was also working on a novel with the tentative title *Infinite Jest*, adding that one reason he wanted to go to the retreat was to "try to determine just where and why the stories leave off and the novel begins." Likely, by then, the Incandenza family's follies were already in draft. Stylistically, they follow closely in the hyperverbal footsteps of the Beadsmans:[17] Hal, the family's "tennis and lexical prodigy," corresponds to Lenore of *Broom*; his father, the brilliant suicide James, a filmmaker, tracks to Lenore's great-grandmother, another absent genius. In addition, without the Incandenzas the title on the Yaddo application makes little sense. You can't have *Hamlet* without a ghost.[18]

But at Yaddo, Wallace clearly found writing "Westward" more urgent, and it was likely not for several years that he returned to the novel. The third strand, the pages on Don Gately, could not have been begun before early 1990, by which time Wallace had entered the real-life counterpart to Ennet House. By fall 1991 he had likely begun interweaving his narrative; the delicate design of the novel was beginning to fall into place. On one side were the Incandenzas led by Avril, the dominating and complex matriarch. Hal, addicted to pot, is the youngest of her three sons, the emotional center of this part of the book, except that one of the points of the book is that that center is empty:

> Hal himself hasn't had a bona fide intensity-of-interior-life-type emotion since he was tiny; he finds terms like *joie* and *value* to be like so many variables in rarified equations, and he can manipulate them well enough to satisfy everyone but himself that he's in there, inside his own hull, as a human being ... when in fact inside Hal there's pretty much nothing at all, he knows.

Hal's two older brothers are Orin, a professional football player and womanizer in Phoenix, and Mario, who suffers from a cognitive and physical disability. Avril is now in a relationship with her late husband's brother, another of the many whiffs of *Hamlet* in the story.

The family runs the Enfield Tennis Academy, where perfection is the goal and the best of the players are trained to satisfy, through their tennis games and commercial endorsements, the appetite of the consumerist culture they came from. On the other side are the residents of Ennet House, led by Gately. The Ennet House addicts are not being cultivated to feed America's obsessions; they are the people who've OD'd on them.[19] The two worlds, as in real life, live in parallel, interacting only when they have to, with only a "tall and more or less denuded hill" separating them. Yet they are thematically joined—the Enfield Academy world is preppy, team-focused, and saturated with drugs; the Ennet House world is poor, crime-ridden, and shattered by drugs. Both are hemmed in by self-absorption: for the Enfield players their solipsism is narcissism, the risk that all the attention being focused on them will make them believe they are blessed in some more than ordinary way; for the Ennet House residents the solipsism is that of despair, but also the self-centeredness at the heart of therapy and recovery, a world where the self is so damaged that nothing else can get near it. Character after character there sees his or her wounded past and nothing else, while up the hill player after player sees only his or her potential. Overseeing both sides, literally, are Marathe and Steeply, competing (or possibly cooperating) secret agents, whose function in the novel is to sound the themes as well as give a motor to the plot, which centers on the idea that before committing suicide James Incandenza had made a movie so absorbing that anyone who watches it succumbs to total passivity. The original of the video cartridge—Wallace imagines cartridges as something like minidiscs—has disappeared and if the Quebecois find it they will have the ultimate terrorist weapon to use against their decadent neighbors to the south.

For Wallace to orchestrate his material was enormously complex, and as he rewrote scenes he must have had to work hard to keep straight the various voices he was using. He had always been good at mimicry, but the voices in the recovery house chapters are subtler and truer than in the other sections. They seem to descend from a caring narrator rather than be roused up as proof of his talent. Wallace created dozens of characters, many capturing aspects of how he saw himself. There is Kate Gompert (her name borrowed from a woman who had played on the junior tennis circuit with Wallace and would subsequently sue him unsuccessfully for libel). Addicted to pot and brutally depressed, Gompert casts a practiced eye on the psych ward where she finds herself:

> Kate Gompert was on Specials, which meant Suicide-Watch, which meant that the girl had at some point betrayed both Ideation and Intent, which meant she had to be watched right up close by a staffer twenty-four hours a day until the supervising M.D. called off the Specials.[20]

Another pot addict, Ken Erdedy, embodies a different side of Wallace. We first meet him barricaded in his apartment as he waits for an obliging young female acquaintance to bring dope—"a fifth of a kilogram of marijuana, 200 grams of unusually good marijuana." The woman—the friend of a dealer—has promised it to him so he can go on one last binge before quitting for good, spurring an obsessively branching set of contingencies in Erdedy's mind:

> Where was the woman who said she'd come. She said she would come. Erdedy thought she'd have come by now. . . . He did not use the phone to call the woman who'd promised to come because if he tied up the line and if it happened to be the time when maybe she was trying to call him he was afraid she would hear the busy signal and think him disinterested and get angry and maybe take what she'd promised him somewhere else.[21]

Once Wallace had his setup, he seems to have worked with remarkable speed because by April 1992 he had 250 finished pages for Nadell. He was not just in the grip of inspiration. The point was to get a contract for the book. It was "the bravest thing" he had done since getting sober, he would later tell an interviewer, but he believed the work was going so well that he could deal with the pressure. "Life is good. I'm trying to get together enough of this Long Thing to plead for an advance," he wrote Brad Morrow with uncharacteristic confidence that March.

As promised, on April 15, 1992, he was ready with his proposal and partial manuscript of *Infinite Jest*, "a novel," he noted in his cover letter, "although structurally it's not much like any other novels I've seen." "Plotwise," he added, "this thing proceeds according to something more like a broad arc than a Freytagian triangle. The low gear in which plot stuff proceeds in sections 1 and 2 is intentional." He warned of footnotes that were "just brutal." He addressed his note to "Bonnie and Gerry and Whatever Other Trusted and Hopefully Trustworthy Persons End up Reading this," and urged everyone to mail the manuscript back or destroy it when they were done. He sent the package off to Nadell.

Wallace's literary rebirth did not coincide with any calming of his conviction that he had to be with Karr. Indeed, the opposite. In fact, one day in February, he thought briefly of committing murder for her. He called an ex-con he knew through his recovery program and tried to buy a gun. He had decided he would wait no longer for Karr to leave her husband; he planned to shoot him instead when he came into Cambridge to pick up the family dog. The ex-con called Larson, the head of Granada House, who told Karr. Wallace himself never showed up for the handover and thus ended what he would later call in a letter of apology "one of the scariest days of my life." He wrote Larson in explanation, "I now know what obsession can make people capable of"—then added in longhand after—"at least of *wanting* to do." To Karr at the time he insisted that the whole episode was an invention of the ex-con and she believed him.[22]

By the spring of 1992, Karr's marriage was finally at an end and Wallace had new hope he could be at her side. He was ecstatic. He was ready to leave Boston. He had come to hate "this soot-fest city," as he called it to Morrow. And he was sick of teaching. If he could get an advance, he could have the life and the woman he wanted. He had suffered beyond what he knew possible for her, and the suffering felt like an act of absolution.

In April, just before sending in the manuscript pages for Nadell and Howard, Wallace took the train down to Swarthmore College, outside of Philadelphia. Franzen was teaching a class there and had invited him to judge a fiction competition. Wallace also read from *Infinite Jest*. Playing to his young audience, he chose a section about Don Gately that predates his admission to Ennet House. In the segment, the young addict and a partner break into a local assistant district attorney's house, take pictures of themselves with toothbrushes up their anuses, and send the pictures to him. Beforehand, Wallace asked for a chalkboard and wrote down words and abbreviations that might not be familiar to the students. *Infinite Jest* was filled with the languages Wallace had learned in Boston—from drug addict lingo to Alcoholics Anonymous slogans. One word that Wallace had recently learned was "shunt"—to disarm an alarm system by creating a new circuit for the electricity. Wallace had gotten the word in an interview with a retired burglary detective whom Mark Costello had met working as an assistant district attorney. Wallace had listened for an hour, overwhelmed by the fact-heavy conversation. When Costello looked, "shunt" was the only word he had written in his notebook.[23]

At Swarthmore, Wallace stayed with Franzen, who remembers "an endearingly eccentric figure," a tobacco chewer with a love of showering,

Diet Dr Pepper, and blondies. They hardly knew each other, despite having become, as Wallace would later put it in a letter to his friend, the "best of pals and lit combatants." Wallace was urging Franzen and his then wife to join him and Karr in Syracuse, and after the reading the two young men headed north in Franzen's old Saab to check out the city, Wallace upset he had left his favorite scarf, in the colors of the family tartan, behind.[24] They took turns driving, the weather was bad, and Franzen was amazed at how much wiper fluid his friend used.

When they got to Syracuse, Wallace was surprised to find himself relegated to Karr's floor for the night alongside Franzen. She appeared not to have the same expectations for his visit that he had. And when Wallace, Franzen, and Karr drove through the town, she asked him to crouch down out of view—apparently she was worried that news of his arrival would reach her husband, who was still nearby. Wallace and Franzen drove back down to Swarthmore the next day, discussing the purpose of literature nearly the whole way. Wallace argued that it was to alleviate loneliness and give comfort, to break through what he characterized in *Infinite Jest* as each person's "excluded encagement in the self." He wanted Franzen to know that he had become a different person and a different writer in the four years they'd known each other. After he got home, he wrote Franzen that their chat had been "among the most nourishing for me in recent memory" and suggested that his friend read Brian Moore's *Catholics*, a story of a man who pledges everything for his faith. Franzen read the book and was unimpressed—his disciple had surpassed him in his quest for sincerity—but then Wallace rarely did things by halves.

A month later, in May 1992, Wallace packed up what little he had and drove to Syracuse. He had rented a first-floor apartment in a house around the corner from Karr and a few blocks from the main campus. It was in a typical graduate-student neighborhood, full of warping clapboard houses and semi-kempt lawns and right across from the food co-op. But being near the woman he loved made all the difference. "Syracuse," he wrote Debra Spark later in the month, "is very cheap (not to mention lovely to live in, with grass and trees and terrific parks and absurdly little traffic and M. Karr)." Costello came up and brought Wallace's old college computer. Wallace, he saw, was scribbling eagerly in his spiral-bound book whenever he had a moment. They went with Karr and her son for a tour of the hippie thrift shops in the tiny towns of Onondaga County. Costello bought a leather jacket, and the couple teased him. He also noticed that Wallace and Karr behaved like friends rather than lovers, probably because Karr wanted things to look ambiguous to her son or maybe because they were still ambiguous. "He really could have been her gay friend, from body language," Costello remembered.

To Costello's eyes, Karr seemed like a tougher version of Gale Walden. She had his friend's number. When she would tease him about his work he would put up with it, to his old roommate's surprise. He also saw how much Wallace liked being with Dev, Karr's young son. Wallace told the boy there were talking spiders in his beard and, when Dev asked, explained that the purpose of his bandana was to keep his head from exploding. Children had a quality Wallace would increasingly crave in those around him: they were drawn to him without crowding him. They were part of that group of people—students, recovery friends, ordinary people unconnected to the fiction business—whom he admitted to his circle because they left him room. Such people, he wrote to Franzen, "make me feel both unalone and unstressed."[25] Costello spent the weekend nights of his visit on chair cushions in his friend's tiny apartment, Wallace in the bed. He explained that he was banned from sleeping at Karr's while Dev was there.

With Karr still not quite available, Wallace made do as best he could. He lived on chocolate Pop-Tarts and soda, too poor to eat properly. Getting fed was a priority. So when he met Stephanie Hubbard and Doug Eich, a couple in the orbit of the recovery group he had just joined, his interest was both literary and culinary. He would go to Hubbard's house, where she would cook and he and Eich discussed language and fiction. Eich misused nauseous for nauseated and Wallace corrected him, adducing his mother. Eich, a graduate student in linguistics, called his new friend "a smug prescriptivist douche-bag." Wallace was chewing tobacco again, which he would spit into a soda can, apologizing profusely to Hubbard and Eich while enjoying their attention. Then he would take a toothbrush he kept in a Ziploc bag in his sock and brush his teeth in their bathroom. The three would discuss the day's recovery meetings. Eich and Wallace shared a passion for DeLillo and also Cormac McCarthy. Wallace had discovered McCarthy late, when he was teaching at Amherst. "Something like Faulkner on acid," he had written Richard Elman at the time, in excitement. Eich and Wallace agreed that the gritty portrait of the alcoholic in *Suttree* was far more interesting than the self-pitying Consul in Lowry's *Under the Volcano.*[26]

The three would talk for hours. The conversation often turned to faith. Wallace said he was trying to pray, because, even though he did not necessarily believe in God, it seemed like a good thing to do. Karr had become attracted to Catholicism—for her baptism would be a key moment in her recovery from alcohol. So for a time Wallace too hoped to receive the sacraments, thinking that if he and Karr were to marry they could have a religious wedding. (Ultimately the priest told him he had too many questions to be a believer, and he let the issue drop.) Wallace's real religion was always language anyway. It alone could shape and hold multitudes; by comparison God's power was spindly. That was why he was obsessed with grammar; as he put it in a letter to Franzen, "If words are all we have as world and god, we must treat them with care and rigor: we must worship."

At first, in Syracuse, Wallace had trouble pushing *Infinite Jest* forward. Change always derailed his writing. Costello had added a new keyboard to Wallace's college computer. "I simply have to *pound* to get the letters to register," he complained to Franzen. He couldn't read some of his old drafts; he was too poor to buy a table to put it on; there were too many distractions. Wallace was, he wrote Franzen, "in a real funk about the Project" and worried his current inertia would "become a stasis that threatens to accumulate its own inertia, etc." Franzen had made a second visit to Syracuse, this time with his wife, to look at the possibility of moving there again. The three drove down the street on which Raymond Carver had lived when he taught at the university in the 1980s. His old house was for sale. They were amazed to learn that the price was $10,000 higher because it had once been the home of a famous writer.[27] Now Wallace again tried to lure him, advertising that "it's awfully pretty here now—60s, clear, sunny, every kind of floral scent known to Linnaeus floating around."

Over the next few months Wallace fell back into his routines. He would get up and go to a 7:15 sobriety meeting, then come back and work, next go to a gym to work out. Seeing the size of Big Craig and the other men in Granada House had made him serious about weight lifting: he now drank a protein shake every morning with raw egg in it, which he called his "breakfast vomit."[28] In the evening there was another sobriety meeting and then he would go back to work, altering and typing into his old computer what he'd written in the morning. This arrangement brought out his best writing, he felt, because the process of writing by hand and then transcribing forced his brain to wait for his hands. When he tried composing directly on a PC, it felt wrong.[29]

The work moving forward again, Wallace discovered that his tiny apartment felt just right, a counterpart to the bungalow in Tucson and his senior single at Amherst, places where he didn't feel his ass in the chair. He had gotten hold of the silver velour recliner and put it in the living room. He piled his books and papers on his bed. To sleep he moved them to the floor. He was so happy he sent Franzen pictures of his narrow slice of paradise.

For evening company, there was, by August, Mary, with whom a relationship had finally begun in earnest. "The Era of Skulking seems to be drawing to a close!" Wallace told Spark, reporting that Karr's estranged husband had begun seeing someone. They would watch action movies together at night, both loving, as Karr told a later interviewer, "movies where shit blew up." They worked out together and played tennis. Karr cooked for both of them and for her students. They read books out loud to each other and exchanged drafts (Karr was working on *The Liar's Club* and he poached material from her life.) This was their happiest time. They went to her twentieth high school reunion in Texas and "had big big fun," Wallace told Spark. Wallace even was willing to dance, though only to the slow music.

But no sooner were he and Karr finally a couple than problems emerged. By the fall he was mad at her for never quite integrating him into her family; she was mad at him for never thinking about anyone's needs but his own. He responded with more protestations of love, writing from around the corner, as she remembered. "I want you to know that I AM here," he wrote her, "I AM with you. . . . Mary, I am going nowhere but to you if you will have me. As you move closer to being available to me . . . I become more, not less, devoted to you and to my love for you and to my desire to have a life with you if you want me."

He went on in loving quasi-complaint:

What I feel is that I'll find no other woman whom I love this way, who makes my nervous system shimmy and Poor Old say Sig Heil as you do, who makes me laugh as belly-deep, who teaches me in so many ways she doesn't know—as people who are real to each other teach each other, without intent or agenda—with whom I disagree in such interesting ways.

Wallace turned to his recovery groups for companionship. His sponsor, a garrulous older real estate investor with, as others remember, a spectacular sock collection, was there to give him counsel. Mostly Wallace talked to him about Karr and their unhappy relationship. "I had the impression of hurling things," the man remembers; "you could not please Mary." He invited Wallace to join a men's group he was involved in, which Wallace nicknamed "the catacombs." They would meet at different members' houses each week, and when they got to Wallace's they sat amid the tower of manuscript pages and piles of books. He told them he had always looked on how to get women into bed as "a physics problem"; Mary, though, obeyed no law he understood.

That fall Mark Leyner was invited to Syracuse as part of a reading series at the university. Leyner was at the height of his celebrity. He had just published *Et Tu, Babe* and been on the cover of the *New York Times Magazine*, where he had been surprised to find Wallace, with whom he had previously been friendly, call him "a kind of antichrist." Now he smoothly worked his way through his material to the large crowd. As he riffed, he bobbed back and forth like a boxer, or the writer of the moment he was. He singled Wallace's fiction out for praise but then made fun of alcoholism and said that people who wore bandanas reminded him of the cabin boys on *The Love Boat*. He insisted that the goal of writers was "to entertain," if "in a very unique way." At the very end, a hand came up from the back row: it was Wallace, scruffy, in a bandana. "Is it sufficient to entertain people as spectacularly as you have," he asked now, in his thin voice, "or should there be a further moral purpose to your work?" Leyner replied that he felt entertainment was itself a moral goal and mentioned the well-known moment in

Preston Sturges's *Sullivan's Travels* in which a Mickey Mouse cartoon helps convicts forget their hard lives for a moment. Wallace clearly wasn't satisfied with Leyner's answer—to give addicts more of the drug wasn't to cure them—but time was up. Karr drove Leyner to the train station. Wallace, along for the ride, seemed to him grateful to be in her presence.

Ever since Boston, Wallace had been seeing therapists. Unsurprisingly, during these sessions his attention came to rest on his mother. Sometime in therapy he became certain that his mother had been abused as a child by her father. As he understood it, she had repressed the memory of the transgression and thus repression and control had become her way of dealing with the world, including the problems in her marriage. From this Wallace grew convinced, as he wrote Karr, that his mother's hidden life— "so much hidden pain and lying"—was key to understanding his own situation. Her insistence that all was well, her desire to protect him, he believed, had set the stage for the denial of his own pain that lay behind his drug use and alcoholism. The link was so clear, he wrote Karr, that his mother might just as well have taught him "how to bartend and de-seed dope." Once her story was unearthed, the healing might begin. The truth hurt, he wrote Karr, but, he was convinced, "it heals too."

Wallace had entered therapy with some trepidation. He was not from a culture that routinely dug up past upsets. But Karr had encouraged him in his investigations,[30] and by the time that he left for Syracuse he had blossomed into a committed therapand, as eager to ferret out the roots of his personal malaise as he'd once been to crack logical paradoxes. He went to group therapy and also had a private therapist, whom he paid cash because he had no health insurance. His hope was that his background or upbringing might at least partly explain his depressions and addictions. Yes, he had a chemical imbalance, but why? What had happened to make him into this anxious, agitated, and needy thirty-year-old?

He wrote some speculations in the margins of Alice Miller's *The Drama of the Gifted Child*, a book Karr gave him. He recognized himself in Miller's description of the unhappy, talented child. "Ouch" and "Gulp," he speckled in the margins. After Miller wrote:

As soon as the child is regarded as a possession for which one has a particular goal, as soon as one exerts control over him, his vital growth will be violently interrupted.

Wallace penciled "SFW," his mother's initials. (Inadvertently proving her reach, next to the word "effect" in the same paragraph, he wrote, "s/b [should be] affect.") He ascribed his current predicament to having a "narcissistically-deprived Mom." There is an intemperateness to Wallace's explorations of his childhood here, the anger he felt at his mother's supposed obfuscations unleashed again as he discovers his own—but then he had come to believe the one had led directly to the other.

He read John Bradshaw's *Bradshaw on the Family*, a pop bestseller on dysfunction and childhood, and where Bradshaw wrote that low-self esteem translated into "believing that your worth and happiness lie outside of you," he noted, "Writing Success Fame Sex." Wallace wanted to become the sort of person for whom desire for the last three did not motivate the first. That was one of the goals of the therapy, as it was, indirectly, of recovery. As he worked his way through his past, on the advice of a therapist he told his mother that they should stop talking, which led to an estrangement that would last on and off for some five years.

As the fall turned into a remarkably snowy winter, Wallace's relationship with Karr deteriorated further. The two fought bitterly. Karr, Wallace wrote Franzen, was prone to "terrible temper-outbursts." She found him spoiled, a mama's boy using rehab as an excuse for self-absorption. Her needs were more concrete—food, money, child care for her son. He still wrote her constantly, even though he was just around the corner. He printed out in huge letters on a computer the words "MARRY ME" and added, "No shit, Mary Karr, do not doubt my seriousness on this. Or the fact that I'm a gila-jawed bulldog once I've finally made a commitment, a promise. My expectation is not that it would be easy, or all the time pleasant. My expectation is that it would be real, and illuminated." Karr knew it would not work out, she remembers, when one day she asked Wallace to pick up Dev from school and Wallace said he needed his car to go to the gym instead. Thinking back on all his failed relationships, in the margin of *Bradshaw* he blamed them on his "fantasy bond" with his mother.

*   *   *

In April 1992, Nadell submitted the first 250 pages of Wallace's novel— "structurally . . . not much like any other novels I've seen," as Wallace had written in his cover letter—to Howard at Norton. The submission contained the major lines of the novel—the Incandenza family, Gately and Ennet House, and the plot to find the master copy of "Infinite Jest," a movie so absorbing that watching it could kill you. In a country addicted to television, it would be the ultimate weapon, an entertainment neutron bomb. The novel was set in the near future but no reader could mistake it for anything other than a commentary on the present day. Reading the manuscript, Howard was amazed by the changes he saw in his author's writing. Wallace had gone from a clever writer to a profound one, from one with lots of ways to say little to one with one way to say something important. He now saw Wallace's addiction, descent, and recovery as "a ceremony of purification." He was eager to publish the new work, but Norton was a conservative house. Its taste was mainstream (it would soon have a huge success with Patrick O'Brian, the purveyor of seafaring tales), and did not put out much in the way of avant-garde writing—*Girl with Curious Hair* was an exception, but it had sold only twenty-two hundred hardcover copies. Howard went to his editorial board and asked how much he might offer. They authorized him to pay an advance of $35,000. Wallace calculated what would be left to live on after expenses and his agent's commission. He was taking the psychic risk of asking for an advance so he could write without teaching, but $5,000–$6,000 a year wouldn't do it.

Nadell quickly found another bidder, Michael Pietsch, an editor at Little, Brown, who in June 1992 bought the book for $80,000. Pietsch had worked with other innovative writers like Rick Moody and had been quietly supportive of Wallace's work when few were—when Wallace had just graduated from Arizona he had tried to help him place some stories in magazines. Pietsch told Nadell he wanted to publish *Infinite Jest* "more than I want to breathe." Wallace wrote Pietsch to accept his offer, citing his "gut instinct (I have so few gut instincts I am reverent when one manifests)." He thanked him for advancing enough money that he could "get health insurance and fix my car if it breaks and buy books so I can mark them up."

Wallace avoided confrontation with authority figures, so it is a testimony to his faith in his judgment this time that he now wrote Howard with frankness, assuring the editor who had been through so much with him that his decision to sign with Little, Brown was not "a . . . go-for-the-gold-type pressure situation." He explained, "I not only wanted to quit dicking around with teaching and try to be a professional writer, but also wanted to try to live like a grown-up while I did so. . . . If that compromise seems venal or ungrateful," he added, "so be it." He said he was "qualmless" but finished on a more conciliatory point for the editor who had meant so much to him:

> You have believed in me and supported me and given me good counsel and good faith at every turn; you are more important to me than I bet you could believe.

With Pietsch, Wallace had some immediate damage control to do: his new editor also edited Leyner. How to tell him that in his essay on television, still forthcoming, he spent a half dozen pages flaying one of Pietsch's best-known writers? *Harper's* and he had finally agreed that the television piece was wrong for the magazine, but Steve Moore had picked it up for the *Review of Contemporary Fiction* and, titled "E Unibus Pluram" ("Out of One, Many"), it was to come out the next summer. Wallace wrote to his new editor to explain what he found missing in Leyner's writing, almost as if writing a review of his earlier self:

> Brains and wit and technical tightrope-calisthenics are powerful tools in fiction, but I believe that when they're used primarily to keep the reader at arm's length they're being abused—they are functioning as defense mechanisms. Leyner is a hidden writer, as so many exhibitionists and actors and comedians and intellectuals are hidden. I do not wish to be a hidden person, or a hidden writer: it is lonely.

He promised Pietsch that *Infinite Jest* would supply the element missing in Leyner's work, would make, as he'd written about *Wittgenstein's Mistress*, "the head throb heartlike":

I want to improve as a writer, and I want to author things that both restructure worlds and make living people feel stuff, and my gut tells me you can help me.

As an editor, Pietsch was used to being *in loco parentis*; he felt no need to take sides. He responded, "My notion about Mark Leyner is that he doesn't feel any compulsion to do more in his work than entertain, surprise, and dazzle. . . . It's fine to want more from a book but that doesn't lessen the legitimacy of his accomplishment." But he added, "All that notwithstanding, it was with delight I read of your intention to pursue selves and stories."

Wallace returned to work. "I am both bogged down and forging ahead on the Project, if that's coherent," he wrote Franzen in September. "Word on the streets is that fall here is beautiful but very brief: snows swirl by Halloween." He worried what winter would be like, though on the plus side his apartment was so small that his body heat or "at the very outside one space heater is apt to warm the whole facility." To escape the town he had taken to calling "Drearacuse," he sometimes drove to New York for the weekend and stayed with Costello. He would make an arrangement to meet a young woman for coffee and then, as Costello remembers, come back Sunday night and get his bag.

Other than women and his old friend, New York held little interest for Wallace. ("My whole nervous system seems to be on the outside of my body when I'm in NYC," he would later protest to Alice Turner.) One exception was a community garden on Avenue B and 6th Street in the East Village, near where Costello lived. There a street sculptor was engaged in building a monument called the "Tower of Toys." Homeless and barefoot, the sculptor would climb up and nail or attach yet one more plank or pole. While he watched the seemingly endless project, Wallace would complain to Costello about Karr.

In the spring of 1993 Wallace got an unexpected job offer. The English department at Illinois State University in Bloomington-Normal, about an hour from where he had grown up, was hiring. The school was an oddity, a large public college with an interest in avant-garde fiction. The English department ran something called the Unit for Contemporary Literature,[31] under which auspices it hosted the *Review of Contemporary Fiction* and the Dalkey Archive Press, the publisher of *Wittgenstein's Mistress*. When he had heard of the job opening, Steve Moore had contacted Wallace. Wallace had promised himself not to teach while he finished *Infinite Jest*, but he had been writing the manuscript steadily and successfully. So in bandana and boots, he went for a brief interview at the MLA conference in New York in December 1992. He was unusually self-confident, perhaps buoyed by a sense that *Infinite Jest* was on target. "You should know I am really really smart," he told the English department members who met him. He sent a résumé with his publications and on the second page added entries for "REVIEWS IF ANYBODY CARES . . ." and "PRIZES &c (IF ANYBODY CARES . . .)." In February he flew to Illinois for two days of interviews and readings. To a small group of faculty and students he read the Don Gately crime scene and a section about Lyle, the guru who haunts the Enfield Academy weight room licking sweat off the players and dispensing advice in return. During a question-and-answer session, when a faculty member asked why they should hire him, he responded, "Who else?" Then the faculty committee went out with him to a local Chinese restaurant, where he told the department chair, Charlie Harris, a Barth expert, that Barth was dead.

By now the department was getting the idea that this was not the same author who had written *Girl with Curious Hair*, but they did not mind, it seemed. They found Wallace stunningly smart and committed. In "E Unibus Pluram," Wallace quoted Emerson that once or twice in a lifetime one met a man who "carries the holiday in his eye." Wallace seemed to them such a person.

Good as the visit was, Wallace still did not expect to get the job. "I alert you in advance," he had joked in a note to Harris when he first applied, "that I am both caucasian and male." The department was under pressure to hire more women, but everyone was deeply impressed with Wallace. They did not know what had happened in Arizona or Amherst or Boston, though Wallace's fragmented teaching history must surely have suggested problems in the past. "What we wanted was the writer," remembers Curtis White, a professor in the department who had helped organize the Unit for Contemporary Literature. "We hoped for the best on the rest of it."

Wallace wanted the job as much as ISU seemed to want him to have it; he was ripe to go somewhere. He had been working at maximum speed. Fiction wasn't the problem, for once. "Full-time writing is going OK volume-wise," he wrote Debra Spark at the time, "but I find the isolation and lack of contact with people awfully hard to take." He explained, "Things are sad here. Mary and I have agreed, not as amicably as one might wish, that we do not work as a couple. . . . We are both angry at one another, though in my case the anger's just about been replaced by a very dark sadness. She was my best friend in the world, and we both gave up a lot and worked very hard to try to make this work." One night Wallace tried to push Karr from a moving car. Soon afterward, he got so mad at her that he threw her coffee table at her. He sent her $100 for the remnants. She had a friend who was a lawyer write back to say she still owned the table, all he'd bought was the "brokenness."

Portions of *Infinite Jest* were beginning to appear in literary magazines. "Three Protrusions," the excerpt in which Ken Erdedy waits for his pot, had been the first in a widely read one, appearing in *Grand Street* in the spring of 1992. It was a virtuoso, voicy story, not dissimilar in style to Wallace's earlier work. A year later, a more intriguing excerpt about Ennet House appeared in *Conjunctions*, in its "Unfinished Business" issue. Wallace wrote a preface assuring readers his would not remain so: "NYC guys in serious business suits have paid $ for something they're legally entitled to by 1/1/94." Aware that he had an opportunity to introduce a different David Foster Wallace, a writer with deeper goals and purer motivations, he continued:

Under fun's new administration, writing fiction becomes a way to go deep inside yourself and illuminate precisely the stuff you don't want to see or let anyone else see, and this stuff turns out (paradoxically) to be precisely the stuff all writers and readers everywhere share and respond to, feel. Fiction becomes a weird way to countenance yourself and to tell the truth instead of being a way to escape yourself or present yourself in a way you figure you will be maximally likable.

The fifty pages that followed were a kaleidoscope of first-person testimonials—stories of "hitting bottom"—lifted from Alcoholics Anonymous meetings, with rummies and meth heads taking over a fictional world where, since he began tearing through his senior thesis, no one had ever known pain deeper than a breakup before. Gately made his appearance too, another new kind of character for Wallace:

> And that was the first night that cynical Gately willingly took the basic suggestion to get down on his big knees by his undersized Ennet House bunk and ask for help from something he still didn't believe in, ask for his own sick spidered will to be taken from him and fumigated and squished.

The response to the *Conjunctions* publication was highly favorable. "Fun's new administration" was finding Wallace readers. And as the *Conjunctions* excerpt appeared, Illinois State had written to offer Wallace a job that would lead to tenure. Wallace was thrilled, even more so when Charlie Harris agreed to let him teach just two classes a semester. The arrangement was so generous that Wallace immediately worried it wouldn't last. He had visions of a replacement department head "upping it to three or four and you being in Burma or something" on sabbatical. Could he get, he asked Harris, kind of joking, a letter "preferably notarized by at least an appellate-level jurist" confirming the arrangement? Harris promised him it was forthcoming.

Despite, as he wrote to Don DeLillo, with whom he had struck up a correspondence with the encouragement of Franzen, "a certain icky sense about availing myself of academic patronage," he felt he had made a good decision.[32] It did not bother him overmuch that, as he wrote Washington, he would be "the least weird writer there." He explained to Dale Peterson at Amherst, "The chairman is a dreamboat, everybody seems at once passionate and low-ego about teaching writing, and there was an utter absence of the Machiavellian politics that made Arizona such a gnarly place to be. . . . If I do not like teaching at ISU," he explained, "I won't like it anywhere, and I can retire from the field assured that I've experienced academia at its nicest."

CHAPTER 6

"Unalone and Unstressed"

In July 1993 the director of the Dalkey Archive, John O'Brien, and his son, met Wallace in front of his new house on North Fell Avenue in Bloomington. The two groaned as they carried Wallace's weights up the stairs. Wallace had rented the house sight unseen from one of the members of the search committee. It turned out to be pretty, with a fireplace and a screened-in porch, opposite a park. Wallace brought his silver velour recliner, put a spit can nearby, and papered the bathroom with manuscript pages from *Infinite Jest*, tennis competition charts, and an adult diaper wrapper.[1]

Returning to the Midwest brought mixed feelings for the thirty-one-year-old writer. He was particularly wary about being so close to his mother while he was fictionalizing her in his novel. He was drawing her as the lens of therapy had revealed her to him. Avril Incandenza is the seductive puppetmaster of Enfield Tennis Academy. When she speaks, Wallace wrote, everyone inclines their heads to her "very subtly and slightly, like heliotropes."

And Wallace missed Karr. He had spent the last few months of his time in Syracuse mostly in exile, anxious he'd have to be recording the arrival and departure of "different masculine-model cars" in front of her house, as he wrote Corey Washington in March. He had brought her with him though as a character in his book. Joelle Van Dyne, also known as Madame Psychosis, is a radio show host and drug addict in recovery at Ennet House, a woman who keeps her face veiled either because it is hideously disfigured or because she is so beautiful that every man who sees it falls in love with her. She stars in "Infinite Jest," the lethal video cartridge.

Predictably, Wallace worried about going back to teaching. He had been writing at an unequaled pace for two years and feared the change to his routine. But he was also an adult now, a man three and a half years sober with a job and a house and an advance for the book he was well under way with. That's what it meant to live under the new administration of fun: no more irony and distance, commitment not spectation (a favorite word of his), *involvement*. And even, where possible, the hope of redemption. "Really good fiction could have as dark a worldview as it wished," he told Larry McCaffery in the *Review of Contemporary Fiction* interview, which came out just as he arrived in Bloomington, "but it'd find a way both to depict this world and to illuminate the possibilities for being alive and human in it." The writer's job was to give "CPR to those elements of what's human and magical that still live and glow despite the times' darkness." He added, "Fiction's about what it is to be a fucking human being." Wallace had always preferred certainty to unclarity, passion to incrementalism, and now he was a full-fledged apostle of sincerity. He had no tolerance for the person he was and gave no quarter to writers whom he thought were like the writer he used to be. When Steve Moore wrote him to recommend a novel he was publishing, praising its "sardonic worldview perfect for the irony-filled nineties," Wallace shot back that this was "like saying 'a kerosen[e]-filled fire extinguisher perfect for the blazing housefire.'"

Wallace was particularly allergic to those who dreamt of fame instead of achievement. He took every opportunity to point out to young writers the snares of the sort of early success he had had. He wrote Washington that whenever younger people asked him how to become an author his reaction was to be "polite and banal." He pointed out, "The obvious fact that the kids don't Want to Write so much as Want to Be Writers makes their letters so depressing." To one such inquirer, a young man in his early twenties, he gave some unbending advice: "Take this time to learn to be your own toughest critic and best friend. . . . I wish I had. . . . Concentrate on the work, loving it and hating it and making it the best and truest expression of yourself it can be; the publishing stuff will come." He added, "I'm mostly saying this to myself at 22, 23." When Washington asked him if he himself had a swelled head, Wallace demurred: "Even a marginal soap-opera actor receives exponentially more mail than Bellow, I'm sure.

And I'm no Bellow," adding by hand "(yet!)," then a trademark smiley face
to deflate his own boast. He went on:

> I did, very briefly, at an artist colony called Yaddo in 1987, meeting
> McInerney and some of the other celebs, get a big head and believe
> for a few months that I was destined for celebrity, Letterman ap-
> pearances. Etc. The rather brutal intervening years have taught me
> that, though there's nothing de facto wrong with that stuff, it's not
> for me, simply because it's low-calorie and unstimulating and also
> highly narcotic. McInerney's big job now is acting as a custodian for
> the statue of himself that celebrity has constructed.

Alone in the summer heat of the Illinois flatlands, Wallace tried to make
life as much like Syracuse as he could. He found tennis courts, a gym, a
therapist, and a substance abuse recovery group. The group Wallace liked
met in a church on Oakland Avenue at noon. It was made up mostly of
working-class people. He was a surprise to them. When he walked in for
the first time, in his torn T-shirt, work boots, and bandana, several members took him for homeless. Soon he had become a literal fixture there—he
took the same seat at every meeting. The members loved the way he
talked—for many he was the most articulate person they had ever met—
and felt his elaborate, run-on narratives of the daily battle to maintain the
equanimity that kept him sober expressed what they were thinking, only
better. As ever, it fell to them to tell him not to live so much in his head.
They made fun of him for being too analytical and offered him slogans like
"Keep It Simple" and "Be Nice to Myself" and "Stop Trying to Figure Everything Out." For God, they'd suggest, he should just substitute "Good Orderly Direction." "A grateful heart will never drink," they might add. The
banality of the responses maddened Wallace, but here he was drug- and
alcohol-free after almost four years, thanks to people like them. "It starts to
turn out that the vapider the AA cliché, the sharper the canines of the real
truth it covers," he would write in *Infinite Jest*. "I don't know how recovery
works," he would tell friends, "but it works." He was always available to help
other members with both spiritual and practical questions, rewriting their
job applications or professional correspondence. He attended a second recovery meeting at the Lighthouse Institute, where he sponsored addicts

who had been ordered by courts to attend a recovery program. It came under the rubric of "pay it forward" that he had learned at Granada House: if you help someone, when you need help someone will be there for you too.

The other members began looking after him in turn. They saw him—and he played to this—as a sort of holy fool. A former judge started giving Wallace his cast-off clothes. The daughter of another recovery member brushed Wallace's long, unruly hair (he refused her offer of conditioner). If his computer crashed, someone from recovery came and rescued his files. Familyless, he was adoptable—one couple hung a stocking for him every Christmas. Wallace went through a number of sponsors until he found one he liked, a man who had entered the program after falling out of a tree while high. The accident had broken his back, made it necessary for him to use two metal canes. He was incontinent and had to go to the "john," Wallace wrote a friend in a later letter, "like every fifteen minutes." But Wallace used him to tamp down his own self-absorption. "He's extremely helpful," he explained, "as just a plain nonverbal model of what Real problems are when I think I've got Problems."

Since junior year of college, Wallace had never been without a girlfriend for very long. These women filled an important gap in his life. They were the clock by which he noted time's passing and the mirror in which he examined his character. When he was having problems with Karr back in Syracuse, for instance, he had written to Franzen, "I'm having to countenance the fact that I just may be constitutionally unable to sustain an intimate connection with a girl, which means I'm either terribly shallow or mentally ill or both."

As the summer wore on, Wallace was still getting his ex out of his system. His male friends in Syracuse had been enormously relieved when ISU had offered him a job; to them the Karr relationship seemed wholly dysfunctional. "Run for your life," his sponsor, John F., remembers telling him. He now affected to have left Karr behind in letters to friends. "Unpacking, trying to write, chasing tail," he boasted to Morrow, summarizing his activities his first summer in Illinois. But in fact several months after arriving many of his thoughts were still of Karr; he bought her expensive lingerie and perfume and mailed it anonymously. He even bought the right to name a star after her. He wrote in a notebook, "Now she's in the sky and a little bit of her will always be overhead." He sent her the box with the certificate. Around the same time, he wrote a Syracuse friend that he was "off sex" and promised himself he would never be in such a poisonous relationship again. "I won't sleep with anybody who lives far away anymore," he wrote her, "whom I can't be with—I hope—from now on."

Fortunately, his department head, Charlie Harris, and Harris's wife, Victoria, also a professor of English at ISU, stepped in. Victoria had their twenty-four-year-old daughter Kymberly in mind for Wallace. Kymberly was an actress and aspiring playwright who lived in Chicago. On Wallace's first visit Victoria had shown him her picture. "Isn't she beautiful?" she'd said. "You should marry her." The two began corresponding, and soon Harris, leaving behind personal problems in Chicago, had moved home. Wallace and her mother invited her out the next day to a movie. He chose *Jurassic Park*. The three went to downtown Normal's theater to watch the blockbuster. Wallace was, as ever, also doing research. Steven Spielberg, the movie's director, was someone Wallace had always been interested in. Though he'd seen the movie twice before in Syracuse, he enjoyed it again, getting, as he would say, his "dose." Kymberly, on the other hand, had been so bored she'd walked out. Afterward, they went to the Gallery, a club where Wallace refused to join her on the dance floor. Despite their differences the two began hanging out; Wallace gave her sections of *Infinite Jest* to woo her, and soon they were a couple. In the empty Midwest, she felt, he was the most interesting man she knew; Wallace enjoyed her vibrancy and physicality.

Both in therapy, they spent a lot of their time discussing their painful pasts and how they had come to be the way they were—a catalog of ex-lovers and family, with Wallace focused on Karr and his mother. They talked about wanting community and children. Kymberly was astonished at the intense way Wallace listened. He had become interested in Buddhism through a woman he met in Syracuse and gave Kymberly works on the religion that had been suggested to him, plus the Big Book. One day Victoria Harris found them deep in conversation on the couch in the Harrises' living room. "Stop talking about your relationship and start having it!" she admonished them.

*   *   *

Michael Pietsch read the portion of *Infinite Jest* that Wallace sent as soon as he got it in May 1993. He made his way through the 750 pages Wallace had mailed off and responded just as Wallace was getting ready to leave Syracuse. His letter was remarkably insightful, given how little time he'd been able to spend thinking about the partial manuscript of a very complicated book:

> You ask what I think it's about. Since it's not all here my answer to that (and all my suggestions) will have to be tentative. . . . It's a novel made up out of shards, almost as if the story were something broken that someone is picking up the pieces of. This fits with the broken lives the novel's about; also as a way of recreating two worlds, the halfway house and the tennis academy. . . . [O]ccasionally there surfaces through the stories an "I" who may be the one trying to put everything together.

Pietsch wrote Wallace that he was "seriously loving being inside" the "huge roiling story about addiction and recovery, their culture and language and characters, the hidden world that's revealed when people come in and tell their stories." But he also saw a major problem on the horizon: length. Good as it was, the book was on its way to being too long. Wallace had tried to trick him with narrow margins and a tiny font in sending the first 400,000 words, but Pietsch had pulled out a calculator and tallied that if what he had on his desk was two-thirds of the finished book, *Infinite Jest* would be twelve hundred pages, at the least. He doubted the marketability of such a tome. "This should not," he lectured Wallace, "be a $30 novel so thick readers feel they have to clear their calendars for a month before they buy it." He urged Wallace to "try cutting now," even while he finished his story. His other major editorial worry related to the physics of reading. The fragmentary structure of the book—three plot strands that seemed to come to the fore and then recede without pattern—was a lot. A little structural innovation was enriching, but too much and you lost the reader entirely. This was a harder problem for Wallace to solve, because the book consistently confounded the reader's expectations on purpose. If reality was fragmented, his book should be too. It was also in keeping with Wallace's insistence that the story not be so amusing that it re-create the disease he was diagnosing. It must not hook readers too easily, must not allow them to fall into the literary equivalent of "spectation." *Infinite Jest* had to be, as he subtitled it, "a failed entertainment." To the extent the novel was addictive, it should be self-consciously addictive. That was one reason he'd structured the story like a Sierpinski gasket, a geometrical figure that can be subdivided into an infinite number of identical geometrical figures. The shape of the book—following Wallace's natural cast of mind—was recursive, nested. Big things—*Infinite Jest*, a novel you keep having to reread to understand—find their counterpart in smaller things: "Infinite Jest," the video cartridge, which itself plays in an endless loop. One character fears she is blind, so she never opens her eyes. Another has an answering machine message that is like one of those infinite man-holding-a-book-whose-cover-is-the-man-holding-a-book visual regressions: "This is Mike Pemulis's answering machine's answering machine." The effect is to emphasize the characters' isolation, their lives in a funhouse that isn't all that fun. As in *Broom*, the apparent casualness of the structure was intensely thought through.

What Pietsch found most off-putting was the political overlay Wallace had given the book centering on the attempts by Quebecois terrorist groups to wrest back their province from O.N.A.N. "Almost everything that matters emotionally works without reference to the time frame or the interAmerican huggermugger," Pietsch noted, wondering about the necessity of what he called "the ornately bizarre-to-goofy superstructure" of the book. He warned, "the dog is awfully shaggy already." The letter left Wallace upset and unsatisfied. "He seemed to agree with most of it, glumly," Pietsch scribbled on a copy of the letter he later sent to Nadell.

Wallace had not been waiting for Pietsch's response to resume writing. By the time he left for Illinois in July 1993, as he later told an interviewer, he had reached the scene in which Gately is shot protecting his charges at Ennet House, nearly three-quarters of the way through the story. Likely Wallace had more in rougher form. But the combination of the memo and the move to Illinois deflated him. He was home in Illinois again, or nearly, and near home he often found his momentum dissipating. He spent many summer days staring at the ceiling of his new home. He asked a friend from Syracuse to call him every night to make sure he had written, hoping that guilt would spur him to productivity, but the trick did not work.

Wallace had been stumped in a similar way when he moved to Syracuse, and he drew again on the patience and endurance he had learned in recovery to try to get past the roadblock. But as he was settling down to get back to work, a distracting nonfiction project came his way. The editors at *Harper's* were longtime fans of his writing. In 1991, they had published "Tennis, Trigonometry, Tornadoes," his fanciful remembrance of his high school sports life, and, a year later, an adept parody of John Updike's Rabbit books called "Rabbit Resurrected." Updike had been an early love of Wallace's, before he had awoken to literature, and even now he was stunned by the grace and ease with which Updike wrote. But as he'd changed his attitude toward his own work he had reconceived of Updike as part of the American problem, and of Rabbit Angstrom, his principal character, as symptomatic of the prison of self-absorption and egoism that afflicted so many Americans. There was nothing outside his priapic neediness. Rabbit had died in the fourth installment in the series, *Rabbit at Rest*, published in 1990. Wallace imagined the next chapter in the pages of *Harper's*, resurrecting Rabbit into "a solipsist's heaven, full of his own dead perceptions." Rabbit asks, "Would there be vaginas, where he was going, vaginas finally freed from the shrill silly vessels around them, bodiless, pungent, and rubicund, swaddled in angelic linen . . . the odd breast or two, detached, obliging?"

Despite not having taken his television essay, the *Harper's* editors were again on the lookout for assignments to give Wallace. So, soon after they learned he was returning to the Midwest, they asked him if he wanted to go to the state fair. The fair was a massive event, with thousands of booths and tens of thousands of visitors attending its 4H shows, dance competitions, and junior boxing tournaments. Wallace hesitated. He worried that he had never done reporting—to his mind the failed pornography piece no longer counted. But he was intrigued too, eager to make some money, and happy for the chance to escape his own head and see a different side of his native region.

Wallace cast around for someone to go with him, asking Costello, Charlie and Victoria Harris, and in the end chose their daughter, whom he then barely knew. In August, in the sweltering Midwest summer heat, he and Kymberley drove to Springfield, the state capital. At the fair, they visited the Horse Complex and the Swine Barn, and then went on to the amusement ride section. Harris took a ride called the Zipper, a steel cage that spun at the end of a long elevated arm. Wallace was not thrilled to watch his new friend get lifted away, and was thoroughly mortified when the ride operators—he called them "carnies"—kept flipping the cage around to make Harris's skirt fall up. When they finally brought her back to earth, Wallace was furious. He wanted to press charges. Harris told him it was no big deal, but Wallace remained upset. Harris went home the next day, and Wallace continued his reporting. He chatted with the local evangelists and watched a car race without interest ("Certain cars pass other cars, and some people cheer when they do"). A dance competition touched him more deeply, when he saw how sincere was the pleasure the ordinary midwestern couples took in it, a moment worthy of *Sullivan's Travels*.

Back home in Bloomington, surrounded by his *Infinite Jest* research material, he sat down to try to organize his notes. He put a layer of myth over his experience. In Wallace's telling, the Illinois fair grew increasingly Boschian as the days went on. Drawing on his gift for comic exaggeration and not particularly worried by veracity, by the end, bald men farted as they arm-wrestled, vomit spewed from the mouths of patrons being spun in the Ring of Fire, and, at the "Illinois State Jr. Baton-Twirling Finals," the insanity reaches a kind of climax as

a dad standing up near the top of the stands with a Toshiba video camera to his eye takes a tomahawking baton directly in the groin and falls over on somebody eating a funnel cake, and they take out good bits of several rows below them.

Harris became an old heartthrob, someone who "worked detasseling summer corn with me in high school." She was in real life neither "a Native Companion," as Wallace called her in the article, nor a graduate of Urbana High—that was more Susie Perkins or his sister. And when it was time for Native Companion to speak, Wallace gave Harris the voice of the woman whose star still twinkled over his head. "Oh for fuck's sake," Native Companion reproofs the upset Wallace after being exposed during the Zipper ride, "it was fun—son of a bitch spun that car *sixteen* times. . . . Buy me some pork skins, you dipshit."

Wallace took pleasure in writing the piece. For him, the challenge in nonfiction was always what to leave out, but the state fair was a subject with natural boundaries and one that invited a light style that moved to bigger, more serious questions: What made Americans so obsessed with entertainment? Could whatever void they were trying to plug ever be filled? It helped that at the fair the people were gluttons and the animals miserable. It was another chance to assert the thesis of *Infinite Jest*, to anatomize the unending American quest for distraction, the failure of his countryman, as Remy Marathe, the Quebecois terrorist agent,[2] says in *Infinite Jest*, "Choose with care. You are what you love. No?"[3]

Shortly after, Wallace sent in his long draft, several times the possible length of the piece. Colin Harrison, the editor, set to work cutting with Wallace. The process reminded Harrison of a game of tennis, the prospective edits turning into "here's-what-I-think, what-do-you-think rallies that sometimes went on for many minutes," as he wrote in a remembrance, and ended with a cut accepted or partially accepted or traded off for a cut somewhere else. Wallace was strategic and aggressive, but when he lost a point, he moved on. Together they shortened the piece almost by half. Harrison, an experienced editor, was aware that Wallace sometimes embellished. At one point, he asked Wallace if a vial of crack that Wallace reported had fallen out of the pocket of a young man on the Zipper had really "direct-hit a state trooper alertly eating a Lemon Push-Up on the midway below." Wallace was coy. "I'm going to give you this one," Harrison remembers saying. He wanted Wallace to pursue his comic vision. "I drank the Kool-Aid," he recalls. So if Wallace wrote it, it aided the narrative energy, and could not be disproven when the piece was fact-checked, it could run.[4, 5]

The article, which came out the next July, also unveiled a new Wallace to readers, neither the creator of elaborate fictional worlds nor the Cavellian essayist but someone more of a piece with the characters in his fiction. At one point, Wallace describes being too afraid to go into the Poultry Building, explaining that as a child he had once been attacked by a chicken "without provocation, flown at and pecked by a renegade fowl, savagely, just under the right eye." The story was likely made up, but its exaggerated stance toward the traumas of childhood captured something readers began to want from him. They, too, this affluent and confused generation, had felt the large reverberations inherent in small events. That Wallace was a slightly more neurotic version of his reader helped forge a bond, a bond that would carry over when he published his very big novel.

For the fall 1993 semester, Wallace was assigned a fiction workshop for undergraduates and another for more advanced writers, mostly graduate students. He taught around thirty pupils in all. He gave his classes in Stevenson Hall, a midcentury building that hummed with overhead lights. Claiming that his time as a security guard at Lotus had made fluorescent lighting unbearable for him, he asked his students to bring in lamps, creating a cocktail lounge atmosphere in the classroom. Then, with the excuse that there were not enough plugs for them, he moved the class to his home, where the students made themselves comfortable amid *The Compendium of Drug Therapy* and *Psychiatric Nursing* and wondered at the junior circuit tennis championship chart on his wall. In his bandana and untied work boots, a cup at hand to spit into, he was like no professor they had ever met. During smoking breaks, he would go to the bathroom and brush his teeth.

Wallace's informal, rule-bending appearance was misleading. He had revived as a teacher since Emerson, just as he had revived as a writer, and ran his class tightly, a pedagogic hardass. He penalized for lateness and for absence and grammar and spelling errors, trying to wean a lazy generation from dangling participles and subject/verb disagreements. "Don't give your talent the finger," he would tell the students. For tricky grammar questions, he would step out of his office and call his mother—even when they were supposedly not speaking, they could speak about this.

In his undergraduate class, Wallace was kind to the clueless but cruel to anyone with pretensions. When a student claimed that her sentences were "pretty," he scribbled lines from her manuscript on the blackboard and challenged, "Which of you thinks this is pretty? Is *this* pretty? And *this*?" He continued to battle any young man who reminded him of his younger self. When one student wowed his classmates with a voicy, ironic short story, he took him outside the classroom and told him he had "never witnessed a collective dick-sucking like that before." Wallace promised to prevent the "erection of an ego-machine" and strafed the student with criticism for the rest of the semester. The young man, Ben Slotky, found it odd that Wallace kept inviting him to play tennis though he did not know how. Wallace took pleasure in telling undergraduates who expected creative writing to be a gut that they should get out before they learned they were wrong. No one could call themselves a writer, he added, until he or she had written at least fifty stories.

He asked for a high level of commitment, but he gave it too. No one worked harder. He read every story three times and marked it up with each pass—once for first impressions, a second time to evaluate how well it did as a work of fiction, and a third time as if it were about to go to press. He would append long letters of analysis and critique to even routine undergraduate efforts. And for the graduate students, many of whom had been drawn to ISU by its reputation as a safe place for theoretical fiction, the first day of class Wallace sometimes put the names of major literary theorists on the blackboard and said, "I know about all this stuff. You don't need to remind me of it." Anyone who thought he was going to champion the department's tradition soon realized he or she was wrong; his goals were traditional. The story should connect reader and writer. "Go somewhere it is difficult to get to. Try to tell about something you care about," he would say. Or, "What is at stake in this story?" he would ask, parroting just the question he'd found so irksome from the professors at Arizona almost a decade before. If a story shied away from its emotional potential, Wallace would write on their papers, "This is a skater. See me." And to those who insisted on the intellect over the heart, he'd order, "Write about a kid whose bunny died." He was making a clear statement about the purpose of fiction. If the heart throbbed, who cared what the head did?

Wallace was relieved to find he could work on *Infinite Jest* and teach at the same time. The first semester he taught he was also moving forward again on the book. As he had with Karr, he gave Kymberly Harris new sections to read and comment on. But Harris had not come to Bloomington to be a muse or literary widow; she wanted Wallace to go out with her for dinner, to see her in plays, to be available for conversation. Wallace wanted to work. They broke up, got back together, each iteration making their mutual need more intense, a pattern he knew from Walden and Karr. He closed the door and wrote; she went out without him. Yet he did not want to be as alone as this left him. Writing all day was too solitary; being with Kymberly was too much company. So Wallace adopted a rescued Labrador pup that he named Jeeves (formally, Very Good Jeeves, the name of a story collection by P. G. Wodehouse that Wallace had loved as a boy). The dog gave Wallace great pleasure. He had the run of the house, slept in Wallace's bed, and ate food out of his mouth; Wallace particularly liked a little sideways dance Jeeves did before he got his dinner. He understood that a dog was not a relationship with another person and yet he saw the advantages. Dogs didn't have acting careers; they didn't compete with you for grant money; and when you lavished love on them it made you feel good about yourself. As he would tell an interviewer after *Infinite Jest* came out, "It's just much easier having dogs. You don't get laid; but you also don't get the feeling you're hurting their feelings all the time."

But it turned out that Wallace was too busy for the demands even a canine made. Jeeves would chew on his foot while he typed, then hump the velour recliner. He would relieve himself in the living room. Harris would come over to find her $100 pairs of shoes ruined and her underwear eaten. And Jeeves's barking drove Wallace crazy; he tried to wear earplugs while he worked, then added airline headphones. He found himself unable to set limits. In some way Jeeves was an avatar of him—or of how he saw himself—ungainly, honest, quick to give his love, a rebounder from constant disappointment. Any form of discipline for Jeeves just seemed to him cruelty; he felt keenly the least whimper of pain from the animal. It was easier for him to be mean to a person than a pet.

In desperation, Wallace reached out to his friends from the university and in his recovery group. John O'Brien sent over his dog trainer, but Wallace couldn't bear to see Jeeves disciplined. His sensitivity became a joke among his friends—this was after all farm country. Finally, a retired engineer from his recovery group started taking the Lab puppy for walks in nearby Miller Park, while Wallace strove to work. Still, he complained when Jeeves came home covered with green slime from the pond there. "What am I supposed to do," he demanded, "send him through a car wash?"

Gale Walden had appeared in Illinois to look after her grandfather in Champaign, who was ill. She had also gotten a job at the *Review of Con-*

temporary Fiction. She and Wallace had barely been in touch since he had warned her away in Boston. Sometimes the two would meet now at diners, halfway between Champaign and Bloomington. They picked corn together on her grandfather's land, and she cooked it for him. A more mature friendship was emerging. She would sometimes come by his house and be amazed at the chaos—"papers, file cabinets, multiple *Harper's* magazines, toys Jeeves had torn up, and really a lot of herbal tea, which I thought was probably a female influence," she remembers. He had papered the bathroom with pages from his novel. He told Walden he was putting everything he had into it. To her he seemed happy in a new way.

As 1993 drew to a close, Wallace had nearly finished his draft. He had made some of the cuts Pietsch had suggested and he had continued to expand Don Gately's role, so that Gately was beginning to take the book over from Hal Incandenza. The change limned his own journey post-sobriety, from clever to mindful. Late in the novel, Gately is shot trying to protect his Ennet House charges and lies in a hospital, enduring the pain without morphine. In what is effectively the climactic scene of a novel without climaxes, he resists artificial pain relief with great effort:

> He could do the dextral pain the same way: Abiding. No one single instant of it was unendurable. Here was a second right here: he endured it. What was undealable-with was the thought of all the instants all lined up and stretching ahead, glittering. And the projected future fear. . . . It's too much to think about. To Abide there. But none of it's as of now real. . . . He could just hunker down in the space between each heartbeat and make each heartbeat a wall and live in there. Not let his head look over. What's unendurable is what his own head could make of it all. . . . But he could choose not to listen.

In November, Wallace returned to Boston for a panel at the Arlington Center for the Arts. The subject was the future of fiction. There were about thirty people in the audience and the host was Sven Birkerts. Birkerts and Wallace had met once since the former had given *Girl with Curious Hair* its first serious consideration, during Wallace's short stint as a student at Harvard. At the time, Birkerts had been stunned by Wallace's rapid-fire thought, enthusiasm for postmodernism, and need for cigarettes. Birkerts had also invited Franzen. To the audience, Wallace seemed the most cheerful of the three participants, the one with the most sense that successful fiction was still possible. Stranded overnight on the way home at O'Hare Airport, he wrote a long note ("HOPE THIS IS READABLE; I USED BLOCK CAPS, IN HOPES") to Birkerts, trying to explain just how much he had changed. He told Birkerts that the critic cared more for "Little Expressionless Animals" than the author did now. The note also contained an early suggestion that capturing human verities when you had Wallace's racing, recursive mind might at times be hard:

> This long thing I'm 90% done with—I wanted to make a kind of contemporary Jamesian melodrama, real edge-of-sentimentality stuff, and instead I find it buried—like parts of "L.E.A."—in Po-Mo formalities, the sort of manic patina over emotional catatonia that seems to inflict the very culture the novel's supposed to be about.[6]

He added, "I have never felt so much a failure, or so mute when it comes to articulating what I see as the way out of the ironic loop."

That fall Wallace asked Moore to look over the manuscript and see whether the cuts Pietsch had wanted in June made sense to him. He was pleased when a month later Moore responded with suggestions for more modest condensing. Even better, his ideas were, by Wallace's estimate, "80% different from Little Brown's, meaning I get to go with my gut more." Wallace's gut was that when Pietsch read all the pages he'd see better how they all fit together. He had also realized by now that he was not going to be able to get the book in by the end of the year and had apologetically asked Pietsch for an extension; there were only so many hours in the day. As a professor, he penalized students for late papers, but to his surprise, Pietsch was happy to give him more time. "The trick in a case like this," Pietsch wrote back, "is to make sure we have to ask for only one extension." They agreed in the end to a new due date of April 15, five months away. Still, feeling guilty after the fact, in January, Wallace sent the excuses he ought to have put in the first note: the surprising Illinois cold, a lithium battery in his 1980s-era computer so old it was "no longer manufactured outside like Eastern Europe," and most of all Jeeves:

I thought getting a puppy would make it easier to spend 3 or 4 months in high-stress isolation, but it turns out the puppy does *not* go into suspended animation or reversible coma when I need to work, and shits about 17 times a day, and barks.

He was back at work by now, among other things expanding the "inter-American huggermugger" that Pietsch had found too complicated, believing that the book needed it. *Infinite Jest* might be a "Jamesian melodrama," but it was also the big shit he'd been working on for almost ten years, his bid for a seat at the table with Pynchon, and for that he had to preserve his unfamiliar political setting. He also around this time wrote what would become the beginning of the novel, the memorable scene, set a year after the end of the rest of the book, in which Hal Incandenza has a nervous breakdown during an admission interview at the University of Arizona. What transpires is an exaggerated version of Wallace's own experience on his college tour fifteen years before, when he threw up at his Oberlin interview. At his own interview, Hal is seized by terror and literally can no longer speak. He is rushed to an emergency room in the midst of a psychotic episode, the end of which trip he imagines in detail:

It will start in the E.R., at the intake desk . . . or in the green-tiled room after the room with the invasive-digital machines; or, given this special M.D.-supplied ambulance, maybe on the ride itself: some blue-jawed M.D. scrubbed to an antiseptic glow with his name sewn in cursive on his white coat's breast pocket and a quality desk-set pen, wanting gurneyside Q&A, etiology and diagnosis by Socratic method, ordered and point-by-point. There are, by the *O.E.D. VI*'s count, nineteen nonarchaic synonyms for *unresponsive*, of which nine are Latinate and four Saxonic. . . . It will be someone blue-collar and unlicensed, though, inevitably—a nurse's aide with quick-bit nails, a hospital security guy, a tired Cuban orderly who addresses me as *jou*—who will, looking down in the middle of some kind of bustled task, catch what he sees as my eye and ask So yo then man what's *your* story?

Wallace saw that the scene was a better lead-in for the novel than the discussion between Hal and his father posing as a professional conversationalist that had stood at the book's beginning for so long. It captured the sense of terrified isolation that is key to the story, the worry that what we feel we can never express. And it held out a hope rarely signaled in Wallace's earlier work but dear to his recovery experiences: the possibility that telling a story can heal.

But beginning the chronology of the book a year after the earlier draft had ended also presented a problem, one that offered an opportunity that excited Wallace. Telling Pietsch about it was likely the real purpose of his letter complaining about Jeeves. Wallace acknowledged as much in his note: "A lot of this is stalling before a query." If Hal was a crack-up in the first scene of the novel, the reader might reasonably wonder how he had gotten that way. There were several possibilities. Hal may have seen the devastatingly absorbing video his father made or be detoxing from marijuana or have taken a potent kind of hallucinogenic fungus known as DMZ (nicknamed "Madame Psychosis"). Hints for all three of these plot twists are in the text. But Wallace wanted to tell Pietsch that he was never going to let the reader settle on one. *Infinite Jest* was meant to be a failed entertainment, not a potted amusement. He now warned his editor that he wasn't going to tie up his story in a nice little bow: "Any sort of conventional linear ending for this stuff is in my opinion going to seem either linearly thrillerish in a way that doesn't go with the rest of the book; or else incredibly prolix and complicated." Reminding Pietsch that the plot of the book he'd bought "has always been more of an arc than a terminating line," he proposed

an almost Artaud-ish blackout-type ending. . . . One that might look truncated or even violently ablated. . . . That is to say (I am not at my clearest on this, I know), a conceived ending that's not so much anticlimactic as aclimactic? I can (but hopefully will not) give you about 4300 thematic/theoretical reasons why an aclimactic close here will be best—e.g. resonating echoes w/themes of stasis, annulation, paralysis, undecidability, clarification of questions > solutions to questions etc.

Wallace had dealt with enough New York editors by now to worry how such high-concept talk would strike even the supportive Pietsch. He asked for help, reminding his editor that "your loyalties to readability and readerly pleasure are one of the reasons why your editorial input here and elsewhere is of value." There was an element of flattery here—Wallace played tennis in his letters too—but also truth. He so much wanted to help the reader to a more engaged life that he feared losing him or her on the way. He went back to writing and rewriting, cutting and then adding back in more than he had cut, taking breaks only to teach his classes. He could not have worked harder, as he let Pietsch know, but even so, he saw he would not finish the manuscript by April 15 and asked for more time at the beginning of that month. His letter requesting an extension was penitent, whether from exhaustion, memories of his tangle with Viking Penguin, or the usefulness of imagining Pietsch as an unforgiving authority figure so he would get the book written:

> I'm mortified to have essentially lied to you about 4/15; the date seemed an almost GOP-ishly staid and conservative projection back in January. I now want to say late April or May. I'm not saying this: I'm saying I want to say it. I canceled class for these two weeks, but now I know I won't be done by 4/18, and then I have to make up all the classes I'd canceled.

He imagined apocalyptic consequences to being late connected to the meaning of April 15:

> If I don't file my taxes I might go to jail—though this is also a sort of late-night terror I have, about Little Brown's parent company's lawyers sending me to jail because of some Kafkaesque boilerplate clause I neglected to see at the bottom of the legal document I know I signed, and was given $ by you guys. I know this is just a dark fantasy.

But ever recursive in his thinking, he added:

> I also know there['s] something doubly annoying about a letter like this: it's so anxious and cringing that it kind of forestalls a stern re-

sponse on your part, since the letter might now make a stern response seem like kicking somebody who's already kicking furiously
at himself and telling you to go ahead and kick because he's such a
dork he deserves it.

Wallace's apology-cum-meta-apology prompted words of comfort from
Pietsch, who reassured his author that everyone at Little, Brown was
happy to wait for the novel and eager to read it. Wallace, relieved, wrote
back with thanks for Pietsch's "extremely analgesic letter," while quietly
claiming a little more time to work on his book:

> I am writing this thing; or rather except for the last ten pages have
> written the whole thing, and am w/ all due haste putting it together
> in a seamlessly tight bag. . . . [P]lan your own schedule for this thing
> hitting your mahogany by late june at the very latest. I will finish the
> final draft by then or be dead.

As ever, his letter contained news. (The negotiations on due dates were
just to soften Pietsch up.) He had a new scheme ("I'm telling you this in
advance to like prepare you emotionally"), a way to shorten the book without having to cut it beyond where it could be cut: endnotes. At the back of
the book in smaller type they could stick "harder stuff—data, medical
lore, 19th-century asides, ESCHATON math calculations (which I'm attached to because darn if I did find a neater and more elegant way to prove
the Mean Value Theorem for integrals than anything that's in the texts)
and certain scenes."
He went on:

> I've become intensely attached to this strategy and will fight w/all
> 20 claws to preserve it. it allows me to make the primary-text an
> easier read while at once 1) allowing a discursive, authorial intru-
> sive style w/o Finneganizing the story, 2) mimic the information-
> flood and data-triage I expect'd be an even bigger part of US life 15
> years hence, 3) have a lot more technical/medical verisimilitude 4)
> allow/make the reader go literally physically "back and forth" in a
> way that perhaps cutely mimics some of the story's thematic con-

cerns . . . 5) feel emotionally like I'm satisfying your request for compression of text without sacrificing enormous amounts of stuff.

Aware that he was wandering back into the experimental terrain he had worked so hard to exit, he added, "I pray this is nothing like hypertext, but it seems to be interesting and the best way to get the exfoliating curve-line plot I wanted."

Finally, in late-June 1994, Wallace had the full manuscript, some roughly 750,000 words, complete with Artaud-ish ending and hundreds of endnotes. He promised to bring the bundle to New York on June 30 "handcuffed to a wrist." He was exhausted:

> If further stuff needs to be cut I'm apt not to fight but to ask for an enormous amount of help, because everything in it's connected to everything else, at least in my head. The whole thing may be incoherent for all I know. At this point I have no idea. It's like not knowing what your family looks like: you live right up close to something so long and it blinds you. I just want it done.

In New York, he met up with Costello and they went to see Gus, a polar bear at the Central Park Zoo whose constant neurotic circumambulations of his holding cage were attracting attention from the press, including a mention on *Letterman*. Wallace felt saddened to see the tourists gawking. He flew to Arizona on a visit, where he saw Ashby, who was surprised at how much bigger and shaggier Wallace had gotten with the years. For Wallace it felt strange to be away from a story that had kept him busy nearly night and day for three years. "I am sad and empty, as I always am when I finish something long," he wrote Franzen, whom he saw in Chicago on the way back. He went on:

> I don't think it's very good—some clipping called a published excerpt feverish and not entirely satisfying, which goes a long way to describing the whole experience of writing the thing. I pray Pietsch doesn't want major changes, mostly because I don't want to have to be engaged with the thing again, not at all.

* * *

That summer Amy Wallace was going to be married in upstate New York. She was thirty now and had found someone to settle down with, which made Wallace feel left behind, the unmarried older brother. Amy's upcoming wedding brought forward another fear, one he had been evading during his feverish work on the book. He wrote Franzen that he was scared that "stuff in the mss" would hurt his mother. The portrait of Avril Incandenza had considerable ferocity. She was now an arch grammarian "engaging in sexual enmeshments with just about everything with a Y-chromosome." Wallace had placed her at the center of a comic but painful scene in which, dressed in a cheerleader's uniform, she pretends to be blowing a whistle while one of the Enfield Academy tennis players assumes a three-point stance in nothing but football helmet and jockstrap. Wallace had even put in a suggestion that Avril had committed incest with Orin, Hal's brother, thus triggering Orin's own satyriasis.

Wallace calmed himself with the thought that *Infinite Jest* was after all fiction and that all the "rococo lit-flourish" surrounding her portrait would make the parallels hard to see. One flourish that packed particular power for him was the dedication, which would ultimately read: "For F. P. Foster: R.I.P.," a coded condemnation of his mother's father. (In an earlier draft, Wallace had made the attack more emphatic: "For Fenton Foster RIP, (P) [Rest in Peace (Please!)].")

At Amy's wedding, in July, David was a "bridesman," his hair gathered in a ponytail. Everyone found him in good spirits. His "dread [of] the various eddies of such a confluence" (his phrase to Franzen) did not show, and if anyone noticed that things were cool between him and his mother, no one said anything.

Wallace was looking forward to the start of the fall 1994 semester. The department was allowing him to teach an undergraduate introductory course in literature. This had been his quiet wish since coming to ISU. Now after a year of hard labor, he was to be let out of the ghetto of creative writing classes. The equation that the more he taught the less he wrote had never entirely disappeared from his mind, and it was also true that the simpler what he taught was, the lower the impact on his own creativity; the course would grow to be a favorite of his over the years. After the formal description of the course in the syllabus, he told his students what he was really hoping to have happen:

> In less narcotizing words, English 102 aims to show you some ways to read fiction more deeply, to come up with more interesting insights on how pieces of fiction work, to have informed intelligent reasons for liking or disliking a piece of fiction, and to write—clearly, persuasively, and above all interestingly—about stuff you've read.

This was a return to teaching's first purpose. Wallace liked to sit in his classes, flannel shirt tied around his waist, straddling a backward-facing chair, rocking, as he discoursed on character and pacing. He reminded one student of "an engineer of literature," pulling out the building blocks of stories—voice, narrative structure, point of view. He often used writers of popular fiction—Jackie Collins, Thomas Harris, and Tom Clancy among others—for this purpose, because the components of their fiction were easy to identify and it also made the point that a story did not have to be hard to be worth reading.

Meanwhile, Pietsch was reading Wallace, while Wallace brooded and waited for a response through the months. He wrote Franzen that Pietsch kept cracking "ominous hernia-jokes." Pietsch had in fact had the manuscript tentatively set in type and confirmed that the novel, if printed as Wallace had written it, would be almost twelve hundred pages long. To make money on it, the publisher would have to charge more for each copy than anyone was likely to want to pay. He finally wrote a note to his anxious author in October 1994 warning him that though he loved "having this monster in my head," there was going to have to be more cutting. Also, he pointed out that there were areas that had confused him in April that having a complete draft had not clarified: the book took too long to get going, and the characters at the Enfield Tennis Academy blurred in his mind. He still didn't buy the back-and-forth among the merged United States, Mexico, and Canada and the angry Quebecois separatists. "There is no part of the novel I'm looking forward to rereading less than the sequence of colloquys between Marathe and Steeply on the mountain," he wrote of the two secret agents. Then he responded to the two innovations Wallace had proposed in earlier letters: he was not excited by the idea of endnotes—footnotes would be easier on the reader, he felt—nor by the "Artaud-ish" ending. "Hundreds of pages of killer cartridges and stalking Canadians," he objected, "and moving furniture and Avril's affairs and James's suicide—all those dingleberries in the air— and we don't get to find out who or how or why?" But by the time he finished reading the manuscript a second time in December, he was cheerier. He acknowledged that he was beginning to see how tightly everything fit together. What looked arbitrary now worked. He even found the ending satisfying:

> Hal's breakdown, the one at the start of the novel, is approaching clearly enough that I finished the book guessing how he got from here to there. . . . The revelation that Hal's known all along of his mom's many affairs seems like a key to it all . . . I'm assuming now that this part of the story isn't resolved more clearly . . . because Hal's still avoiding it.

He added that "Gately's hitting bottom . . . is gorgeous and very very powerfully sad," and saw that endnotes might be better than footnotes—less "academic and daunting." Maybe, he thought, Little, Brown could package the book with a bookmark so readers could keep their places.

Happier though Pietsch was, he still felt the book was too long. He wanted the same effect achieved with less. So just before Christmas he added hundreds of specific suggestions for cuts. And in February 1995, Wallace responded with a sixteen-page letter of his own, acceding, rejecting, and counterproposing, wheedling, in a bath of faux mea culpa language for having birthed such a complicated and long book. "I guess," he wrote, "maybe I have an arrogance problem—I think I'd presumed in some of this stuff that it was OK to make a reader read the book twice." But he dug in on the ending, where Pietsch still wanted more clarification: "We know exactly what's happening to Gately by end, about 50% of what's happened to Hal, and little but hints about Orin. I can give you 5000 words of theoreticostructural argument for this, but let's spare one another, shall we?"

Some of the new round of cuts Wallace took eagerly, other times with an undertone of reluctance. "Mugging of Joe D. in Cambridge. Cut, although it introduces three different characters and starts four different plotlines," he groused at one point, agreeing to cut back one of the characters who dated all the way back to the Hammerhill boxes that had held some of his early attempts at the novel. Sometimes he wanted to keep a scene simply because it had been in the book for so long. Other times he threatened that if material were removed, longer, duller rewriting would rise up to plug the gap. Another of his favored tactics was to respond to a request for a cut with a condensation, turning ten pages into five or five into two, or taking the unwanted material and putting it in the endnotes, where some of his favorite passages went to make their last stand. Pietsch also hesitated to put the words "A Failed Entertainment" on a book people were supposed to buy. Wallace suggested it might go on the "frontispiece" instead. Pietsch objected that the problem with calling *Infinite Jest* "A Failed Entertainment" anywhere was "it's not," and it quietly disappeared from the manuscript.

The winter of 1994–95 Wallace took a major step. After almost a decade of an itinerant life, he bought a house. It was the largest asset he had ever owned and he thought of it as much as anything as a down payment on his maturity. The house had three bedrooms and a little patio in front and a yard in the back that he had fenced off for Jeeves. It was made of brick, allaying a fear of tornadoes that dated back to his childhood. The house stood at the edge of town, near trailer parks and a slaughterhouse and also open land; down the street were cornfields, much as with his childhood home in Urbana. He was particularly pleased that his mail address was "Rural Route 2," rather than a street address. Wallace moved in with his books and manuscripts and soon letters from Franzen and DeLillo and then a copy of the Saint Francis prayer appeared on the walls.

Wallace had never owned anything bigger than a car before and he approached his new possession as if everything to do with it were a cause of wonder, a stance that also served to reassure him that though he was now a homeowner he had not totally sold out. "I bought a house," he wrote to Don DeLillo in May, it's small and brick and next to a horse pasture. It has what seems like a 6-acre lawn, and I bought the house in the winter and it didn't occur to me that the grass in this lawn grows and will have somehow to be dealt with. I haven't mowed a lawn since I folded my childhood lawn-mowing business at 13, and I see all my neighbors mowing their own 6-acre lawns like every fourth day, and Weed-Whacking, and dispersing seed and nitrates through devices that look like enormous flour-sifters on wheels, and I am not keen on becoming a lawn-obsessed homeowner. But it's nice to own a house and not pay off a landlord's mortgage.

Wallace's recovery friends were much in evidence in his new home. Many of them were handy, and they were vigilant that the impractical Wallace not get ripped off by their own. His best friend from recovery, Francis B., built his bookshelves. Another put in a cutoff switch for his main electrical cable; Francis B.'s mother volunteered to clean Wallace's house; soon she was doing his wash, with Wallace hiding his underwear from her before she got there. She would cook for him or pick up a roast chicken at his favorite restaurant and stick it in his empty fridge while he was teaching or at a meeting. One time when the handle on his screen door came off, Wallace called Francis B.: "How much is a new screen door going to cost me?" His friend came by with a screwdriver. Wallace exaggerated his helplessness. It was at once a gesture of generosity and of selfishness. The others took pleasure in helping, and Wallace got things done that he didn't have time or aptitude for.

In March 1995 Colin Harrison asked Wallace to go on a Caribbean cruise and write about it for *Harper's*. He and Kymberly were split up, at least for the moment. Spring break was coming and, offered the chance to get away from the cold and the never-ending revisions to *Infinite Jest*, he accepted. Once again he would join the American hordes dosing themselves on fabricated amusements. He would sample shuffleboard, endless buffets, on-board talent shows, and whatever else came his way. But, as ever, he was unsure how to proceed. The hopes of editors always made him nervous. He asked Costello and Franzen if they would join him, but neither was available, so alone he flew to Fort Lauderdale, from which the ocean liner MV *Zenith*—dubbed by him the *Nadir*—was slated for a weeklong circuit around the Gulf of Mexico. From the ship, Wallace called Harrison and asked what the magazine was looking for. Harrison told him to just "Be yourself. Enjoy. You'll find the story."

There was an immediate problem. Shipboard life was full of alcohol and Wallace didn't drink. There would also be no recovery meetings on board. In compensation he smoked plenty of cigarettes. "Prospects for an acute and fecund belle-lettristic essay on cruising in '95 are looking bleak," Wallace wrote Franzen from Playa del Carmen. "Everything but the shuffleboard court is restricted. The atmosphere summons images of a floating range of Poconos." Wallace felt lonely, awkward, and on a false footing and spent most of his time in his cabin or in the ship's library. He was relieved when the trip was over and he was back on shore. On his way home in late March he stopped in New York, visiting Pietsch to talk about his manuscript, and stayed with Franzen for a few days in Jackson Heights in Queens, where his friend was now living. Franzen tried to get Wallace to cut back on the blondies, while Wallace made fun of the tidiness of his friend's household. They bickered but more affectionately—work was on the whole going well for both of them now. Wallace was still wary of anything to do with cities and sophisticated city people but one night Franzen took him to a gathering hosted by *Open City*, a literary journal, at a Manhattan nightclub. It was not a scene Wallace felt very comfortable in, a party full of alcohol and drugs. During the evening he met Elizabeth Wurtzel, a writer whose memoir of depression, *Prozac Nation*, was a current hit. Wurtzel had struck a provocative pose on the cover of her book in a flesh-colored T-shirt, mid-riff exposed, and when Wallace questioned why, she told him it was what you had to do to sell a book. He demurred, citing his duty to art and other DeLilloesque objections. But Wallace was smitten by her silver lamé leotard and walked her home. In the lobby of Wurtzel's building, as she remembers, he spent more than an hour trying to persuade her to let him come upstairs. He told her it would be a therapeutic favor. She told him if he stopped chewing tobacco he'd have a better chance.

Trivial as the encounter was, it stayed on Wallace's mind. Wurtzel was a breathing symbol of temptation to him, Salome to Leyner's antichrist.

He had never met anyone as self-involved as he was, someone, moreover, with a history of depression, yet whom fame and drugs had not pushed into collapse. It was another glimpse of the alternative universe he had last seen at Yaddo with McInerney in 1987, the lure that the decisions he'd made about celebrity were not the only ones possible. He quickly inscribed a copy of *Broom* to her. "Not my best thing, by a long shot, believe me," he noted on the title page. Wallace was in a happy time in his life, but all the same Wurtzel prompted a long letter full of recursive agonizing that he wrote soon after he got back to Bloomington:

> I go through a loop in which I notice all the ways I am—for just an example—self-centered and careerist and not true to standards and values that transcend my own petty interests, and feel like I'm not one of the good ones; but then I countenance the fact that here at least here I am worrying about it, noticing all the ways I fall short of integrity, and I imagine that maybe people without any integrity at all don't notice or worry about it; so then I feel better about myself (I mean, at least this stuff is on my mind, at least I'm dissatisfied with my level of integrity and commitment); but this soon becomes a ve-hicle for feeling superior to (imagined) Others. . . . It has to do with God and gods and a basic sense of trust in the universe v. fear that the universe must be held at bay and micromanaged into giving me some smidgeon of some gratification I feel I simply can't live without. It's all very confusing. I think I'm very honest and candid, but I'm also proud of how honest and candid I am—so where does that put me.

He told her how hard it was for him when he wrote to discern the differ-ence between caring about the reader and caring that the reader cared about him:

> The crux, for me, is how to love the reader without believing that my art or worth depends on his(her) loving me. It's just about that sim-ple in the abstract. In practice it's a daily fucking war.

By now, the cruise ship experience had begun to cohere for him. He was merging the miserable time he had had on board into his larger themes. He produced an overstuffed meditation, twenty-four pages in the magazine, on the mistaken American belief that pleasure can do anything other than stoke the need for more pleasure. Early in the article he declares:

> I now know the difference between straight bingo and Prize-O. I have seen fluorescent luggage and fluorescent sunglasses and fluorescent pince-nez and over twenty different makes of rubber thong. I have heard steel drums and eaten conch fritters and watched a woman in silver lamé projectile-vomit inside a glass elevator.[7]

Wallace explored the various types of cruise self-indulgence, from shuffleboard ("thanatopic," he called it) to the daily "eleven gourmet eating ops" to skeet shooting. He told the story of having missed a clay pigeon by a wide margin and watching it sink into the ocean: "Know that an unshot discus's movement against the vast *lapis lazuli* dome of the open ocean's sky is sun-like—i.e., orange and parabolic and right-to-left—and that its disappearance into the sea is edge-first and splashless and sad."

"Sad" became the tocsin ringing through the piece, sadness as the consequence of too much plenty: sad waiters, sad cruise ship–goers taking pointless videos of other sad people pointing video cameras at them from their own cruise ships, and sad, senseless attempts by Americans to amuse themselves in the absence of any larger spiritual idea. "Choose with care," Marathe warns in *Infinite Jest*. "You are what you love. No?" Wallace's cruise ship piece was about the price of failing to choose well.

To underpin this note, Wallace quoted the saddest story of all, one that had been in the news just before departure:

> Some weeks before I underwent my own Luxury Cruise, a sixteen-year-old male did a half gainer off the upper deck of a Megaship. The news version of the suicide was that it had been an unhappy adolescent love thing, a ship-board romance gone bad. But I think part of it was something no news story could cover. There's something about a mass-market Luxury Cruise that's unbearably sad. Like most unbearably sad things, it seems incredibly elusive and complex

in its causes yet simple in its effect: on board the Nadir (especially at night, when all the ship's structured fun and reassurances and gaiety ceased) I felt despair. The word "despair" is overused and banalized now, but it's a serious word, and I'm using it seriously. It's close to what people call dread or angst, but it's not these things, quite. It's more like wanting to die in order to escape the unbearable sadness of knowing I'm small and weak and selfish and going, without doubt, to die. It's wanting to jump overboard.[8]

In April 1995 *Infinite Jest* was back on Wallace's desk—Pietsch had had the novel set in sample type again and realized the book was still too many pages. He sent a list of possible new cuts. To DeLillo, whom he increasingly turned to as his authority on literary matters, Wallace voiced a growing worry:

> I am uncomfortable about making cuts for commercial reasons— it seems slutty—but on the other hand LB is taking a big gamble publishing something this long and this hard and I feel some obligation not to be a p.-donna and fuck them over. Maybe I'm writing because I want your general aestheto-ethical imput on this. I don't know.

He added that he would probably wind up "cutting 40% of what they ask and making the font slightly smaller and hoping to fool them." DeLillo wrote back that he had to follow his instincts; as Wallace summarized his advice back to Pietsch, when "you feel incipient bladder tumors at the thought of cutting something don't cut it."

The edits Wallace agreed to left Pietsch in, as he wrote Wallace in mid-May, "a state of editorial ecstasy . . . the veil lifted." But ten days later he was back with more unwelcome news. "Here's what happened," he wrote Wallace, "I got to the end of *Infinite Jest* Friday a week ago and mailed that letter to you. Then over the weekend I was struck by the realization that I hadn't actually edited the manuscript yet. Only now do I feel that I know the novel well enough to make more detailed suggestions." Anticipating his author's response, he added, "I know this is harrowing for you, but I believe that this is the work you want me to do. This is my best editing, David."

A new round of editing followed, focusing on the first five hundred pages. "I'm prepared to thumbwrestle you over every one of these cuts," Pietsch challenged Wallace, having absorbed the latter's language of playful combat. He chopped at endnotes, and went after more of the "inter-American huggermugger" in the back, where Wallace had stashed it. Wallace quickly responded to the edits, as he did when agitated, with a circle signifying "total acquiescence to demand" and a dash meaning "bared teeth," "dickering," or that a proposed cut had to be discussed on the phone.

Pietsch was also still worried about how the parts fit together. This was a novel in which, with the possible exception of Gately's story, the plot reaches no conclusion. You don't know for sure if the terrorists find the lethal cartridge. The reader never learns what drove Hal mad. Is Avril Incandenza an agent for the Quebecois terrorists? There were hints that she and John "No Relation" Wayne,[9] the top player in the school, both were. Wallace insisted that the answers all existed, but just past the last page. The novel continued in time in the reader's mind—that is, it meant for it to have the trajectory of a "broad arc" rather than a Freytagian triangle. Pietsch asked for one clarification now. He wanted some indication of the fate of Orin Incandenza, who may be responsible for sending out the lethal cartridge to get back at his mother.

Wallace, amid all the cutting and rewriting, gave it a try. "Potential insertion into page 1229 about which I'm not exactly qualmless," he faxed Pietsch on June 11 and sent a scene, with overtones of *1984*, in which Quebecois terrorists trap Orin under a surreally massive inverted "tumbler" and unloose roaches on him—his "special conscious horror." The goal is to suffocate him—a fate similar to that which he inflicted on the roaches infesting his bathroom several hundred pages earlier.

Another set of alterations was forced by a phone call. In May, Mary Karr, who had read some of the portions of the novel serialized in magazines, called Pietsch to point out that many of the Ennet House scenes were taken either from what Wallace heard or saw at Granada House and in recovery meetings, where conversations were supposed to be private. For Wallace, an accusation of this sort could elicit maximum anxiety, the threat of new exposure and problems. He might find himself once again in *Girl with Curious Hair* territory. But this time things went far more smoothly. He changed some names in the manuscript, altered other details, and added a strongly worded but evasive denial to the copyright page that the events in the novel were disclosed at confidential recovery meetings.[10]

Wallace flew to New York once more at the end of June with the manuscript in a box on his lap. Kymberly Harris came with him this time. Their relationship had revived in the spring. Wallace had even requested a sitdown with her parents and, arriving highly nervous, asked if it would be okay for Kymberly to live with him. "David is asking for my thumb," she joked. The Harrises gave their consent, amused by Wallace's formality, but he had been serious, in a way; a midwestern rigor in certain matters was still within him and this was a major step in his mind. Kymberly had moved in with her clothes and furniture in April, but, now just a couple of months later, she planned to audition for the Actors Studio in New York. Wallace dropped in on Pietsch and handed off his bundle and was back in Bloomington a week later. Soon after, the Actors Studio wrote Kymberly to say she had been accepted. Wallace pronounced himself thrilled, delighted that she had gotten into the "Yale Medical School of Acting," then, quickly less thrilled, asked her to wait a year before she went east. At first she agreed, but by August she realized that the more deeply she got involved with Wallace the less likely she would be ever to leave Bloomington. She told him she was going to New York, with him or not, and four friends came and moved her and her things out, leaving him the silver velour recliner, Jeeves, his old bed, and little else.

Soon Wallace found other companionship. One day he was out jogging and a dog appeared by his side. Wallace realized it was a stray and decided to take it home. "The Drone," as he named him after the mythic club in P. G. Wodehouse's novels, was a black Lab mix, as Jeeves was.[11] He was more rebellious than Jeeves, less of a house pet.[12] Together the two ruled the house, their chew toys and fur everywhere. Their water came from the cooler. If Wallace was away for more than a few hours, he brought in a sitter.

To Wallace's surprise, Little, Brown had already produced a brochure with a short piece by Wallace on writing and a brief excerpt from the novel and distributed it at the annual booksellers' convention in late spring. And just a few weeks after he brought his final manuscript to New York with Harris, Pietsch sent him bound copies for subsidiary rights sales and pre-publication quotes. After discussion, the cover was a picture of blue sky with puffs of clouds. It was inspired by the "wallpaper scheme" of the administrative offices' waiting room at the tennis academy that incites Hal's agoraphobia, with its "fluffy cumuli arrayed patternlessly against an over-enhancedly blue sky."[13] Wallace wrote to DeLillo that the book had "a cover that's (troublingly, to me) identical to the passenger safety card on American Airlines flights."

The work of *Infinite Jest* almost done, Wallace was casting around for new projects. The state fair piece and the sections of *Infinite Jest* that had run in journals had made him in demand. He said no to a week at a nudist colony and a chance to attend the launch of a scent endorsed by Elizabeth Taylor at an air force base, the similarity of these offers sparking the suspicion, as he later told an interviewer, that all the magazine editors in New York read each other's mail.[14] Wallace was vulnerable to being wanted and he had liked all the new readers his magazine work got him. So he agreed to write a piece for *Details* about the tennis star Michael Joyce (it was ultimately published in *Esquire*), and another on the U.S. Open for *Tennis*, a magazine that he'd devoured as a teenage player. Both magazines were looking for a piece of the Wallace voice, that tone of a sensitive, sincere genius operating in second gear. His nonfiction persona was, as Wallace told an interviewer, "a little stupider and shmuckier than I am." He became adept at the back-and-forth of magazine work, limiting the psychic cost of the editing by calling and leaving long messages at night on his editors' voice mails.

Wallace also began a review of Joseph Frank's four-volume biography of Dostoevsky for the *Voice Literary Supplement*, where Lee Smith, the editor of *Signifying Rappers*, was now working. Wallace had over the years become deeply attracted to the Russian's writing and life. The parallels between Dostoevsky's and his own certainly caught his eye, as they had at Granada House. Wasn't his time there comparable to Dostoevsky's exile in Siberia, where the Russian had first seen how much he had in common even with the most desperate souls? He left this implied in the lengthy article he produced:

> What seems most important is that Dostoevsky's near-death experience changed a typically vain and trendy young writer—a very talented writer, true, but still one whose basic concerns were for his own literary glory—into a person who believed deeply in moral/spiritual values.

Wallace spent most of July on the essay and became more and more impressed. Here was a writer impossible in modern America, one earnestly and unapologetically moral. He wrote in a notebook around this time.

> Hyperc[onsciousness] makes life meaningless [. . .]: but what of will to construct OWN meaning? Not the world that gives us meaning but vice versa? Dost embodies this—Ellis, Leyner, Leavitt, Franzen, Powers—they do not. Their fictions reduce to complaints and self-pity. Dostoevski has BALLS.

He wanted to extend the point he had made in "E Unibus Pluram" two years before. Then he had mostly diagnosed a disease; now he was giving a model for the cure. American writers were still content to describe an ironic culture when they should be showing the way out. They had still not discovered, as he wrote in *Infinite Jest*, that "what looks like the cage's exit is actually the bars of the cage." "Who is to blame," he concluded in his *VLS* piece, "for the unseriousness of our serious fiction? The culture, the laughers? But they wouldn't (could not) laugh if a piece of morally passionate, passionately moral fiction was also ingenious and radiantly human fiction."

In August the copyedited manuscript of *Infinite Jest* arrived. Wallace had been dreading this day. He had written Pietsch in the winter that if his editor would give him the name of "your/our copyeditor . . . I'll start sending candy and sweet nothings now." He had sent a prophylactic note along, almost a compendium of Wallace stylistic tics, in the hopes he could limit disagreement:

To Copyeditor:

Hi. F.Y.I., the following non-standard features of this mss. are intentional and will get stetted by the author if color-penciled by you:

—Single quotation marks around dialogue & titles, with double q.m.'s inside—reversal of normal order.

—Such capitalized common nouns and verb-phrases as *Substance, Disease, Come In, Inner Infant, etc.*

—Neologisms, catachreses, solecisms, and non-standard syntax in sections concerning the characters Minty, Marathe, Antitoi, Krause, Pemulis, Steeply, Lenz, Orin Incandenza, Mario Incandenza, Fortier, Foltz, J.O. Incandenza Sr., Schtitt, Gompert.

—Multiple conjunctions at the start of independent clauses.

—Commas before prepositions at the end of sentences.

—Hyphens to form compound nouns.

—Sentence-fragments following exceptionally long sentences.

—Inconsistent paragraphing, with some extremely long paragraphs.[15]

Now he braced himself for several months of unraveling the mistakes and foolish consistencies of people who knew grammar less well than he, a fear that was shortly confirmed. He wrote his Boston friend Debra Spark in October that he was "in the 8th circle of page-proof-proofreading hell. Never again anything over 150 pages." He wheedled and begged Pietsch for more time, presenting evidence that it was the publisher who had messed things up. "The more I proof these page proofs, the more convinced I get that it would be a *mistake* to disseminate bound galleys before typos and solecisms are corrected," he wrote Pietsch. "I'm going over each word and line with a loupe, almost," he assured him. To Alice Turner, to whom he sent the bound proofs, he claimed in December to have caught "about 47,000 typos in the bound galley." (Later he would tell an interview from *Time* that he had corrected all but one of "about 712,000.") One of his graduate students, Jason Hammel, remembers going over to Wallace's house to find him with loose pages of *Infinite Jest* spread out in front of him, watching the movie *Beethoven* over and over on a TV/VCR combo from Rent-A-Center. He told Hammel it was the only way at this point he could bear to read the book. His eyes, by now, he complained to the chief copy editor, were "wobbling like a vestibulitiser's."

Wallace was not the only member of his family to play copyeditor. He had also tried to test-drive the family's response to the book by hiring his sister for that task even before the manuscript had been finished. She immediately saw what was going on and asked him if he really felt this was the right way to deal with his anger at his mother; Wallace just shrugged. But he still felt he had to give his mother the manuscript to read. He sent it to Urbana and waited. In December, six weeks later, he wrote Alice Turner that he was worried still to have heard nothing, "wholly ominous given our family's normal communication grid; I fear someone sees more autobiography in it than there is."[16]

As the February publication of *Infinite Jest* neared, Wallace felt neither he nor his book was ready. Any hint of impending clamor made him glad he was in Illinois, safe from curious eyes and the intoxications of admiration and publicity. But Little, Brown had the job of making sure Wallace felt necessary or at least familiar to literary readers. He had not had a book of fiction come out since 1989. The massiveness of the novel was the central fact to be dealt with. It became a joke at the publisher's marketing meetings to ask, as one participant remembers, "Has anyone here actually read this thing?" Soon Little, Brown realized that the obstacle could be made the point. To read *Infinite Jest* was to accept a dare. It began a campaign of postcards sent to four thousand reviewers, producers, and bookstore owners. With each round of postcards a bit more of the title was revealed against the toneless blue sky of the jacket. One postcard had glowing quotes from earlier Wallace books, another promised "the biggest literary event of next year" and a third promised, "Just imagine what they'll say about his masterpiece." This was too much for Wallace, and in a mid-September letter, in the midst of the "*fucking, fucking* nightmare" of the page proofs, as he would later call it, he begged Little, Brown to stop. "'Masterpiece'? I'm 33 years old; I don't have a 'masterpiece,'" he wrote Pietsch. "'The literary event of '96?' *What if it isn't? What if nobody buys it?* I'm getting ready, inside, for that possibility; but are you guys?" At least, he begged, could they reduce the size of his name on the publicity material? A deeper worry, though, was that in the cascade of edits, the nebulous, fine-veined schema of the novel had been compromised. Wallace himself wasn't sure anymore. When David Markson wrote him to say how much he enjoyed the advance copy of the book he got but there were parts he couldn't figure out, it touched a chord in the author and he answered, a bit ungratefully:

> About the holes and lacunae and etc., I bet you're right: the fucker's cut by 600 pages from the first version, and though many of the cuts (editor-inspired) made the thing better, it fucked up a certain water-tightness that the mastodon-size first version had, I think.

Seven years after *Girl with Curious Hair* had come out *Infinite Jest* was to be published into a very different literary terrain. Minimalism had vanished. Postmodernism was a yet more distant memory: no recent graduate of a writing program would have bothered to make one of its authors the patriarch for his patricide. Importantly, the American political climate had changed, changing the literary climate. Both minimalism and postmodernism, as Wallace had noted in his "Fictional Futures" essay, were forms of social protest, and as the 1990s progressed, just what was to be protested grew harder to define. Ronald Reagan had left office at the beginning of 1989, the Berlin Wall had been pulled down the next year, and the Soviet Union had dissolved in 1991. Political worry was replaced by economic abundance. Americans had never felt more masterful than in the mid-1990s, living in the space between the Cold War and the time of ill-defined threats that was to come.

Wealthy eras usually repair to realism, at least for a while. This was true too of the 1990s. The well-wrought short story—"no character without Freudian trauma in accessible past," as Wallace wrote in "Fictional Futures"—returned to the fore, if indeed it had ever been anywhere else. Lyrical realist novels like Jane Smiley's *A Thousand Acres*, E. Annie

Proulx's *The Shipping News*, and Richard Ford's *Independence Day* dominated awards lists. Cormac McCarthy became the best-known literary author of the decade, but it wasn't the intense McCarthy Wallace loved of
Blood Meridian and *Suttree* but the more romantic one of *All the Pretty
Horses*, the story of a young cowboy who crosses into Mexico to look for
love and a friend's stolen horse.

No time of calm is without its undertone of introspection and angst;
affluence has its victims too. Wallace was by no means the only one nor
the only one trying to give them voice. Certainly anyone as attuned to
television as Wallace was could witness the damaged and the distressed
telling their stories all day long.[17] And something similar was going on in
writing by non-Anglo American writers, many of whom were presenting a
vivid world of stories drawn from their own histories. But these were not
authors to whom Wallace has a strong response; his remained the world of
the 1970s novel, predominantly male, Caucasian, and highly erudite.[18]
There a sense of anxiety was more muted, though not absent. Rick Moody
was writing *Purple America*, a novel that deploys shifting consciousnesses
to define a damaged and polluted America, and William Vollmann was
pursuing the reportorial inquiry into the darker side of American life he
had begun with *The Rainbow Stories*, an investigation similar to one that
Denis Johnson was conducting in books like *Jesus' Son*. These were a few
of the authors who shared or even anticipated *Infinite Jest*'s sense that the
focus on consumption and pleasure in modern American life would end
badly. None of them, though, combined such a stance—the anti-hedonistic
strain in American fiction—with the promise of redemption that lies at
the center of *Infinite Jest*.

Indeed, earnest storytelling seemed to nearly everyone but Wallace an-
tithetical to proving oneself worthy of taking on questions of societal unease; Don Gately is a character one can't imagine any of the others creating.
Literature—especially from the sorts of writers Wallace felt in conversation with—was about delving, extracting, and then layering a complicating layer of language on observed life; there was nothing evangelical about
it. The literary gesture existed almost as an inverse to the narrative of recovery meetings, where as Wallace wrote in *Infinite Jest*, "an ironist . . . is a
witch in church. . . . Same with sly disingenuous manipulative pseudo-
sincerity." In *Infinite Jest*, Wallace was proposing to wash Pynchonian ex-

cess in the chilling waters of DeLillo's prose and then heat it up again in Dostoevsky's redemptive fire. "Look man," Wallace told Larry McCaffery in the *Review of Contemporary Fiction* interview,

> we'd probably most of us agree that these are dark times, and stupid ones, but do we need fiction that does nothing but dramatize how dark and stupid everything is? In dark times, the definition of good art would seem to be art that locates and applies CPR to those elements of what's human and magical that still live and glow despite the times' darkness.

Infinite Jest then didn't just diagnose a malaise. It proposed a treatment, answering a need that Wallace saw perhaps better than any other writer of his time. The book is at once a meditation on the pain of adolescence, the pleasures of intoxication, the perils of addiction, the price of isolation, and the precariousness of sanity. (Wallace never forgot David Lynch's *Blue Velvet* and the skein that separates unremarkable from abnormal in America.) It spoke of the imminence of collapse and the possibility that one can emerge stronger from that collapse. It offered faith apart from religion. Its multiple voices jibed with an America that no longer spoke as one, an America in which, as in James Incandenza's films, "you could bloody well hear every single performer's voice, no matter how far out on the . . . narrative periphery they were." It captured a new generation of young people—especially young ones, especially male—who in the midst of plenty felt misunderstood or ignored, who with each decade had less and less idea how to make their rich inner selves visible, who understood what Hal meant when he objected:

> I'm not a machine. I feel and believe. I have opinions. Some of them are interesting. I could, if you'd let me, talk and talk. Let's talk about anything.

But the book also had the range to get beyond the much-trafficked literary realm of the misunderstood young. It captured another America, the millions felled by the "input too intense to bear" that Wallace had signaled in "Westward," the Don Gatelys of the world, charismatic and full of fallow potential, people "damaged or askew," calling out to the reader from inside their broken lives, as they call out to Hal's sensitive brother Mario as he visits Ennet House:

> Mario likes the place: it's crowded and noisy and none of the furniture has protective plastic wrap. . . . The inside of it smells like an ashtray, but Mario's felt good both times in Ennet's House because it's very real; people are crying and making noise and getting less unhappy, and once he heard somebody say *God* with a straight face and nobody looked at them or looked down or smiled in any sort of way where you could tell they were worried inside.

There was no need to decide which *Infinite Jest* you were reading, since, after all, these two main strands both emanated so clearly from the same concern: how to live meaningfully in the present. There is a generosity to the world created by this 1,079-page novel. A great intelligence hangs above it and seems not entirely uninterested in our survival. It watches from the walkway about the courts at the Enfield Academy and lurks in the communal rooms at Ennet House, explains the rise of O.N.A.N. and the fall of network advertising, the composition of tennis rackets, the Boston street names of controlled substances, and the history of videophony. *Infinite Jest*, for all its putative difficulty, cares about the reader, and if it denies him or her a conventional ending, it doesn't do so out of malice; it does it out of concern, to provide a deeper palliative than realistic storytelling can, because, just as in Ennet House, you have to work to get better. The book is redemptive, as modern novels rarely are (there is a reason Wallace had to reach back to Dostoevsky for a model). Gately abides, taking on, almost in a Christlike way, the sins of his flock, and Christ implies a God. Wallace never forgets his pledge, as he told McCaffery, that "all the attention and engagement and work you need to get from the reader can't be for your benefit; it's got to be for hers."

All this makes it seem as if the critical success of *Infinite Jest* were predetermined. True, the book appeared at a moment in which critics were looking for big novels, for some way of summing up the world at the turn of the millennium, but *Infinite Jest* did not seem immediately what they wanted. It was too difficult, felt too headlong, its calculated casualness confused. The prepublication notices straddled the fence between admiring and wondering whether the reviewer wasn't being had. *Publishers Weekly* called the work a "brilliant but somewhat bloated dirigible of a second novel," while *Kirkus* was slightly warmer, admiring what was "almost certainly the biggest and boldest novel we'll see this year and, flaws and all, probably one of the best." Predictably, most reviews emphasized the dimensions of the book, both literal and metaphorical. Sven Birkerts captured this amazement in the *Atlantic*, where he noted that *Infinite Jest* had "mov[ed] toward us like an ocean disturbance, pushing increasingly hyperbolic rumors before it: that the author could not stop writing; that the publisher was begging for cuts of hundreds of pages; that it was, qua novel, a very strange piece of business altogether." *Library Journal* warned its readership that *Infinite Jest* was "not for the faint-hearted or the weak-wristed."

Most reviewers who wrote about the book liked it, but there was an undertone of obedience to their writing, of being relieved they could answer in the affirmative the dare Little, Brown had laid down. "Challenging and provocative," wrote the *Orlando Sentinel*. The *Chicago Tribune* called the novel "brashly funny and genuinely moving . . . worth the long haul." The novelist Jonathan Dee in the *Voice Literary Supplement* praised Wallace as "the funniest writer of his generation." All agreed *Infinite Jest* was significant—or, at least, a novel others would think was significant, so their readers should know about it. Walter Kirn, a mischievous novelist who reviewed it for *New York*, sped the plow: "Next year's book awards have been decided. The plaques and citations can now be put in escrow. The competition," he wrote, "has been obliterated. It's as though Paul Bunyan had joined the NFL or Wittgenstein had gone on 'Jeopardy!' The novel is that colossally disruptive. And that spectacularly good." *Esquire* praised the book but criticized the publicity campaign. (Wallace, who happened to be in New York when the piece came out, in a note to Markson called it "that sneery thing in *Esquire* about the so-called 'Hype of the Huge.'") All these developments were positive from the publisher's point of view. "I'm very happy with the launch so far," Michael Pietsch wrote to Bonnie Nadell, "all our drum beating seems to have been heard."

The book began selling well, especially given its size, and the publisher quickly went back for several small reprints. Yet the novel was certainly not sweeping everything away in its path. Jay McInerney reviewed the book for the *New York Times Book Review* with little enthusiasm. He missed the inventiveness of *Girl with Curious Hair* and found Wallace's sentences more interesting than his plot. In the end he was not convinced that Wallace had successfully yoked two different kinds of books: "The overall effect is something like a sleek Vonnegut chassis wrapped in layers of post-millennial Zola," he objected.

The most significant negative note came from Michiko Kakutani of the daily *Times*, who had expressed qualified affection for *Broom*. Faced with a behemoth in which narrative strands consume hundreds of pages and then fade away for several hundred more, in which the two principal plots of the story don't clearly intertwine until more than six hundred pages into the book, in which the reader is consistently distracted by the need to thumb the back for endnotes that often offer information no reader seems to really need, in which digressions, playlets, urban legends, quasi-science, and pseudo-history break up the narrative, she found herself skeptical that she had read a masterpiece: "The book seems to have been written and edited (or not edited)," she wrote, "on the principle that bigger is better, more means more important, and this results in a big psychedelic jumble of characters, anecdotes, jokes, soliloquies, reminiscences and footnotes, uproarious and mind-boggling, but also arbitrary and self-indulgent." The end or non-end of the book particularly bothered her:

> At the end, that word machine is simply turned off, leaving the reader—at least the old-fashioned reader who harbors the vaguest expectations of narrative connections and beginnings, middles and ends—suspended in midair and reeling from the random muchness of detail and incident that is *Infinite Jest*.[19]

But such reviews did not dampen the impression, especially among the sort of critic interested in the dialogue among modernism, postmodernism, and whatever was coming after, that something new was being communicated. Birkerts in the *Atlantic*, who had welcomed *Girl with Curious Hair* as the first book truly to absorb the schizogenic vision of the writer writing in the media-saturated age, saw *Infinite Jest* as a brilliant extension of that preoccupation into the era of the Internet, with its manifold, overwhelming sources of image and information. So what others considered incoherence or sloppiness was to him a sign of a talent struggling to absorb the news:

> To say that the novel does not obey traditional norms is to miss the point. Wallace's narrative structure should be seen instead as a response to an altered cultural sensibility. The book mimes, in its movements as well as in its dense loads of referential data, the distributed systems that are the new paradigm in communications. The book is not *about* electronic culture, but it has internalized some of the decentering energies that computer technologies have released into our midst.

These comments came at just the moment when the importance of computer-based communication was exploding. Indeed, in the eight or nine years from the inception of *Infinite Jest* to its publication, the Internet had gone from a tool primarily for academics and the technologically adept to something approaching the limitless repository of information it is today. Few novelists or cultural critics had had time yet to think about what this transformation meant, least of all Wallace, and he was surprised to learn he had written a cybernovel. Asked by the *Chicago Tribune* whether his book was meant to reflect life as it was experienced in the computer age, he demurred. "This is sort of what it's like to be alive. . . . You don't have to be on the Internet for life to feel this way," adding that he had never been. (He was wise enough to see a snare in it for an addict like himself. He felt, he told a friend, that he had already been exposed to enough ads for one lifetime and saw it as another insistent bleat creating the modern atmosphere of information overload, the state of affairs he would later call "Total Noise.") Of course, "what it's like to be alive" felt different for Wallace than it did for most people. Beset by anxiety and whipped by consciousness, his was a mind more drawn to the flat bright outlines of personhood than the nebulous contours of personality; it would be too simple to say that life for Wallace looked even more like the Internet than it did like television, but there is truth to it. In any event, the Internet Age was a gift that the post-millennial world gave to Wallace as a writer in search of readers. Collage and pastiche were gaining currency, and caricature and portrait were drawing closer together in people's minds. Wallace's characters—modern in their very sketchiness—felt realer to many readers than what realists were writing. As the culture collapsed into the anecdote and sound bite, *Infinite Jest* was one of the few books that seemed to anticipate the change and even prepare the reader for it. It suggested that literary sense might emerge from the coming cultural shifts, possibly even meanings too diffused to see before.

Wallace knew that he could not hide out in Bloomington forever. On publication day he would have to pack up and head east to face what he liked to call, referencing his old Tolkien reading, "Sauron's great red eye." But in fact Sauron was coming his way.

His first interview was with *Details* magazine. Wallace had never been interviewed by the mainstream media in depth before—the only feature magazine piece written on him had been by a friend of his agent for *Arrival* in 1987. So he left up the letters from Franzen, DeLillo, and others— "a whole wall of letters that help me or are important," as he later wrote to DeLillo. The reporter, David Streitfeld, who was on staff with the *Washington Post*, told him he should take them down, because a journalist could see them and quote from them. He also told Wallace that rambling self-analysis might not be the ideal approach to conversations for publication; an interview was not the place for confidences. "I was wildly indiscreet about stuff like drug histories and M. Karr," Wallace wrote DeLillo after, "and he stopped me in the middle and patiently explained certain rules about what to tell reporters." About his time in substance abuse programs, he needed no coaching, since Karr had already warned him about it via her phone call to Pietsch. When *Newsweek* soon after asked him how he knew so much about recovery, he trickily replied:

I went with friends to an open AA meeting, and got addicted to them. It was completely riveting. I was never a member—I was a voyeur. When I ended up really liking it was when I let people there know this and they didn't care.

By the time the *New York Times Magazine* came to see Wallace in Bloomington on the eve of his book tour, he was cannier. All the same, some of his personality came through. The reporter, Frank Bruni, got to watch Jeeves eat a bologna sandwich from Wallace's mouth. "They pretend they're kissing you," Wallace said, "but they're really mining your mouth for food." And he went along to a dinner at the home of a couple named Erin and Doug Poag. They ate Kentucky Fried Chicken and heroes on trays and watched *The X-Files*, a taste of Wallace unbuttoned. Wallace did not mention that his connection to the Poags was from his recovery circle—he claimed to have met them at a "Mennonite church." And, understandably, without that information, Bruni was left with the impression that Wallace's fondness for ordinary midwestern people might be a put-on. In all, Bruni's article grappled with—and never quite decided—whether the author of *Infinite Jest* was more "shtick" or "soul" or a combination of both that was generationally unique.[20]

Next came the book tour, which began in Manhattan in mid-February. Erin Poag went with him to steady her friend while he was away from both his home and his recovery group. One reporter mistook her for either his mother "or the Illinois version of a publicist." Walking up the rickety stairs to his first New York reading, Wallace tried to turn around and go back down. "I don't think I can do this," he told Poag. She answered, "If you get up and don't like it, we don't have to stay," and, a solidly built woman in her fifties, she put her hand on his back and pushed him along. Wallace had the strange feeling as he walked into the room of the crowd parting. The *Times Magazine* noted the turnout:

> The critics aren't the only ones angling to prove that they get it. Wallace's contemporaries have shown up at his public appearances in force. When he read at K.G.B., Elizabeth Wurtzel, the author of "Prozac Nation," claimed a spot near the front of the room.[21] The following night, at another jam-packed reading, this time at Tower Books in the Village, Ethan Hawke lurked in the back.

Soon afterward, Gerry Howard recalls bumping into a long line of fans waiting to see Wallace read at a Rizzoli's bookstore on West Broadway. He was amazed that this writer, whom he had always thought destined for a small, essentially intellectual, literary public, had become a phenomenon. "There was this adoration," Howard remembered. "He had reached people in this highly personal way." The *Times Magazine*, trying to pin down this connection, dubbed *Infinite Jest* "The Grunge American Novel," signaling the link between a fragmented novel of fragmented souls and a cultural movement led by singers like Kurt Cobain of Nirvana characterized by a similar affect. There was considerable truth to it; both proffered an awkward sincerity. They shared an allergy to façades, to disco-type slickness. *Infinite Jest*'s jagged multiple-conjunction-opening sentences held the same promise of authenticity as the primitive musical arrangement and bad amping of Seattle garage bands. Both music and novel implied that communication had gotten harder and harder, hitting walls of isolation too high to scale, reducing us to diminished gestures, preferences, grunts. As Wallace would tell an interviewer around this time, "there's a way that it seems to me that reality's fractured right now; at least the reality that I live in." The chorus of "Smells Like Teen Spirit" paralleled Wallace's portrait of a generation addicted to media with its assertion that everyone was "stupid and contagious. . . . Here we are now, entertain us."[22]

There was a shared look between writer and singers too. The unwashed hair with bandana, unlaced work boots, and old plaid shirts that Wallace had been wearing since Arizona were also now practically a uniform for anyone who felt disenchanted with the post-Reagan American culture of buying and owning. Wallace's "impulse to second-guess every thought and proposition" had become, as Howard notes, "something like a generational style." "When I was younger," Wallace told an interviewer for the *Boston Phoenix*, "I saw my relationship with the reader as sort of a sexual one. But now it seems more like a late-night conversation with really good friends, when the bullshit stops and the masks come off."[23]

The possibility that Wallace himself was going to become famous filled him with confusion, though of course he saw the irony of what was happening. He wanted his work to be fully experienced, not lightly absorbed with all the other noise of the culture. When a fellow English professor at ISU congratulated him on the cruise ship piece in *Harper's*, Wallace pointed to his mouth with one hand and made a butt-wiping gesture with the other. To anyone who praised his achievement, he would only repeat that he had "worked really really hard on" *Infinite Jest*, as if he were a child talking about his artwork. He posted a sign on his office door at ISU during his book tour: "D.F. Wallace is out of town on weird personal authorized emergencyish leave from 2/17/96 to 3/3/96 and from 3/5/96 to 3/10/96."

The low point of Wallace's rise was his publication party. Little, Brown wanted to mark the arrival of the book with a media gathering at the Limbo Lounge, a trendy East Village club. Nadell had not loved the idea. *Infinite Jest* was "not a hip downtown kind of book," she wrote the publisher. "It is a major literary novel." But Little, Brown believed that to ignite enthusiasm for the novel it had to establish the book's of-the-moment credentials. The party wound up being held at the Tenth Street Lounge, if anything a more glamorous destination. A large crowd of editors and writers gathered there on February 21. The *New York Times Magazine* filed this report:

> And at the official book party two nights later at an East Village club, M. G. Lord, the author of "Forever Barbie," can be seen chatting up another novelist of the moment, A. M. Homes. Between puffs of their cigarettes, many people whisper what Wallace says he does not want to hear: he is the current "it" boy of contemporary fiction.

Wallace spent much of the time upstairs in a private room, watching the proceedings from a window that looked down on the main floor, with Charis Conn, his fiction editor from *Harper's,* and Costello. His frequent trips to the bathroom led the uninformed to suspect cocaine use, though in fact he was pulling out chaws of tobacco. "I think I made it a project *not* to look in the mirror during that party," he later told an interviewer, "because I knew that a whole lot of other people were looking at me, and if I thought about what I looked like, I was going to go crazy." Wallace and Costello were sneaking out of the club together when a young blonde woman followed them from the party and presented herself to the author. "Do you want to meet my puppy?" she asked. Wallace went off, leaving his friend behind.

Afterward, Wallace wrote to DeLillo of how little he had enjoyed the gathering. The party, he told his *miglior fabbro*, had been "packed and scary. . . . It's the only Pub Party I've ever been to, and if God's in his heaven it will be my last." The ensuing publicity tour had been the subject of careful negotiation with Little, Brown. Wallace had agreed to visit, as he wrote DeLillo, "some dozen cities" for readings and interviews. He had turned down the *Today* show, agreeing as compensation to a *Rolling Stone* interview, because, as he wrote DeLillo, "I argued (compellingly, I think) that Rolling Stone was essentially TV anyway." The *Rolling Stone* reporter was the journalist David Lipsky. The two got along well, and Lipsky, also a novelist, took in what was left of the private Wallace in his home: chew toys on the floor, a copy of *Cosmopolitan*, which Wallace swore he subscribed to, claiming that "reading 'I've Cheated—Should I Tell?' a bunch of times a year is fundamentally soothing to the nervous system." There was a Barney towel doubling as a window curtain, a postcard of Updike, and a Scottish battle scene painting. A large poster of Alanis Morissette, the intense, confessional female soloist, was on one wall. To someone who did not know Wallace, the décor might have looked like conventional professorial po-mo mockery of the middlebrow. But Wallace was serious—at least sort of—when he told Lipsky he liked to listen to Enya, the sugary Irish singer. He referred to Kymberly in the present tense as his girlfriend and said she had taught him to appreciate Ani DiFranco and P. J. Harvey, "and what's her name? Tori Amos," though he preferred Morissette. He was effectively underscoring to hipsters that he wasn't one of them. *Infinite Jest* wasn't just an assertion of anomie, the way grunge was. It was also supposed to be an answer to despair, a corrective to the misery of youth, a recipe for personal growth. Wallace could observe grunge and note its impact, but its undemanding hopelessness flew in the face of his recovery theology; it was too self-pitying. If you were as stupid as "Teen Spirit" asserted, there was only one person who could make you smarter.

Rolling Stone did not in the end save Wallace from TV. The public-TV talk show host Charlie Rose also wanted him on. Wallace asked the people he trusted whether he should do it. Franzen told him he had to, because, as Wallace wrote in summary to DeLillo, to whom he next appealed, "you guys made your bones in a different time, when the author's own personal person wasn't as necessary a part of a PR machine that itself wasn't necessary to sell books." He told DeLillo his inclination to avoid TV was "not out of integrity so much as an awareness that I do a fair amount of writing about TV and spectation and that I wanted to stay on my side of the screen and that I'd fuck up future work if I didn't."

Wallace wrote the letter in March, during a break between the two parts of his publicity tour. He had been to eleven cities by then, to Seattle, to read at Elliott Bay, an important independent bookstore, then to San Francisco, Los Angeles, Houston, where he couldn't sleep, and Iowa City, where he ran out of petty cash and a member of the audience stood up and accused him of being insensitive to those with disabilities, because in the mini-essay that Little, Brown had asked him for he had quoted an observation by Bill Gray, the blocked novelist in DeLillo's *Mao II*, that writing a book was like having a "hideously deformed infant that follows the writer around, forever crawling after the writer."

Wallace was accumulating regrets as he went. In Los Angeles, he and Nadell got into an argument with a dealer when he refused to sign hundreds of books, magazines, and memorabilia. And at the Tower Books reading in New York, the one Ethan Hawke had attended, Wallace, flying high on what must have felt like a toxic gust of celebrity, had added the name of the director Richard Linklater to the list of directors of the sorts of projects second-tier actors who were hired to be stand-ins for video phone conversations might be involved in. The ad lib got a knowing laugh from the crowd, but later Wallace heard that his "brain fart," as he described it later, had offended Hawke, who had just starred in a Linklater film. Wallace's sense of having been "a *serious* asshole" had a self-referential cast: "This poor guy can't even go in the back. He didn't want to be acknowledged. He just wanted to listen to a reading."

Wallace was learning that all sorts of relationships that had been simpler—if never quite simple—when he was more or less unknown were tricky now. In Seattle, he had told Corey Washington he could not hang out because he was too exhausted to see even an old friend. Costello was furious at having been abandoned at the Tenth Street Lounge party. Elizabeth Wurtzel had continued during the past year to entrance Wallace.

One time he had called Franzen from a payphone at 3 a.m. when they were out together to say, "I'm with a girl who has heroin in her possession. This is not good." Then after the KGB reading, she brought him back to her apartment and took him up to her loft bed, but at the last minute changed her mind about sex. Wallace, suspicious that she had only brought him home in the first place because of his rising fame, grew furious. "You're going to make me drink again!" he shouted at her. He threw on his clothes and stomped out, ending the friendship.

Even before Wallace's tour was over, Little, Brown had reprinted the book six times for a total of forty-five thousand copies. Pietsch wrote Wallace that readers were calling him at the office to try out theories about the ending. "It reminds me of the exhilaration I felt finishing *Gravity's Rainbow* for the first time and finding someone else who'd read it to knock brains with," he wrote his author. There was even movie interest in the book. The director Gus Van Sant wanted to option *Infinite Jest*. Wallace worried it seemed whorish—he knew that serious writers did not sell their work to the movies—but a friend in the business told him he had nothing to worry about; no one could ever make a movie from that novel.[24]

By April, Wallace was at last all but done. He had had a fantastical success, and he was far from sure the experience had been a pleasant one. He was too self-aware not to see the paradox that his attempt to condemn seduction had proven so seductive. He had tried to write a splintered entertainment, to remind people of the dangers of spectation, and instead he had wound up prying open their wallets with Leyner-like adroitness. He had hoped readers would read his book twice, but whether they had read it at all was the question. Had *Infinite Jest* become another entertainment cruise ship, bright lights on an empty sea? Wallace turned to DeLillo to try to make sense of the experience, alluding to a media stampede satirized in his novel *White Noise*:

> I . . . tried my best to tell the truth and to be kind to reporters who hadn't read the book and wanted only to discuss the "hype" around the book and seemed willfully to ignore the fact that articles about the hype were themselves the hype (for about a week there it seemed to me that the book became the Most Photographed Barn, everyone

tremendously excited over the tremendous excitement surrounding a book that takes over a month of hard labor to read).

When JT, his buddy from Tucson, wrote to congratulate him, he wrote back, "WAY MORE FUSS ABOUT THIS BOOK THAN I'D ANTICI-PATED. ABOUT 26% OF FUSS IS WELCOME. AS YOU SAID YEARS AGO, 'YUPPIES READ.'"

CHAPTER 7

"Roars and Hisses"

As soon as Wallace got home, he pulled the tour schedule off his wall and threw it away. Being back was a relief. He felt again the "weird warm full excitement of coming home," the pleasure, as he had written Alice Turner just before his book tour, of a world where his neighbors were "lumber salesm[e]n and Xerox copier repairmen," and hoped he would never have to go anywhere again. "The Icky Brothers"—Jeeves and The Drone—were waiting. He wrote poetically to DeLillo about the "horses in the yard of the doctor's manse next door," of spring in Bloomington, and apologetically to Corey Washington. He left a two-word message with Costello's secretary: "I'm sorry."

He was glad again to attend his regular meeting and reinsert himself in the world of recovery, with its emphasis on community and cooperation. The lessons of recovery were never far from his thoughts. When David Markson wrote in June to complain about an author's getting an award he thought should have been his, Wallace gently warned him away from the pitfall of envy: "Mostly I try to remember how lucky I am to be able to write, and doubly, triply lucky I am that anyone else is willing to read it, to say nothing of publishing it. I'm no pollyanna—this keeping-the-spirits-up shit is hard work, and I don't often do it well. But I try. . . . Life is good."

Little, Brown wanted to publish a volume of Wallace's magazine pieces right away. The idea was to get the book out before the red eye of Sauron moved on. Even before the last "spasms-trips" of Wallace's tour, as Wallace called them, Pietsch was asking for the manuscript. Wallace, trying to show his gratitude, promised to work fast on "the lump." For him it also represented an opportunity. He had never liked magazine editing, though he accepted it. Now he had, as he would later explain to DeLillo, a chance to undo the cuts editors had imposed on him to "make extra room for Volvo ads." He added back in what had been taken out, sometimes doubling the published length of the pieces, reestablishing their verbal exuberance and their scope.[1] He tinkered until the last minute, offering again to pay for corrections and reminding Pietsch that he still owed him for the ones at the last minute for *Infinite Jest*, but Pietsch pointed out that *Infinite Jest* was certain to generate royalties beyond its advance and the cost of the changes could come from those funds. Wallace responded that there would be more corrections forthcoming for the paperback.

A Supposedly Fun Thing I'll Never Do Again came out in February 1997. Wallace told DeLillo he liked only the first and last essays in the book—"Tennis, Trigonometry, Tornadoes," to which he gave back his original title with its mathematical overtone, "Derivative Sport in Tornado Alley," and the cruise ship piece. Yet the response to the publication of what were to Wallace a group of older, maybe not so interesting anymore essays, was surprising. *Infinite Jest* had left in equal amounts goodwill and frustration. How many readers had gotten to page 70 and given up? But they all the same wanted more of Wallace. If nothing else, the title he gave the collection—it was the original title of the cruise ship piece restored—captured well his generation's ambivalence toward pleasure and marketing and the marketing of pleasure. There was something stunning about the experiential aspect of the essays in the book too, the ones whose technique Wallace described in an interview as "basically an enormous eyeball floating around something, reporting what it sees." Their very length spoke of commitment, discomfort, the importance of caring in a world urging you constantly to lighten up. It was like listening to your best friend in grad school, tirelessly willing to absorb, reason, confront, embrace but never accept.

In general, critics felt less ambivalent toward Wallace's nonfiction than they did toward his fiction. The *San Francisco Chronicle* saw "a passionate and deeply serious writer" amid the hijinks, and James Wood in *Newsday* noted a fruitful divide between Wallace the postmodern essayist and the journalist "eager to notate reality (though in funky ways)," concluding,

"His contradictions are his strength, and if one wants to see the zeitgeist auto-grappling, in all its necessary confusions, one must read every essay in this book." For Laura Miller of Salon.com, the articles were confirmation of the promise hinted at by *Infinite Jest*. Writing in the *New York Times Book Review* she noted that *A Supposedly Fun Thing* "reveals Mr. Wallace in ways that his fiction has of yet managed to dodge: as a writer struggling mightily to understand and capture his times, as a critic who cares deeply about 'serious' art, and as a mensch."

Wallace did not want to go on tour for the paperback of *Infinite Jest*, but since it came out the same month as *A Supposedly Fun Thing*, he could do so without appearing to. He went to ten cities as the new book appeared on many bestseller lists and sold roughly fifteen thousand copies in hardcover. One night Wallace read at the Brattle Theatre in Cambridge, Massachusetts, and then went to the *Harvard Lampoon* castle to receive an "Author of the Millennium" award, which he accepted only after making sure it was made up. There were long lines everywhere he went. At the end of the *Infinite Jest* book tour, despite misgivings, he had gone on Charlie Rose's talk show. The spur was not his novel but a recent essay by Franzen on the state of fiction. The two had faced off with Mark Leyner and the experience had been relatively painless. So Wallace now said he'd appear on the show again for his essays. This time, without foils, the encounter was uncomfortable, as Wallace rocked back and forth in his white bandana, battling the urge to spew out the churning contents of his mind—to be on TV talking about the power of TV left him particularly confused: it was the kind of recursion he could not ignore. Friendly but insistent, Rose asked him about his pre-recovery days:

DFW: ... Here's why I'm embarrassed talking about it, not because—

ROSE: I want to know why.

DFW: Not because I'm personally ashamed of it, because everybody talks about it. I mean, it sounds like—

ROSE: In other words, everybody—

DFW: It sounds—

ROSE: Everybody talks about it for themselves or everybody talks about you?

DFW: No, everybody talks—it sounds like some kind of Hollywood thing to do. "Oh, he's out of rehab and—"

ROSE: No, I—

DFW: "—back in action."

ROSE: —didn't say anything about rehab.

After a second successful book, Wallace again wanted to be sure that nothing fundamental had changed. Francis B. asked him to go with his wife's preteen daughter to a movie and Wallace took her to *Titanic* and told her to cover her eyes during the nude scene. As ever, he admired those who lived as he could not: one member of his group worked twelve-hour shifts in a tire factory without air-conditioning, his only comfort the Serenity Prayer. "I mean," he wrote a friend, "can you see why I LOVE some of these people?" At school he wore his bandana, devoted time in his classes to Grammar Rock, his mini-lessons on usage, and spat tobacco delicately into a red plastic cup. He edited students' stories three different times, encouraging the timid and rebuffing the febrile. He made vocabulary word lists: "Birl, cause to spin rapidly with feet." "Musth, period of heightened sexual drive in elephants (Vulcans) when they're more aggressive." He wanted to disappear again into the obscurity of being a difficult writer in a regional midwestern city.

Yet the world was different. What he liked about Bloomington was that he could live his life there "blissfully ignorant of most of the Red Hot Center's various roars and hisses," as he had written Alice Turner, adding, "My best kids are farm-kids who didn't even know that they liked to read until I persuaded them they did." But still they or their parents got *Time* and *Newsweek*. They had seen the pictures of Wallace and knew that the outside world regarded him as a personage. But students who wanted to talk about how it felt to be famous did not get far, and anyone who thought they would get points for reading *Infinite Jest* soon learned to do it out of their teacher's sight.

His fame occasionally impinged on the campus. A man from Chicago called his department office, wanting to arrange a tennis game. Another came to the school and asked how he could meet the author of *Infinite Jest* and proceeded to wait the whole day, making the staff of the English department nervous. Some students from the University of Chicago arrived on a scavenger hunt, one requirement of which was to get their picture taken with Wallace (he was nowhere to be found).

Wallace began to change his phone number every few months. He would make restaurant reservations under fanciful names—one he particularly liked was Jim Deatherage, the name of a friend's high school creative writing teacher. John O'Brien, the Dalkey Archive Press director, had thirteen dogs. They would come over and play with Jeeves and The Drone or Wallace would bring the Icky Brothers over to his house on the outskirts of the city. One day he complained to O'Brien that he no longer knew what to make of people: "People come up and say they love the book and I don't know if they've read it. I don't know who to trust anymore."

Students had begun applying to the graduate program specifically to study with him. He was becoming a beacon for a kind of writing, not the postmodernism of the rest of the department and not the realism of Iowa and everywhere else, but a third approach, uncomfortable but sincere realism for a world that was no longer real. Making the head throb heartlike had the potential to become a literary movement. Different names were bruited for it, from the New Sincerity to Post-postmodernism. Occasionally one heard Grunge Fiction.

But Wallace did not seek acolytes. He was too competitive, too solitary, too recursive, felt his journey too painful to wish on others. For him teaching was just instilling basic skills; the student had to do the rest. He was starting to wonder how happy he really was in Bloomington anyway. "I find myself saying this year the same thing I said last year and—and it's a little bit horrifying," he had told Rose on his show, pointing out that most teachers stopped learning from their teaching after "about two to three years." He became interested in yoga and meditation and practiced them regularly. With some of his recovery friends he went to a Jesuit retreat near St. Louis for a few days. The monastery observed silence to encourage reflection, and Wallace took advantage of this by bringing a bag full of work. He'd always wanted to see the Mississippi River up close, though, so he convinced Francis B. to descend with him to the riverbank below the cliffs on which the monastery stood. Disappointingly, when they got there, the flats held nothing but a dead gar. "This isn't what I expected," Wallace complained. At that moment, a cabin cruiser went by and a group of women lifted up their shirts. "Now that was spiritual," Wallace said.

Sex, and the intense, complicated interchanges it brought with it, filled a place in Wallace that nothing else could. Promiscuity had been part of his life for a long time now. But being famous increased the number of women who would sleep with him or perhaps his sense that he needed to sleep with them. At his readings there were long lines everywhere he went, abundant "audience pussy"—a phrase Mary Karr used. He came back from one reading in New Orleans to tell Francis B. he had slept with a girl who was underaged. Corey Washington went to a reading in Washington, D.C., and saw two hundred people there, Wallace sedulously signing copies of *A Supposedly Fun Thing*. A young woman came up to them afterward. "I told you not to come here," Wallace snapped. He was, he wrote a friend, "literally crazy" on the subject of sex. Once talking to Franzen he wondered aloud whether his only purpose on earth was "to put my penis in as many vaginas as possible."

When Kymberly had left, she had speedily been replaced by another woman in recovery, who was also taking one of his classes in the English department. But one day when he wasn't in the house, she read through his journal and he broke up with her. She was in turn replaced by her best friend, who was also a friend of Kymberly's. She had two children, a favored arrangement for Wallace, part of the "fetish for conquering young mothers," as he phrased it, that he had given to Orin Incandenza in *Infinite Jest*.[2] The young woman chewed tobacco and they dated for more than a year. But Wallace was badly suited to relationships by now. He had been alone too long and become, to quote his description of the tennis academy in *Infinite Jest*, "abundantly, embranchingly tunneled." Over time he had added idiosyncratic touches to his house. He painted one room black, where he expected to work, and put his silver velour chair in it. "I've wanted a black room since I was a kid," he explained to Brad Morrow in a letter. He filled it with lamps, many removed from his parents' house. He put his computer in the living room for rewriting and revising and covered it with the wedding veil of a friend, as if it were the site of a sacral mystery. Wallace knew himself well enough to know he did not want a

TV—until he did. Then he would buy one and insist it stay unplugged. Or he would put it out at the curb for collection or give it to some of his friends from recovery. His behavior was so noticeable that the local paper, the *Pantagraph*, mentioned it in an item.

All this might have suggested a man not well suited to relationships, but his dedication—sexily flawed—to what might be called single-entendre connections was extremely intoxicating to some women. For them, as several remember, he was "like a drug."[3] He played Trivial Pursuit with one undergraduate and her friends in their dorm. To another he read *The Velveteen Rabbit*. "Real isn't how you are made," the Skin Horse tells the Velveteen Rabbit, "it's a thing that happens to you." With a third it was charades. The women would wind up sharing his bed with him, Jeeves, and The Drone for a time, cajoling him about what one called "the food with no color" in his fridge—crackers, cream cheese, cereal—and then, sooner or later, they were sent on their way. "That's a three-day weekend I'm still paying the credit card bill on," he said of one young woman, unchivalrously. Wallace affected not to care that some of the women were his students. He told his friend Corey Washington he was trying to get himself fired.

Wallace continued seeing therapists in Bloomington, partly to try to resolve issues with his mother, partly for his own relationship problems. Worried that he was becoming a stock Romeo, he insisted he was ready for commitment, and for an end to what he called in a later letter "serial high-romance and low-intimacy" relationships that never got truly intimate. Other than the classroom, his favored venue for meeting women was St. Matt's, the church in whose rectory his recovery group met. His listening skills and his own practiced efforts at self-disclosure often led to breaking the rules against "thirteenth stepping." Other recovery members warned him to stop, citing the emotional dangers of dating the newly sober, which, from his crazed relationship with Mary Karr, Wallace was no stranger to. "The odds are good but the goods are odd," went an old recovery saw. But Wallace could not stop himself. He wrote a friend that there were times he'd walked into the twelve o'clock recovery meeting and found that he had slept with three of the ten women there, "and come close" with one or two others. His behavior seemed, even to him, at times hard to justify; he was leaving a lot of hurt in his wake. But his bigger worry was that all this seducing was most damaging to himself. He saw that the need to make every woman fall madly in love with him had made him highly manipula-tive, a man who went around trying to make women feel the same, as he put it in a letter to a friend, "tuggy stuff" he always felt in that moment. To him this was the most wretched of transactions—tricking someone into needing you by pretending to care. It was the thing he had written *Infinite Jest* in part to expose. It made you, he realized, not so different from "the people selling Tide."

By the time Wallace returned to Illinois State from his *Supposedly Fun Thing* book tour in the spring of 1997, he was already worried about his fiction writing. Predictably the effort to produce *Infinite Jest* had left him feeling wrung out. This sense of depletion had not surprised him at first. He had crafted the beginning of the novel in Boston in the early 1990s, expanded and improved it in Syracuse, and by the time he got to Bloom-ington in July 1993 he was mostly rewriting and responding to Pietsch's edits. That had taken up the next year or so. But by 1995 he had been hoping—expecting—to start something else. It was his assumption that the new thing would be a novel too. The novel was the big form, the one that mattered, that reviewers and other authors cared about and by which he could fulfill his compact with readers. DeLillo's published writing con-sisted almost entirely of novels; so did Cormac McCarthy's.

The freedom success now brought left Wallace uneasy; in his life, he had worked to narrow his choices, to give himself a simple set of instructions—don't drink or smoke pot; don't try to impress others to make yourself feel better. But on the page things were more complex. He knew that he had to write for himself and not think about the reader, but that was easier to enunciate than to enact. He would have conversations during this period with Costello where he would complain about how hard it was now to get the words down in the right order. Since Amherst, he and Wallace had had as a touchstone of good writing John Keats's poem "This Living Hand":

> *This living hand, now warm and capable*
> *Of earnest grasping, would, if it were cold*
> *And in the icy silence of the tomb,*

So haunt thy days and chill thy dreaming nights
That thou would wish thine own heart dry of blood
So in my veins red life might stream again,
And thou be conscience-calm'd—see here it is—
I hold it towards you.

Wallace would talk about wanting in his writing to "make the hand come out," and then, in disappointment afterward, "The hand, Mark—there's no hand." Costello worried that his friend was being too negative about his own work, that success had tipped his delicate internal balance.

When *Infinite Jest* was done, Wallace found himself more comfortable with shorter fiction. The value of this writing was unclear to him, though, and did not make him feel he was using his time well. "Writing is going shittily here," he wrote to DeLillo in September 1996. "I've spent all summer doing dozens of obscure ministories that seem neither comprehensible nor interesting to anyone else." He told Brad Morrow at *Conjunctions* that he spent his days in his black room, writing "weird little 1-pagers." Some were about "the spiritual emptiness of heterosexual interaction in post-modern America," as he would phrase it in a later interview, others almost metaphysical aperçus about the hazy intersection of cognition and the world, vignettes he grouped together under the heading "Another instance of the Porousness of Certain Borders." What had made the scope of his imagination contract so radically? He blamed himself, rather than, say, fatigue or age. He thought perhaps other authors had less trouble. The year before he had turned back to the writer whom he most admired for help. He had a "jejune" question for DeLillo—like "some kind of tentative hand in the back row of a writer's classroom visit or something." He went on, "Do you have like a daily writing routine? Do you set off certain intervals as all and only time for fiction-writing? More important, do you then honor that daily obligation, day after day? Do you have difficulties with procrastination/avoidance/lack of discipline? If so, how do you overcome them?"

I ask because I'm frustrated not just with the slowness of my work but with the erratic pace I work at. And I ask you only because you seem at least on this end of the books, to be so steady—books every couple or so years for over two decades and you don't seem to have an outside job or teaching gig or anything that might relieve (what I find to be) the strain of daily self-starting and self-discipline and daily temptations to dick around and abandon the discipline. Any words or tips would be appreciated and kept in confidence.

DeLillo wrote back to reassure the thirty-three-year-old Wallace that centering yourself to write got easier over time, though it never got easy. "The novel," he wrote his younger friend, "is a fucking killer. I try to show it every respect." This perhaps satisfied Wallace for a time, but his hand was up again a month later. Why, he asked his adopted role model, did the route to maturity have to be such a struggle?

> Maybe what I want to hear is that this prenominate war is natural and necessary and a sign of Towering Intellect: maybe I want a peptalk, because I have to tell you I don't enjoy this war one bit. I think my fiction is better than it was, but writing is also less *Fun* than it was.

"All right," DeLillo replied, a bit more sharply this time, "your first book was more fun but that doesn't mean you've left pleasure behind forever." For him, at least, it was the act of writing that carried him forward: "I have fun when I find myself gliding on language and when the story seems to drive itself forward and when I'm able to give a character his or her most unexpected expression," he wrote. Still, novel writing, with its isolation and the uncertainty about what one had achieved, was never going to be a picnic. Wallace had to understand that. He offered a kind of buck-up, disputing Wallace's distinction between his "bad" early work and his "good" later work:

> And I don't see that the occasional acrobatics in Girl with Curious Hair are a form of exhibitionism. And I don't see anything in the early pages of [*Infinite Jest*] that would lead me to believe that you are dying of funlessness. But of course reader and writer are dealing from different perspectives. Where you see fun in my work, I re-

member doubt, confusion and indecision, and now experience considerable regret, particularly over the earlier books.

And he ended with a compliment, meant to give Wallace a sense of belonging to an elite for whom this sort of suffering was the price of membership:

> When I say the novel is a killer, I am reserving this designation for writers who are smart enough, sensitive enough and good enough to realize the dangers and consequently to respect the form. You have to be good before you even sense the danger, or before you can understand what it takes to succeed. Let the others complain about book tours.

It's unlikely this comforted Wallace. For him there had to be a huge difference between the tone of his early work and *Infinite Jest*—not just his literary development but his actual physical survival was embodied in the difference. Now Wallace cast about for different ways to motivate himself. He invited Charis Conn from *Harper's* to stay with him for a semester to work on her novel, putting at once a competitor and a watchdog in his spare bedroom. (He dubbed his house "Yaddo West.") He quit smoking, took it up, quit it again. He tried teaching new classes to spur his interest in his day job. In the spring of 1997 he taught a course with Doug Hesse, a colleague in the English department, on creative nonfiction, which they defined in a handout they gave the class as "a somewhat problematic term for a broad category of prose works such as personal essays and memoirs, profiles, nature and travel writings of a certain quality, essays of ideas, new journalism, and so on."[4] The same semester he designed and taught a class on great novels of the twentieth century, "basically," as he wrote in the course syllabus, "a contrived, excuse/incentive to read several interesting, difficult U.S. novels. . . . The class is to function as a large, sophisticated, energetic reading group." "I'm gearing up to do 2 DeLillo, 2 Gaddis, 2 McCarthy . . . and 1 Gass. Death by fiction," he wrote Steven Moore with pride.

When extra teaching didn't stimulate his creativity, Wallace thought about not teaching. He had not forgotten that he had done his best work away from the classroom. Other times he blamed his lack of discipline. He imagined a more perfect version of himself and scribbled it on a sheet of paper one day:

What Balance Would Look Like:
2–3 hours a day in writing
Up at 8–9
Only a couple late nights a week
Daily exercise
Minimum time spent teaching
2 nights/week spent with other friends
5 [recovery meetings a] week
Church

"I'm back to thinking IJ was a fluke," he wrote on another sheet:

> I feel nothing lapidary inside. "Until there is commitment, there is only ineffectiveness, delay." Goethe. How to make a commitment— to writing, to a somewhat healthy relationship, to myself. How to schedule things so that a certain portion of each day is devoted to writing. How to save money so that I can take Fall '97 off.

This last he acted on. He asked DeLillo to recommend him for a Guggenheim Fellowship, then four days later canceled the request. "A weird lightning-bolt fellowship" had come his way, he reported. The Lannan Foundation in Santa Fe had awarded him $50,000, "which means," he wrote Steven Moore, who had helped arrange the grant, "I can take an unpaid year off next year and face writing fears head on." But the prospect of a whole year without classes, Wallace wrote DeLillo, caused him "basically to have projected my own superego out onto the world and thus imagine that THEY expect-nay-demand an exhilarant piece of novel-length prose at the end of my grant time, which I know is horseshit but still makes it hard to breathe." He asked again why he could not find DeLillo's discipline—"you quiet, deeply serious guys who take time and publish only finished, considered stuff." He was becoming as afraid of having too much time as not enough.

God, as Wallace liked to point out, being "nothing if not an ironist," the year after he won the Lannan, the MacArthur Foundation gave him an award of $230,000, which, together with the Lannan money and the income from his books, effectively freed him from the need to teach. The receipt of a so-called genius award was acutely uncomfortable for Wallace. It sat just the wrong side of his worry that he was a high-level entertainer who could be bought by what he called, in a letter to Markson, "the blowjobs the culture gives out." He did not like the idea of being celebrated for who he was, as opposed to what he had written or was currently trying to write. Accepting the award was as risky as taking an advance on a book—worse psychologically, really, because you got to keep the funds either way. The only one who could punish you for not living up to expectations would be yourself. He did not really need the money either. His only big cost was health insurance, which ISU provided. He went nowhere and bought little—he drove an old car, and malls, he told friends, made him sad. To expiate the burden, no sooner did he have the funds than he tried to get rid of them. He lent money to ex-girlfriends and gave it away to friends in his recovery group to pay for their children's college tuition. He offered to fund other friends' worthy projects—one wanted money to help her write a study of childhood sexual abuse. He bought a pickup truck. One day in class he mentioned he couldn't figure out where it had gone. He was embarrassed when a student brought forward the keys and told him he had lent it to her several weeks before.

Anxiously, he went into his year off. "I am getting some writing done," he wrote Moore in September 1997, after a summer on his own, "though not of course as much or as well as I like." He wrote in the margins of a notebook around the same time, "I am a McArthur [sic] Fellow. Boy am I scared. I feel like throwing up. Why? String-free award—nothing but an avowal of their belief that I am a 'Genius.' I don't feel like a Genius." He spent a lot of time writing letters in procrastination, many of them about procrastination, as he cast around for what was keeping him from feeling he could write anything bigger or braver than his "microstories." He came to blame the fame that adhered to him since *Infinite Jest*. He came back to an image of celebrity that had absorbed him since he'd worked on that book. In those pages, an assistant coach lectures a reporter about why he feels the need to protect his players from the media:

For you it's about entertainment and personality, it's about the statue, but if they can get inculcated right they'll never be slaves to the statue, they'll never blow their brains out after winning an event when they win, or dive out a third-story window when they start to stop getting poked at or profiled, when their blossom starts to fade.

Now Wallace was wondering whether he hadn't become a literary statue, "the version of myself" as he wrote a friend at the time, "that I want others to mistake for the real me." The statue was "a Mask, a Public Self, False Self or Object-Cathect." What made the statue especially deadly to Wallace was that it depended for its subsistence on the complicated interplay between writer and public. Not just: You are loved. But also: You love being loved. You are addicted to being loved.

Wallace had known for some time what he wanted to write, he continued in the letter, but he was "paralyzed" by fear of failure. He worried that whatever "magic" or "genius" people said they'd seen in his last two books would not be in evidence. He would, he worried, be "obliterated or something (I say 'obliterated' because the fear most closely resembles some kind of fear of death or annihilation, the kind of fear that strikes one on the High Dive or if one has to walk a high tightrope or something)." He was now frozen by his own need to be the person others saw him as. They could let go of it more easily than he could. And since the success of *Infinite Jest* the problem had gotten worse, so that he feared the "slightest mistake or miscue" would knock the statue down. The prospect terrified him. He concluded that since the publication of *Broom*—"the date of the erection/unveiling of the statue of DFW as Author"—he had only been able to do "truly good work" on "rare" occasions.

He was being too hard on himself. For Wallace, self-examination and self-flagellation often overlapped—and were also often a spur to possible literary inquiry. What turned an author into a statue? And wasn't even inquiring in this way an attempt to polish it up, clever custodial work? As he'd written to Wurtzel, "I think I'm very honest and candid, but I'm also proud of how honest and candid I am—so where does that put me."

Comparable examples of recursion beset him all the time; they were his default mental setting. He was working on another of his "Porousness of Certain Borders" pieces, which began:

As in those other dreams, I'm with somebody I know but don't know how I know them, and this person suddenly points out to me that I'm blind. Or else it's in the presence of this person that I suddenly realize I'm blind. What happens when I realize this is I get sad. It makes me incredibly sad that I'm blind. The person somehow knows how sad I am and warns me that crying will hurt my eyes somehow and make them even worse, but I can't help it—

He was appalled at how much time it took to yield such vignettes. The exception were two stories that came out of his own experience more directly. The first was "The Depressed Person." The story, published by *Harper's* in 1998, was a genre Wallace hadn't tried since "Westward," revenge fiction. It was his way of getting even with Wurtzel for treating him as a statue (or, she would say, refusing to have sex with him). Freed from desire, he now saw that her love of the spotlight was just ordinary self-absorption. "The Depressed Person" of the title is a spoiled young woman, who repulses the reader with her obsessive neediness, much as she repulses her friends in the story. "The depressed person was in terrible and unceasing emotional pain," the story begins, "and the impossibility of sharing or articulating this pain was itself a component of the pain and a contributing factor in its essential horror." Through the course of story, the unlovable protagonist shuttles fruitlessly between friends and therapists, looking for a sympathetic ear—the same ear the narrator denies her—as her clinical symptoms are revealed to be nothing more than narcissism.[5]

The second story, "Self-Harm as a Sort of Offering" (collected later as "Suicide as a Sort of Present"), was a meditation on his difficult relationship with his mother. Wallace was always looking for some sort of catharsis in their connection. In the story—as, he believed, in his own life—a mother's intense love for and disappointment in her son is the root of his neurosis. The need she holds for him to excel is itself the result of the belief her own parents inculcated in her that she needs to be perfect. The destructive cycle then gets passed to the next generation:

The child appeared in a sense to be the mother's own reflection in a diminishing and deeply flawed mirror. Thus every time the child was rude, greedy, foul, dense, selfish, cruel, disobedient, lazy, fool-

ish, willful, or childish, the mother's deepest and most natural inclination was to loathe it. But she could not loathe it. No good mother
can loathe her child or judge it or abuse it or wish it harm in any
way. The mother knew this. And her standards for herself as a
mother were, as one would expect, extremely high. . . . Hence the
mother was at war. Her expectations were in fundamental conflict.
It was a conflict in which she felt her very life was at stake: to fail to
overcome her instinctive dissatisfaction with her child would result
in a terrible, shattering punishment which she knew she herself
would administer, inside. She was determined—desperate—to succeed, to satisfy her expectations of herself as a mother, no matter
what it cost.

The story ends ambiguously—it is not clear who gives the present of
suicide to whom—but in its intense distancing sentences one feels Wallace examining the shards of his childhood again and again, trying to construct a whole without bringing it so close it will hurt him again.

Wallace always wrote in the midst of busyness. There were classes, and
even without classes there were recovery meetings, errands for friends
and friends of friends, and demands from his dogs. He himself now sponsored many participants in recovery and made it a point to always be
available. Charis Conn was amazed to see that whenever Wallace had a
few free minutes, he would sit down, cross his legs, and work on a story
(one explanation for the shortness of so much of his work during this
time). He sent a few of his "1-pagers" to the more innovative magazines
with which he had connections, where, despite his reputation, the result
was tepid. Most found his efforts obscure. How had a marquee maximalist
become a jotter of haikus? Wallace wrote to Steven Moore in late 1996
that he had recently sent out four little stories and they'd all been rejected,
a situation that felt familiar and that, combined with his failure to be
nominated for the National Book Award for *Infinite Jest*, led him to believe
that his "15 minutes are over and things are back to normal."

When Wallace was not happy with his fiction, nonfiction grew in appeal.
There were always offers. The *New York Observer* now asked him to review

Updike's *Toward the End of Time*, a story, like Wallace's two novels, set in the near future, and he agreed. Wallace's one-sided conversation with Updike was long-running. Admiration and dislike were always in competition, usually mixed together. Updike was an extraordinary writer, Wallace acknowledged, but there was something too insistent about the way he always declared his genius. The self-conscious beauty and elegance of his prose, Wallace wrote to DeLillo in January 1997, "paw ... at the reader's ear like a sophomore at some poor girl's bra." Now faced with the master's new book, Wallace felt only disdain and a whiff of pity. How, he asked the *Observer* readers, could so gifted a writer write a book as bad as *Toward the End of Time*?

> *Toward the End of Time* concerns an incredibly erudite, articulate, successful, narcissistic and sex-obsessed retired guy who's keeping a one-year journal in which he explores the apocalyptic prospect of his own death. It is, of the total 25 Updike books I've read, far and away the worst, a novel so mind-bendingly clunky and self-indulgent that it's hard to believe the author let it be published in this kind of shape.

Wallace evinced a particular dislike for the protagonist's "bizarre adolescent idea that getting to have sex with whomever one wants whenever one wants is a cure for ontological despair," a line of thought no doubt well known to Wallace.

He received much congratulations when the piece ran in October 1997, and the remark that he attributed to "a friend" in the article, that Updike was "just a thesaurus with a penis," was widely circulated. Wallace did not like overly personal literary criticism, but he felt within his rights in this case because of his sense that Updike's flaws had gone beyond the literary to the moral. His characters—well, the author himself—were forgetting that literature was not about showing off; it had to be a service to the inner life of the reader. How then to justify creating characters

> who are also always incorrigibly narcissistic, philandering, self-contemptuous, self-pitying and deeply alone, alone the way only a solipsist can be alone. They never belong to any sort of larger unit or

community or cause. Though usually family men, they never really love anybody—and, though always heterosexual to the point of satyriasis, they especially don't love women. The very world around them, as beautifully as they see and describe it, seems to exist for them only insofar as it evokes impressions and associations and emotions inside the self.

After the review ran, Wallace was sorry. He knew that *Toward the End of Time* was hardly representative of Updike's best work, his attack seeming after the fact like another brain-fart. "It makes me look like a punk taking easy shots at a big target," he wrote an admirer who praised the review. "Never again, ami, a book review of a titan." (On the other hand, he included it in his next essay collection, *Consider the Lobster*, published in 2005.)

As he was finishing the Updike piece, *Premiere* asked Wallace to cover the awards ceremony the adult entertainment industry held every year in Las Vegas. Wallace loved the idea—pornography was a subject that never stopped interesting him. It was where the false pleasures and relentless marketing of America met, a metonym for what was toxic in the nation. "My opinions are only that the love you of this country speak of yields none of the pleasure you seek in love," lectures Marathe in *Infinite Jest*. The piece was also a way to intellectualize an appetite a less guilt-ridden man might have just enjoyed. Rather than look for the movies locally, Wallace asked *Premiere* to rent them in New York and send them to his home. There he watched them in preparation and quickly shipped them back.

In January 1998 he went to the convention. He met the "gonzo porn" producer Max Hardcore and Jasmin St. Claire, known in the industry as "the gang-bang queen." He was able to compare his penis size to those of male porn stars in the men's room and take in a spectacle tackier than he had ever seen before. What always amazed Wallace about real life was the overload of information. He did not see how anyone could really capture what went on in a single moment. He wrote to a friend in frustration, "Writing about real-life stuff is next to impossible, simply because there's **so much!**" He spent a great deal of time in the hallway of the convention, propped against a wall, scribbling in his notebook. (He was as interested in recording his reaction to what he was seeing as in what he was in fact seeing.) At night he would lie awake in his bed looking at himself in the ceiling mirror.[6]

Where Wallace didn't find the remarkable, he invented or borrowed. He made use of interviews from his long-ago unpublished *Playboy* research. *Premiere* had asked a writer from *Hustler*, Evan Wright, to help out, and, with his permission, Wallace mined his research as avidly as his own. Wright told Wallace of a scene from two years before in which a porn star, angry at something he had written, put him in a headlock. For his article Wallace moved it to the present and improved the moment by giving Wright a pair of "special autotint trifocals" that the headlock sent "in an arc across the room and into the forbidding décolletage of Christy Canyon never to be recovered." Wright had written in the *LA Weekly* about a woman at an industry charity bowling event who had valves under her arms through which she was slowly augmenting her bust size with silicone. Wallace turned them into air valves that would allow her to grow or shrink her breasts at whim, a character out of Philip K. Dick. In all, the convention left him with much the same feeling as the Caribbean cruise had: how sad the world was when you opened your eyes, how much pain it contained. "Some of the starlets are so heavily made up," he wrote in the article, "they look embalmed. They have complexly coiffed hair that tends to look really good from twenty feet away but on closer inspection is totally dry and dead." When he got back to Bloomington, he was relieved. He described his trip to DeLillo as "three days in Bosch's hell-panel." "I don't think I'll have an erection again for a year," was his comment to Franzen.

Bit by bit Wallace scratched out enough short fiction so that by late 1997 he thought he had a new collection. He told Pietsch he was surprised how dark the stories were since he hadn't been feeling "particularly dark" in the past few years. He knew that the mini-tales might not please all the readers of his last two books. They were funny but they were not playful or redemptive, qualities many readers had come to associate with his name. He immediately looked for reassurance that the publication of the collection would not become a replay of *Infinite Jest*, a chance for Little, Brown to cash in on what he called his "late 90s notoriety." "I don't think the book could stand up to that kind of hype," he wrote Nadell. "It'd be slim, strange and a bit slight. A small book." But the reflexive cast of his mind immediately set him to wondering whether his modesty meant he really didn't think the book deserved readers at all. "Do I," he asked Nadell, "secretly think it's not strong enough to publish, meaning I should wait a few years or however long it takes to have some Bigger or more reader-friendly stories? Or am I a whore to think that way?"

With Wallace a desire to be published usually won out. Moreover, as he began organizing and revising the stories for a collection, he became more excited by how powerful they were as a group. They centered on fear, longing, anxiety, depression, and boundaries, the challenge of being human in an inhospitable time. Many of the stories examined courtship behavior—his, of course, which was particularly nauseating to him at times—but also the entire back-and-forth that he had witnessed between men and women, fortified by the many stories he'd heard in recovery and in relationships.

The set-up for the core of the collection is consistent: they are little plays, conversations, most between a woman and various men she is interviewing. The interrogator's questions are never written, though; it is up to the reader to figure them out.[7] The tales are designated only by place and date, as if they were jailhouse or psych ward interviews B.I. #59 04-98 HAROLD R. AND PHYLLIS N. ENGMAN INSTITUTE FOR CONTINUING CARE EASTCHESTER NY B.I. #15 MCI-BRIDGEWATER OBSERVATION & ASSESSMENT FACILITY BRIDGEWATER MA. The men are not named.

One man tells a story to a friend about seeing a woman get off an airplane and wait at the gate for someone who doesn't show; he picks her up, exploiting her disappointment. A second invites women to let him tie them up; he claims an almost perfect ability to sense which women secretly want to be dominated in this way, comparing it to "chicken-sexing."[8] In a third, a man uses his withered arm—his "Asset," he calls it—to get women to sleep with him out of pity: "I see how you're trying to be polite and not look at it," he challenges the interrogator. "Go ahead and look though. It don't bother me. . . . You want to hear me describe it? It looks like a arm that changed its mind early on in the game when it was in Mama's stomach with the rest of me. It's more like a itty tiny little flipper." In a fourth, a man tells the interviewer that men who spend a lot of time focusing on the sexual needs of women—"going down on a lady's yingyang over and over and making her come seventeen straight times and such"—are actually as narcissistic as men who only want to orgasm. "The catch is they're selfish about being generous," he lectures. "They're no better than the pig is, they're just sneakier about it."

The men in the stories not only seem to feel nothing; they seem to feel nothing about feeling nothing. They have creepy amounts of self-awareness but no ambition for catharsis. Their hideousness is beyond question. But Wallace was also making a point about women and their endlessly disappointed hopes for sane connections in the era of relative equality (if indeed it was sane connections they wanted and didn't just say they wanted). It was as if he were challenging women, saying, You think men are disgusting? I'll show you disgusting men. "How exactly the cycle's short pieces are supposed to work is hard to describe," the narrator of one story, "Octet," avers, addressing himself. "Maybe say they're supposed to compose a certain sort of '*interrogation*' of the person reading them somehow—i.e. palpations, feelers into the interstices of her sense of something, etc. . . . Though what that 'something' is remains maddeningly hard to pin down, even just for yourself as you're working on the pieces." Wallace would call the stories in a letter to his old Amherst teacher Andrew Parker "a parody (a feminist parody) of feminism," though they were also a postmodernist parody of postmodernism, as one nameless male chauvinist makes clear:

> Today's postfeminist era is also today's postmodern era, in which supposedly everybody now knows everything about what's really going on underneath all the semiotic codes and cultural conventions, and everybody supposedly knows what paradigms everybody is operating out of, and so we're all us individuals held to be far more responsible for our sexuality, since everything we do is now unprecedentedly conscious and informed.

"I see that Hal is not the last sad character you'll be inventing," Pietsch had responded to the first batch of stories he read, which Wallace sent in

February 1997. Wallace added the remainder in mid-August 1998, just before he had to go back to teaching after his anxious sabbatical. He wrote his editor with uncharacteristic enthusiasm:

> I feel pretty good about the mss.'s constituents and their order as they stand. I like the way they play off one another and the way certain leitmotifs weave through them (see for example the child-perspective-self-pity of "The Depressed Person" vs. the parent-perspective-self-pity of "On his Deathbed . . . Begs a Boon" vs. the more quote-unquote objective intrafamily pain of "Signifying Nothing" and "Suicide . . . Present," or the way p. 149's "Yet Another Example . . . (Vi). . . . arcs back to "The Depressed Person," etc.)

Publication was set for May 1999, at the end of the school term, so Wallace could tour.

The week that Wallace mailed off the full *Brief Interviews with Hideous Men* manuscript to Pietsch, the Poags invited him to dinner to meet a woman. Nearing thirty-seven, Wallace felt ready for a change. The birth of his sister's first child in February had reminded him he was no closer to the alluring stability of family life. Writing *Brief Interviews* had also shaken him up. The book, he told friends, had made him look at aspects of himself he didn't find very appealing. He had recently broken up with yet another girlfriend and wrote a friend that he felt like he had been through the experience so many times by now that it left him dispirited—"not about the thing not working out but low vis a vis DFW and his existential state."

Wallace had told the Poags he wanted to be with either a nurse or a social worker, and the woman they invited, Juliana Harms, worked for the Department of Children and Foster Services. For Wallace the meeting was a date, but the Poags told Harms Wallace was interested in interviewing her for some work he was doing, which, given Wallace's hunger for material, was also true. Wallace was an inveterate interviewer. He went to a tire factory, trailed an exterminator, and even had watched Francis B. propose to his girlfriend. Now the foursome had Chinese food for dinner and sat on the Poags' front porch afterward. From across the street they heard a baby's cry: Harms tensed up. "That's not normal," she said. When the baby calmed down, so did she. Wallace was impressed.

Soon they met again, and before long the pretense of an interview was gone and they were seeing each other. Harms was more like Susie Perkins than like the women Wallace had dated over the past decade; she was not depressed, nor did she have a history of drug or alcohol problems. She had liked *Girl with Curious Hair* but most of all remembered looking at the picture on the back, taken when Wallace lived in Somerville, and thinking, "User"—a drug abuser. Wallace was fascinated by her job, which included entering houses under police protection to remove endangered children, and pressed her for every detail about how she did it.

Immediately, Wallace had wanted to go to bed with her. This was how he usually dated. Harms resisted, though; so instead they would go for long walks; she lived in an apartment on the other side of town from him. They spent hours talking into the night. She loved Kokopelli, a Hopi trickster and fertility god. He had a large one on his wall. The *Oxford English Dictionary* held pride of place on the shelves in his living room. On the first birthday of hers that they celebrated together, a month after they met, Wallace gave Harms the two-volume version, with, as she remembers, "salivating excitement." They became involved. Wallace's "Mary" tattoo had faded over the years. "Who's Marv?" they would joke.

Wallace was in a "post-partum funk," as he called it, after finishing *Brief Interviews*. The Drone was sick with lymphoma and despite a course of chemotherapy was not getting better. "I've been going around crying like a toddler at the prospect of him suffering or dying," he wrote Brad Morrow. Harms helped him through these difficult moments. In November Wallace took her to Jamaica. The gesture was a counterphobic one— he hated travel, and tourism even more. But Wallace saw a chance to start afresh, a way to slough off his own hideousness. The couple arrived at the Beachcomber Resort in Negril. They swam together, Wallace lulled by the promise that there could be no sharks so close to shore in the Caribbean, and ate spicy food and walked on the beach, where, attracted by his long hair, marijuana sellers swarmed him. "They always come to the addict," he said. But as often as he could, Wallace barricaded himself in the coral pink bathroom to write. Never liking to be without a project, he had started on a long essay on language which was giving him the usual trouble. "We snorkeled," he wrote Franzen in quiet panic on his fifth day at the resort, "Juliana got menaced by a sting ray. She is easy to be with, and that's good, because except for the 2 hours a day I flail away (futilely) on the usage article, we're together all the time." Harms was surprised to find that her new friend locked the door to work even when he was alone.

Back in Bloomington, Wallace settled down to his article. The piece was tied to the publication of a new dictionary of American usage, but he wanted to write about the function of language more broadly, what it really meant to speak of "a common language." Grammar, he saw, was agreement, community, consensus. "Issues of usage, looked at closely even for a moment," he wrote DeLillo, "become issues of Everything—from neurology to politics to Aristotelian *pisteis* to Jaussian *Kritik* to stuff like etiquette and clothing fashions." Not surprisingly, as soon as he opened himself up to such vast considerations, Wallace found himself overwhelmed: "Every argument seems to me to sprout several potential objections, each of which feels like it has to be handled or the whole argument falls like a pine." He invoked an image from Faulkner that writing a novel was like building a hen coop in a hurricane and asked DeLillo to remind him never to do nonfiction again. "The whole thing needs to end," he added.

The relationship with Harms continued to go well. She got him to cut his hair for the first time in a year and they went to the office Christmas party for the Department of Children and Foster Services, Wallace wearing one of her plastic tortoiseshell headbands. Drone died in mid-December. Wallace held his dog in his arms and cried as the veterinarian gave a lethal injection. The body could not be cremated for three weeks and so he would go by the veterinary office and sit outside the freezer where his dog lay. He sent DeLillo a holiday card with the emendation, "It is a sad Christmas."

Again Harms was there to comfort him. Wallace asked Harms not to fly in winter; he was afraid of losing her in a crash. Soon Harms moved into his house at the edge of town, bringing her cat. They bought a king-sized bed, because the old one was too small. The two shared corny pop songs they loved, like Edwin McCain's "I'll Be Your Crying Shoulder." (Wallace boasted he had the musical taste of a high school girl.) He bought her expensive gifts, happy that the books and the fellowships had made him well-to-do. The couple got engaged and picked out a setting for their

rings. They talked about having a child and agreed that if Harms got pregnant they would be pleased.

But there were issues. Harms wouldn't let him use a pen on the couch.
He was allergic to her cat. She would come home from work and zone out.
He worked all day on his fiction.[9] At Harms's urging, Wallace checked
himself into an addiction center in Pennsylvania to try to get off nicotine
entirely. He had been at various times a smoker, a tobacco chewer, and a
patch user—sometimes all three in quick succession—since graduate
school.[10] The stay lasted more than a week, and Wallace came home highly
agitated. He wished he had a major project under way; he wished he were
smoking. He wondered about the Nardil. He never felt quite himself on it.
It left him somehow slightly detached from reality. He had in recent years,
he believed, become hypoglycemic too, and so his historic diet of prepack-
aged blondies was replaced by sugarless jelly spreads.

Wallace had managed to keep television at bay for many years now, but
in order to relax after her grueling days, Harms ordered satellite TV service with, as she remembers, 75 channels. Wallace would sit and click
through the stations, landing on one, then moving on to the next, always
afraid he was missing something better and so really watching nothing.
By now, between the loss of The Drone, the availability of TV, the lack of
nicotine, and the scarcity of privacy, he was stupefied. But he was engaged
and committed to Juliana.

Juliana was an active Catholic. She and her fiancé discussed his convert-
ing. Wallace, who never lost his hope that he could find faith, signed up for
an ecumenical Christian program called cursillo: the goal "to bring God
from the head to the heart." But his new attempt to join a formal religion did
not get much further than the one with Karr. At the final ceremony, when
the participants were meant to attest their belief in God, Wallace expressed
his doubts instead. Faith was something he could admire in others but never
quite countenance for himself. He liked to paraphrase Bertrand Russell that
there were certain philosophical issues he could bear to think about only for
a few minutes a year and once told his old Arizona sponsor Rich C. that he
couldn't go to church because "I always get the giggles."[11]

He was back at school now teaching and could be short-tempered, perhaps resenting the time it took up. In one creative writing class he shoved
a student who had shown him attitude and then threatened to fail him: "I

too have used outrage, abrasiveness, and irritation as a way to keep people at arm's length," he wrote Lee Freeman in a note. "So trust me: it is a bush-league defense, and painfully obvious in the terror it betrays."

By now the new relationship energy with Harms had completely dissipated. Wallace bolted himself in his dark workroom, and when Juliana came home she watched TV alone. Costello was worried by how praising Wallace was when he talked of Harms. He knew, as he remembers, that "admiration was always the tomb" of his friend's relationships. Wallace and Juliana went to St. Louis to visit Franzen, who felt like Wallace's interest in her was largely theoretical.[12]

Harms, too, saw that Wallace was pulling away. The search for the ring had stopped. He got a rescued puppy to replace The Drone, but he found the presence in the house of the new dog, Werner, a pit bull mix, unbearable. "I can't work," he complained to Harms. "I have to take care of him all day." The couple went to a MacArthur Fellowship reunion in Chicago, and Wallace stayed in the hotel room, trying to write. "I need to be ready to write," he explained to her. But to Costello he acknowledged, "Clean pages are safe around me." He told Juliana he felt like he was always disappointing her, then got mad when she said he had all the qualities she could hope for in a partner. She grew suspicious—she guessed he was hiding something larger.[13]

Harms confronted Wallace, who denied being involved with another woman. She pulled out all his papers. A trained investigator, she knew where to look. She found several notes from a graduate student in Wallace's department. "I haven't had a physical affair with her but I'm contemplating it," Wallace explained sullenly. Harms had had enough. A few weeks later, in early January 2000, Doug Poag helped her move out. Wallace contributed to the down payment for her new house out of his MacArthur money and then was peeved when a new boyfriend quickly moved in.

The graduate student became Wallace's girlfriend. They exchanged books—he gave her *The Screwtape Letters*, she gave him the J. D. Salinger collection *Nine Stories*—"She was a girl who for a ringing phone dropped exactly nothing" was a line he loved. Things grew increasingly intense, but as ever the work came first for Wallace and the relationship faltered.

*   *   *

In April 1999, Salon.com asked Wallace for his list of underappreciated novels, and in his response he included longtime loves like *Omensetter's Luck*, *Wittgenstein's Mistress*, and *Blood Meridian*, but added Jerzy Kosinski's little-known *Steps*, "a collection of unbelievably creepy little allegorical tableaux done in a terse elegant voice that's like nothing else anywhere ever. Only Kafka's fragments get anywhere close."

Kafka's fragments may have been the comparison he wanted reviewers to make when they read *Brief Interviews*. He had written a book that was, as he told an interviewer, "mean to just about everyone it's possible to be mean to," and had to hope for thoughtful readings. He was, though, resigned to what might come, perhaps even to being ignored. He wrote Brad Morrow that he was glad to be out of the spotlight: "The big Attention eyeball has mostly passed on to other poor schmo's." Still, Little, Brown asked him to go on a book tour and he obliged, as long as it was short. "I'm in the midst of the world's smallest tour," he boasted to Steven Moore in June. "Just four cities." Even short book tours filled him with misgivings. "The Statue Talks!" he joked to a friend.

He avoided interviews as much as he could and tried to show as little of himself as possible when obligated to sit down for them. He met a writer from *Book* magazine at the Cracker Barrel by the I-55 interchange in Bloomington, where he grouchily averred that he "just want[ed] to be left alone to eat my meatloaf." *Publishers Weekly* found him at a K-Mart. In Los Angeles, he went on *Bookworm*, a radio show hosted by Michael Silverblatt. Silverblatt was special—he had been so excited by *Infinite Jest* he had called Michael Pietsch to ask to read the outtakes. In their conversation now, Wallace suggested that the collection was meant as a corrective for those readers who had misunderstood his last novel:

> I wanted to do a book that was sad. . . . It's something I tried to do in *Infinite Jest*. Everybody thought that book was funny, which was of course nice, but it was also kind of frustrating. I designed this one so that nobody is going to escape the fact that this is sad.

Silverblatt gave a persuasive explanation of how Wallace was attempting to effect this:

Here, it felt as if, in reading these stories with eyes wide open, I was being asked to revolve so much that I would get dizzy. And that, in the fall, in the dizziness, a kind of compelling sadness— that the sadness is itself formed by the obligation to have no stable position. That everything has to spin on itself, until a kind of weariness, attrition, ecstasy, exhilaration, humor, terror, become compounded. And the emotion bomb, as the therapists say, is left in the reader.

To which Wallace answered, "Wow. You're giving—I mean, this is why I look forward to coming to L.A.—is you tend to give interpretations of the stuff that's real close to what I want."

The country's reviewers on the whole were more positive than Wallace expected. He was welcomed to the short story form (although in fact this was his second collection), and critics tended to play up his formal inventiveness and shy away from the knotty problem of what the reader was supposed to come away with. Benjamin Weissman in the *LA Weekly* praised this "full-scale harassment of the short story form," while Andrei Codrescu in the *Chicago Tribune* admired Wallace's "seemingly inexhaustible bag of literary tricks." Adam Goodheart, writing in the *New York Times Book Review*, sounded a mixed note, comparing Wallace to Edgar Allan Poe, "another mad scientist of American literature." But Michiko Kakutani of the *New York Times* chose to do unto Wallace as he had done unto Updike:

No doubt these portraits are meant as sardonic commentaries on our narcissistic, therapeutic age, but they are so long-winded, so solipsistic, so predictable in their use of irony and gratuitous narrative high jinks that they end up being as tiresome and irritating as their subjects.

She accused Wallace of writing an "airless, tedious" book that failed to live up to the promise in "E Unibus Pluram" to reanimate the "deep moral issues that distinguished the work of the great 19th-century writers." "The NY Times just slaughtered the book," Wallace wrote Moore afterward, "just panned it, in a review that caused my editor pain (he actually called me about it)." Wallace was in fact also devastated and could recite several sentences in it from memory.

The *New York Review of Books* soon afterward published the first major overview of Wallace's mature work, taking a stance between impressed and skeptical and implicitly psychoanalyzing the author along the way. "The Panic of Influence," by A. O. Scott, emphasized Wallace's anxious relationship with post-modernism and also his expectation he could have things both ways, pursuing the questionable tactic of writing cleverly to assert the superiority of sincerity in a world wedded to cleverness. Scott also accused Wallace of fencing off all possible objections to his work by making sure every possible criticism was already embedded in the text. *Brief Interviews*, especially, the critic wrote, was not so much anti-ironic as "meta-ironic," driven much like the characters in its stories by the fear of being known. This sort of writing, he continued, was clearly connected to the self-centered self-absorbed culture of late-twentieth-century America, but "does Wallace's work represent an unusually trenchant critique of that culture or one of its most florid and exotic symptoms? Of course, there can only be one answer: it's both." Wallace was not pleased but he was impressed. In the margins of a draft of the story "Good Old Neon," which he began around this time, he noted (punningly), "AO Scott saw into my character."

Brief Interviews, though, sold well, which made Little, Brown happy and, for better or worse, helped buff the statue. Though Wallace claimed he no longer read reviews, he printed out a post by a critic for *Slate's* book club to tape inside his composition notebook: "The difference: BIWHM's just too much telling, not enough showing. He needs to combine that urge to confront what matters with his ability to spin a wonderful tale. When that book comes out, I'll be waiting in line."

Wallace had been mulling the possibilities for a third novel since the mid-1990s, even as he began the stories that would form the heart of *Brief Interviews*. The setting had come early, possibly even before the publication of *Infinite Jest*: he knew he wanted to write about the IRS. The agency fit well with Wallace's Pynchonian appetite for clandestine organizations and hidden conspiracies. And like the tennis academy and recovery house in *Infinite Jest*, it was a world unto itself, where characters would be in charged apposition to one another. Wallace himself had had numerous small brushes with the agency over the years, usually involving trivial errors on Form 1099s that he or his accountant had to get corrected. These encounters touched off the same anxiety within him as communications from lawyers and fact-checkers. He had an idea as well of the IRS as a secular church, a counterpart to Alcoholics Anonymous in *Infinite Jest*.[14] But, finally, he probably settled on the IRS for the most obvious reason: it was the dullest possible venue he could think of and he had decided to write about boredom.

Wallace had no direct knowledge of life at the IRS or indeed in any office—he had never worked in one—and his grasp of accounting was shaky, but he was an avid study, so, soon after the publication of his novel, he began taking classes at the university. He went from beginning financial accounting in the fall of 1996 ("Examines the nature of accounting, basic accounting concepts, financial statements, accrual basis of accounting . . .") to federal income taxation in summer 1997 and advanced tax that fall. He read countless agency publications and books on accounting and the IRS, from *West Federal Taxation* to D. Larry Crumbley's *The Ultimate Rip-Off*. He interviewed real-life IRS employees and went to Peoria, where the agency had a large facility. He boasted to Costello that he was only a few credits short of passing the state accounting exam.

As Wallace moved forward, he acquired vocabulary and context for his novel, much as he would for one of his nonfiction pieces. He used to tell his classes that a novelist had to know enough about a subject to fool the passenger next to him or her on an airplane; Wallace easily surpassed that benchmark. He learned that what outsiders called an IRS agent might actually be an examiner, an auditor, or an investigator. He read that the IRS had changed its focus in the Reagan era from an agency primarily involved with compliance to one engaged in revenue maximization; a fiscal mission had replaced a civic one. He thought there might be something in that conflict to dramatize. When something wasn't true that would be good, he made it up. He decided junior employees were called "wigglers" or, dismissively, "turdnagels." (This became his email address for a time, after he started using email in the early 2000s.) "'Snout'=IRS Investigator /

'Immersive'=Talented IRS examiner," he wrote in a notebook. He imagined that all IRS agents got a new social security number when they entered the agency. Wallace found a prose poem by Frank Bidart that suggested a clever epigraph for this rebirth: "We fill pre-existing forms and when we fill them we change them and are changed."

His research in pornography over the years was still on his mind. Wallace's original conceit for the novel may have involved not just tedium but pleasure. He made notes for a plot in which a group of rich businessmen run a video porn operation. They go into business with Drinion, an IRS immersive so talented that he sometimes floats above his seat while he works. Drinion had helped seize the business on behalf of the service for unpaid taxes. He comes now to double as their male lead in the movies. His great virtue is that he is so pale that he can be digitally erased and the porn viewer can have his own image replace it.[15] It was the "Infinite Jest" videocartridge one iteration further along: what could be more addictive than watching yourself act out an addiction?[16]

The Bidart poem neatly connected to Wallace's core interest in the IRS: how does it change a person's internal life to work at something as dull as monitoring tax returns? The agents' jobs were tedious, but dullness, in Wallace's conceit, was what ultimately set them free. The lack of stimulation gave them a chance to open themselves up to experience in the largest sense of the word. The idea connected to Buddhism—Eastern religious practices had been a growing interest of Wallace's for many years. (He liked to practice sitting meditation, he wrote Rich C., with "weird cultish Sikh and Buddhist groups, most of whom are very crazy in a very attractive way.") The goal of the discipline was crucial to him—the inability to slow down his whirring mind was part of what he felt made his life so hard. As a character notes in the story "Good Old Neon," which Wallace wrote around 2000, "What goes on inside is just too fast and huge and all interconnected for words to do more than barely sketch the outlines of at most one tiny little part of it at any given instant." In the process of writing the novel he came to call *The Pale King*,[17] he laid out its central tenet in one of his notebooks:

Bliss—a-second-by-second joy and gratitude at the gift of being alive, conscious—lies on the other side of crushing, crushing boredom. Pay close attention to the most tedious thing you can find (Tax Returns, Televised Golf) and, in waves, a boredom like you've never known will wash over you and just about kill you. Ride these out, and it's like stepping from black and white into color. Like water after days in the desert. Instant bliss in every atom.

Wallace had explored this state briefly in *Infinite Jest*, partly through Lyle, the levitating guru in the weight room, and partly through John "No Relation" Wayne, the top player at the tennis academy, whose skill comes not from Wallace- or Hal-like cunning but from "frustrating mindless repetitive practice and patience and hanging in there."[18] With the help of researchers, Wallace assembled hundreds of pages of research on boredom, trying to understand it at an almost neurological level. He pulled down his *Oxford English Dictionary* and was intrigued to find that "bore" appeared in English in 1766, two years before "interesting" came to mean "absorbing."

Wallace had four offices to write his novel in: his black room at home, a university office (rarely visited), a room put aside for him in Francis B.'s mother's house, and a rented space in town.[19] He was usually flummoxed by his lack of progress. DeLillo, to whom he wrote in worry, reassured him that a novel was "a long march to the mountains." He took a second year-long leave in 2000 and spent the first half of it trying to work and seeing a lot of movies. (Movies, he liked to say, were an addict's recreation of choice.) Then he wrote letters about the movies. DeLillo was his chosen correspondent and his opinions were anti-elitist and mildly contrarian. For instance, he saw and loved the cyberthriller *The Matrix*—"visually raw and kinetic and riveting in a way that only something like Bochco's Hill Street Blues was in '81," he wrote his friend—and hated the acclaimed *Magnolia*, which he found pretentious and hollow, "100% gradschoolish in a bad way." That summer he went to a retreat run by the Lannan Foundation in Marfa, Texas. There Wallace spent a pleasant month. He borrowed a nearby rancher's two golden retriever puppies to walk and turned the books by the retreat's alumni to the wall. This was his moment to approach the novel head-on, but the writing didn't go particularly well, at least in retrospect. To Franzen, on his return, he wrote, "Almost everything I did there will have to be thrown away, but that, too, is good, in a way." To Rich C., he was more downbeat: "I'm scared I can't do good work anymore."

Wallace was ever more in demand for his nonfiction. In the fall of 1999, *Rolling Stone* asked him if he wanted to write about a candidate in the upcoming presidential elections and he chose John McCain, the independent-minded Republican who was opposing George W. Bush for the presidential nomination. Wallace was politically fairly conservative; he'd voted for Ronald Reagan and supported Ross Perot in 1992, telling his friend Corey Washington, "You need someone really insane to fix the economy." He came to combine midwestern conventionality with girlfriend-pleasing campus liberalism. In 2000 he voted for Bill Bradley in the Illinois primary. In truth politics did not generally matter much to him. He did not think who won an election could change what was broken. But in McCain Wallace saw another chance to explore the hollowing out of the American character. McCain's campaign, which prided itself on openness and truthfulness, raised two intriguingly recursive questions in his mind. Was McCain genuinely honest or just portraying himself as genuine? If the former, were Americans so steeped in the complex double-talk of advertising they could not see genuineness when it appeared? And if the latter, were they so used to being tricked that it was now its own source of pleasure?

Wallace spent a week on the campaign trail in early February 2000 and, as was his style, ignored the top-level operatives to focus on the techies and hacks in the bus that followed McCain's bus, the Straight Talk Express, dubbed (probably by Wallace) the Bullshit 1. He exaggerated on the way to make his point. He painted the major newspaper reporters—he called them "the twelve monkeys"—as haughtier and more alike one another than they even were and pretended the McCain campaign strategist was so afraid of him he would duck around the corner to avoid encounters (in fact they got along well; the gesture was playful, as the campaign strategist told a reporter for *Salon* in 2010.) And did two separate reporters really mistake Wallace for a bellboy and tell him to carry their suitcases? It seemed unlikely, but all this falsity contributed to creating a portrait of

Wallace as an outsider, someone who could convey a truth readers weren't getting elsewhere, real straight talk. In the end, what Wallace wanted to capture was what

> the brief weird excitement [that the campaign] generated might reveal about how millennial politics and all its packaging and marketing and strategy and media and spin and general sepsis actually makes us US voters feel, inside.

McCain's campaign was fast folding. After he lost the primary elections of early March to Bush, *Rolling Stone* needed the article in a hurry. Wallace took only three weeks to write twenty-seven thousand words. The piece—cut by more than half in three days of frantic editing by phone—was in print by mid-April, a speed that Wallace found both liberating and upsetting. In the end Wallace used his unaccustomed ringside seat at American history to further preoccupations that dated back to his "E Unibus Pluram" essay. His conclusion was that McCain was America looking in the mirror. "Whether he's truly For Real," he ended, "depends now less on what's in his heart than on what might be in yours."

The article would win a National Magazine Award, but Wallace always felt his take on the "three months that tickled the prostate of the American Century," as he called the campaign in a letter to DeLillo, was just a vacation from the novel he was supposed to be working on. "I do not know why the comparative ease and pleasure of writing nonfiction always confirms my intuition that fiction is really What I'm Supposed to Do," he added as "The Weasel, Twelve Monkeys and the Shrub" was about to appear, "but it does, and now I'm back here flogging away (in all senses of the word) and feeding my own wastebasket, and taking half-hours off to write letters like this and still calling it Writing Time."

In June 2000, an editor from Atlas Books approached Wallace with the idea of writing a volume on mathematics for its Great Discoveries series, which it was copublishing with Norton. Jesse Cohen suggested as subjects either Georg Cantor, a pioneer in set theory, or Kurt Gödel, who authored the incompleteness theorems, which state that no matter how much one knows about a system there is yet more to know. That knowledge has limits that are themselves the product of our knowledge was the sort of thing that Wallace never stopped thinking about. "Obvious fact," he would later write in the book, "never before have there been so many gaping chasms between what the world seems to be and what science tells us it is." Cantor, though, held the prospect of something even more appealing: an inquiry into a man who took on a puzzle of the sort that had always fascinated and worried Wallace—in this case, the nature of infinity. Most investigations into thinking of this sort, Wallace knew, led to paralysis, the a.p.-s's (adolescent pot smoker's) solipsism he always feared. Cantor though had broken through to the other side by showing that there are different sized infinities and that they can be thought about almost like ordinary numbers. He had turned a fearsome unknown into a quantity that mathematicians could manipulate. Cantor also presented the more achievable challenge. "I know [enough] about Gödel's proof to know that the math and notations alone would take me years to get proficient at," Wallace wrote Cohen. He added in a stern fax he sent shortly after from Marfa that if he did undertake the book it would be "on the side as a diversion from other contracted stuff." All the same, he couldn't resist thinking how rewarding such an effort would be:

Did you know that the implifications/ramifications of Cantor's diagonal proof are huge, especially for contemporary computer science (e.g. "trans-computational problems," etc.)? Did you know that it would take 500 pages even to outline these consequences and ramifications? Would the book just be a bio of Cantor and contemporaries and discuss the Proof and its context, or would you also expect a Consequences discussion?

When Cohen wrote back that the book was meant to be a book of ideas, the thrust being on "Cantor and the sheer mindbending quality of his theories," Wallace was hooked. This was the part of him he had left by the side of the road when he became a fiction writer, the part he had tried to breathe life back into when he went to Harvard, the part that made him the smartest guy in the room. He had slid into lightweight magazine work, offering insights on porn and tennis. The information that the advance might be as high as $100,000 did not hurt either. That was a bigger advance than he had gotten for *Infinite Jest*. He said yes.

It was now the fall and Wallace was more than halfway through the second leave that was supposed to be devoted to his fiction. He started research on the infinity book. His efforts on what he had taken to calling "the Long Thing" did not go well. "Most of my own stuff I've been delivering to the wastebasket," he wrote Markson in November. "It looks good in there." All the same he was so glad not to be teaching that when he found out that the university was accidentally still paying him, he wrote his department head to say he wouldn't cash the checks in case they tried to make him pay them back with classes later. But in the spring of 2001, he was back in the classroom, trying to balance his nonfiction, his fiction, and his fears. The article on American usage he had begun when he was with Juliana finally appeared in *Harper's*. The magazine ran less than half of what he had originally written but he acknowledged in a note to DeLillo that Colin Harrison, his longtime nonfiction editor there, "did a pretty good cut."

That summer he went with friends to a two-week meditation retreat at Plum Village near Bordeaux, France, under the Zen master Thich Nhat Hanh. The retreat required abstention from both coffee and smoking. Wallace wanted to understand more deeply what it was he was proposing in *The Pale King*. What did the bliss that followed great boredom actually *feel* like? He found that writing about mindlessness and achieving it for oneself were two different things; he left early, blaming the food, and was home as soon as he could be. He wrote to DeLillo on his return, "Highlights: 1) Went AWOL from Viet-Buddhist monast[e]ry's retreat. . . . 2) watched 2 of 4 drunk Peruvians drown in Dordogne off St. Foy La Grande. 3) Ate a snail on purpose." He mentioned that Franzen, whose third novel, *The Corrections,* was coming out in mid-September, was "gearing up for his turn at having Sauron's great red eye upon him."

The morning of September 11 found Wallace at his usual activities, going to his meeting, running errands, planning to write. At the actual moment of the attacks, he was showering, "trying to listen to a Bears postmortem on WSCR Sports Radio in Chicago," as he remembered. He did not know whether he had feelings about the attacks beyond the ordinary, but when *Rolling Stone* approached him for a piece on his response, he felt drawn to try. In three days, he wrote a short, delicate essay—"Caveat. Written very fast and in what probably qualifies as shock," he appended to the draft. "The View from Mrs. Thompson's" is a piece of oblique social analysis, a tribute both to the heartland and recovery. (It was first punningly called "A View from the Interior.") He once more disguised his recovery group circle as friends from church. Thus Mrs. Thompson, his pseudonym for the mother of Francis B., became "a long-time church member and leader in our congregation." He captured the essence of her and her friends' diffuse, gentle articulations as they viewed the awful events, their worries about family in or near Manhattan, and their tears as they watched the towers collapse on television. "What the Bloomington ladies are," Wallace wrote,

> or start to seem, is innocent. There is what would strike many Americans as a bizarre lack of cynicism in the room. It doesn't once occur to anyone here to remark on how it's maybe a little odd that . . . the relentless rerunning of horrific footage might not be just in case some viewers were only now tuning in and hadn't seen it yet.

He contrasted the sincerity of the women with the attitude of a young man named Duane, also present, whose "main contribution was to keep iterating how much like a movie it is." Wallace ended, "I'm trying to explain the way part of the horror of the Horror was knowing that whatever America the men in those planes hated so much was far more my own—mine . . . and poor old loathsome Duane's—than these ladies'." Did a certain part of America then deserve what it got? This was a point Wallace of course had to sidestep, but for anyone who had absorbed the lessons of *Infinite Jest* it was present all the same.

"It's been a couple of very humbling years," Wallace wrote Michael Pietsch soon after, admitting the novel was not going forward but insisting he had the maturity now to withstand fallow times: "When there's sufficient humility and non-seriousness-about-self, it's not all that bad, more like when the two guys are laughing existentially . . . at the end of *Treasure of the Sierra Madre*." It did hurt, though, that the turn of the millennium had brought with it an abundance of large literary efforts that threatened to push *Infinite Jest* to the edge of the stage. Dave Eggers's memoir, *A Heart-breaking Work of Staggering Genius*, had appeared in 2000, with a quote from Wallace on the jacket praising this "merciless book." The work sought that characteristic honesty beyond honesty of Wallace's essays.[20] Eggers was also the editor of a new magazine, *McSweeney's*. With its self-conscious sense of pleasure and wariness of hype, *McSweeney's* shared Wallace's goal of recording real life in a media-saturated age. (He in fact contributed three stories.) The admiration was mutual: Wallace proposed Eggers to Little, Brown to design *Brief Interviews with Hideous Men*.

And in September 2001, *The Corrections* was finally published, a novel Franzen had worked on—as Wallace noted with admiration to Pietsch a month later—for ten years, including "two periods when he threw [away] nearly-completed books he just knew in his gut weren't right." Wallace watched with amazement as the book became a bestseller. "I apologize in advance for the fact that I will never make you, me, or our joint employers," Wallace wrote Pietsch, looking for reassurance, "anything even close to the amount of money he's making FSG [Farrar, Straus & Giroux], by the way." In truth he was happy for his friends—sort of—but knew (and cared and didn't care) that his role as one of the founders of a new kind of writing was threatening to slip into the historical.[21] At the same time as he was being pushed aside as its leader, he was being held responsible for its flaws. For many years, critics had asked Wallace if he saw himself as part of a movement, and for as many years he had said no. Back in the early 1990s, he had written Morrow, half-jokingly, to suggest an issue of *Conjunctions* designed to show how he, Vollmann, and Franzen had nothing in common. When *Salon.com* inquired at the time of *Infinite Jest* what he and Franzen, as well as Donald Antrim, Jeffrey Eugenides, Rick Moody, and Richard Powers shared, Wallace responded, "There's the whole 'great white male' deal. I think there are about five of us under 40 who are white and over 6 feet and wear glasses." Then, in August 2001, James Wood warned in a review of Zadie Smith's *White Teeth* in the *New Republic* that there was a disturbing new trend in fiction: "A genre is hardening. . . . Familial resemblances are asserting themselves and a parent can be named." Wood dubbed the new style "Hysterical Realism," its principal characteristic being a desire to abolish stillness, as if ashamed of silence. . . . Stories and sub-stories sprout on every page, as these novels continually flourish their glamorous congestion. Inseparable from this culture of permanent storytelling is the pursuit of vitality at all costs. Indeed, vitality is storytelling, as far as these books are concerned.

Wood believed this freneticism came at the price of intimacy and psychological acuity, the true gifts of the novel. Wallace wasn't the father of this undesirable new movement in fiction—that was Dickens, in Wood's conceit—but he was named as one of the louche uncles, corrupting literary youth. And the next year would bring two more additions to the family: Gary Shteyngart's *The Russian Debutante's Handbook* and Jonathan Safran Foer's *Everything Is Illuminated*, both debut novels that seemed to owe their exuberance—their commitment to "vitality at all costs"—to *Infinite Jest*. The irony was that Wallace had now spent half a decade trying to slow down not just literature's pulse but his own.

Wallace was beginning to feel like time was passing him by. He read in the *New York Review of Books* about electronic publishing and wondered what it meant that he didn't like the idea, was wed to the artifact— "the traditional galleys-and-proofs-and-pub-dates-and-real-books-with-covers-you-hate" approach, as he wrote to DeLillo. He used to welcome change, he remembered: "The whole thing makes me feel old, sort of like the way Heavy Metal music or cum-shots in mainstream movies make me feel." When his high school class in Urbana had celebrated their twentieth reunion the year before, Wallace hadn't been able to attend— he was at Marfa—but sent a check for a floral arrangement for classmates who had died and asked for someone to videotape the event. Shortly afterward, he came through Urbana and was absorbed by the images of his classmates celebrating, which he watched in the home of the class reunion chair. He apologized to her for not having been more sensitive to her depression when they were students, and when he found out she worked with the man whom as a boy he had tormented with snowballs, he wrote a letter apologizing to him too. He made amends wherever he could, sometimes to excess.[22] He wrote to his Arizona sponsor that "I struggle a great deal, and am 99.8% real," then crossed that out and wrote in "98.8%," noting in a parenthesis in the margin, "Got a bit carried away here."

Wallace knew it was time to leave Illinois State. His writing was stuck and his relationships with women were falling into a pattern so predictable that even he saw the humor in them.²³ The university had also begun to back away from "the Unit," the oasis for experimental literature in the prairie. Wallace cared little by now for this kind of writing, but the people who had worked so hard to create it mattered to him.

Ever since *Infinite Jest*, various high-level writing departments had put out feelers to him in the hopes that this well-known author, so obviously wasted on a second-tier midwestern university, would be willing to move. In the fall of 2000 he received a letter from Pomona College, in Claremont, California, which had just created a chair in creative writing. Wallace responded to the English department chair with caution. The department head, Rena Fraden, reassured him that the post was designed for a full-time fiction writer. On a later call he joked that all his friends had gotten a letter too, including Franzen (who said he was not interested and recommended Wallace). He and Fraden agreed that he would visit the school in December and give a reading and teach a class to see what he thought of the school. When he came, the students at the class, as one remembered, sat "in a narcotic state of awe." Wallace taught a workshop and said if he could leave them with one thing it was the difference between "nauseous" and "nauseated." He gave a reading to a small group in Crookshank Hall and met the faculty and liked them. He went to a dinner at Fraden's house, where the participants each talked about a book that had affected him or her deeply. One mentioned *Clarissa*; another Thomas Malory's *Morte d'Arthur*. Wallace surprised all by naming a popular page-turner (no one can remember quite which).

Wallace quickly bonded with Fraden. She was the sort of sympathetic, uncompetitive academic whom he could count on to provide the special conditions that helped him to work, a successor to Dale Peterson, Mary Carter, and Charlie Harris. Pomona began to look like a place where he could make a new start. He and Fraden discussed that evening what it would take to get him to leave Bloomington. He asked for as little teaching as possible; Fraden agreed. The department voted to end the interview process and offer him the job. A month later, Wallace accepted. "The students actually appear to like to read and write, which will be a welcome change," he wrote to Peterson. "I have gotten very tired (and sometimes impatient) with having to be a disciplinarian in order to get ISU students (the bulk of them, anyway) simply to do their homework." He had promised ISU that he would teach a full year after his second leave, and he meant to keep that promise, but he was already looking forward to a new start. He pointed out to Morrow that he had been "home" for almost a decade and explained to Curtis White, his colleague in the department, that it was time for him to grow up.

CHAPTER 8

The Pale King

In midsummer 2002, Wallace left Bloomington in the Volvo he'd bought with some of his MacArthur money, Werner and Jeeves in the back. It had been nine years since he'd last changed jobs. Francis B. and his mother raced him to his first stop, a hotel in Columbia, Missouri, so that when Wallace looked up at the front desk, he found his friend signing the registry. The joke fell flat, though: it turned out the forty-year-old author was traveling, not with professional dog movers hired by Pomona, as he had told them, but with Sarah Caudle, a young mother who had been a long-time friend and was now his girlfriend. It took the couple six days to drive west. During the trip they ate in their motel room so that the dogs were never alone. In St. George, Utah, Wallace wanted to go to a recovery meeting. He found a listing in the phone book, but by the time the sponsor called back it was too late.

When they got to Claremont, bleary-eyed and anxious, they drove up and down the streets. The Mission-style strip malls astonished Wallace—he wondered, as he always did when faced with something new, if he had made a mistake. Wallace told Caudle he was afraid that the bland weather would sap his "will to live." "What kind of zip code starts with '9,'" he had written DeLillo plaintively just before leaving the Midwest. And, in the winter, he would write Morrow to claim he missed "yellow snow and flowing mucus." But there was posturing in this homesickness: in reality Wallace's sense of being uprooted passed quickly this time. The house the college had arranged for him was pretty, on the main street, Indian Hill Boulevard, and near the campus. It was fenced all in, with lemon trees in the back and a giant palm tree Wallace happily measured to be eleven and a half feet around.

The first few days brought two visitors. Fraden came with one of her daughters, and fruit and baba ghanoush. And Karen Green also dropped by. When Wallace was still in Bloomington, Green, a visual artist, had asked him for permission to turn "The Depressed Person" into a grid of illustrated panels. Now she brought the finished artwork, along with a housewarming gift of Ikea ice trays. The story, Wallace's act of anger against Elizabeth Wurtzel, ends without hope: the depressed person cannot break out of the cage of solipsism that her "terrible and unceasing emotional pain" has placed her in. Green had reimagined the story, so that in the last panel of her painting she is cured. When Wallace saw what Green had done, he was pleased. He told her that she had turned it into a story that people would want to read. That day in Claremont he offered to make lunch for her. There were lamps scattered everywhere—she counted fourteen—and towels stretched out to dry on the furniture: the place looked to Green "like an office with a laundry." His fridge turned out to contain only hot dogs and goldfish crackers. When Green asked if Wallace had mustard, he told her, "I'm not that into condiments." They went to a park and Werner jumped on her and tore out her belly-button ring. She came back a few weeks later, the day before her birthday, with a mutual friend, and Wallace prepared her hot dogs and put them in the frilly paper cuffs that usually attire lamb chops.

On the car ride west Wallace had invited Caudle and her daughter to move in with him. But soon he called her in Illinois and said he wanted to end their contact. And when Karen Green's own marriage ended in November, Wallace offered to help. "I'll be your hideous man expert," he said. Expecting that they were going to begin a relationship and determined to start on an honest footing this time, he wrote her a series of letters—Grim Letter I, Grim Letter II, he called them—where he laid out his psychiatric history and his history with women.[1] "I don't want to be Satan," he explained. She drew a picture of Satan on him with a Sharpie and at his insistence added the words, "But I mean well."

Soon Green invited him to spend Christmas with her in Hawaii. He was sad—Jeeves had just died ("the closest thing to a child that I had," he wrote Morrow). To make sure they could get along when they got there, he had first visited her for a day in Marin County, where she lived. They had fun, and he amazed her afterward by writing a letter describing every detail of her house, down to the paint-splattered shoes in the hallway. He told her the depressed person was really him. Wallace wanted to go slow, so to encourage him in Hawaii, Green sent him a sheet with a hole already cut out. In December they left, surprising Wallace's friends, who knew how little he liked to travel. In Hawaii, they watched movies and walked on the beach and talked constantly. Green swam, while Wallace avoided the water. He found the islands, he wrote Morrow afterward, "much less touristy or vulgar than I'd thought, and haunted and sad in a good way." He also liked that there were no bugs. Before they returned home, he asked Green if she would marry him. But Green had a teenage son, Stirling, who danced, and she wanted to be near a good ballet program. On his return Wallace told Morrow that he was "pretty much hopelessly in love with a female in Marin County who's a showing painter."

Wallace settled in to Claremont. He found a recovery group he liked and, touched by California culture, drank his "breakfast vomit," lifted weights, ran with Werner, and even bought a new tennis racket. He festooned his walls with shark attack clippings and pages of the Long Thing. When school began, he found he liked teaching at Pomona more than he had expected. For one thing, there were no graduate students (and thus no budding literary theorists), and the undergraduates were more capable than at Illinois State—he was in the "land of 1600 SAT scores, apparently" as he described Pomona to Morrow. He found Fraden, the department head, exactly how he hoped she'd be. They soon had a standing date to watch *Buffy the Vampire Slayer* every Tuesday night at her house. As ever, Wallace tried to tamp down any sense that he was special; when the students in his fiction class had a "Dress Like DFW Day," he let it be known that it was only sort of funny.

Best of all, he only had to teach one course each semester and never had to sit on a committee. "We're hiring you to write—you have to keep writing," Fraden had told him. "I have a lottery-prize-type gig at Pomona," Wallace bragged to the *Believer* in 2003. "I get to do more or less what I want." Any grumblings among the faculty, for whom undergraduate education was a calling, were soon laid to rest as word of Wallace's unmistakable dedication to teaching emerged—for example, the eleven impromptu mini-papers he required from students in "Literary Interpretation," or the comments in different-colored inks for each reading that he scrawled in the margins of students' stories. He took teaching seriously and made sure his students did so too. Once, when the school registrar wanted to audit Wallace's course, on the literary essay, Wallace turned her down because she would have had to miss too many classes for faculty meetings.

His grammar obsession quickly became well known. "On a scale of 1 to 10, this is an 11," he would tell students, seeing a particular blunder. Or, "This actually hurts my brain." He would consult his mother's book, *Practically Painless English*, to answer any challenges and would sometimes trot out her old feint of fake-coughing when a student fell into a grammatical solecism. He used the modifier "only" in class to show the power careful usage wielded:

> You have been entrusted to feed your neighbor's dog for a week while he (the neighbor) is out of town. The neighbor returns home; something has gone awry; you are questioned.
> "I fed the dog."
> "Did you feed the parakeet?"
> "I fed *only* the dog."
> "Did anyone else feed the dog?"
> "*Only* I fed the dog."
> "Did you fondle/molest the dog?"
> "I *only* fed the dog!"

His voice cracked with pleasure as he spoke the last line.

Wallace stood out in Claremont. His earnestness, part midwestern childhood, part defense mechanism, was unusual on a campus where the tone was muted cool, sun-drenched Ivy. Wallace once tried to get approved a course called "Extremely Advanced Essay Writing," but the registrar objected that no "Advanced Essay Writing" class had been offered before. Still, Wallace's arrival was a triumph for both the department and the university, this middle-aged *monstre sacré* in his iconoclastic outfits—bandana, beaten-up hiking shorts, and double athletic socks inside unlaced hiking boots. The *Los Angeles Times*, in covering his arrival, noted with approval his Pomona College sweatshirt with the arms cut off.

Wallace very much wanted Green to be in the same city with him. He did not want to wait until Stirling graduated high school in 2005. In the summer of 2003, Green bought a house in Cave Creek, Arizona. Wallace made the six-hour drive once a week. He worked in an upstairs room and read Tom Clancy novels by the pool, "burning his shoulders to a crisp," as Green remembers. There was a local recovery group he liked too.

In August 2003 Wallace went to Maine with Green on an assignment for *Gourmet*. She had never met his parents before but his relationship with his mother had gotten easier with time and they bonded as a group. His editors were hoping he would reprise his role as the elite's correspondent in the heartland, but, having promised to do his "own eccentric researching," he came back with something decidedly more delicate than the state fair or the cruise piece. He had always been interested in what animals feel—their inability to protect themselves touched him as human pain didn't—and over the years he had begun to wonder what right we had to be cruel to them. In Maine he found a scene worthy of Hogarth: thousands of lobsters being boiled alive at the "enormous, pungent and extremely well-marketed Maine Lobster Festival," where "friend and stranger alike sit cheek by jowl, cracking and chewing and dribbling. It's hot, and the sagged roof traps the steam and the smells." Who, he wanted to know, gave us such dominion? But Wallace was and had always been averse to hectoring—it seemed rude to him—and in the piece he took pains to distance himself, physically and rhetorically, from the PETA representative, "Mr. William R. Rivas-Rivas," who, he writes, papered the festival at the harbor with his leaflet "Being Boiled Hurts." Instead, Wallace posed the problem with lobster eating as a series of ethical questions, writing in the faux-naïve voice of the curious midwestern boy he still in some ways was: "Is it all right to boil a sentient creature alive just for our gustatory pleasure?" He went on slyly:

> For those Gourmet readers who enjoy well-prepared and -presented meals involving beef, veal, lamb, pork, chicken, lobster, etc.: Do you think much about the (possible) moral status and (probable) suffering of the animals involved? If you do, what ethical convictions have you worked out that permit you not just to eat but to savor and enjoy flesh-based viands? . . . If, on the other hand, you'll have no truck with [such] confusions and convictions . . . what makes it feel truly

okay, inside, to just dimiss the whole thing out of hand? That is, is your refusal to think about any of this the product of actual thought, or is it just that you don't want to think about it? And if the latter, why not? Do you ever think, even idly, about the possible reasons for your reluctance to think about it? I am not trying to bait anyone here—I'm genuinely curious. After all, isn't being extra aware and attentive and thoughtful about one's food and its overall context part of what distinguishes a real gourmet?

Wallace was not under the illusion that his investigation would change anyone's behavior (it did not change his own—at the festival one evening, Green remembers, he enjoyed two lobsters for dinner), but there was pleasure in and of itself in expanding the fight against American complacency.

In general, Pomona had a mellowing effect on Wallace. In September 2002, for instance, he had gone east for the *New Yorker* festival. He was to read alongside Franzen, and the two, who had never shared a stage before, jockeyed for the order, with Wallace feigning not to know that the second reader had the more prestigious slot. For Franzen, it was a microcosm of something that always bothered him in their friendship: Wallace didn't like acknowledging how competitive they were. In the end, Wallace went first in the heat and read two sections of his long, unfinished novel. One was about Leonard Stecyk, the smarmy young man whose desire to behave perfectly with everyone leads to a wedgie in school (he grows up to be an IRS agent),[2] and the other was a Kafkaesque story about an implacable infant who turns up in an agency office and drives the examiners crazy. "My audit group's Group Manager and his wife have an infant," the narrator, an unnamed auditor, recounts, "I can describe only as— fierce. Its expression is fierce; its demeanor is fierce; its gaze over bottle or pacifier or finger—fierce, intimidating, aggressive."[3] The crowd was highly appreciative; Wallace had brought a towel for his own perspiration and was happy to see his friend also sweating. "I . . . did not think he could," he wrote DeLillo afterward. But, graciously, Franzen had spared him the news that the author they both most admired was himself in the audience. "He's kind in his way," Wallace acknowledged afterward of his friend.[4]

*   *   *

Wallace had had three significant projects to work on as he settled in at Pomona: the ever-present Long Thing, a new story collection he had proposed to Pietsch, and a round of editorial queries on his book on Cantor and set theory. On the math book, he had pushed himself hard in the spring of 2002, his last semester in Bloomington, devoting almost all his time to it and getting a draft in just before leaving. Characteristically, the project had gone from a dare ("I'm doing a book about math!" he'd written Moore. "You?") to a task (to DeLillo, just before moving to Pomona, he called it his "wretched math book"). But all the same, after a lot of effort he felt he had done good work and struck a balance between the biographical and the mathematical. He had hired a University of Illinois graduate student to go over the equations and technical details to make sure they were accurate too. But in September 2002, he wrote DeLillo in frustration that what had seemed done was not. "Both the math-editor and the general editor want repairs," he complained. A book he had thought would take him four months of part-time work had now taken eleven of nearly full-time work. "I never want to see another Fourier series as long as I live," he added, pride peeking out from beneath the irritation. And the copyedit was living up to his nightmares. Nine months later he was back to DeLillo with this new complaint: "The galleys for this blasted math book were such a mess that they're having to typeset the whole thing over." When the publisher asked for a small essay for its catalog on how he had come to write the book, Wallace responded with a meta-refusal:

> The obvious objection to such promotional ¶s is that if the booklets are any good at all . . . blurblets are unnecessary; whereas, if the booklets aren't any good, it's hard to see how my telling somebody that as a child I used to cook up what amounted to simplistic versions of Zeno's Dichotomy[5] and ruminate on them until I literally made myself sick, or that I once almost flunked a basic calc course and have seethed with dislike for conventional higher-math education ever since, or that the ontology and grammar of abstractions have always struck me as one of the most breathtaking problems in human consciousness—how any such stuff will help.

Wallace's publisher printed the disclaimer. It also asked another mathematician to review the manuscript. He expressed serious reservations and pointed to errors, some small, some larger, in it. Much as during his time at Harvard, Wallace was beginning to wonder if he had gotten into deeper water than he had realized.

Everything and More was finally published in October 2003. In the book Wallace covered the history of infinity as a philosophical and mathematical concept, beginning with Zeno's dichotomy and moving through calculus and axiomatic set theory, the idea that all of mathematics is derivable from a handful of simple axioms, and on to Cantor. Cantor had suffered from severe mental illness; Wallace took pains to point out that the mathematician's willingness to delve deep into questions of recursion and paradox was not the cause. "The real irony is that the view of ∞ as some forbidden zone or road to insanity—which view was very old and powerful and haunted math for 2000+ years—is precisely what Cantor's own work overturned," he wrote. He noted:

> In modern medical terms, it's fairly clear that G.F.L.P. Cantor suffered from manic-depressive illness at a time when nobody knew what this was, and that his polar cycles were aggravated by professional stresses and disappointments, of which Cantor had more than his share. Of course, this makes for less interesting flap copy than Genius Driven Mad By Attempts To Grapple With ∞. The truth, though, is that Cantor's work and its context are so totally interesting and beautiful that there's no need for breathless Prometheusizing of the poor guy's life. . . . Saying that ∞ drove Cantor mad is sort of like mourning St. George's loss to the dragon: it's not only wrong but insulting.

Wallace had written *Everything and More* in a slightly different voice than usual, that of an amateur delighting in his subject and eager to communicate his enthusiasm, Cavell on holiday. He adduced a made-up high school math teacher, Dr. Goris, as his guide and threw in his customary mixture of high and low vocabulary, as well as a lot of math notations. He hoped that the playful tone of the book would help critics and professionals identify *Everything and More* as the college bull session it was meant to be. A few were charmed. The distinguished math writer John Allen Paulos in the *American Scholar* praised Wallace's "refreshingly conversational style as well as a surprisingly authoritative command of mathematics," but many felt otherwise. One, a philosopher of mathematics, writing in the *New York Times Book Review*, thought the book suffered from some of the same flaws as *Infinite Jest*: "One wonders exactly whom Wallace thinks he is writing for," noted David Papineau of King's College, London. "If he had cut out some of the details, and told us rather less than he knows, he could have reached a lot more readers." Papineau was kinder than some of the other experts. *Science* wrote of the book that "mathematicians will view it with at best sardonic amusement. Crippling errors abound." The magazine's reviewer, Rudy Rucker, who had given *Broom* a glowing notice in the *Washington Post* in 1987, went on to enumerate a host of technical errors: providing the wrong definition of uniform convergence, botching the crucial Zermelo-Fraenkel axioms that form the basis of much of set theory, and conflating Cantor's continuum problem with his continuum hypothesis. Wallace-l, an electronic mailing list devoted to Wallace's work, became a repository for suggested corrections by various professional mathematicians. Wallace's publisher now asked one of the list's contributors, Prabhakar Ragde of the University of Waterloo, Ontario, to re-review the book before paperback publication. He sent back a three-page memo. Some of his suggestions Wallace took, but he also finally cried enough: there was a distinction between trying to write for general readers and specialists. "Dr. Ragde, who is clearly one sharp hombre," he wrote the editors, "has nailed many of the book's crudities—it's just there are lots of crudities that I decided were more perspicuous for lay-reader purposes." The book became one of the publisher's bestselling titles all the same, on the strength of Wallace's name and its engaging style, though he always had the disquieting feeling that he had been mugged for trespassing.

Oblivion was a far smoother process. The collection consisted of eight stories, some of which came from the notebooks Wallace was using to write portions of *The Pale King* and probably began as sections of it. Wallace had downplayed the stories when he had first tentatively suggested a new collection to Pietsch in October 2001, calling them "the best of the stuff I've been doing while playing hooky from a certain Larger Thing." But Pietsch, as ever his ideal reader, responded immediately to the portraits of "unhappy, complicated, intellectualizing men." In the following two years, while Wallace worked on *Everything and More,* he also wrote the last story in the collection, "The Suffering Channel," the story of a man for whom great art comes so easily that he can defecate it, and Pietsch began organizing the pieces for publication. "I don't feel like much of an editor here," Pietsch admitted to Wallace in October 2003, "but these stories didn't strike me as needing many red-penciled queries.... Overwhelmingly, these stories do what they do with irresistible force." Privately, he marveled at the creative pain and stress evident in his author's newest effort.

The stories were mostly successors to those of *Brief Interviews.* They too concerned themselves mostly with middle-aged, middle-class white men in middle America.[6] Though the subjects share their antecedents' condition of total self-absorption, their pride in themselves—whether in their sexual politics or just in their sexuality—has by now been replaced by a sullen silence. These men are aware of themselves as over-the-hill, culturally disempowered, on their way to nowhere, especially vis-à-vis women. It is no accident the first story is called "Mr. Squishy." Even irony has lost its power to protect them. They seem able to see everything but what's in front of their eyes and to talk about everything but what actually matters to them.

The stories in *Brief Interviews* are afraid of expansion, so unattractive or unstable are the interiors of their subjects; the stories in *Oblivion* seem afraid of compression, as if the title were a threat that could only be defended against by the relentlessly engaged consciousness. Words cover the stories, coating them in thick layers of verbiage, perspectives shift, and there are disorienting chronological jumps. "It's interesting if you really think about it, how clumsy and laborious it seems to be to convey even the smallest thing," the narrator of "Good Old Neon" writes. There is only one way to halt the onrush of data, to slow it down so you can find its meaning: "Think for a second what if all the infinitely dense and shifting worlds of stuff inside you every moment of your life turned out now to be somehow fully open and expressible afterward, after what you think of as *you* has died ... ?"

"Good Old Neon" is the most uncomfortable of the stories in an uncomfortable volume, a narrative about an advertising executive who deliberately kills himself by crashing his car into a concrete bridge abutment. Neal is a familiar type in the Wallace world, a young man whose personality is built on the need to impress others. And the more he succeeds in impressing them, the more of a fraud he feels. Like Wallace, he feels frozen by the need to control how others see him, "condemned to a whole life of being nothing but a sort of custodian to the statue." Suicide appears to him the only escape from this recursive nightmare. "Self-loathing isn't the same thing as being into pain or a lingering death. If I was going to do it, I wanted it instant," he assures us. Strangely, his is a death testified to by David Wallace, a year behind him at the same Aurora, Illinois, high school, leafing through their yearbook. It is a story where a ghost tells his remembered self about David Wallace's imagining why the ghost's remembered self killed himself. [7]

"Good Old Neon" is the only story in *Oblivion* explicitly about a suicide, but many in the collection have a tamped-down sense of doom, of thoughts distorted by words and words constrained by personality and personality deformed by culture.

"The Suffering Channel" is about that culture and the cluster of editors and writers in New York who help create it. Much of the story takes place at *Style*, a lightweight celebrity magazine whose cheery denizens plan the next issue's pabulum in offices on the sixteenth floor of 1 World Trade Center. "The Suffering Channel" can be read as a prequel to "The View from Mrs. Thompson's"; it re-creates the heyday of irony less than three months before the fatal attacks. But it is also a story about personal shame and the confused sources of an artist's art. In the tale, the celebrated defecator, whom we first think so gifted he can just shit a classic, turns out to be beset by self-hatred. To go to the bathroom is to remember the childhood abuse and humiliation that led to his creativity. He is asked to give a performance on the Suffering Channel, a new station devoted entirely to "real life still and moving images of most intense available moments of human anguish." Yet at story's end it turns out to be impossible to broadcast his agony; his shame and his art both are to remain private:

> There's also some eleventh hour complication involving the ground level camera and the problem of keeping the commode's special monitor out of its upward shot, since video capture of a camera's

own monitor causes what is known in the industry as feedback glare—the artist in this case would see, not his own emergent *Victory*, but a searing and amorphous light.

Oblivion, published in June 2004, met with what was by now a familiar duality. Wallace had a public that awaited his books—he filled bookstores, and an event at the Public Theatre in Manhattan where he was interviewed by George Saunders sold out. The book sold well—in all eighteen thousand hardcover copies in its first year—and was on several bestseller lists. Wallace found the author tour painless, he preferred having company onstage. The collection got the customary respectful reviews accorded an important writer in the daily press, but there was also an undercurrent of irritation, even anger, on the part of critics—Wallace was denying them the full enjoyment of his great talents. Why, for instance, did all the protagonists sound the same? Where had the Dickensian scope of *Infinite Jest* gone? What had happened to its comic genius? Reviewers remembered that Wallace had promised readers something different: a single-entendre writing that felt redemptive. That hardly seemed the achievement, let alone the aim, of *Oblivion*. Michiko Kakutani in the *New York Times* again brought up this gap, criticizing the collection for offering "only the tiniest tasting of [Wallace's] smorgasbord of talents. Instead, he all too often settles for . . . [the] cheap brand of irony and ridicule that he once denounced."

More sympathetic critics acknowledged that there was something interesting about using deadened language to convey deadened states, that the ironization of irony had merits, but they too wondered whether what Wallace was writing was of more than academic interest. "Another Pioneer," contained the words "evection," "canescent," "protasis," "epitatic," "hemean," "nigrescently," "ptotic," "intaglial," "catastasis," and "extrorse," not to mention "thanatophilic" and "omphalic." It had a single paragraph twenty-three pages long. The same thing might be said about the stories as is said in *Infinite Jest* about Jim Incandenza's disdained experimental cartridges, that there was "no sort of engaging plot, no movement that sucked you in and drew you along." Or maybe that they were less stories than forms for stories, much as one character in "The Suffering Channel" is described as "not a body that occupied space but rather just a bodyshaped area of space itself."

The eagerly awaited next novel was on reviewers' minds as well. Where was it? The *Houston Chronicle* hypothesized, generously, that it was already written, imagining a "forest-killing manuscript à la the thousand-page *Infinite Jest*" that was at that very moment "devouring the time and energy and quite possibly the soul of a senior New York editor." Wyatt Mason in the *London Review of Books*, after a skillful elucidation of the title story, wrote:

> Wallace has the right to write a great book that no one can read except people like him. I flatter myself to think that I am one of them, but I haven't any idea how to convince you that you should be, too; nor, clearly, does Wallace. And it might not be the worst thing in the world, next time out, when big novel number three thumps into the world, were he to dig deeper, search longer, and find a more generous way to make his feelings known.

Chiding notices were harder for Wallace than the pans, which he expected by now—he could ignore critics calling for more salt in the soup—because for him, too, all roads led back to his "more generous" Long Thing, *The Pale King*. He had hoped at times while he was writing them that the stories in *Oblivion* would show a way out of the dead end *Infinite Jest* seemed to have left him in. He boasted to Costello that in writing it he had "looked straight into the camera." He meant that he had finally surmounted the need to have readers love him. The mania was gone; only a studied and mature sadness remained. But to his disappointment he didn't find that the story work suggested how to write a novel of similar honesty. The problem may have been that Wallace's approach to *Oblivion*—the trick-free prose, the Pynchon-free plots, the insistence that the reader work for his or her satisfaction—was simply too pitiless to carry a reader through a novel. And while *Oblivion* was descriptive, *The Pale King* was supposed to be prescriptive. It had to convince the reader that there was a way out of the bind. It had to have a commitment to a solution that *Oblivion* lacked.[8] Wallace had settled on his thesis long before. As he wrote in a notebook:

Maybe dullness is associated with psychic pain because something that's dull or opaque fails to provide enough stimulation to distract people from some other, deeper type of pain that is always there, if only in an ambient low-level way, and which most of us spend nearly all our time and energy trying to distract ourselves from feeling, or at least from feeling directly or with our full attention.

The problem came up when he tried to dramatize this idea. How do you write about dullness without being dull? The obvious solution, if you had Wallace's predilections, was to overwhelm this seemingly inert subject with the full movement of your thought. Your characters might be low-level bureaucrats, but the rippling tactility of your writing would keep them from appearing static. But this strategy presented its own problem: Wallace could make the characters vibrant, but only at the risk of sacrificing what made their situation worth narrating—the stillness at the center of their lives. How could you preach mindful calmness if you couldn't replicate it in prose? A failed entertainment that succeeded was just an entertainment. Yet Wallace had never really found a verbal strategy to replace his inborn one. In more ways than he cared to acknowledge he remained the author of *The Broom of the System*. He wrote to Franzen around this time:

> Karen is killing herself rehabbing the house. I sit in the garage with the AC blasting and work very poorly and haltingly and with (some days) great reluctance and ambivalence and pain. I am tired of myself, it seems: tired of my thoughts, associations, syntax, various verbal habits that have gone from discovery to technique to tic.

Usually when Wallace found work frustrating, his relationships suffered. But this time his love for Green flourished. He had found something as important to him as his fiction. "It's a dark time workwise," he wrote Franzen, "and yet a very light and lovely time in all other respects. So overall I feel I'm ahead and am pretty happy." His fit with Green worked in ways no other ever had. She was herself creative but not a writer. She didn't have his intense competitiveness; she created to create, unshadowed by any statue. When she teased him it was with love. "We used to have this joke about how much can you irritate the reader," Green recalls.

Time was on the relationship's side too. Wallace no longer thought of himself as young. "No more nymphs for me," he had written Steven Moore as he was about to turn forty in early 2002. Wallace had a strikeout drawn through the fading word "Mary" on his tattoo and placed an asterisk under the heart symbol; farther down he added another asterisk and "Karen," turning his arm into a living footnote. He knew he could not sustain the emotional availability of a parent and he was worried about passing on his mental instability, so he did not want to have children anymore, but he enjoyed being with Stirling. They would often play chess, which Green's son usually won. Wallace's whirring mind made him an inconsistent competitor.

As Stirling began his final year of high school, Green and Wallace made plans for her to move to Claremont. They began house hunting. Wallace first asked the university if he could buy his house on Indian Hill Boulevard and was surprised to be told it wasn't for sale. So he and Green looked elsewhere. When he tired of the search, she went alone, eventually choosing a ranch home in a newly developed area at the very northern limit of the town. Like the house in Bloomington, it was far enough from the university to allow for privacy, and from their street they could see the mountains.

Wallace at this point considered Green his fiancée, but other women had had that title before. He emailed Franzen in February 2004, "I hear Kath[y] gaffed and landed you"—Franzen had moved in with Kathryn Chetkovich, a writer from Santa Cruz whom he had been dating. Ever competitive, Wallace saw his own girlfriend as a counterpart to Franzen's, another K from California. A week later he emailed, "I am more and more sure KG and I will get married. Now it's a matter of getting her to be more and more sure."

At the end of 2004, Wallace and Green flew to Urbana for Christmas, staying at the Jumers Castle Lodge, "a sad place with trophies on the walls," as Wallace's sister, Amy, remembers. She and her two daughters had the job of luring his parents to the courthouse, where they discovered their son in a suit, with his companion in a dress. The forty-two-year-old Wallace and Green were married, his nieces as the witnesses. After lunch, the newlyweds walked down a path and Wallace gave a hop and clicked his heels together. Amy photographed the moment, and this became their wedding announcement. They spent the evening watching a *Law & Order* marathon in their "shitty motel," as Wallace reported to DeLillo, assuring him that "my ass is not as big as it looks in the photo."

Six months later, Green moved to Claremont. Wallace had already been living in the house for a while, and by the time his new wife got there, he had taken it over. A jockstrap hung from a lamp, and the town had earlier posted a notice on his door ordering him to remove the weeds on his lawn. Green painted the garage bright red and furnished it with his recliner, a comfortable desk, and Wallace's lamps, his accounting books, the old Scottish battle scene, a poster of Klimt's *The Kiss*, and other miscellanea he had brought from Bloomington. She tore out the wall-to-wall carpeting in the house. He had developed a personality for social interactions that he had never had before. Whenever anyone came over and complimented the décor, Wallace would quickly say it was Green's doing. But Green would see another side at night, when he would beg her not to get sick or die.

Wallace was thrilled that his personal life was finally in order: he took it as evidence that he had matured, left behind his unfocused, hedonistic, self-indulgent past.[9] The couple watched DVDs together—*The Wire* was a favorite; he thought of writing an essay on how the best writing in America was for television shows. Wallace felt strong in his sobriety as he never had before, the pair even keeping wine for guests. Wallace liked to remind Green what a good companion he was. "I took out the garbage. Did you see that?" he would say to her, or "I put tea on for you when you were driving home!" Some of his bachelor ways lingered, though. When he wrote he would go from the garage to the guest room, where there was an extra computer, and on to the family room, to write in longhand with his earplugs in—"scattering debris, intellectual and otherwise," as Green remembers. She was appalled to find his towels and socks hanging from her paintings. Soon they were in couples therapy, working on these issues. He agreed to a clothesline outside.

Wallace often got mail from aspiring authors, many modeling their prose after his, and one day Weston Cutter, a young writer, wrote to ask Wallace, why bother writing? "It's just this: how do you keep hope?" Cutter asked. "How do you not just get tired of all this shit, all the time from every vector, public and private and governmental? And more pressing, how do you not wear yourself out and feel as if you're just another supplier of said stuff?" "This is like listening to a transcript of my own mind," Wallace jotted at the bottom of his letter in response, adding, "Basically—I empathize. I have no answers. I do know I'm easiest when I accept how small I am and how paltry my contribution is as a % of total. But >60% of the time I don't/can't accept it. Go figure."

Shortly after his arrival in Claremont Wallace had told the *Los Angeles Times* reporter, "I'm poised, ready to write, 10 hours a day." But of course being ready to write was not the same as writing. There was always the teaching and the counseling and the sponsoring. He wanted to help those most in need, offering informal advice and complete availability, paying it forward.[10] He wrote in his introduction to English 67—Literary Interpretation:

> Clinically shy students, or those whose best, most pressing questions and comments occur to them only in private, should do their discussing with me solo, outside class. If my scheduled office hours don't work for you, please call me so that we can make an appointment for a different meeting time.

One student, Kelly Natoli, remembers Wallace introducing himself on the first day of a creative writing class: "He said, 'It's going to take me, like, two weeks to learn everyone's name, but by the time I learn your name I'm going to remember your name for the rest of my life. You're going to forget who I am before I forget who you are.'"

In 2005, Kenyon College invited Wallace to give an address at its graduation. The student invitation committee did not know much about Wallace, which may have been just as well, since the real Wallace differed at this point almost 180 degrees from the Wallace of popular imagination; a slacker exterior hid an intense moralist, someone whose long experience in recovery had made him into an apostle of careful living and hard work. Success had to be earned; do your homework; make your bed. How many times had he told his students that the worst thing to happen to them would be to be published before they were forty? At Kenyon, Wallace saw a chance to set out the things he cared about without the frustrating contrivance of the novel. He could just tell the audience to be mindful instead of trying to orchestrate it through his characters. He had a chance to remind that most self-centered of cohorts, college students, to get over themselves—or, better, outside themselves. His point of departure for his speech was similar to the one he'd set out in a letter to a friend in 1999: "You're special—it's O.K.—but so's the guy across the table who's raising two kids sober and rebuilding a '73 Mustang. It's a magical thing with 4,000,000,000 forms. It kind of takes your breath away."

So for the Kenyon College address, he wrote a speech against egoism and egotism, about openness and humility, of apostles who behold but cannot see. He inserted a favorite joke from recovery. Two young fish are swimming along and they happen to meet an older fish swimming the other way. The older fish goes by and calls out to them, "Morning, boys, how's the water?" The younger fish continue side by side for a while and then one stops and says, "What the hell is water?" In other words, it was not hard to be successful in conventional terms; what was hard was to be aware of life as you lived it. "The trick," he underscored, "is keeping the truth up front in daily consciousness." He continued:

> Learning how to think really means learning how to exercise some control over *how* and *what* you think. It means being aware enough to *choose* what you pay attention to and to *choose* how you construct meaning from experience. Because if you cannot or will not exercise this kind of choice in adult life, you will be totally hosed. Think of the old cliché about the mind being "an excellent servant but a terrible master."

He explained to the students that they could stand in a supermarket line and experience nothing but the anxiety and irritation their college-augmented sense of superiority would entitle them to or they could, in the midst of that same experience, open themselves up to a moment of the most supernal beauty—"on fire with the same force that lit the stars—compassion, love, the subsurface unity of all things." It was up to them, of course; they could do as they chose: "But if you've really learned how to think, how to pay attention, then you will have other options."

The truth behind banalities always excited and embarrassed Wallace, filling him with the wonder that, as he wrote in *Infinite Jest*, "clichéd directives are a lot more deep and hard to actually *do*." Over the past twenty-five years his mental life had run a huge circuit through the most astonishing complexities to arrive at what many six-year-olds and nearly all churchgoers already understood. He wasn't sure whether what he had written was deep or unimportant. As he worked on the speech, he and Green joked that she should do a little soft-shoe behind him while he read it from the podium. Wallace delivered his words in his academic robe, bent slightly forward, a lock of hair covering his face, sweat dripping down his neck, in his intense, slightly quavering voice, speaking modestly and hesitantly. It was as if there was nothing more uncomfortable for him than being there, at this podium, but what he had to say was too important to keep it to himself. There was a sense that day that the man speaking these ordinary phrases had earned that right. It was one thing if your aunt told you you weren't the center of the universe just because you thought you were; it was another if the author of *Infinite Jest* did. Wallace was someone whom younger people felt a link to, someone who had defied the corruptions of the adult world.[11]

All this time the reputation of *Infinite Jest* was growing. The novel was connecting with more and more readers, passed along and recommended by word of mouth and on the Internet. This was true even though the world had changed drastically in the decade since Wallace had written it. The current danger was not from total immersion but from relentless fragmentation, not from watching one video to death but from skipping among hundreds. Americans were now not passively but frenetically entertained, and the warning shot turned out to be not Wallace as a child, glued to the four stations of 1960s Urbana, but Wallace in Bloomington, clicking among seventy-five channels of satellite TV, unable to decide which show to watch lest he miss a better one. Instinctively, Wallace was wary of the emerging technology. "I allow myself to Webulize only once a week now," he wrote a graduate student who was helping him with his math book in July 2001, and he didn't become a consistent emailer for several years afterward. "Thank God," Karen Green remembers him saying when they got a new piece of computer equipment, "I wasn't raised in this era."[12]

But changes in technology did not really affect whether one responded to *Infinite Jest*. Video cartridges were the vector of the plot, but they were not responsible for the sadness at its core. What the novel was about was how to feel connected in your own life, and that was still the great struggle. The Web might offer a different hope of escape from the self, but actually escaping was no less futile, as those who spent their time trying discovered. (It was named the "Web" for good reason.) Among the early champions of *Infinite Jest*, in fact, were the technologically elite, the rising generation of information and technology experts, programmers, and webmasters, real-life counterparts to the student engineer in *Infinite Jest* who takes his work break on the roof of the "great hollow brain-frame," of the MIT Union. These readers immediately responded to a writer who saw the afternoon light through the lens of a new reality, as they did:

> The P.M. was moving fast from a chilly noon cloud-cover into blue autumn glory, but in the first set it was still very cold, the sun still pale and seeming to flutter as if poorly wired.[13]

Reading *Infinite Jest* was an act of protest against the future they were creating, the one Wallace had imagined in "Here and There," a world "of the cold, the new, the right, the truly and spotlessly here." Yet paradoxically the Web made *Infinite Jest* an easier read. The cognitive jumps in its pages felt less extreme after a generation of Internet surfing and blogging than they had when the book was published. Wallace's distinctive prose with its rapid ascents and descents in diction and its seemingly endless appetite for expansion, at once erudite and ungainly, yearning for home without ever finding it, turned out to be perfect for a new medium. The Web seemed made for multiple conjunctions at the opening of sentences.

In time these early Internet users took up Wallace for their fan communities too, a transition that particularly discomfited him (though to be fair anything that reinforced the masonry of the statue did). When in March 2003 a member of Wallace-l told Wallace about their email list at a taping of a reading for *The Next American Essay*, a compilation of creative nonfiction edited by John D'Agata that Wallace had contributed to, his response was, "You know, for emotional reasons and sanity I have to pretend this doesn't exist." Yet efforts like it did exist, and their influence looped back into the world of conventional magazines. Chad Harbach, an editor at *N+1*, a literary magazine founded in Brooklyn in 2004, declared in its first issue that "David Foster Wallace's 1996 opus now looks like the central American novel of the past thirty years, a dense star for lesser work to orbit." It was their *Catcher in the Rye*, a *Catcher in the Rye* for people who had read *The Catcher in the Rye* in school. By 2006, 150,000 copies of *Infinite Jest* had been sold and the book continued to sell steadily.

Wallace was becoming a staple in the academy too. In 2003, Marshall Boswell's *Understanding David Foster Wallace* came out, the first book dedicated to Wallace's oeuvre. The same year Stephen Burn's book-length guide to *Infinite Jest* was published. Scholars began examining his works' dense allusions. They focused on narcissism, irony, and recursion. The influence of Derrida, De Man, Heidegger, and, of course, Wittgenstein were looked at. Some of the early efforts had an improvisatory feel, as academics tried to find the appropriate approach to a writer who represented an era in literature when there was as yet no secondary source material. Another problem was that Wallace himself had laid out such a clear explanation of his theoretical aims. That Wallace had abandoned literary theory a decade before opened the question of the theory by which he rejected theory, if he had in fact rejected theory and not just subsumed it. *Infinite Jest*'s debt to other literature was perhaps an easier way to start, from *Gödel, Escher, Bach* to *Tristram Shandy* and, of course, *Hamlet*. In 2007, Timothy Jacobs, a Canadian scholar, wrote a thoughtful paper marking out the links between *The Brothers Karamazov* and *Infinite Jest*. The parallels are multiple, both being novels about a father and his three sons. Orin Incandenza corresponds to Dmitry Karamazov, the nihilistic oldest brother; Hal is Ivan; and Mario is the stand-in for Alyosha Karamazov, the simple, almost holy youngest son, with his "foolish grin" and refusal to lie. Like "the good old Brothers K," as Wallace called Dostoevsky's novel, *Infinite Jest* counterposes sincerity and faith against moral lassitude. Both eschew stylish irony to make a single point: faith matters.

Attention to his past work, though, was not going to help Wallace out of his current hole; in fact it would dig him into it more deeply. Stuck on

The Pale King, he eyed the output of his contemporaries with envy: Franzen, Eggers, and especially Vollmann, who won the National Book Award for his novel *Europe Central* in 2005. "I'm in awe of his productivity," Wallace emailed Franzen in November of that year. "How many hours a day does this guy work?" He felt the field he had once dominated getting more and more crowded. Single-entendre principles, hijinks sentences, prose at once formal and street-smart were no longer his alone. He read Rick Moody's *The Diviners*, a maximalist novel set in Hollywood, thought it good in part but tired in style, and swore to Franzen he would never write like that again. But how, then, should he write? When Franzen told him he was having trouble with his own work, Wallace wrote to commiserate (or perhaps outdo):

> I too have lots of stuff that's been jostling in line inside for years for a book. And many, many pages written, then either tossed or put in a sealed box. What's missing is some . . . thing. It may be a connection between the problem of writing it and of being alive. That doesn't feel quite true for me, though. Mine is more like the whole thing is a tornado that won't hold still long enough for me to see what's useful and what isn't, which tends to lead to the idea that I'll have to write a 5,000 page manuscript and then winnow it by 90%, the very idea of which makes something in me wither and get really interested in my cuticle, or the angle of the light outside. I've brooded and brooded about all this till my brooder is sore. Maybe the answer is simply that to do what I want to do would take more effort than I am willing to put in. Which would be a bleak reality indeed, if that's all it is?

"DeLillo's thing," he added to Franzen, "about the unwritten book following Gray around like a malformed fetus dribbling cerebrospinal fluid from its mouth gets apter all the time. I am dead becalmed—stuff literally goes right into the wastebasket after being torn from the top of the legal pad." More than a year later he was no farther along, writing to Franzen: "I go back and forth between (a) working to assembl[e] a big enough sample to take an advance, and (b) recoiling in despair, thinking that if I had your integrity I'd pitch everything and start over."

Complicating things was that he and Green were having so much fun. They listened to U2 and old Simon and Garfunkel CDs and loved IZ's rendition of "Over the Rainbow." For his forty-fourth birthday, in February 2006, Green got her husband a bootleg of the new season of *The Wire*. That Christmas they had spent with his family on Stinson Beach, Wallace with a pair of binoculars watching out for sharks as Karen swam far from shore. Franzen persuaded Green and Wallace to go to Capri in the summer for a writer's festival, where Wallace discovered octopus and went to parties at sponsors' houses. He seemed, to Franzen's eyes, as "available" as he had ever been. Afterward, Wallace took a detour to Wimbledon to start a piece on Roger Federer for the *New York Times Magazine*. He loved sitting courtside and watching Federer play. When Wallace insisted on using the serial comma, which was against the rules of the *Times*'s style handbook, the issue was settled in his favor by the executive editor Bill Keller.

Wallace was used to contradictions, both in his life and in his work, by now. But he could not pretend after all these years that his real work was going well. He told Michael Pietsch that he had completed "two hundred pages, of which maybe forty are usable." He wrote Franzen at the beginning of 2006 that he had to get serious again in late January, and then again, when he didn't, in the fall.

In September 2006, Green and Wallace adopted a two-year-old dog, whom they named Bella. "It's . . . part-Rottweiler, part Lab (?) or Boxer (?). . . . Very good-hearted, patient, and smart in dealing with Werner," Wallace wrote Franzen. Though Wallace saw Werner as the boss, their friends laughed to see his first female dog subtly take over the pack. Bella made Wallace feel his family was complete again. Yet the specter of his unfinished work was never far from his thoughts. *The Pale King* was wildly overdue now, though the only deadline was in his own mind, since there was no contract. When Little, Brown had invited him to a celebration for the tenth anniversary of *Infinite Jest* in 2006—the book was to be reissued with an introduction by Dave Eggers—he had declined, telling Michael Pietsch he was "deep into something long, and it's hard for me get back in it when I'm pulled away." The next year the New School invited him for a commemoration. "The idea of coming to NYC is appealing," he wrote to

Franzen. "The idea of doing any more public events around a book I don't remember is not."

Stymied in the composition of the novel, Wallace threw his energy into research, though he knew the danger that posed.[14] But he still wanted to be first in his class. The value of meditation and emptying the mind continued to play a key role in *The Pale King*; Wallace still wasn't sure he understood Buddhism and its practices. He began a correspondence with Christopher Hamacher, a young man who had read his Kenyon address and traced some of its roots to Buddhist thinking. Wallace peppered his correspondent, a practicing Zen Buddhist, with questions. He asked about authors he should seek out, mentioning books by Alan Watts, Eckhart Tolle, and Jiddu Krishnamurti. His friend told him don't read, just do: "It's absolutely wonderful that you don't 'know' anything about zen." Wallace wondered was he letting himself off easy when he meditated: "Is it OK to sit in a chair? Or is severe pain part of the (non-) point?" he asked. "What about a 'meditation bench' that lets you kneel with a straight back? Is it half-lotus or nothing? If so, why?" His new friend told him that the lotus position was preferable and the pain would pass, but to use his common sense. Wallace then confessed that there were many times when he didn't much want to sit or sat only briefly. "You're not going to hell if you only sit 15 minutes, sometimes," his friend advised him. "A good rule is to sit exactly as long as you planned, no more, no less." It was still hard for Wallace to understand that Buddhism wasn't a course you tried to ace.

Wallace audited more accounting courses, now at the Claremont Graduate University. "You should have seen him with our accountant," Karen Green remembers. "It was like, 'What about the ruling of 920S?' He had a correspondence with an Illinois accountant, Stephen Lacy, also a former philosophy student, who sent him a famously impenetrable passage, Section 509(A) of the IRS tax code, with a note that seemed to echo Wallace's own premise for the novel:

I find that although I can never quite understand what it says, after I read it several times and concentrate, I can actually get into a kind of weird Zen-type meditation high! (Then again sometimes it provokes a profound anxiety attack.)

Lacy argued that the tax code was postmodern, meaning relativistic and constructed of words, but Wallace did not want to write a postmodern novel about the tax code: in fact the opposite, he wanted to write a pre-modern novel about the tax code, one that took the code as holy writ, a text out of which mystical clarity might emerge. "Tax law is like the world's biggest game of chess," he emailed Franzen in April 2007, "with all sorts of weird conundrums about ethics and civics and consent of the governed built in. For me, it's a bit like math: I have no talent for it but find it still erotically interesting." He added, "I wrote a page today! (Well, more like rewrote/typed, but STILL!)"

In his heart Wallace knew he was temporizing. *The Pale King* had so many ambitions. It had to show people a way to insulate themselves from the toxic freneticism of American life. It had to be emotionally engaged and morally sound, and to dramatize boredom without being too enter-taining. And it had to sidestep the point that the kind of personality that conferred grace was the opposite of Wallace's own. In 2005, Wallace wrote in one of his notebooks, "They're rare, but they're among us. People able to achieve and sustain a certain steady state of concentration, atten-tion, despite what they're doing." By now, his failing to write the book had itself risen to a meta-level—he saw that he could not write it because he could not himself tune out the noise of modern life. He wasn't an adept, an immersive, even after more than a dozen years of sobriety and recov-ery and sitting. He was not as far as he wished to be from the "obscurely defective" young man from Urbana who had arrived at Amherst in 1980. "Work," he wrote Franzen in December 2006, "is like shitting sharp stones, still."

There were many parts of the book all the same that came to some fruition, ones where he polished the sentences over and over. A few sec-tions achieved what he was aiming for, or came close enough for him to allow for their publication. In 2007, the *New Yorker* ran a small part of the novel, entitled "Good People," which dealt with the decision by a future IRS agent named Lane Dean Jr. to commit to his girlfriend, whom he had accidentally gotten pregnant.[15] Another section, a favorite at readings, was the one in which an agent's calm is disturbed by a colleague's surreally menacing baby. It found its way into *Harper's* as "The Compliance Branch" in 2008. The Lane Dean section was poised and uninflected, written with a quiet style reminiscent of Hemingway's "Hills Like White Elephants"; "The Compliance Branch," by contrast, was hectic and exaggerated, not unlike the Incandenza sections of *Infinite Jest*. The disjunct between the two suggested the challenge Wallace was facing in deciding how to tell his story. "My own terror of appearing sentimental is so strong that I've decided to fight against it, some," he wrote his *New Yorker* editor, Deborah Treisman, about "Good People." "But the terror is still there."

He made starts at many other passages and characters. Despite his promise to the reader in an "Author's Foreword" not to write "some kind of clever metafictional titty-pincher," he introduced a character named "David Wallace," who works at the agency as a summer intern.[16] Other agents contained identifiable parts of the real Wallace. There is Stecyk, the unctuous young man who winds up getting a wedgie.[17] And David Cusk, who suffers from anxiety attacks, racing to the bathroom where "the toilet paper disintegrate[s] into little greebles and blobs all over his forehead." In the quiet study of tax forms, they both seek peace.

Wallace came closest to creating the sort of character who fully inhabits the page in Chris Fogle, whose apathy when stoned echoes that of Wallace in his senior year of high school. Fogle, though, has a conversion far neater than Wallace ever experienced, one of the sort he had urged on the students that day at Kenyon College:

I was by myself, wearing nylon warm-up pants and a black Pink Floyd tee shirt, trying to spin a soccer ball on my finger, and watching the CBS soap opera *As the World Turns* on the room's little black-and-white Zenith. . . . There was certainly always reading and studying for finals I could do, but I was being a wastoid. . . . Anyhow, I was sitting there trying to spin the ball on my finger and watching the soap opera . . . and at the end of every commercial break, the show's trademark shot of planet earth as seen from space, turning, would appear, and the CBS daytime network announcer's voice would say, "You're watching *As the World Turns*," which he seemed, on this particular day, to say more and more pointedly each time— "You're watching *As the World Turns*," until the tone began to seem almost incredulous—"You're watching *As the World Turns*"—until I was suddenly struck by the bare reality of the statement. . . . It was as if the CBS announcer were speaking directly to me, shaking my shoulder or leg as though trying to arouse someone from sleep— "You're watching *As the World Turns.*". . . I didn't stand for anything. If I wanted to matter—even just to myself—I would have to be less free, by deciding to choose in some kind of definite way.

Fogle decides to join the IRS, and soon heads off for training in Peoria, after which he is recruited to be part of a team of tax savants—Fogle's ability, never fleshed out in the text but present in Wallace's notes, is to recite a string of numbers that grants him total concentration. Wallace liked the many pages he wrote on Fogle well enough to consider publishing them as a short stand-alone novel. Perhaps someone else reading other sections of the book—Wallace would show them to no one—might have been satisfied with those too, but he could not get out from under the shadow of the statue. To the inside cover of a notebook, he taped an anecdote about T. S. Eliot, who had also suffered from crushingly high standards: "One of [Conrad] Aiken's friends was a patient of the famous analyst Homer Lane, and Aiken told this friend about Eliot's problem. Lane said to his patient, 'Tell your friend Aiken to tell his friend Eliot that all that's stopping him is his fear of putting anything down that is short of perfection. He thinks he's God.'" (The underlining was Wallace's).

Wallace had said again and again how much he loved the reader. But how much did he really care whether people found what they were looking for in his books? And how much did he write for himself? One test was his willingness to create a satisfactory plot. He had never liked plot, that tidying up of life in which, as he had written Howard in 1986, "revelations revelationize [and] things are cleared up." To rely too much on plot risked seducing the reader; it was like selling Tide. Moreover, plots typically involved the gradual maturation of the characters, and that was not how Wallace saw things. His default view of life was more mechanistic than organic. Change in a character—Hal, Gately, Wallace himself at Granada House—was usually a binary flip. Yet he knew an unplotted book violated the physics of reading. So over the years, he slowly cast about for a structure for *The Pale King*. In one of his notebooks, there is a sentence suggesting that he had hit on a framework of interest: an evil group within the IRS is trying to steal the secrets of an agent who is particularly gifted at main-

taining a heightened state of concentration. It was a nice Pynchonian notion, with an echo of the scramble for the "Infinite Jest" video cartridge,
but Wallace didn't follow up on it. Probably it struck him as too clever, a
short cut. Instead he divided the agents into two groups: those who wanted
to automate the agency versus those who still wished to process returns by
hand. His own heart was with the old-fashioned processors. Over the past
decade he had been watching the digitalization of media with ever greater
discomfort. "Digital=abstract=sterile, somehow," he had written to De-
Lillo in 2000. Electronic media facilitated consumerism; it removed ob-
stacles to spectation. It was also that if the IRS was going to be a secular
religion, it needed its priests. To Wallace, so troubled by freedom, there
was nothing more erotic than people who willingly gave up theirs. But
anti-automation was more of an attitude than a plot anyway, as perhaps
Wallace knew. There was also the consideration that if you really wanted
to capture the mindfulness that comes through boredom, the less plot you
had the better. Wallace wrote in a note: "Something big threatens to happen but doesn't actually happen," and elsewhere, characterized the novel
as "a series of setups for things to happen but nothing ever happens."
Maybe different scenes in suggestive apposition may have been all he
wanted for his plot, but if so, he remained worried that the thousands of
pages he had written left the reader still too much on his or her own. "The
individual parts of this book would not be all that hard to read," he wrote
Nadell in 2007. "It's more the juxtaposition of them, the number of separate characters, etc."

And life kept breaking back in. Wallace had become increasingly political over the years, thanks in large part to Green. He was a vocal critic of
George W. Bush's administration. "I am, at present, partisan," he had told
The Believer in 2003. "Worse than that: I feel such deep, visceral antipathy
that I can't seem to think or speak or write in any kind of fair or nuanced
way about the current administration. . . . My own plan for the coming
fourteen months is to knock on doors and stuff envelopes. Maybe even to
wear a button. To try to accrete with others into a demographically significant mass. To try extra hard to exercise patience, politeness, and imagination on those with whom I disagree. Also to floss more." When Bush
won reelection in 2004, Wallace and Green seriously considered leaving
the country, but Wallace felt that would be an overreaction. In the end, he

was a writer, not a political operative. He cared about the moral state of the country, more than which side won.

The thought kept recurring to him that he was no longer the kind of person who could write the novel he wanted to write. *Infinite Jest* had been driven by his dysfunctional yearning for Mary Karr; nothing similar goaded him now. Green had opened up a showroom for her work. She called it Beautiful Crap, a name that happily coincided with the plot of "The Suffering Channel." She loved her gallery, and they discussed jobs he might enjoy. "He talked about opening up a dog shelter," she remembers. It would be what the tennis coach Gerhard Schtitt in *Infinite Jest* meant when he said that the important thing was to "learn to be a good American during a time, boys, when America isn't good its own self." Wallace considered, he wrote Franzen, "forgetting about writing for a while if it's not a source of joy. Who knows. Life sure is short though." He thought about focusing only on his nonfiction.[18]

The Federer piece had been a complete joy. He stopped the nonfiction for a period to see if it made the fiction come easier—was the magazine work dissipating his ability to finish *The Pale King*? "It just made him crazy to think he had been working on it for so long," Green remembers. In his final major interview, given to *Le Nouvel Observateur* in August 2005, he talked about various writers he admired—Saint Paul, Rousseau, and always, Dostoevsky, among them—and added, "What are envied and coveted here seem to me to be qualities of human beings—capacities of spirit—rather than technical abilities or special talents."

Around this time, Wallace wrote Nadell, telling her that he needed "to put some kind of duress/pressure on myself so that I quit futzing around and changing my mind about the book twice a week and just actually do it." Franzen's example had been an influence; he told Wallace that having a contract for *Freedom*, the novel that followed *The Corrections*, had helped focus him. Wallace wasn't sure. He explored the tax consequences of taking a single payment versus spreading the advance out over the years and worried about the alternative minimum tax. And he prepared a stack of about 150 pages of *The Pale King*. There were plenty of equally finished pages—among them the story of the levitating Drinion—which, for whatever reason, he did not include. "I could take a couple of years unpaid leave from Pomona and just try to finish it," he wrote to Nadell. When she encouraged him, he responded more hesitatingly: "Let me noodle hard about it. It may not be until the end of summer that I'd even have a packet to-gether."

Wallace had never been certain that being on Nardil was the right thing, and whenever he was not writing well, he wondered if it played a role. But the memories of how it had saved his life were also always present. He had read widely about other antidepressants but never found one he thought he should change to. In the summer of 2007, Wallace was eating in a Per-sian restaurant in Claremont with his parents and began to have heart palpitations and to sweat heavily. These can be the signs of a hypertensive crisis, although Green thinks he may have merely had an anxiety attack— the chicken and rice dish he ordered was one he had eaten many times; he never saw a doctor for a diagnosis. In any event, he eventually went to a physician, who told him what he already knew: there were a lot of superior antidepressants on the market now. Compared with them, Nardil was "a dirty drug."

Wallace saw an opportunity. He told Green that he wanted to make a change. "You know what? I'm up for it," she remembers answering, figur-ing he could not be stopped anyway. She knew the decision came out of an area of deep conflict for him. "The person who would go off the medica-tions that were possibly keeping him alive was not the person he liked," she says. "He didn't want to care about the writing as much as he did." Soon afterward, he stopped the drug and waited for it to flush out of his body. For the first weeks, he felt that the process was going well. "I feel a bit 'peculiar,' which is the only way to describe it," he emailed Franzen in August, who had checked in to see how he was doing. "All this is to be expected (22 years and all), and I am not unduly alarmed. Phase 4 of with-drawal/titration commences today. It's all OK. I appreciate the monitor-ing." The next month brought "disabling nausea/fatigue" and left him more concerned: "I've been blowing stuff off and then having it slip my mind," he wrote his friend. "This is the harshest phase of the 'washout process' so far; it's a bit like I imagine a course of chemo would be." He remained "fairly confident it will pass in time." *GQ* took his picture for their October 2007 issue, and in it, he looked skinny and unshaven, a grizzled version of his Amherst self. Wallace had never entirely put out of his mind the fundamentalist faction in recovery that regarded prescription drugs as a crutch. The plan was for him to go from Nardil to another antidepressant, but he now decided he should try to be completely drug free. Green was worried. Her husband, she remembers thinking, was expecting "a Jungian rebirth." Soon afterward, Wallace had to be hospitalized for severe depression. When he got out, doctors prescribed new drugs. But he was now too panicked to give them time to work. He took over the job of keeping himself sane, second-guessing doctors and their prescriptions. If he tried an antidepressant, he would read that a possible side effect was anxiety, and that alone would make him too anxious to stay on the drug. He wrote to Nadell in December, "Upside: I've lost 30 pounds. Downside: I haven't even thought about work since like September. I'm figuring I get 90 more days before I even remotely expect anything of myself—the shrink/expert says that's a fairly sane attitude." When his sister, Amy, would call, he would tell her, "I'm not all right. I'm trying to be, but I'm not all right."

He continued to write in a notebook, but he did not have the strength to return to his challenging manuscript. "The Pale King" had once referred to the IRS, and possibly to the state of contentment and focus the book advocated; but now it was a synonym for the depression that tormented him, or death. Not all days were bad. He taught throughout. He emailed friends. He and Green tried to maintain their lives. Always self-critical, Wallace would rate good days as "B-plus" or "cautiously optimistic." They joked about the unthinkable. Green warned him that if he killed himself she'd be "the Yoko Ono of the literary world, the woman with all the hair who domesticated you and look what happened." They made a pact that he would never make her guess how he was doing.

During the spring of 2008, a new combination of antidepressants seemed to stabilize Wallace. It looked like the worst might be over. In February, he had written to Tom Bissell, a writer who was a new friend, "I got really sick over the fall. Pneumonioid-type sick. Lost a scary amount of weight. I'm still not all the way back on my feet. I'm twelve years older than you; I feel more like 30 years older right now. This return letter will probably be the most 'work'-type thing I do today, writing-wise." He added that he had been reading Camus lately: "He's very clear, as a thinker, and tough—completely intolerant of bullshit. It makes my soul feel clean to read him." He taught a class in creative nonfiction that semester. Students who had studied with him before, though, noticed that his comments were terser, his playfulness muted. On the last day of class, he choked up. The students were confused; where was the Wallace they knew? At a coffee shop afterward he cried again. "Go ahead and laugh," he told them, but they knew something was wrong.

That spring *GQ* asked him to write an essay on Obama and rhetoric and he felt almost well enough to do it. Obama gave him hope; he and Green even talked about his being a speechwriter for the candidate. The magazine reserved a hotel room for him in Denver for the Democratic convention and began to make arrangements, but soon he canceled. When the *New York Times Magazine* approached him to write about the Olympics in Beijing that summer, he apologized but said he wasn't feeling well enough. Nadell was busy explaining that her client had a stomach malady. "It had to be severe enough to explain why he couldn't travel," she remembers. Wallace would mine *House* for diseases he could suggest to others he might be suffering from.

Wallace's parents were slated to come visit. His relationship with them was the best it had been in years; he told Green he had no idea what had made him so mad at his family in his thirties. "We'll have big fun," he promised them. But then he asked them to wait. That June, the annual booksellers' convention was in Los Angeles, and Green and Wallace drove the thirty miles of roadway to have dinner with Pietsch, Nadell, the humor writer David Sedaris, and his publicist Marlena Bittner, who also worked on Wallace's books. Sedaris was surprised at how funny and gentle Wallace was, how full of praise for his students. At the end Pietsch asked Wallace how he was doing. "You don't wanna know," his writer replied. When they hugged, Pietsch looked into Wallace's eyes and thought they looked "haunted."

About ten days after the dinner, Wallace checked in to a motel about ten miles from his home and took all the pills he could find. When he woke up, he called Green, who had been searching for him all night. She met him at the hospital and he told her that he was glad to be alive. He was sorry that he'd made her look for him. She had him transferred to the university's hospital, his speech still slurred for a week. The suicide note he'd mailed got to her several days later. She painted their garage door red to match the inside, a promise she'd made him in the hospital. He switched doctors and agreed to try electroconvulsive therapy. He was terrified at the prospect—he remembered how ECT had damaged his short-term memory in 1988—but he underwent twelve sessions.

Franzen came for a visit while the treatments were in progress in July. He now spent part of each summer in nearby Santa Cruz writing. He was astonished at the changes in his friend's body and mind. They would play with the dogs or go outside so Wallace could smoke. Franzen asked what he had been thinking when he tried to kill himself and Wallace winced and said he didn't remember. He was barely able to read, not even the thrillers he ordinarily devoured. Instead he mostly watched TV. After dinner, Werner licked out his mouth.

Wallace's illness was taking a huge toll on Green; she was exhausted. For one nine-day period, she didn't leave their house. When she did go out, Wallace's friends from his Claremont recovery group kept him company. Later in the summer a yard hose went missing and Green found it in the trunk of their car. He had planned to tie it to the exhaust pipe using his bandana. When she confronted him, he insisted he had already decided not to go through with it. She did not believe him and had him hospitalized again.

In August, Stirling suffered an athletic injury, and Green wanted to be with him, so Wallace's parents stayed with Wallace for ten days. He was close to giving up hope. "It's like they're throwing darts at a dartboard," he complained to them about his psychiatrists. They went with him to an appointment; when the doctor suggested a new drug combination, Wallace rolled his eyes. He was a shut-in now, worried he'd run into his students if he went into town. Sally Wallace cooked him the meals he had loved as a child—casseroles and pot pies; they watched *The Wire*. It was obvious to his family that he was in unendurable pain. Before she left, he thanked her for being his mother.

Eventually, Wallace asked to go back on Nardil, but he was too agitated to give it the weeks it takes to work. Franzen would call and encourage him to stick with it—the worst was over. "Keep talking like that," Wallace said. "It's helping." In early September, Nadell spoke with him and thought that he sounded a bit better. He was writing notes to himself, making gratitude lists and lists of symptoms and fears and keeping a journal. In his last entry he wrote that he would stay awake so that when Green got home he could help her with the groceries.

Green believes that she knows when Wallace decided to try again to kill himself. She says of September 6, "That Saturday was a really good day. Monday and Tuesday were not so good. He started lying to me that Wednesday." He waited two more days for an opportunity. In the early evening on Friday, September 12, Wallace suggested that Green go out to prepare for an opening at Beautiful Crap, which was about ten minutes away in the center of Claremont. Green felt comforted by the fact that he'd seen the chiropractor on Monday. "You don't go to the chiropractor if you're going to commit suicide," she says.

After Green left, Wallace went into the garage and turned on the lights. He wrote her a two-page note. Then he crossed through the house to the patio, where he climbed onto a chair and hanged himself. When one character dies in *Infinite Jest*, he is "catapulted home over . . . glass palisades at desperate speeds, soaring north, sounding a bell-clear and nearly maternal alarmed call-to-arms in all the world's well-known tongues."

Green returned home at 9:30 and found her husband. In the garage, bathed in light from his many lamps, sat a pile of nearly two hundred pages. He had made some changes in the months since he considered sending them to Pietsch. The story of "David Wallace" was now first. In his final hours, he had tidied up the manuscript so that his wife could find it. Below it, around it, inside his two computers, on old floppy disks in his drawers were hundreds of other pages—drafts, character sketches, notes to himself, fragments that had evaded his attempt to integrate them into the novel over the past decade. This was his effort to show the world what it was to be "a fucking human being." He had never completed it to his satisfaction. This was not an ending anyone would have wanted for him, but it was the one he had chosen.

ACKNOWLEDGMENTS

David Foster Wallace and I never met. The closest we came was at a party in 1996 for *Infinite Jest*—the publishing party he would later tell Don De-Lillo was the only one he'd ever gone to "and if God's in his heaven it will be my last." I had commissioned a piece on *Infinite Jest* for a magazine where I was a features editor, and so I was there in that large room with several hundred others. I was amazed to see a stocky man with long scraggly hair and a bandana, some sort of grimy shirt, granny glasses, and that expression of a deer who wishes it was anywhere but on this road. He was across a vast dance floor spot-lit. At least that's my memory.

Because we never spoke and because he died so young, when I began to write his biography I had to look for his voice elsewhere I turned to his friends and family. Fortunately for me the vast majority were open and willing to talk and pass on their memories.

I learned in the process of writing this book why the list of acknowledgments in biographies is always so long—because biography is a joint act, an exercise in communal remembering. And if it takes a village to write a biography, it takes a town to write the first biography of someone as complex as David. Herewith, some of the kindly residents. To all I apologize for the countless emails and repeated phone calls, the thing I asked you that I had already asked you before, the desperate requests for clarification right when you were sitting down to dinner. All I can say is Thank You. Thank you.

First, my deepest appreciation to Karen Green, David's gracious and gifted wife.

I received welcome support also from Wallace's family, especially his sister, Amy, a person of caring and poise. To Bonnie Nadell, who was Wallace's superb agent for his entire career (they met in their early twenties), I owe a significant debt of gratitude. I'd like also to point out three of Wallace's friends who gave more help than I had the right to ask for. The first is the novelist Mark Costello, David's roommate at Amherst. A second is Heather Aronson, David's good friend from Arizona and a talented fiction writer too. The philosophical Corey Washington, also a friend of David's from Amherst, showed an inexhaustible willingness to help on everything, from the minutiae of David's Amherst grades to questions of free will and fatalism.

David had deep friendships with two other writers who helped me enormously: Jonathan Franzen, his "best of pals and lit combatant," as Wallace called him, was one who was with him to the end. Mary Karr, the poet and memoirist, played an important role in an earlier part of his life. To Mary I owe a particular debt for helping me try to figure out what went on during David's tumultuous Boston and Syracuse years. Any failure to make sense of these bafflingly complex days is, of course, mine (ditto errors of all sorts that may be in these pages).

There were many other writers whom Wallace knew or corresponded with in his later years. Many were kind enough to give me their recollections, among them Sherman Alexie, Tom Beller, Sven Birkerts, Tom Bissell, Don DeLillo, Dave Eggers, Jeffrey Eugenides, Lewis Hyde, Frederick Kaufman, Brad Leithauser, Mark Leyner, Ruth Liebmann, Richard Powers, George Saunders, David Sedaris, Evan Wright, and Elizabeth Wurtzel.

Now to those kind souls not mentioned above who helped as I worked my way through each of David's ports of call in his too-short life. This list does not aim to be comprehensive—as Wallace wrote about the difficulty of writing about real life, "There's **so much!**"

In Urbana: Mrs. Clare Barkley, Thomas Desmond, the Dessouky brothers, Maged and Yasser, John Flygare, Matt Friedman, David Ghent, Martin Maehr, Michail Reid, Brian Spano, Sherry Thompson (Mrs. McLellan when she taught at Urbana High), and Lolita Zwettler.

At Amherst: Ruth Abbe, Fred Brooke, Sylvia Kennick Brown, David Chinitz, Dave Colmar, Rajiv Desai, Willem DeVries, John Drew, Jay Garfield, Shubha Ghosh, Jonathan Glass, David Hixon, Ann Huse, Dan Javit, Andrea Justus, Nancy Kennick, Nat Larson, Brad Leithauser, Alan Lelchuk, Miller Maley, Charlie McLagan, Andrew Parker, Dale Peterson, and Mark Valladares.

In Arizona: Jaci Aaronson, Forrest Ashby, Robert Boswell, Karen Brennan, Rich C., Andy Crockett, Alice Elman, Alison Hicks Greifenstein, Ron Hansen, Bob Houston, Zita Ingham, JT Jackson, Ken Kalfus, Rick Kempa, Will Layman, Antonya Nelson, Paul Niesen, the late Steve Orlen, Amy Pence, Jonathan Penner, Bruce Petronio, Buzz Poverman, Francine Prose, Kim Roberts, Andy Robinson, Aurelie Sheehan, Charles Sherry, and Ron Steffens.

At Yaddo: Marina Budhos, Kathe Burkhart, Robert Cohen, Stephen Dunn, Marie Howe, Jeanne McCulloch, Jay McInerney, and Michael Torke. I would also like to thank Elaina Richardson and Lesley Leduc for the copies of David's applications to Yaddo.

As a teacher at Amherst: Sue Dickman, Tias Little, Margit Longbrake, John Reid, and Jessamyn West. As a teacher (briefly) in Arizona: Marvin Diogenes, Martha Ostheimer, and Tom Willard. As a graduate student at Harvard: Steven Affeldt, Roy Blumenfeld, Warren Goldfarb, Steven Gross, Mi-Kyoung Lee, Alva Noe, and Dmitri Tymoczko. At Granada House: Big Craig and Deb Larson. At Emerson: Jack Gantos, DeWitt Henry, Don Lee, and Debra Spark. In Syracuse: Doug Eich, John F., Stephanie Hubbard, Stephen J., Christopher Kennedy, Michael Martone, and Linda Perla.

In Bloomington: Francis B. and his wife, Terri, and her daughter Sarah Adams; Susan Barnett; Becky Bradway; Mimi Davis; Tim Feeney; Ron Fortune; Lee Freeman; William Gillespie; Jason Hammel; Juliana Harms; Charlie ("he saved me from the dog") Harris and his wife, Victoria, and daughter Kymberly (the fabulous Harris family!); Amy Havel; Doug Hesse; Greg Howard; Bob McLaughlin; Erica Neely; John O'Brien; Doug and Erin Poag; Marty Riker; Joe S.; Ben Slotky; Curtis White; and Deb Wuliger. A special thank-you to Bill Flick of the *Pantagraph* for searching its archives.

The Pomona years: Margaret Adorno (Pomona's peerless registrar), Kyle Beachy, Daniel Birkholz, Ben Casnocha, John D'Agata, Kevin Dettmar, Maria Donapetry, Kathleen Fitzpatrick, Rena Fraden, Neil Gerard, John Goodson, Kaneisha Grayson, Christopher Hamacher, Patrick Jagoda, Natalie Klein, Robert Lesser, Coty Meibeyer, Kelly Natoli, Ashley Newman, Colleen O'Rourke, Caroline Potter, Jared Roscoe, Paul St. Just, John Seery, Amanda Shapiro, Bryn Starbird, and J. B. Wogan.

From the world of magazines and books, among those who worked with Wallace, special thanks go to Michael Pietsch, his editor at Little, Brown, who answered countless questions and helped me find my way through the labyrinth of *The Pale King,* and Gerald Howard, his editor at Penguin, who took me through David's early years. Also my deep thanks to Jennifer Barton, Adam Begley, André Bernard, Marlena Bittner, Will Blythe, John Bohrer, Mark Bryant, Lisa Chase, Jesse Cohen, Charis Conn, Will Dana, Josh Dean, Peter Desrochers, John Dickerson, Jonathan Galassi, Colin Harrison, Jack Hitt, Tom Jenks, Jay Jennings, Vanessa Kehren, Bill Keller, Glenn Kenny, Stephen King, Jeannie Luciano, Gerry Marzorati, Steven Moore, Eve Rabinovits, Amy Rhodes, Gemma Sieff, Lee Smith, Bill Tonelli, Alice Turner, and Holly Wilkinson.

Sui generis is James Ryerson, who helped me with many thorny questions about Wallace and "Uncle Ludwig" (Wittgenstein). I owe a debt to his thinking and writing on Wallace's philosophy thesis, too, and am grateful he read drafts of my passages. Wherever I went, I met Jamie on the way back, sometimes in the company of Caleb Crain, who also lent a hand in similarly difficult moments where *Everything and More* was concerned.

Stephen Lacy supplied the details of his interesting colloquy on taxes with Wallace, and Jennifer Schuessler supplemented with her own research from her excellent piece on Wallace and the IRS from the *New York Times Book Review.* David Hering of the University of Liverpool kindly shared some of his research on Wallace's earliest drafts of *Infinite Jest* with me and was a generous sounding board to my theories.

The Wallace community is fortunate to have Nick Maniatis's thehowlingfantods website: if you are curious about it and it's about DFW, it's there. I know of no author better served by his Web public. Nick graciously put out a request for letters, and several interesting pieces of correspondence came forth. Wallace wrote honestly to a wide range of people, many of whom he did not know well. Among those I'd particularly like to thank for sharing letters are Weston Cutter, Christopher Hager, Brandon Hobson, Marie Mundaca, and Nick Solomon.

Two noted Wallace scholars helped me as well. Stephen Burn of Northern Michigan University generously forwarded me correspondence and made available some of his own research, as did Marshall Boswell of Rhodes College. Adam Kelly of University College, Dublin, and Harvard lent a hand in interpreting the role of literary theory in Wallace's fiction. Frank Bruni shared his memories of researching his Wallace profile for the *New York Times'* magazine section, and David Streitfeld told me of his visit to Wallace's house for *Details*. Deborah Treisman shared correspondence and memories of Wallace's contributions to the *New Yorker*.

Of the many interviewers who went before and on whom I relied for David's words, I want to particularly signal my debt to David Lipsky, whose long-ago visit with Wallace at the time of *Infinite Jest* for *Rolling Stone* (the piece was never written) he turned into an insightful, enjoyable book, and also to Larry McCaffery, who interviewed David for the *Review of Contemporary Fiction* and kindly made his drafts available. That interview remains the point of departure for all Wallace studies.

Among archivists and librarians, I would like to give a special thank-you to Thomas Staley, the director of the Ransom Center, where David's papers are housed, as well as to his top-notch staff, among them Megan Bernard, Andi Gustavson, Ancelyn Krivak, Molly Schwartzburg, Danielle Sigler, and Jennifer Tisdale, for their kind assistance. David McCartney helped me with the Frank Conroy papers at the University of Iowa, and Rosemary Cullen with the Brad Morrow papers at Brown University. Peter Nelson of the Amherst College archives tabulated David's innumerable academic awards for me and found correspondence and yearbook material. Emily Boutilier put out the word to Amherst alumni who knew David.

Without all these people this book would never have been written, but there is one person who lent truly special support: Michelle Dean, a talented journalist who as my research assistant during the latter part of this work, displayed astonishing energy and commitment, playing a key role in helping to make this complicated story as accurate and comprehensive as possible. I expect to see her between her own hardcovers soon.

Two Wallace aficionados also were indispensable: Matt Bucher, who heads the Wallace-1 email list, selflessly gave of his time and energy. He read draft language and suggested improvements, drawing on his top-level knowledge of DFW. My apologies to Jordan for dragging him away from child rearing to help me again and again. And Jonah Furman, just out of Johns Hopkins University, lent his own gifts as a fact checker, research assistant, deep Wallace reader, and sounding board.

Three other young researchers lent their time and talents too: Shelby Ozer, a talented high school senior; Becky Cooper, world-trotting polymath; and Mark Byrne, who worked as a research assistant for me while also a student in the Literary Journalism program at NYU, under the generous Professor Robert Boynton. I once asked Mark if a friend of his was also a Wallace fan, and he memorably replied: "Honestly, I don't think I've ever had a sustained friendship with someone who's not."

During the latter part of my research and writing I enjoyed the support of a fellowship from the Leon Levy Center for Biography at the CUNY Graduate Center. There I wish to thank trustee Shelby White, Judy Dobrzynski, directors past and present Brenda Wineapple and Gary Giddins, as well as Adam Begley, Madison Smartt Bell, Tom Hafer, Elizabeth Kendall, John Matteson, and Ikuyo Nakagawa. Staff members Caitlin Delohery, Michael Gately, and Alyssa Varner were enormously kind and helpful at this special institution.

At Viking Penguin, my enormous gratitude to Paul Slovak, my editor, whose enthusiasm helped propel me on this complex voyage and whose calm kept me from capsizing; his assistant, David Martin; and indefatigable editor Beena Kamlani. Also to my agent, Elyse Cheney, and her deputy, Alex Jacobs, as well as to Tania Strauss, who arrived still dipped in the glamour of Hollywood, which she got working with my film agent, Howie Sanders at UTA. And in London, my British editor, Philip Gwyn Jones, and his colleague John Freeman, who, coincidentally, once interviewed Wallace himself.

At the *New Yorker*, the editor David Remnick; my long-time editor Daniel Zalewski; and his assistants, Yvette Siegert and Andrew Marantz; editors Henry Finder and Susan Morrison. This book all started with an email from David one long-ago fall evening. There is no more talented editorial team going. They, as Wallace would say, "simply separate sock from pod."

I want to express my appreciation to James Atlas, Patricia Bosworth, Anne Fadiman, Frances Kiernan, Brad Morrow, and Lee Siegel, all special friends and supporters in the creation of this work.

Some old friends who helped in new ways: To Alissa Land, who took a road trip with me to what was Granada House in Brighton and endured the rigors of literary research, and to Bryan Simmons, who helped peel back the mystery from David's brief stint as a security guard at Lotus Development—my thanks. To Shelley and Eames Demetrios, also thanks, for letting me stay in Guthrie's room. Guthrie, thanks!

To the Montclair Public Library, where I did much of this work, partly in their wonderful Terra Tea & Fair Trade cafe, and to Panera's on Bloomfield Avenue and the Chamagudao tea shop (now closed), where I did the rest—thank you for providing a quiet place to think about David and his work and to eat pastries.

To my in-laws, Diana Shahmoon and Charles Blustain, for more pastries and good comments. To my brothers, Eric and Adam, and their wives, Diane and Denise, yes, more baked goods. And concluding in this vein, if less probably, to Katherine Neuman of Cafe Lula, who gave me a whole apple pie (proprietor Jason Hammel, see above).

And finally to my wife, Sarah, who was pushed off the dedication page by our children and who otherwise would be there, again.

NOTES

Chapter 1: "Call Me Dave"

1. Amy Wallace says that she never met "anybody who had the need for television David had."

2. Wallace claimed that as an eleven-year-old he traded lawn mowing with a neighbor for a tutorial on Stendhal's *Le Rouge et le Noir*. The improbable exchange is echoed in *Infinite Jest* where Hal Incandenza offers free mowing to an "oral lyrologist" in return for information on the history of the instrument.

3. In his first published story, "The Planet Trillaphon as It Stands in Relation to the Bad Thing," the protagonist says of his depression, "Some people say it's like having always before you and under you a huge black hole without a bottom, a black, black hole, maybe with vague teeth in it, and then your being part of the hole."

Chapter 2: "The Real 'Waller'"

1. The three roommates also heard the other students in the hall bathroom. Wallace said he could recognize the sounds of different people in the stalls and years later made use of these memories in a story told by the son of a men's room attendant, "Brief Interview #42."

2. This story was mythologized at Amherst in later years such that Wallace so flummoxed a professor with his superior intelligence that the professor snapped shut his briefcase and left the class in the middle of a lesson.

3. In Senior Rhetoric, for instance, Wallace wrote a story about a man who kills his own clone by pushing him out a window. The tale played off of the *Frankenstein* myth and ended with a pun, the creator arrested for "making an illegal clone fall." The teacher told him she was disappointed in the ending but gave him an A-plus.

4. A hint as to other stories Wallace may have been working on at the time is provided in a conversation between two characters at a publishing house in *The Broom of the System*, Wallace's college novel, who are looking through a pile of unsolicited manuscripts for the publisher's quarterly. The stories discussed are "The Enema Bandit and the Cosmic Buzzer," which may be a version of "The Clang Birds," as well as "Dance of the Insecure," "To the Mall," "Threnody Jones and the Goat from Below," "Love" (itself a part of *Broom*), and "A Metamorphosis for the Eighties." Comments one character, "That last one

is actually rather interesting. A Kafka parody, though sensitively done. Self-loathing-in-the-midst-of-Adulation piece. Collegiate but interesting."

5. Wallace's parodies sometimes offended. A piece he wrote about cosseted students at antebellum Amherst arriving with their slaves drew a protest from the Black Student Union.

6. Another philosophical book of the era, *Gödel, Escher, Bach*, by Douglas Hofstadter, impressed Wallace a great deal. Subtitled "an eternal golden braid," the book investigates consciousness, logic, language, and the structures of meaning. Wallace borrowed his father's copy and "actually shoved this book excitedly at people in the eighties," as he remembered in an interview in *The Believer*. *Gödel* is a predecessor to *Infinite Jest*, at least structurally. Mark Costello remembers Wallace when he was working on his novel "going on about the 'braid' or 'fugue' shape—disparate elements making a whole."

7. That "every love story is a ghost story" is a thought that stayed with Wallace from the beginning of his writing career to the end. The phrase appears in a letter he wrote in the graduate program at the University of Arizona, and he is still turning it over in his mind twenty years later when he slips it into a scene in which IRS examiners silently turn pages in *The Pale King*. From "Planet Trillaphon" to the posthumous *The Pale King*, moments of happy love in Wallace's work are rare.

8. That human connections can heal would become the centerpiece of Wallace's mature credo. As he would write one day in *Infinite Jest*, "The truth will set you free—but not until it's done with you."

9. Wallace never republished "Planet Trillaphon" in a collection, probably because it was too revealing. Also, by the time he had sufficient other short fiction for a collection, after publishing *The Broom of the System*, the conventionality of the narrative would have seemed amateurish to him.

10. The other students were entranced by Wallace's recitation of the Underground Man's monologue in the class.

11. The other opening sentence that Wallace considered of surpassing beauty is (slightly misquoted) from a Stephen Crane story, "The Open Boat." It sounds a similarly unsettled note: "None of the men knew the color of the sky."

12. Wallace claimed Lenore's great-grandmother was loosely inspired by a real Wittgenstein disciple, Alice Ambrose, who lived near Amherst. His knowledge of nursing homes come from a stint working in one in high school.

13. Wallace once wrote Jonathan Franzen he was glad everyone focused on his debt in *Broom of the System* to Pynchon, because it meant they didn't see how much he had taken from DeLillo.

14. I owe this observation to Marshall Boswell, in his book *Understanding David Foster Wallace*.

15. Reading his former roommate's manuscript in the spring of 1985, Mark Costello noticed that Lenore seemed like an idealized projection of Amy Wallace, especially in her manner of speech—"the dry wit and the tendency to repeat in less inflated terms what someone has said to her."

Chapter 3: "Westward!"

1. He wrote on his Iowa application that he had also applied to the Johns Hopkins MFA program, where the postmodernist John Barth taught. Unfortunately, the school has no record of an application. If Wallace was rejected, it would lend a more personal slant to his later intense antagonism toward the writer.

2. Containers of waste appear regularly over the years in Wallace's writing and reach an acme in *Infinite Jest*. Most critics would trace the leitmotif to his affection for Pynchon, for whom waste was also a central symbol, but personal exposure certainly played a role.

3. This fascination with spiders would appear in *Infinite Jest*, where the three Incandenza generations that precede Hal fear them. For instance, Hal's great-grandfather refuses to stand under palm trees out of concern they will drop on his head. And the ferocity of the female may have played a part in the portrait of Avril Incandenza, Hal's mother, a venomous widow herself.

4. When "Forever Overhead" was chosen for *Best American Short Stories 1992*, Wallace dismissed it in his contributor note as "straining to make a personal trauma sound way deeper and prettier and Big than anything true could ever really be."

5. When Mary Carter died in 2011, many of Wallace's fellow classmates were surprised to find that she had been in her sixties at the time she ran the writing program.

6. "I completely deny ever once kissing any part of my sister's feet at any time whatsoever," Wallace wrote in his contributor note for "Forever Overhead" in *Best American Short Stories 1992*, setting that record straight at the same time as he claimed the "excruciatingly shaming" trauma of panicking on the top of the high dive for himself, when the person who froze atop the high dive, according to his family, was actually his mother.

7. Though never a Zumbye, Wallace enjoyed singing songs from their album in the shower, especially "Tears of a Clown" and "Since I Fell for You."

8. Minimalism was political too, practically the literary world's univocal response to the Reagan era, as if the cuts in budgets had trimmed countless words and emotions from writers' vocabularies at the same time.

9. When Wallace brought up Derrida and De Man, from his literary theory class, to support his respect for brat pack writers, Elman said he didn't care. He derided him as Herr Doktor Wallace, as Wallace's face flushed and his voice rose. Afterward, Wallace worried that he had transgressed and speedily wrote Elman an apology, explaining he was "passionately interested in this stuff, and I'm afraid I sometimes forget where I am and whom I'm talking to."

10. The evident comic appeal of the excerpt is why Wallace's agent Bonnie Nadell later suggested that he begin the book with it, rather than the original opening, a conversation between Lenore and her great-grandmother that was eventually cut.

11. Wallace's readings in literary theory hang heavily over the story, especially his fascination with Derrida. For Wittgenstein language was speech and without a speaker there could be no meaning. By contrast, Derrida insisted that writing was no less fundamental to language and the absence of the speaker/author was precisely what allowed the reader to assert the meaning of the written words—Derrida's famous dictum that "there is nothing outside the text." In creating a character who is all disembodied speech in a written narrative, Wallace was joining the two approaches.

12. These are Penner's notes. He says he would in the actual class have expressed himself more diplomatically.

13. Penner told Wallace that the fantastical ending of "Solomon Silverfish" was too short, the rest too long, showing he was a more complicated reader than Wallace gave him credit for. All the same, the students had no doubt where his heart lay. "Penner," Robert Boswell remembers, "was really uptight about what was and what wasn't a story; he was the worst person to work with David."

14. Penner has a different interpretation of these words. "As I interpret them," he says, "they mean we'd hate to lose him as a real writer, hate to see him sink to a trivial level. I don't remember telling David that, but I certainly felt it."

15. A small print run of hardcovers, now extremely valuable, was also planned, under the Viking imprint.

16. Soon after selling the book, Wallace confessed to Corey Washington his fear that "only me and Mom will buy the book . . . and my name will be economic and literary mud—even shit."

17. ". . . so that word and reference are unified . . . in absence," Wallace noted to Nadell happily.

18. "He was very polite in ignoring me" is Howard's too-modest memory of his editorial interactions with Wallace. He told Leon Neyfakh of the *New York Observer* after the writer's death, "I'm sure I may have changed a comma to a semicolon or maybe fixed a couple of words in *Broom of the System* but yeah, he knew what he was about, David, even if I didn't."

19. The name of another musician from Placebo Records, Michael Pemulis, would later attach to an important character in *Infinite Jest*.

20. Wallace appended a note on the copy of the story he circulated in his workshop apologizing if the story offended and asking if the grotesqueries seemed unnecessary, because "that would obviously be bad narrative news."

21. Carter made no effort to hide who her favorites were at the event. While she walked Wallace around, she asked Heather Aronson to serve hors d'oeuvres.

22. Julie's autistic brother lives in Tucson. The two children are premature adults, abandoned by their parents and largely ignored by their foster parents (pun surely intended). The setup suggests how upset the fracture in his parents' marriage may have left Wallace.

23. There may also, as ever, have been an element of parody to the story, Wallace trying out the sort of heartfelt encounter that teachers like Penner admired. (If so, it did not work. When he submitted it to his fiction workshop the instructor, Buzz Poverman, another teacher who favored realism, told him, others in the class remember, that it was "not a story.")

24. In the interview Wallace gave to Larry McCaffery, he made a try at explaining the dynamic of his surprising public success: "I'm an exhibitionist who wants to hide, but is unsuccessful at hiding; therefore, somehow I succeed." He cut the comment before the interview was published in 1993.

25. The story went through a number of intriguing titles before settling on "My Appearance." Wallace called it at various times "40," a reference to the actress's age, "All Things to One Man," "Lettermania," and "Late Night."

26. Wallace's acceptance to Yaddo showed some of his academic sleight of hand. Richard Elman was one of his recommenders. "I'll shine your shoes for a week," he'd written his old teacher, asking for his help. He'd also asked Jonathan Penner, who wrote a glowing endorsement.

Chapter 4: Into the Funhouse

1. Wallace may have first encountered the poem in the famous early advertisements for a farm implement, which he knew:

The Plough That Broke the Plains . . . McCormick Reaper
  Westward the Course of Empire Takes Its Way

He was also aware of the painting by Emanuel Leutze that hangs in the Capitol.

2. The fried roses, whose "noisomely oily smell" Wallace confirmed on the family stove, was central enough to his thinking that he chose it for the title of the story and the collection, until Nadell objected.

3. Wallace told Costello that another character in the story, Magda, the orange-faced stewardess—"an aloft waitress, she terms it"—of the story, came from real life. While he was working on "Westward," a flight attendant who was a fan of postmodernism recognized him from the sketch the *Wall Street Journal* had published alongside their article. She took him to her condo in Hartford for three days.

4. The passsage plays off Barth's own essays on literature and generational conflict with their premise that the aesthetic of modernism was no longer useful and something new had to be found.

5. He would add in a 2002 letter to the critic Marshall Boswell, in the course of his by then customary putdown of *The Broom of the System*, "The best thing to come out of that was that I still have the same agent, and she's a dear friend and merciless critic."

6. He would later speak of "sort of an artistic and religious crisis" in these months, words reminiscent of his description of the breakdown that first spurred his creativity at Amherst in 1983.

7. He usually drank alone until he lost consciousness. He would describe himself in a later interview as "sort of a joyless drinker."

8. After *Broom*'s success, the IRS claimed Wallace owed them money. He had always been a careful taxpayer, part of his midwestern upbringing of cooperation and order. "A certain Uncle wants a certain sum far in excess of proper family obligation," he wrote Howard in surprise. The problem was traced to an erroneous 1099 form. Wallace dashed off an explanation and there it ended, though he would have other similar mix-ups with the agency over the years. Perhaps these planted an interest in the agency.

9. These sorts of paradoxes were of absorbing interest to Wallace and extended beyond verbal tricks for undergraduates; they feature in much of twentieth-century mathematical logic. They also play a role in *Broom*, where a plot point revolves around a riddle whose implications Wittgenstein wrestles with in his *Tractatus*: The barber cuts the hair of anyone who doesn't cut his own hair. Who then cuts the barber's hair?

10. Wallace did not overestimate the appeal of this habit. He wrote to Franzen that tobacco chewing "turns the mouth to hamburger in a week, is stupid and dangerous, and involves goobing big dun honkers every thirty seconds."

11. The program Wallace joined stressed anonymity. For that reason I don't identify it by name and use the first name and first letter of the last name when quoting members who spoke about Wallace.

12. He would in a 1990 letter to Jonathan Franzen explain that the role drugs played in his writing was "not working under the influence, but somehow using the influence as a counterpoint to the work—hard to explain." This is somewhat evasive; according to Costello, he also wrote high.

13. "Title imposed by editor," he wrote Brad Morrow, who ran *Conjunctions*, noting that he now found the story "Girl with Curious Hair" "pretty gross."

14. In later years, Wallace would boast about "a seventeen-page letter about literary theory" that he had written to Howard to argue his editorial vision for *Broom*, but there is no such letter; he was either misremembering his explanation to the Viking legal department or trying to make a grim experience more palatable.

15. The nineteenth-century German critic Gustav Freytag designed a widely used triangular representation of a typical story line, in which the action rises to the climax or moment of reversal and then descends through the denouement.

16. Wallace was not always so impressed with the idea that his generation faced unique challenges. He wrote an undergraduate in 1995 that the idea was "a lot of hooha. Kids write about Jeopardy and Letterman exactly the way elders write about trees and the sky-reflecting mudpuddle. It's what's there." Then, reconsidering his reconsideration, he added, "That may be a bit disingenuous."

17. Amy Wallace says her brother exaggerates. Their father came from nonpracticing Catholics. Their mother was from a religious family but her own parents were not church-goers. "David and I were encouraged to believe what we wanted," she says.

18. "Order and Flux in Northampton" is an homage/parody of James Joyce. Wallace shared Joyce's fascination with wordplay though they approached literature from very different perspectives. But he took what he wanted from other writers. He told Mark Costello that he had gotten the idea of the discontinuous interview numbers in *Brief Interviews* after reading in a biography that Joyce loved putting puzzles in his work.

19. His intense sense of competitiveness returned quickly though. Reading the work of William Vollmann, he felt a familiar twinge of envy and anger. When he learned that Vollmann's new book, *The Rainbow Stories*, was also about to be published, he worried that *Girl* was "going to get dwarfed by that fucker Vollmann's coming out only a month sooner," as he wrote Brad Morrow. He also tarred Vollmann's first novel, *You Bright and Risen Angels*, with being, of all things, "too Pynchonian."

20. When Steven Moore mentioned in a letter that he was submitting Wallace's essay "Fictional Futures and the Conspicuously Young" for a $1,000 prize, Wallace joked, "My nose could use the grand."

21. Bangs in turn likely got the image from Pynchon's *Gravity's Rainbow*, in which Roger Mexico's heart "grows erect, and comes."

22. Costello's literary aspirations would bear fruit in a pseudonymous noir novel, *Bag Men*, published in 1997, and *Big If*, which came out in 2002 and was nominated for a National Book Award.

23. This rating should be taken in context. Wallace turned to letters when his fiction was not going well, so his letters rarely report a good day's work. All the same, in mid-1989 he was clearly frustrated. Adrift in his current work, he devalued his old. *Broom* he was embarrassed by, though *Girl with Curious Hair* he still admired. It had furnished "some real personal mind-blowing successes," he wrote his friend Franzen.

24. When *Boogie Nights* came out in 1997, Wallace called Costello and told him the movie was exactly the story that he had been trying to write when they lived together in Somerville.

25. Vollmann's reportage among prostitutes and skinheads in San Francisco for stories like "Ladies and Red Lights" and "The White Knights" likely inspired Wallace's own attempt to mix reporting and fiction in his pornography novel.

26. Franzen did not win the grant until 1996, but he did get a Whiting Award that year thanks in part to Wallace (as did Vollmann).

27. Jim Wallace remembers his son's surprise at the hierarchical nature of the Harvard program. "The students did their professors' laundry and clustered around them, and he thought that was just ridiculous. He was a published author and expected to be treated as an equal."

28. The attentive observation in *Infinite Jest* of Denial Aisle—the back row at recovery meetings full of "catexic newcomers crossing and uncrossing their legs every few seconds and sniffing compulsively and looking like they're wearing every thing they own"—likely comes from this period.

Chapter 5: "Please Don't Give Up on Me"

1. Wallace found it funny that a "marine hospital" should be nowhere near water.

2. Wallace fictionalized Larson with affection in *Infinite Jest*. "It turned out Pat Montesian liked the color black a lot. She was dressed—really kind of overdressed, for a halfway house—in black leather pants and a black shirt of silk or something silky," he writes of the executive director of Ennet House.

3. All the same Wallace liked to quote one of the veteran recovery members, the group known in *Infinite Jest* as "the crocodiles," who told him, "It's not about whether or not you believe, asshole, it's about getting down and asking."

4. Members of recovery groups were supposed to be anonymous. So when *Infinite Jest* with its many scenes set in a thinly fictionalized Granada House came out, Wallace was forced to dissemble. "I mean," he told an interviewer, "I got very assertive research and finagle-wise. I mean, I *hung out*. There were twelve halfway houses in Boston, three of which I spent literally *hundreds* of hours at."

5. Big Craig didn't trust Wallace when he first met him. Marijuana was a lightweight addiction in his eyes. Craig was just out of prison; Wallace was just out of Harvard. "My suspicions were that he was looking for material for a book," he remembers.

6. Wallace was well aware that suffering could help a writer produce his best work. In Somerville he had read Paul De Man's essay "The Rhetoric of Temporality" and wrote "brilliant" when he came upon the following disquisition on authorship: "The mere falling of others does not suffice; he has to go down himself. The ironic, twofold self that the writer or philosopher constitutes by his language seems able to come into being only at the expense of his empirical self, falling (or rising) from a stage of mystified adjustment into the knowledge of his mystification."

7. The exchange was not entirely so serious. Wallace also gave Franzen some practical advice for his upcoming stay at Yaddo: "Seek out the artists and composers. I've found them almost without exception nicer!! Less cliquish, and less apt to fuck with your head than the fiction writers. Poets tend to be OK as long as they're old. Avoid any fiction writer you don't already know. Do not fuck anyone (you'll pay a huge psychic price later)."

8. A few years later he would tell a recovery audience that during this time the only way he could stop his whirring brain was either to masturbate or go to a movie and sit in the front row.

9. Wallace similarly hyped Costello to Karr. "I expected to meet some guy that was like seven feet tall, wearin' a cowboy hat, chewing tobacco, with his dick coming out the bottom of his pant leg," she remembers.

10. "The big reason" for the prohibition, Wallace explained ably in *Infinite Jest*, "is that the sudden removal of Substances leaves an enormous ragged hole in the psyche of the newcomer, the pain of which the newcomer's supposed to feel and be driven kneeward by . . . and intense romantic involvements . . . tend to make the involvees clamp onto one another like covalence-hungry isotopes, and substitute each other for meetings and Activity in a Group and Surrender."

11. Around this time Karr was working on an essay on poetry called "Against Decoration," published in *Parnassus* in 1991, where she took as the twin poles of authorial error "absence of emotion" and "lack of clarity." She urged poets to move their readers, writing that emotional response was the main goal of art, and was not shy in passing on the same message to Wallace. When he told her he had put certain scenes into *Infinite Jest* because they were "cool," she responded, "that's what my fucking five year old says about Spider-man."

12. The book was a platform for some of the themes Wallace had first tried out in Arizona, especially the damage wrought by irony. "Serious rap's so painfully real," he wrote, "because it's utterly mastered the special 80s move, the 'postmodern' inversion that's so much sadder and deeper than just self-reference: rap resolves its own contradictions by *genuflecting* to them."

13. Big Craig had a role in inspiring the climactic scene in *Infinite Jest* too. He had his wisdom teeth out with only Novocaine.

14. A typical line from an ad featuring the pathologically inaccurate spokesman: "Hi, I'm Joe Isuzu and I used my new Isuzu pickup truck to carry a two-thousand-pound cheeseburger." The prospect that horrified Wallace most was that Americans were so used to being lied to that any other relationship with media would feel false.

15. When the critic Marshall Boswell wrote to Wallace in May 2002 to ask when he had started *Infinite Jest*, Wallace replied, "It doesn't work like that for me. I started *IJ* or somethin' like it several times. '86,'88,'89. None of it worked or was alive. And then in '91–'92 all of a sudden it did."

16. At Arizona Wallace wrote a character sketch, which he called "Las Meninas," in which a young African American woman named Wardine is beaten by her mother, who is jealous that her boyfriend is attracted to her daughter. Likely for some years the sketch stood alone, but in *Infinite Jest* it becomes connected to other stories. Wardine's mother's boyfriend lives in the same housing project where an addict named Poor Tony goes to buy drugs (the project was actually close to Granada House). Poor Tony, a transvestite, in turn winds up visiting a store run by a pair of Quebecois terrorists.

17. There exists an early two-page draft of a scene from *Infinite Jest* titled "What Are You Exactly." In the brief scene, Hal (called "David") goes for a visit to a man described as a professional conversationalist, who turns out to be his father in disguise. The scene is reminiscent of the therapy sessions between Lenore and Dr. J. in *Broom*; both share an unacknowledged sadness and a brittle despair.

18. The word "Incandenza" also appears on a list of character names Wallace made on the title page of *Erotic Communications*, a collection of readings that he used in Somerville for his research on pornography.

19. The addicts' time at Ennet House is in some way therapy for an overdose of consumerism. In the margins of his copy of Lewis Hyde's *The Gift*, Wallace noted, "AA's = those driven mad w/ fear by the paradigm of scarcity in a commodity/capitalist economy; require return to basically 1st-century communism of spirit."

20. She diverges from Wallace grammatically when she asks her psychiatrist, "Listen, have you ever felt sick, I mean nauseous? Like you knew you were going to throw up?"

21. Both Gompert and Erdedy wind up in Ennet House, along with others of Wallace's troubled legions, the facility proving an effective fictional device for Wallace. For where else do addicts congregate but a rehab house? It is their Rick's.

22. In the letter to Larson, sent nearly two years after the incident, Wallace says that he kept his plan from Karr for fear she'd think he was "crazy and reject me."

23. He also went to various locksmiths in Boston and explained that he was a postmodern novelist doing research on how to disarm a burglar alarm system. "Finally," remembers Mark Costello, "the fifth didn't throw him out."

24. Wallace had an interest in his family's Scottish origins. He went to see *Braveheart*, the story of William Wallace, the national hero, when it came out in 1995. And as he moved from city to city, among the few possessions he brought with him was a painting of a Scottish battle scene his father had given him.

25. As Rick Vigorous comments in *Broom*, "It's when people begin to fancy that they

actually know something about literature that they cease to be literarily interesting, or of any use to those who are."

26. "Poor me, poor me, pour me a drink" was a standard warning against self-pity in recovery, one that Wallace would cite in *Infinite Jest*.

27. Wallace admired Raymond Carver, whom he distinguished from his minimalist acolytes (Wallace dismissed them as "crank turners"). He was a man who had outrun alcohol in moving from a deflected style to a more sincere one, and Wallace doubtless saw the relevance to his own story.

28. Hints of effeminacy always brought out a bit of Wallace's anxiety. When he moved to Illinois he placed a special order from a Bloomington store for T-shirts with dark squares on the front meant to hide what he saw as his flabby chest.

29. As he explained in a later letter to the critic Sven Birkerts, he found writing directly onto a computer to be like "think[ing] out loud onto the screen," adding, "Writing by hand and typewriter not only brings out the best in me—it brings out stuff I never would have dreamed was there. . . . It is this—not improvement, but transfiguration of the contents of my head that I am addicted to. It is astonishing when it happens—magical— and it simply doesn't happen on a computer."

30. A hint as to Karr's motive is to be found in *Infinite Jest*, where her stand-in, Joelle Van Dyne, comments, "Never trust a man on the subject of his own parents. As tall and basso as a man might be on the outside, he nevertheless sees his parents from the perspective of a tiny child, still, and will always. And the unhappier his childhood was, the more arrested will be his perspective on it. She's learned this through sheer experience."

31. The name was a source of some amusement to Wallace, viz this from *Infinite Jest*: "That in metro Boston the idiom of choice for the male sex-organ is Unit, which is why Ennet house residents are wryly amused by E.M.P.H. Hospital's designations of its campus's buildings."

32. Typically, Wallace met DeLillo through worries about plagiarism. He was concerned that DeLillo's work was a too obvious source for the Eschaton scene in *Infinite Jest*, in which Ennet Academy students pretend to wage a nuclear war with computers and tennis balls. DeLillo, who admired Wallace's writing, responded that it was not, a generous gesture given the scene's overlap with his novel *Endzone*.

Chapter 6: "Unalone and Unstressed"

1. In *Infinite Jest* the government sells naming rights to each year. The year in which the key action in the story takes place is the "Year of the Depend Adult Undergarment," which most Wallace researchers agree was 2009. There is, however, one bit of data that points to 2011, possibly an error, possibly a deliberately misleading clue on Wallace's part.

2. Marathe is an example of the pleasure Wallace takes in recursion: He is a quadruple agent whose Quebecois bosses think he is a triple agent. In other words, he pretends that he is only pretending to betray the people he is in fact betraying.

3. In *Infinite Jest*, Wallace traces Americans' neediness with a Freudian touch to the original mother-infant bond. The lethal "Infinite Jest" cartridge is said to consist of a baby looking up at a mother's face, the mother intoning, "I'm sorry. I'm so terribly sorry. I am so, so sorry. Please know how very, very, very sorry I am."

4. "Ticket to the Fair" was not the first time Wallace had improved on reality. In "Tennis, Trigonometry, Tornadoes," for instance, he says he was born in Philo, Illinois, a claim that later found its way onto websites and into books on the author. And who but an East

Coast reader would have believed that a tornado could blow up out of nowhere and suddenly sweep Wallace and his tennis opponent over the net, "blown pinwheeling for I swear it must have been fifty feet over to the fence one court over"? As Amy Wallace remembers, in the Wallace family, "We quietly agreed that his nonfiction was fanciful and his fiction was what you had to look out for."

5. Wallace was aware that he had transgressed, and many times he hinted to journalists that their rules weren't his, as in an interview he gave to a writer for the *Boston Phoenix* in 1998: "The thing is, really—between you and me and the *Boston Phoenix's* understanding readers—you hire a fiction writer to do nonfiction, there's going to be the occasional bit of embellishment."

6. The problem of how to use an innovative writing style to carry out a conservative fictional purpose would become Wallace's biggest artistic challenge and would prove insurmountable in *The Pale King*.

7. One suspects the silver lamé outfit was borrowed from Wurtzel and the vomit, as at the Illinois State Fair, was invented, both being, in magazine fact-checking parlance, on author. A description of losing to a nine-year-old girl at chess in the ship's library that only appears in the book version of the piece also has the sort of headlong specificity that characterized Wallace's enhancements for effect, viz: "My first inkling of trouble is on the fourth move, when I fianchetto and Deirdre knows what I am doing is fianchettoing and uses the term correctly. . . . My second ominous clue is the way her little hand keeps flailing out to the side of the board after she moves, a sign that she is used to a speed clock. She swoops in with her developed QK and forks my queen on the twelfth move."

8. The news reports Wallace refers to were probably about Grant Medeiros, fourteen, of Saanich, British Columbia. On February 17, 1995, on the last night of a cruise aboard the *Royal Princess*, Medeiros vanished. His eyeglasses and shoes were found on the deck, and he left his necklace and a note in his parents' cabin, but no one saw him jump, and his body was never found. The press ascribed his misery to fighting with his parents over having to join them on the cruise. The part about a "a ship-board romance" was likely Wallace's invention.

9. On the junior circuit, Wallace and his friends had run into a player with the name of the movie star; this spurred them to make lists of ordinary people with famous names.

10. When Big Craig read the novel after it was published he remembers thinking, "Holy crap! The bastard was just looking for information." For all that Wallace subscribed to the ethos of anonymity in recovery, his fiction always came first. "You didn't get sober to fuck people over [but] it's a hazard in writing," he wrote a friend.

11. Another source for the name may have been the nickname he and Costello shared for junior lawyers, "compliance drones."

12. He wrote in a notebook a few years later, "My dog-emotions shifted when Drone came—there was sort of one to break my heart w/ goodness and one who was 'trouble.'"

13. Blue is a dominant color in *Infinite Jest*. One character is killed drinking Drano, "blue like glittershit"; another reveals "a blue string" behind an eyeball; Joelle vomits "blue smoke" into "the cool blue tub" when she hits bottom; the Charles is transformed to "robin-egg's blue" by the Clean US Party; the skies of the novel range from "Dilaudid-colored" to "pilot-light blue"; one section begins simply, "The following things in the room were blue."

14. Wallace was becoming a brand of his own. "I think he will fulfill Nick's request for a big-name writer," an editor at *Tennis* wrote a colleague after approaching Wallace to write a piece on the U.S. Open for the magazine.

15. The point of his style he omitted. Perhaps he thought it was self-evident, but in a

similar fax to *Harper's* before the editing of a piece he published in 1998 on Kafka, he explained that his goal was to "preserve an oralish, out-loud feel" to his writing. That piece began as a talk, but it is also true of *Infinite Jest*. You are meant to think of it as a story being spoken rather than written—or even better, thought.

16. As Amy Wallace remembers, when mother and son discussed *Infinite Jest* that winter, Wallace insisted to his mother that Avril Incandenza was not based on her. She was not persuaded, and the parts of the book about Avril left her deeply upset.

17. Rock music was the cultural venue in which signs of disaffection and dis-ease first appeared with serious energy. In the early 1990s bands like Pearl Jam and Nirvana sang of alienation and sophisticated frustration. Their music emphasized the personal rather than the political, much as Wallace's fiction did.

18. At a panel discussion on ethnicity and literature in 1998 held in Seattle, Wallace indicated that he understood his privileged status. When the moderator announced that the authors—the others were Sherman Alexie, Cristina García, and Gish Jen—would discuss their experience as members of marginalized minorities, Wallace picked up his chair and with comic exaggeration moved it to the side of the stage.

19. Younger readers had an easier time with *Infinite Jest*'s structure. It was in fact an undergraduate who captured Wallace's strategy best. In the fall of 1995, Christopher Hager, who was studying literature with Gilbert Sorrentino at Stanford University, wrote to the author to discuss *Girl with Curious Hair*. Wallace offered him a galley of his next work instead if Hager would get his friends to buy the book when it came out, joking that if they bought ten copies among them, it would increase Little, Brown's net sales "by at least 25%." In "On Speculation: Infinite Jest and American Fiction after Postmodernism," his undergraduate thesis, Hager captured the novel's "incomplete" ending with delicacy:

The resolution that reviewers complain the novel lacks isn't *in* the text, but sits chronologically & spatially in front of the novel proper, which, as a satellite dish, serves to focus myriad rays of light, or voices, or information, on that central resolution without actually touching it.

Wallace was thrilled; battered by critics who said the novel just sort of stopped, he was waiting for just this type of reading. He offered a similar thought about the book in an online chat room for the e-zine *WORD* in May, saying that "there is an ending as far as I'm concerned. Certain kind of parallel lines are supposed to start converging in such a way that an 'end' can be projected by the reader somewhere beyond the right frame. If no such convergence or projection occurred to you, then the book's failed for you."

20. Journalists in general were unsure what to make of the sincerity Wallace had worked so hard to earn. Interviewing him for *Infinite Jest*, Laura Miller of Salon.com described him as having the manner of "a recovering smart aleck." Wallace, though, was clear in his own mind that the change from who he had been was real. When an interviewer asked him what the old Wallace would have thought of his new writing, he answered, "I don't think he would have hated it—I just don't think he woulda *read* it. I think he would've looked at the first two pages and gone, 'Huh! Wonder who likes this kind of stuff?' And then looked for something else."

21. "Using skills . . . only Elizabeth has," as Wallace would comment in a later interview.

22. Perhaps more apropos to Wallace's own struggle was Nirvana's mournful ballad "All Apologies," whose last chorus, repeated over and over, is often quoted as "All alone is all we are." (The official version on the liner notes reads: "All in all is all we are.")

23. The grunge references probably irritated Wallace, who told friends he'd never heard of Nirvana until after the suicide of Kurt Cobain, the band's lead singer, in April 1994. "A grad student lent me some tapes," he remembered in a letter to a friend written

in the late 1990s, "and I came rushing in the next day saying I thought these guys were kind of brilliant and had anybody ever heard of them . . . the students were too embarrassed for me even to laugh. (That's a true story, by the way.)" Which most friends doubt it is.

24. Similar assurances allowed Wallace to give Nadell free rein to do with his film rights as she saw fit throughout his career.

Chapter 7: "Roars and Hisses"

1. When he went over his 1993 piece on television, "E Unibus Pluram," he added—or more likely, restored from the draft of the article—another dig at Mark Leyner, changing his identification from "writer" to "New Jersey medical ad copywriter," in fact one of the jobs Leyner had held before he became a novelist.

2. Wallace told one young mother he was dating he was jealous that her breasts were "no longer public property," but in less petulant moods he acknowledged a worthy competitor. "Babies," he told Mark Costello, "are famous to themselves."

3. Wallace was an extraordinary listener, with "a way of attending that is at once intense and assuasive: the supplicant feels both nakedly revealed and sheltered, somehow, from all possible judgment." (The description is of Lyle, the weight room guru in *Infinite Jest*.)

4. The syllabus averred, "If, in a piece of creative nonfiction, an event is claimed to have happened, it must happen." But in the classroom Wallace was known to be the less dogmatic of the two teachers when it came to literal accuracy, and one senses his hand in a later sentence on the syllabus: "And yet, the 'creative' half of the title suggests an impulse rather than Enlightenment perspicuity motivates the writer and shapes the writing."

5. An alternate reading of "The Depressed Person" is that the author sympathizes with her. The space he gives to narrating her experiences confers a validity to them, a gift that mimics at the same time the gift of therapy.

6. When from Las Vegas he called Francis B. to complain the mirror on the ceiling was keeping him from sleeping, his friend told him to roll over.

7. Wallace liked the way unwritten questions forced the reader to use his or her imagination. He had practiced the form in a six-page endnote in *Infinite Jest* in which Hugh Steeply, the O.N.A.N. agent, posing as a female journalist, interviews Orin Incandenza. The only voice we hear is Orin's.

8. Wallace had first come upon the story of a man who specialized in finding such women in *Cracking Up*, a psychoanalytic casebook published in 1996.

9. The problem with the relationship might be captured on either side by the comment the outraged male narrator of "Here and There" makes about his girlfriend: "She regarded the things that were important to me as her enemy, not realizing that they were, in fact, the 'me' she seemed so jealously to covet."

10. His habit was worsened by Nardil, which increases nicotine's addictiveness.

11. In 1999, he sent DeLillo a card with the words, "May the peace and blessing of almighty God descend upon you and remain with you forever" on it and added the quip, "Today's Catholic isn't afraid to send cards like this." Later he mailed another one, with a token indicating he had made an offering at mass, with the words, "Already paid for—like a sort of cosmic gift certificate."

12. Franzen would later capture his impression of the relationship in one of a suite of stories called "Break-Up Stories," published in the *New Yorker*, in which a Heidegger-

spouting university instructor insists he is going to marry his girlfriend even as he is scouting around for the next woman.

13. At some point in the late 1990s, Wallace hired a prostitute. It was a logical step for a writer who was interested in the point where sex and marketing met. Plus it was an opportunity for a new experience. Wallace negotiated a price of $200 but when he got into bed with the woman he lost his desire. "We sort of 'cuddled and talked' instead," he wrote Evan Wright, who had helped him with his adult entertainment awards article for *Premiere* in 1999; "she was nice about it."

14. Gale Walden's father, whom Wallace admired, had left the ministry to become an IRS agent, a living metaphor.

15. In a notebook entry, Wallace suggests that Drinion might be the child in the micro-story "Incarnations of Burned Children," and that his penis photographs better than one that has not been scarred by scalding water.

16. It is likely that this plot about a porn performer whom the viewer can digitally replace with himself dates back to the pornography novel that Wallace abandoned in the late 1980s; he mentions the video technology in *Signifying Rappers*, which he was working on around the same time.

17. Other names the novel had, at least briefly, included *Glitterer*, *Net of Gems*, *What Is Peoria For?* and *Sir John Feelgood* (Drinion's nom de porn).

18. The theme of the novel is anticipated in an essay Hal Incandenza submits for "Mr. Oglivie's seventh-grade Introduction to Entertainment Studies" in *Infinite Jest*, about a future television hero who represents the conclusion of a lineage that begins with the "hero of action" (Steve McGarrett of *Hawaii Five-O*) and passes on to the "hero of reaction" (Frank Furillo of *Hill Street Blues*). "We await," Hal writes, "I predict, the hero of *non*-action, the catatonic hero, the one beyond calm, divorced from all stimulus, carried here and there across sets by burly extras whose blood sings with retrograde amines."

19. Its previous tenant had been Planned Parenthood. Wallace told Costello that if he got bombed or shot there, the police should look for right-to-lifers with an outdated phonebook.

20. The earnest authenticity that was Wallace's core literary voice had by now spread far. It was even in the process of being appropriated by advertising, no doubt to Wallace's horror. But the change was bigger than this. The 1980s era of masculine hyper-certainty that had spawned Wallace in rebellion was far in the past. He had helped to move the culture and, with the culture moved, the question he had to answer was what new to write against.

21. Wallace told the *New York Times Magazine* that Franzen exercised in black socks, but then felt ashamed, as he wrote DeLillo. (The comment was not used in the article.)

22. "He spent his entire life apologizing to me," Amy Wallace remembers. "Almost every time I saw him he'd apologize."

23. As did others. The *Onion*, the satirical newspaper, ran a parody with the headline "Girlfriend Stops Reading David Foster Wallace Breakup Letter at Page 20" in February 2003, shortly before he left Bloomington.

Chapter 8: The Pale King

1. But, as Wallace himself would have asked, was he writing these letters to be open and honest or merely to make Green believe he was open and honest—which would actually make him the opposite?

2. Stecyk's flaw, in Wallace's eyes, was the same as that of the men described in *Brief*

Interviews who are so busy worrying about pleasing their sex partners that they get no pleasure themselves; being pleased is an indispensable part of giving pleasure, just as being helped is an indispensable part of being helpful.

3. The story may have been inspired by an episode of Lars von Trier's *The Kingdom*, a show Wallace loved.

4. Wallace had met DeLillo only one time before for a dinner set up by Franzen at an East Village restaurant in 1998. He was amazed then at how much the older writer looked and sounded like his father.

5. Zeno's dichotomy is the idea that motion is impossible because it requires an infinite series of submotions. To get somewhere, you must first get halfway there, but to get halfway there you must first get halfway *there*, and so on.

6. The two longest are set in offices. What drew Wallace to office life were its codes of conduct, the implicit restraints on the individual that were so lacking in his own life. For him office life bore the same relation to real life that literature did. It was a beguiling simulacrum, a cleaned-up imitation, a playful variation with rules.

7. A draft of "Good Old Neon" ends, "Ghosts talking to us all the time—but we think their voices are our own thoughts."

8. After Costello read *Oblivion* he told Wallace it could be the road map for *The Pale King*. Wallace snapped back, "You don't understand how tough the problem actually is."

9. This was a past he made mild attempts to deny over the years. To an acquaintance who read in Marshall Boswell's *Understanding David Foster Wallace* that the author had had a promiscuous period in the late 1980s, he responded, "Huh? I've never been 'promiscuous' though I would have loved to. . . . Where do people get this stuff[?]" To another he refuted stories about Elizabeth Wurtzel: "I know her, may have been at the same table as her at a coupla dinners. But we have never 'dated.'"

10. Wallace enjoyed having younger sponsees in particular. "Sometimes he finds out he believes something that he doesn't even know he believed until it exits his mouth in front of five anxious little hairless plump trusting clueless faces," the narrator reflects on Hal in *Infinite Jest*, where his job is to be a Big Buddy to younger players.

11. The speech, transcribed from a recording made by a member of the Wallace-l email list, moved around the Internet quickly, to Wallace's surprise. When an acquaintance mentioned seven months later that he had read it, Wallace wrote back, "I never gave Kenyon a transcript of it. Much of it was handwritten. I don't get it."

12. From the notebooks for *The Pale King*: "Would that we scrutinized our technology the way we do our people."

13. This passage updates nicely Wallace's insistence in his "Fictional Futures" essay that successful contemporary writing must recognize "a loss of innocence about the language that is its breath and bread."

14. In 2007, when a former colleague from Illinois State University, Becky Bradway, asked him to explain for a textbook she was writing the role research played in a novel, Wallace wrote back, "What's tricky is just what you're asking: how much is enough? You can drown in research. I've done it. I'm arguably doing it now."

15. In a later section of the novel, a picture of the infant on his desk comforts Dean, an evangelical Christian, in a moment of despair. Dean is processing forms, trying to visualize a sunny beach as the agency taught him to do during orientation, but he cannot maintain the image—it turns in his mind to a gray expanse covered with "dead kelp like the hair of the drowned." Overcome with boredom, he considers suicide. "He had the sensation of a great type of hole or emptiness falling through him and continuing to fall and never hitting the floor."

16. Wallace informs the reader that during a suspension from college he was hired by the IRS as a wiggler. "I arrived for intake processing at Lake James, IL's I.R.S. POST 047, sometime in mid-May of 1985," he writes. Upon arriving at the intake center, he is mistaken for another David Wallace—a high-powered accountant transferring to the facility from Rome, New York. For much of the chapter, everyone at the IRS thinks that David Foster Wallace is the other Wallace, a double to his fictional double.

17. From a notebook: "Beneath S[tecyk]'s niceness is incredible rage. Sadism. Waiting only to be unleashed. His rage is a secret within a secret—a secret even from himself."

18. In keeping with his new maturity, Wallace also became more straitlaced about the need for literal accuracy in nonfiction. When Becky Bradway, his former colleague at Illinois State, wrote him for her textbook on creative nonfiction in 2007 and asked what his standard of accuracy was in his writing, he answered, "We all knew, and know, that any embellishment is dangerous, and that a writer's justifying embellishment via claiming that it actually enhances overall 'truth' is *exceedingly* dangerous, since the claim is structurally identical to all Ends Justify Means rationalizations."

Works by Wallace

Throughout this book I quote liberally from David's work. To avoid clutter, unless otherwise indicated in the chapter-by-chapter notes that follow, quotations are drawn from the following editions of David's work.

FICTION

David Foster Wallace, "The Planet Trillaphon as It Stands in Relation to the Bad Thing," *Amherst Review*, 1984.

———. "Solomon Silverfish," *Sonora Review*, Fall 1987.

———. *The Broom of the System* (New York: Penguin, 1987).

———. *Girl with Curious Hair* (New York: W. W. Norton, 1989).

———. *Infinite Jest* (New York: Little, Brown, 1996).

———. *Brief Interviews with Hideous Men* (New York: Little, Brown, 1999).

———. *Oblivion: Stories* (New York: Little, Brown, 2004).

———. *The Pale King* (New York: Little, Brown, 2011).

NONFICTION

———. "Fictional Futures and the Conspicuously Young," *Review of Contemporary Fiction*, Spring 1988.

——— and Mark Costello, *Signifying Rappers: Rap and Race in the Urban Present* (New York: Ecco Press, 1990).

———. "The Horror of Pretentiousness," *Washington Post*, February 19, 1990.

———. "The Empty Plenum: David Markson's 'Wittgenstein's Mistress,'" *Review of Contemporary Fiction*, Summer 1990.

———. "Tennis, Trigonometry, Tornadoes," *Harper's*, December 1991.

———. "Rabbit Resurrected," *Harper's*, August 1992.

———. "E Unibus Pluram: Television and U.S. Fiction," *Review of Contemporary Fiction*, Summer 1993.

———. "Ticket to the Fair," *Harper's*, July 1994.

———. "Shipping Out: On the (Nearly Lethal) Comforts of a Luxury Cruise," *Harper's*, January 1996.

———. "Feodor's Guide," *The Village Voice*, April 9, 1996.

———. "John Updike, Champion Literary Phallocrat, Drops One," *New York Observer*, October 13, 1997.

———. "Neither Adult nor Entertainment," *Premiere*, September 1998.

———. "The Weasel, Twelve Monkeys, and the Shrub," *Rolling Stone*, April 13, 2000.

———. "The View from Mrs. Thompson's," *Rolling Stone*, October 25, 2001.

———. "Tense Present: Democracy, English and the Wars over Usage," *Harper's*, April 2002.

———. Everything and More: A Compact History of ∞ (New York: W. W. Norton/Atlas Books, 2003).

———. "Consider the Lobster" in *Consider the Lobster: Essays* (New York: Little, Brown, 2005).

A NOTE ON SOURCES

Much of what I know about David came from my interviews with his many friends, family, and professional associates thanked in the acknowledgments section. A second source are his books and the third avenue are his extraordinary letters, loaned to or copied for me by dozens of correspondents. David may have been the last great letter writer in American literature (with the advent of email his correspondence grows terser, less ambitious). Happily several of these collections are now or about to be available at the Ransom Center at the University of Texas in Austin, where Wallace's papers are housed and where scholars and researchers can consult them. In addition, much of Wallace's juvenilia and marginalia from which I quote are now at The Ransom.

ADDITIONAL SOURCES, BY CHAPTER

Chapter 1: "Call Me Dave"

3   "My father's got," from David Lipsky, *Although of Course You End Up Becoming Yourself* (New York: Broadway, 2010) at 49.
6   "This schizogenic," from an interview with Larry McCaffery for the *Review of Contemporary Fiction*, Summer 1993.
7   "a really serious jock," from Lipsky, *Although of Course*, at 52.
8   "imposter syndrome," from a letter to Rich C., September 19, 2000.

Chapter 2: "The Real 'Waller'"

18   "a way to hide," from Stacey Schmeidel, "Brief Interview with a 5-Draft Man," *Amherst Magazine*, Spring 1999.
23   "foppish aesthetes," from the McCaffery interview.
24   "not trusting me with reality," from a letter to Mary Karr, circa January 22, 1992.
25   "special sort of buzz," from McCaffery interview.

25	"required thumbing-the-nose," from an appearance on *The Charlie Rose Show*, March 27, 1997.
26	"Any relationship" and "The Sabrina Brothers in the Case of the Hung Hamster," from *Sabrina*, Fall 1982.
28	"the smell of flowers" and "dealing with, yes," from a letter to Corey Washington, June 30, 1983.
29	"practically rammed," from a letter to Corey Washington, August 20, 1983.
30	"Pretty [as Updike's prose was]," from the McCaffery interview.
30	"God damn Charlie," from a letter to Corey Washington, July 1, 1983.
30	"Don't do LSD," from a letter to Corey Washington, August 5, 1983.
31	"It comes into your dreams," from Thomas Pynchon, *The Crying of Lot 49* (New York: Harper Perennial, 1999) at 73.
31	"so much so that," from a letter to Steven Moore, March 7, 1988.
32	"a kind of midlife crisis," from the McCaffery interview.
32	"The same obsessive studying," from the Schmeidel interview.
32	"a teenyweeny bit," from a letter to Corey Washington, August 20, 1983.
33	"I came very close," from a letter to Corey Washington, November 1, 1983.
34	"You now see before you," from a letter to Corey Washington, October 4, 1983.
35	"a weird kind of forger," from Lipsky, *Although of Course*, at 258.
37	*Roses are Red*, from a letter to Corey Washington, December 4, 1983.
38	"almost like having," from an appearance on *The Charlie Rose Show*, March 27, 1997.
39	"A mite better than," from Alan Lelchuk, *Miriam in Her Forties* (New York: Houghton Mifflin, 1985), at 329.
40	"It's really ulcer-city," from a letter to William Kennick, February 4, 1985.
41	"It seems sort of cheaty," from a letter to Corey Washington, July 15, 1983.
43	"Blob-like" and "out of control," from a letter to William Kennick, February 4, 1985.
44	"I got to wondering," from a letter to Gerry Howard, January 21, 1986.
44	"the loss of the whole external world," from the McCaffery interview.
44	"The world is everything," from Ludwig Wittgenstein, *Tractatus Logico-Philosophus* (New York: Cosimo Classics, 2010) at § 1.
44	"This book will perhaps," from Wittgenstein's *Tractatus*, at 27.
45	"the sensitive tale," from the McCaffery interview.

Chapter 3: "Westward"

50	"Instead of the 'guru' system," from a letter by Mary Carter, February 12, 1985.
50	"I don't have any money," from a letter to John Leggett of the Iowa Writers' Workshop, April 9, 1985.
53	"a vast sprawl," from Pynchon, *Crying of Lot 49*, at 14.
53, 54	"A real blast," "I'm not ready or able," "a kind of urine-yellow," and "Perhaps only half true," from a letter to Corey Washington, August 25, 1985.
54	"replete with poisonous spiders," from a letter to William Kennick, undated, circa November 6, 1985.
54	"You use a propane torch," from a letter to Corey Washington, August 25, 1985.
55	"trapping little inspirations," from "Westward the Course of Empire Takes Its Way."
55	"I love it here, Corey," from a letter to Corey Washington, September 14, 1985.

57   "I was a prick," from Loren Stein, "David Foster Wallace: In the Company of Creeps," *Publishers Weekly*, May 3, 1999.

60   "rung his cherries," from an interview with Laura Miller for Salon.com, March 9, 1996.

65   "I've been advised," from a letter to Frederick Hill Associates, September 28, 1985.

66   "I defy you," from a letter to Bonnie Nadell, November 7, 1985.

66   "I would have called myself Seymour Butts," from a letter to Don DeLillo, circa February 2, 2001.

67   "as a newly hatched chick," from Leon Neyfakh, "Gerry Howard on Discovering, Editing, and Hatching David Foster Wallace, *New York Observer*, September 17, 2008.

67   "not, of course, letting her know," from a letter to Corey Washington, December 30, 1985.

68   "If this seems fast" and "neurotic and obsessive," from a letter to Gerry Howard, January 21, 1986.

68   "This Carver/Apple joke" and "The more you condense," from a letter by Gerry Howard, January 10, 1986.

69   "while potentially disgusting" and "a whole set of readers' values," from a letter to Gerry Howard, January 19-20 1986.

70   "You cheat yourself," from a letter by Gerry Howard, January 10, 1986.

70   "made an enormous, haunting impression," from a letter to Gerry Howard, January 19-20, 1986.

70   "I admit to a potentially irritating," from a letter to Gerry Howard, January 16, 1986.

70   "geriatrics emerge," from a letter to Gerry Howard, January 16, 1986.

70   "I am young and confused," from a letter to Gerry Howard, January 19-20, 1986.

71   "It is a great joy," from a letter by Gerry Howard, to Bonnie Nadell, January 13, 1986.

71   "Rick, Lenore, and the G.O.D.," from a letter to Gerry Howard, January 16, 1986.

74   "two broken cars limping across the desert," from Gale Walden, "Road Trip," published in *Wisconsin Review*, 2010.

74   "the next three years at least," from a letter to Corey Washington, September 14, 1985.

76   "Wallace does not," from an essay in *Wigwag*, republished in Sven Birkerts, *American Energies* (New York: Random House, 1994).

77   "It's hot, here," from a letter to Corey Washington, July 13, 1986.

77   "copy-edit the copy-editor," from a letter to Bonnie Nadell, April 29, 1986.

77   "Hoping Very Much I'll Never," from a letter to Gerry Howard, July 2, 1986.

77   "No autobiography, no cocaine," from a letter by Gerry Howard to Don DeLillo, July 16, 1986.

77   "As wild elk produce many elkins" and "You must not," from a letter by Richard Elman, February 20, 1986.

77   "I would be hard put," from a letter by Richard Elman to Gerry Howard, December 19, 1986.

79   "going through both a lawsuit," from a letter to Bonnie Nadell, March 28, 1987.

79,   "I got darned little work done" and "I leave at dawn," from a letter to Corey Wash-
80   ington, September 6, 1986.

81   "a puerile Pynchon," from *Kirkus Reviews*, January 1, 1986.

81   "The guy seemed downright angry," from a letter to Gerry Howard, January 2, 1987.

81   "Maybe they never found out," from a letter to Gerry Howard, January 30, 1987.

81   "a hot book ... a terrific novel," from Rudy Rucker, "From the Mixed-Up Files of Lenore Beadsman," *Washington Post*, January 11, 1987.

81   "an enormous surprise," from Caryn James, "Wittgenstein is Dead and Living in Ohio," *New York Times*, March 1, 1987.

82   "rich reserves," from Michiko Kakutani, "Life in Cleveland, 1990," *New York Times*, December 27, 1986.

82   "I didn't think," from a letter to Gerry Howard, January 2, 1987.

82   "kind of down," from a letter to Gerry Howard, January 2, 1987.

82   "Bonnie, I've never had more difficulty," from a letter to Bonnie Nadell, March 28, 1987.

82   "You would think," from Helen Dudar, "A Whiz Kid and His Wacky First Novel," *Wall Street Journal*, April 24, 1987.

83   "Nice, in a condescending way," from a letter to Bonnie Nadell, April 30, 1987.

83   "I'm so nervous about the reading," from a letter to Bonnie Nadell, March 28, 1987.

83   "The reading went really well," from a letter to Bonnie Nadell, April 6, 1987.

84   "I guess the engagement," from a letter to Bonnie Nadell, April 14, 1987.

84   "Could you give," from a letter to Dale Peterson, circa April 18, 1987.

84   "I'm not interested in fiction," quoted in William R. Katovsky, "Hang 'Im High," *Arrival*, April 1987.

85   "It was my first hint," from Lipsky, *Although of Course*, at 170.

85   "w/r/t the fact," from a letter to Gerry Howard, April 25, 1988.

87   "try . . . to fuck," from a letter to Bonnie Nadell, April 6, 1987.

87   "I am working on a lot," from a letter to Dale Peterson, February 15, 1986.

87   "I think they're good," from a letter to Bonnie Nadell, February 11, 1986.

87   "Not a nice noise, Bonnie," from a letter to Bonnie Nadell, September 7, 1987.

87   "too smart for its own good," from Alice Turner, quoted in a letter to Bonnie Nadell, April 30, 1987.

87   "Wallace clearly is," from a letter by C. Michael Curtis to Bonnie Nadell, June 2, 1986.

88   "cruising . . . at a wildly" and "Maybe to Breadloaf," from a letter to JT Jackson June 9, 1987.

Chapter 4: Into the Funhouse

89   "God I feel lucky," from a letter to JT Jackson, June 9, 1987.

90   "It is . . . important to" from John Barth, "Lost in the Funhouse" in *Lost in the Funhouse* (Anchor, 1988) at 74.

90   "The diving would make" from Barth, "Lost in the Funhouse," at 82.

91   "this tiny, infinitely dense thing," from Lipsky, *Although of Course*, at 229.

95   "I've never been," from a postcard to JT Jackson, August 6, 1987.

96   "Who's Who in the Cosmos 1987," *Esquire*, August 1987.

98   "like, a week," from Patrick Arden, "David Foster Wallace Warms Up," *Book Magazine*, 1999.

98   "I'm sure page for page," from a letter to Bonnie Nadell, September 20, 1987.

98   "in my view far and away" and "If the story seems pretentious," from a letter to Jonathan Franzen, August 13-14, 1989.

99   "I actually cried in front," from a letter to Bonnie Nadell, September 20, 1987.

99   "like a real person," from a letter by Dale Peterson, August 7, 1987.

100   "less seedstrewn accommodations," from a letter by Dale Peterson, July 27, 1987.

100   "Her little ticker didn't," from a letter by Dale Peterson, August 7, 1987.

100   "a horror show," from the McCaffery interview.

100   "I wanted something," from a letter to Jonathan Franzen, August 13-14, 1989.

101   "a kind of suicide note," from Lipsky, *Although of Course*, at 61.

101   "picked up a bit," from a letter to JT Jackson, September 20, 1987.

101   "not really all that nice," from a letter to Corey Washington, September 25, 1987.

101   "I'm squatting amid boxes," from a letter to Bonnie Nadell, September 2, 1987.

101   "Please please get me," from a letter to Bonnie Nadell, September 20, 1987.

103   "I'm basically on my own," from a letter to Forrest Ashby, September 13, 1987.

103   "The view from my apartment," from a letter to a freind, November 9, 1987.

104   "just so *unbelievably* bad," from Lipsky, *Although of Course*, at 62.

104   "I've hurt not just me," from a letter to a friend, November 9, 1987.

105   "gorgeous new poetesses," from a letter to JT Jackson, September 20, 1987.

105   "I think I've again," from a letter to Forrest Ashby, February 8, 1988.

105   "too hung over," from a letter to Corey Washington, February 8, 1988.

106   "Much fiction," from a letter by Alice Turner, April 29, 1988.

107   "p. 148 David," from a letter to Gerry Howard, April 25, 1988.

109   "They didn't even think," from Lipsky, *Although of Course*, at 225.

109   "daunting . . . but that obviously," from a letter to Steven Moore, October 26, 1987.

112   "I miss the heat," from a letter to Corey Washington, May 17, 1988.

113   "I'm enclosing a small," from a letter to Dale Peterson, September 5, 1988.

115   "I'm having a lot of trouble," from a letter to Jonathan Galassi, June 21, 1988.

116   "remote," from a letter to Jonathan Franzen, September 11, 1988.

116   "By now I expect maybe you've heard," from a letter to Bonnie Nadell, October 23, 1988.

117   "They were unpleasant," from a letter to Rich C., December 30, 1988.

117   "Isn't it a marvelous feeling," from a letter by Gerry Howard, December 21, 1988.

118   "far and away the worst," from a letter to Rich C., December 30, 1988.

118   "I have only very recently," from a letter to Steven Moore, January 18, 1989.

118   "Personally I love sending," from a letter to Brad Morrow, February 9, 1989.

119   "I figure if I ever," from a letter to Brad Morrow, March 7, 1989.

119   "95% Portuguese and Brazilian," from a letter to Jonathan Franzen, May 2, 1989.

120   "It's lovely and crowded" and "I may well be," from a letter to Steven Moore, April 17, 1989.

121   "the exact part of my nose," from a letter to Steven Moore, May 1, 1989.

123   "Boston is *fun*," from a letter to Bonnie Nadell, May 26, 1989.

123   "fuck strangers," from Lipsky, *Although of Course*, at 63.

123   "I'm bogged down," from a letter to Jonathan Franzen, May 2, 1989.

124   "You'd be surprised," from a letter to Bonnie Nadell, May 11, 1989.

125   "Alice has been marvelous," from a letter to Bonnie Nadell, May 26, 1989.

125   "was not meant to carry," from a letter to Steven Moore, August 18, 1989.

125   "Stay Fly, and Shit," from a letter to Bonnie Nadell, July 5, 1989.

126   "The thing I like about," from a letter to Steven Moore, May 12, 1989.

126   "carve out two days," from a letter to Steven Moore, May 25, 1989.

126   "Fine prep. For the innumerable," from a letter to Steven Moore, August 18, 1989.

127   "looking into celibatee," from a letter to Bonnie Nadell, August 22, 1989.

127   "Thank God I don't," from a letter to Kathe Burkhart, August 1, 1989.

127   "You seem doomed," from a letter to Kathe Burkhart, August 24, 1989.

127   "toddle off with my Get Smart," from a letter to Jonathan Franzen, undated, circa summer 1989.
127   "intro german plus," from a letter to Steven Moore, May 12, 1989.
128   "short journalistic version," from a letter to Bonnie Nadell, August 22, 1989.
128   "horribly long," from a letter to Bonnie Nadell, August 22, 1989.
128   "This magazine is way," from a letter by Alice Turner, July 5, 1989.
128   "confusion, misunderstanding, deception," from a letter to Alice Turner, July 11, 1989.
128   "I must say," from a letter by Alice Turner, July 17, 1989.
128   "too much impressed," from *Kirkus Reviews*, July 15, 1989.
128   "a real brown helmet," from a letter to Brad Morrow, July 3, 1989.
128   "a dynamic writer of extraordinary talent," from Jenifer Levin, "Love Is a Federal Highway," *New York Times*, November 5, 1989.
129   "What is the fiction writer," from an essay in *Wigwag*, republished in Sven Birkerts, *American Energies* (New York: Random House, 1994).
129   "A lot of it is like being," from a letter to Steven Moore, September 5, 1989.
130   "the best young writer going," from a letter to Steven Moore, May 1, 1989.
130   "simply separates sock from pod," from a letter to Jonathan Franzen, May 2, 1989.
130   "more than a bubble," from a letter to Jonathan Franzen, May 25, 1989.
130   "By merely abstracting," from a letter by Jonathan Franzen, July 22, 1989.
131   "This Jonathan Franzen guy," from a letter to Steven Moore, August 25, 1989.
131   "sentimental pretentious pseudo-autobiographical," and "extensively explained dislike," from a letter to Jonathan Franzen, August 13/14, 1989.
132   "The book is not yet out," from a letter to Bonnie Nadell, November 1, 1989.
132   "a kind of shrill," from Lipsky, *Although of Course*, at 229.
132   "This book is dying," inscription in book for Rich C., October 17, 1989.
133   "as though the entire," from Lipsky, *Although of Course*, at 68.
134   "The lovely medical staff," from a letter to Brad Morrow, October 30, 1989.

Chapter 5: "Please Don't Give Up on Me"

135   "Armageddon," from the McCaffery interview.
136   "hard-core recidivist" and "I am getting booted," from a letter to Bonnie Nadell, November 28, 1989.
138   "every bad '60s novel," from Lipsky, *Although of Course*, at 233.
138   "Give me a little time," from a letter to Steven Moore, January 3, 1990.
138   "I'm not going anywhere," from a letter to Brad Morrow, December 18, 1989.
138   "I am" and "Most of the guys," from a letter to Dale Peterson, December 21, 1989.
139   "a motorhead from the South Shore," from a letter to David Markson, July 29, 1990.
139   "It's a rough crowd," "I try hard to listen," and "I'm scared," from a letter to Rich C., December 21, 1989.
140   "They gave me Librium," from a letter to Rich C., August 24, 2000.
141   "nobody is as gregarious," from Lipsky, *Although of Course*, at 138.
141   "going from Harvard to here," from a letter to Dale Peterson, December 21, 1989.
142   "I think part of why WM" and "one a vapid gushy," from a letter to Steven Moore, January 3, 1990.
143   "The bald fact," from a letter to Jonathan Franzen, May 1, 1990.
144   "some laffs and companionship," from a letter by Jonathan Franzen, May 5, 1990.

144   "a kind of a ripping" and "the humble, unpaid work," from a letter to Jonathan Franzen, May 21, 1990.

145   "[f]iction for me is a conversation," from a letter to Jonathan Franzen, August 13-14, 1989.

145   "I'd love to hear more," from a letter to Jonathan Franzen, May 21, 1990.

146   "so blank and depressed," from a letter to David Markson, June 7, 1990.

146   "I cannot sit still," from a letter to David Markson, July 29, 1990.

148   "a hip kids' college," from a letter to David Markson, October 18, 1990.

148   "Teaching is going OK," from a letter to Jonathan Franzen, September 9, 1990.

148   "We spend most of our time," from a letter to David Markson, October 18, 1990.

149   "rather like asking the Consul," from a letter to David Markson, July 29, 1990.

149   "would be 'sumptuous,'" from a letter to David Markson, October 18, 1990.

149   "They're all 'television' majors," from a letter to David Markson, January 6, 1991.

149   "I want to start trying," from a letter to Steven Moore, November 20, 1990.

151   "I've gone from thinking," from a letter to Steven Moore, October 26, 1990.

151   "I am the best copyeditor," from a letter to Steven Moore, November 20, 1990.

151   "couldn't even take," from a letter to Steven Moore, December 14, 1990.

151   "every shred of will," from a letter to David Markson, April 21, 1991.

152   "flat and strained," from a letter to Jonathan Franzen, November 5, 1990.

152   "The people I've known there," from a note to Jonathan Franzen, April 21, 1991.

152   "I think that eventually," from a letter by Jonathan Franzen, July 22, 1991.

152   "I finally told Mary," from a letter to Jonathan Franzen, June 7, 1991.

152   "Nothing is new," from a letter to Fred Brooke, June 27, 1991.

153   "The apartment is strange," from a letter to Jonathan Franzen, October 4, 1991.

153   "back to back in the afternoon," from a letter to Jonathan Franzen, October 4, 1991.

154   "Please don't give up on me," from a letter to Bonnie Nadell, Spring 1991.

155   "slowly trying some fictional stuff," from a letter to Forrest Ashby, August 8, 1991.

155   "writing quite a bit and enjoying it," from a letter to Dale Peterson, August 23, 1991.

157   "mostly just to see what you think," from a letter to Jonathan Franzen, September 19, 1990.

158   "decided that maybe being really sad," from Lipsky, *Although of Course*, at 237.

158   "The key to '92 is that MMK was most important," from the marginalia in Wallace's copy of Ernest Kurtz, *The Spirituality of Imperfection*.

158   "The writing is going," from a letter to Mary Karr, undated, circa spring 1992.

162   "the bravest thing," from Lipsky, *Although of Course*, at 241.

162   "Life is good," from a letter to Brad Morrow, February 29, 1992.

162   "a novel," from a letter to Bonnie Nadell and Gerry Howard, April 5, 1992.

163   "one of the scariest days," from a letter to Deb Larson, December 6, 1993.

163   "this soot-fest city," from a letter to Brad Morrow, February 29, 1992.

164   "best of pals and lit combatants," from a letter to Jonathan Franzen, June 8, 1992.

164   "among the most nourishing for me," from a letter to Jonathan Franzen, April 10, 1992.

164   "Syracuse," from a letter to Debra Spark, May 27, 1992.

165   "make me feel both unalone and unstressed," from a letter to Jonathan Franzen, June 8, 1992.

166   "If words are all we have," from a letter to Jonathan Franzen, July 15, 1992.

166 "I simply have to *pound*," and "it's awfully pretty here," from a letter to Jonathan Franzen, June 8, 1992.

167 "The Era of Skulking seems," from a letter to Debra Spark, August 19, 1992.

167 "movies where shit blew up," quoted in Evan Hughes, "Just Kids," *New York*, October 9, 2011.

167 "I want you to know that I AM here," from a letter to Mary Karr, undated, circa 1992.

169 "so much hidden pain and lying," from a letter to Mary Karr, circa January 22, 1992.

169 "it heals too," from a letter to Mary Karr, undated, circa spring 1992.

170 "terrible temper-outbursts," from a letter to Jonathan Franzen, September 12, 1992.

170 "MARRY ME," from a letter to Mary Karr, undated, circa fall 1992/winter 1993.

171 "gut instinct (I have so few gut instincts . . .)," from a letter to Michael Pietsch, June 22, 1992.

172 "a . . . go-for-the-gold-type," from a letter to Gerry Howard, June 30, 1992.

172 "Brains and wit and technical tightrope-calisthenics," from a letter to Michael Pietsch, June 22, 1992.

173 "My notion about Mark Leyner," from a letter by Michael Pietsch, July 8, 1992.

173 "I am both bogged down," from a letter to Jonathan Franzen, September 12, 1992.

173 "My whole nervous system," from a letter to Alice Turner, December 11, 1995.

174 "I alert you in advance," from a letter to Charlie Harris, December 26, 1992.

175 "Full-time writing is going OK," from a letter to Debra Spark, undated, circa winter 1992/spring 1993.

176 "upping it to three or four," from a letter to Charlie Harris, April 5, 1993.

176 "a certain icky sense about availing myself," from a letter to Don DeLillo, March 14, 1993.

176 "the least weird writer there," from a letter to Corey Washington, March 2, 1993.

176 "The chairman is a dreamboat," from a letter to Dale Peterson, February 28, 1993.

Chapter 6: "Unalone and Unstressed"

177 "different masculine-model cars," from a letter to Corey Washington, March 2, 1993.

178 "sardonic worldview perfect for the irony-filled nineties," from a letter to Steven Moore, April 10, 1993.

178 "polite and banal", from a letter to Corey Washington, April 16, 1993.

178 "Take this time to learn to be," from a letter to Brandon Hobson, March 31, 1993.

178 "Even a marginal," from a letter to Corey Washington, April 16, 1993.

180 to the "john," from a letter to a friend, March 13, 1998.

180 "I'm having to countenance," from a letter to Jonathan Franzen, September 12, 1992.

180 "Unpacking, trying to write," from a letter to Brad Morrow, August 17, 1993.

181 "off sex," from a letter to Linda Perla, October 15, 1993.

182 "You ask what I think it's about," and "Almost everything," from a letter by Michael Pietsch, June 10, 1993.

186 "here's-what-I-think," from "Finite Jest," *Slate*, September 17, 2008.

189 "It's just much easier having dogs," from Lipsky, *Although of Course*, at 97.

191 "HOPE THIS IS READABLE," from a letter to Sven Birkerts, November 14, 1993.

191   "80% different from Little Brown's," from a letter to Steven Moore, January 25, 1994.
191   "The trick in a case like this," from a letter by Michael Pietsch, November 18, 1993.
191   "no longer manufactured outside like Eastern Europe" and "A lot of this," from a letter to Michael Pietsch, January 16, 1994.
194   "I'm mortified to have essentially," from a letter to Michael Pietsch, April 2, 1994.
195   "extremely analgesic," from a letter to Michael Pietsch, April 29, 1994.
196   "handcuffed to a wrist," from a letter to Michael Pietsch, May 27, 1994.
196   "I am sad and empty" and "stuff in the mss," from a letter to Jonathan Franzen, July 23, 1994.
198   "ominous hernia-jokes," from a postcard to Jonathan Franzen, circa July 1994.
198   "having this monster in my head," from a letter by Michael Pietsch, October 21, 1994.
199   "Hal's breakdown, the one," from a letter by Michael Pietsch, November 30, 1994.
199   "I guess maybe" and "frontispiece," from a letter to Michael Pietsch, February 19, 1995.
199   "we know exactly," from a response to a letter by Michael Pietsch, circa May 1995.
200   "it's not," from a letter by Michael Pietsch, May 12, 1995.
200   "I bought a house," from a letter to Don DeLillo, May 1995.
202   "Prospects for an acute and fecund," from a postcard to Jonathan Franzen, circa March 1995.
203   "I go through a loop," from a letter to Elizabeth Wurtzel, circa April 1995.
205   "I am uncomfortable," from a letter to Don DeLillo, circa May 1995.
205   "you feel incipient bladder," from a letter to Michael Pietsch, circa May 1995.
205   "a state of editorial ecstasy," from a letter by Michael Pietsch, May 12, 1995.
205   "Here's what happened," and "I'm prepared to thumbwrestle," from a letter by Michael Pietsch, May 22, 1995.
206   "Potential insertion into page 1229," from a fax to Michael Pietsch, June 11, 1995.
208   "a cover that's (troublingly, to me)," from a letter to Don DeLillo, September 10, 1995.
208   that all the magazine editors in New York, from the Schmeidel interview.
208   "a little stupider and shmuckier," from Lipsky, *Although of Course*, at 41.
209   "your/our copyeditor," from a letter to Michael Pietsch, February 19, 1995.
210   "To copyeditor: Hi," from a letter to Mike Mattil, undated, circa fall 1995.
210   "in the 8th circle of page-proof-proofreading hell," from a letter to Debra Spark, October 1995.
210   "The more I proof these page proofs," from a letter to Michael Pietsch, October 1995.
210   "about 47,000 typos," from a letter to Alice Turner, December 11, 1995.
210   "about 712,000," from R. Z. Sheppard, "712,000 Typos!" *Time*, February 19, 1996.
211   "wobbling like a vestibulitiser's," from a letter to Mike Mattil, October 8, 1995.
211   "wholly ominous given our family's," from a letter to Alice Turner, December 11, 1995.
211   "*fucking, fucking* nightmare," from Lipsky, *Although of Course*, at 248.
211   " 'Masterpiece'? I'm 33 years old," from a letter to Michael Pietsch, September 20, 1995.
212   "About the holes and lacunae," from a letter to David Markson, November 28, 1995.
216   "brilliant but somewhat bloated," from *Publishers Weekly*, January 29, 1996.

216   "almost certainly the biggest and boldest," from *Kirkus Reviews*, December 1, 1996.

216   "mov[ed] toward us like an ocean disturbance," from Sven Birkerts, "The Alchemist's Retort," *The Atlantic*, February 1996.

216   "not for the faint-hearted," from *Library Journal*, January 1996.

216   "Challenging and provocative," from John Harper, "A Wordy, Wacky World View," *Orlando Sentinel*, March 17, 1996.

216   "brashly funny and genuinely moving," from Bruce Allen, "Future Imperfect," *Chicago Tribune*, March 24, 1996.

216   "the funniest writer of his generation," from Jonathan Dee, "Infinite Fest," *The Village Voice*, March 1996.

216   "Next year's book awards," from Walter Kirn, "Long Hot Novel," *New York*, February 12, 1996.

216   "that sneery thing in *Esquire*," from a letter to David Markson, November 28, 1995.

216   "Hype of the Huge," from Will Blythe, *Esquire*, December 1995.

216   "I'm very happy with the launch," from a letter by Michael Pietsch to Bonnie Nadell, January 23, 1996.

217   "The overall effect," from Jay McInerney, "Infinite Jest," *New York Times Book Review*, March 3, 1996.

217   "The book seems to have been written," from Michiko Kakutani, "A Country Dying of Laughter. In 1,079 Pages," *New York Times*, February 3, 1996.

218   "To say that," from Birkerts, "The Alchemist's Retort."

218   "This is sort of what it's like to be alive," quoted in Mark Caro, "The Next Big Thing," *Chicago Tribune*, February 23, 1996.

219   "Sauron's great red eye," from a postcard to Don DeLillo, August 21, 2001.

219   "a whole wall of letters that help me or are important," from a letter to Don DeLillo, March 16, [1996].

219   "I went with friends," from David Gates, "Levity's Rainbow," *Newsweek*, February 12, 1996.

220   "They pretend they're kissing you," from Frank Bruni, "The Grunge American Novel," *New York Times Magazine*, March 24, 1996.

220   "or the Illinois version," from Valerie Stivers, "The Jester Holds Court," stim.com, May 1996.

221   "there's a way that it seems to me," from an appearance on *The Charlie Rose Show*, March 27, 1997.

221   "When I was younger," from the Scocca interview.

222   "not a hip downtown kind of book," from a letter by Bonnie Nadell to Beth Davey, November 3, 1995.

222   "I think I made it a project *not* to look," from Lipsky, *Although of Course*, at 178.

223   "packed and scary," from a letter to Don DeLillo, circa March 16, 1996.

224   "you guys made your bones," from a letter to Don DeLillo, circa March 16, 1996.

224   "brain fart," from Lipsky, *Although of Course*, at 98.

224   "a *serious* asshole," reading " 'I've Cheated,' " from Lipsky, *Although of Course*, at 99.

225   "It reminds me of the exhilaration," from a letter by Michael Pietsch, April 18, 1996.

225   I . . . tried my best to tell the truth," from a letter to Don DeLillo, circa March 16, 1996.

226   "WAY MORE FUSS," from a letter to JT Jackson, circa April 1996.

Chapter 7: "Roars and Hisses"

227   "weird warm full," from Lipsky, *Although of Course*, at 283.

227   "lumber salesm[e]n and Xerox," from a letter to Alice Turner, December 11, 1995.

227   "The Icky Brothers," from a letter to a friend, December 28, 1997.

227   "horses in the yard," from a letter to Don DeLillo, March 16, 1996.

227   "Mostly I try to remember," from a letter to David Markson, June 24, 1996.

227, 228   "spasms-trips" and "the lump," from a letter to Michael Pietsch, April 10, 1996.

228   "make extra room," from a letter to Don DeLillo, June 25, 1997.

228   "basically an enormous," from an appearance on *The Charlie Rose Show*, March 27, 1997.

228   "passionate and deeply serious," from Brigitte Frase, "A Writer Flails His Way Toward Honesty," *San Francisco Chronicle*, March 9, 1997.

228   "eager to notate," from James Wood, review of "A Supposedly Fun Thing I'll Never Do Again," *Newsday*, 1989.

229   "reveals Mr. Wallace," from Laura Miller, "A Supposedly Fun Thing I'll Never Do Again," *New York Times*, March 16, 1997.

229   "Here's why I'm embarrassed," from an interview with Charlie Rose, March 27, 1997.

230   "I mean, can you see," from a letter to a friend, June 27, 1998.

230   "blissfully ignorant of," from a letter to Alice Turner, December 11, 1995.

231   "I find myself," from an interview with Charlie Rose, March 27, 1997.

232   "literally crazy," from a letter to a friend, December 28, 1997.

232   "fetish for conquering," from a letter to Michael Pietsch, February 19, 1995.

232   "I've wanted a black room," from a letter to Brad Morrow, November 24, 1996.

233   "Real isn't how," from Margery Williams, *The Velveteen Rabbit* (Doubleday, 1958) at 5.

233   "serial high-romance," from a letter to Rich C., August 24, 2000.

233   "and come close," from a letter to a friend, December 28, 1997.

234   "tuggy stuff" and "the people selling," from a letter to a friend, December 3, 1997.

234   "This living hand," from "This living hand, now warm and capable," John Keats, *Selected Poems* (Penguin Classics, 2007) at 237.

235   "writing is going," from a letter to Don DeLillo, September 7, 1996.

235   "weird little 1-pagers," from a letter to Brad Morrow, November 11, 1996.

235   "the spiritual emptiness," from the Stein interview.

235   "jejune," from a letter to Don DeLillo, September 10, 1995.

236   "The novel is a fucking killer," quoted in a letter to Don DeLillo, September 19, 1995.

236   "Maybe what I want," from a letter to Don DeLillo, October 10, 1995.

236   "All right, your first book," from a letter by Don DeLillo, November 6, 1995.

237   "I'm gearing up," from a note to Steven Moore, January 13, 1997.

238   "A weird lightning-bolt," from a letter to Don DeLillo, September 11, 1996.

238   "which means I can take," from a letter to Steven Moore, October 8, 1996.

238   "basically to have projected," from a letter to Don DeLillo, May 20, 1997.

239   "nothing if not," from a letter to Rich C., August 24, 2000.

239   "the blow-jobs the culture gives," from a letter to David Markson, June 24, 1996.

239   "I am getting some writing," from a letter to Steven Moore, September 16, 1997.

240   "the version of myself," "a mask," "obliterated or something," "slightest mistake or

"paw at the reader's ear," from a letter to Don DeLillo, January 19, 1997.

"It makes me," from a letter to Alex Pugsley, May 15, 1998.

"Writing about real-life," from a letter to a friend, January 17, 1998.

"three days in Bosch's hell-panel," from a postcard to Don DeLillo, January 30, 1998.

"I don't think," from a postcard to Jonathan Franzen, January 10, 1998.

"particularly dark," from a letter to Michael Pietsch, August 17, 1998.

"late 90s notoriety," from a letter to Bonnie Nadell, August 29, 1998.

"Do I," from a letter to Bonnie Nadell, August 29, 1998.

"a parody (a feminist parody)," from a note to Andrew Parker, April 20, 1998.

"I see that Hal," from a letter by Michael Pietsch, February 6, 1997.

"I feel pretty good," from a letter to Michael Pietsch, August 17, 1998.

"not about the thing," from a letter to a friend, February 22, 1998.

"post-partum funk," from a letter to a friend, October 25, 1998.

"I've been going," from a letter to Brad Morrow, April 4, 1998.

"We snorkeled," from a postcard to Jonathan Franzen, November 4, 1998.

"Issues of usage," from a letter to Don DeLillo, November 25, 1998.

"It is a sad Christmas," from a card to Don DeLillo, December 1998.

"I always get the giggles," from a letter to Rich C., August 24, 2000.

"I too have used," from a note to Lee Freeman, Fall 1998.

"She was a girl," from J. D. Salinger, "A Perfect Day for Bananafish," in *Nine Stories* (Little, Brown, 1953) at 3.

"a collection of," from "Overlooked," *Salon*, April 12, 1999.

"mean to just about," from an interview with Michael Silverblatt on KCRW, August 12, 1999.

"The big Attention eyeball," from a letter to Brad Morrow, April 4, 1998.

"I'm in the midst of," from a letter to Steven Moore, June 4, 1999.

"The Statue Talks!" from a letter to a friend, December 28, 1997.

"just want[ed] to," from the Arden interview.

"I wanted to do," from an interview with Michael Silverblatt on KCRW, August 12, 1999.

"full-scale harassment," from Benjamin Weissman, "A Sleek and Brilliant Monster," *LA Weekly*, April 28, 1999.

"seemingly inexhaustible bag," from Andrei Cordescu, "Literary Cure," *Chicago Tribune*, May 23, 1999.

"another mad scientist," from Adam Goodheart, "Please Phrase Your Answer in the Form of a Question," *New York Times*, June 20, 1999.

"No doubt these," from Michiko Kakutani, "Calling Them Misogynists Would Be Too Kind," *New York Times*, June 1, 1999.

"The NY Times just," from a letter to Steven Moore, June 4, 1999.

"meta-ironic" and "Does Wallace's work," from A. O. Scott, "The Panic of Influence," *New York Review of Books*, February 20, 2000.

"The difference," from Seth Stevenson, "David Foster Wallace's Hideous Men," *Slate*, June 3, 1999.

"We fill pre-existing forms," from Frank Bidart, "Borges and I," in *Desire: Poems* (FSG, 1999) at 9.

257   "weird cultish Sikh," from a letter to Rich C., August 24, 2000.
258   "a long march," from a letter to Don DeLillo, November 3, 1999.
258   "visually raw," from a letter to Don DeLillo, March 21, 2000.
258–59   "Almost everything I," from a letter to Jonathan Franzen, circa summer 2000.
259   "I'm scared I can't," from a letter to Rich C., September 19, 2000.
260   "the brief weird excitement," from the optional foreword to "Up Simba," in *Consider the Lobster* (Little, Brown: 2005) at 159.
260   "three months that tickled" and "I do not know," from a letter to Don DeLillo, March 21, 2000.
261   "I know [enough]," from a letter to Jesse Cohen, June 29, 2000.
261   "on the side" and "Did you know," from a fax to Jesse Cohen, August 4, 2000.
261   "Cantor and the sheer," from a fax by Jesse Cohen, August 7, 2000.
262   "Most of my own," from a letter to David Markson, November 3, 2000.
262   "did a pretty good," from a letter to Don DeLillo, April 26, 2001.
262   "Highlights" and "gearing up for" from a postcard to Don DeLillo, August 20, 2001.
263, 264   "It's been a couple," "two periods," and "I apologize in advance," from a letter to Michael Pietsch, October 13, 2001.
264   "There's the whole," from an interview with Laura Miller, in *Salon.com*, March 9, 1996.
264, 265   "A genre is hardening" and "vitality at all costs," from James Wood, "Human, All Too Inhuman," *The New Republic*, August 30, 2001.
265   "the traditional galleys-and-proofs," from a letter to Don DeLillo, April 28, 2000.
265   "I struggle a great deal," from a letter to Rich C., August 24, 2000.
267   "The students actually," from a letter to Dale Peterson, March 2, 2001.
267   "home," from a letter to Brad Morrow, April 31, 2001.

Chapter 8: The Pale King

268   "What kind of zip code," from a letter to Don DeLillo, July 3, 2002.
268   "yellow snow," from a letter to Brad Morrow, March 21, 2003.
269   "closest thing to a child," from a letter to Brad Morrow, December 1, 2002.
270   "much less touristy or vulgar" and "pretty much hopelessly in love," from a letter to Brad Morrow, January 6, 2003.
270   "land of 1600 SAT scores," from a letter to Brad Morrow, April 30, 2001.
270   "We're hiring you," from Paul Brownfield, *Literary Star Out of Limelight, Los Angeles Times*, April 27, 2003.
270   "I have a lottery-prize-type gig," from an interview with Dave Eggers, *The Believer*, November 2003.
272   "own eccentric researching," from an email to Bonnie Nadell, April 4, 2003.
272   "enormous, pungent and extremely well-marketed," from "Consider the Lobster," *Gourmet*, August 2004.
273   "My audit group's," from *The Pale King* (New York: Little, Brown, 2011) at 387.
273   "I . . . did not think," from a letter to Don DeLillo, circa November 2002.
274   "I'm doing a book about math!" from a postcard to Steven Moore, January 13, 2002.
274   "wretched math book," from a postcard to Don DeLillo, July 3, 2002.
274   "both the math-editor," from a postcard to Don DeLillo, September 1, 2002.
274   "The galleys for," from a postcard to Don DeLillo, June 4, 2003.

276   "refreshingly conversational style," from John Allen Paulos, "Electrified Paté," *American Scholar*, Winter 2004.

276   "One wonders exactly whom," from David Papineau, "Room for One More," *New York Times*, November 16, 2003.

276   "mathematicians will view it," from Rudy Rucker, "Infinite Confusion," *Science*, January 16, 2004.

276   "Dr. Ragde," from a letter to Jesse Cohen, circa early 2004.

276   "the best of the stuff," from a letter to Michael Pietsch, October 13, 2001.

277   "unhappy, complicated, intellectualizing men," from a letter by Michael Pietsch, November 28, 2001.

277   "I don't feel much like an editor here," from a letter by Michael Pietsch, October 3, 2003.

279   "only the tiniest tasting," from Michiko Kakutani, "Life Distilled from Details, Infinite and Infinitesimal," *New York Times*, June 1, 2004.

280   "forest-killing manuscript," from Steve E. Alford, "Wordy Wallace Has New Stories," *Houston Chronicle*, June 13, 2004.

280   "Wallace has the right," Wyatt Mason, "Don't like it? You don't have to play," *London Review of Books*, November 18, 2004.

281   "Karen is rehabbing," and "It's a dark time," from an email to Jonathan Franzen, July 16, 2005.

282   "No more nymphs," from a postcard to Steven Moore, February 2, 2002.

282   "I hear Kath[y]," from an email to Jonathan Franzen, February 11, 2004.

282   "I am more and more," from an email to Jonathan Franzen, February 18, 2004.

283   "shitty motel," from a letter to Don DeLillo, January 26, 2005.

283–   "It's just this" and "Basically—I empathize," from a letter to Weston Cutter, un
84   dated.

284   "I'm poised, ready," from Brownfield, "Literary Star, Out of the Limelight."

285   "You're special," from a letter to Evan Wright, October 17, 1999.

286   "I allow myself," from a letter to Erica Neely, July 3, 2001.

288   "David Foster Wallace's 1996 opus," from Chad Harbach, "David Foster Wallace!," *n+1*, Issue 1, July 2004.

289   "I'm in awe," from an email to Jonathan Franzen, November 18, 2005.

289   "I too have," from an email to Jonathan Franzen, January 3, 2006.

289   "DeLillo's thing about," from an email to Jonathan Franzen, January 29, 2006.

289   "I go back and forth," from an email to Jonathan Franzen, June 6, 2007.

290   "It's . . . part-Rottweiler," from an email to Jonathan Franzen, September 26, 2006.

291   "It's absolutely wonderful," from a letter by Christopher Hamacher, March 7, 2006.

291   "Is it OK," from a letter to Christopher Hamacher, February 22, 2006

291   "You're not going," from a letter by Christopher Hamacher, July 8, 2006.

291   "I find that although," from a letter by Stephen Lacy to Wallace, September 5, 2005.

292   "Tax law is," from an email to Jonathan Franzen, April 22, 2007.

293   "Work is like," from an email to Jonathan Franzen, December 1, 2006.

292   "My own terror," from an email to Deborah Treisman, January 12, 2007.

294   "revelations revelationize," from a letter to Gerry Howard, January 16, 1986.

295   "Digital=abstract=<u>sterile</u>," from a postcard to Don DeLillo, dated July 21, 2000.

295   "The individual parts," from an email to Bonnie Nadell, April 23, 2007.

295   "I am, at present," from the Eggers interview.

296   "forgetting about writing," from an email to Jonathan Franzen, April 16, 2007.

296   "What are envied," from an unpublished interview with Didier Jacob. *Le Nouvel Observateur,* August 2005 (unpublished).
296   "to put some kind," from an email to Bonnie Nadell, April 20, 2007.
296   "I could take a couple of years," from an email to Bonnie Nadell, April 20, 2007.
297   "Let me noodle hard," from an email to Bonnie Nadell, April 23, 2007.
297   "I feel a bit 'peculiar'," from an email to Jonathan Franzen, August 4, 2007.
297   "disabling nausea/fatigue," from an email to Jonathan Franzen, September 20, 2007.
298   "Upside: I've lost," from an email to Bonnie Nadell, December 4, 2007.
298   "I got really," from a letter to Tom Bissell, February 16, 2008.
299   "We'll have big fun" and "I am not all right," quoted in David Lipsky, "The Lost Years and Last Days of David Foster Wallace," *Rolling Stone,* October 30, 2008.

NOTES

312   "None of the men," quoted in Lance Olsen, "Termite Art, or Wallace's Wittgenstein," *Review of Contemporary Fiction,* Summer 1993.
313   "passionately interested," from a letter to Richard Elman, circa September 23, 1985.
313   "there is nothing outside the text," from Jacques Derrida, *Of Grammatology,* trans. Gayatri Chakravorty Spivak (Baltimore: Johns Hopkins University Press, 1997) at 163.
314   "only me and Mom," from a letter to Corey Washington, January 14, 1986.
314   ". . . so that word," from a letter to Bonnie Nadell, October 31, 1985.
314   "I'm sure I may," from Leon Neyfakh, "Gerry Howard, on Discovering, Editing, and Hatching David Foster Wallace: 'He Was the First Person Who Ever Called Me "Mister,"'" *New York Observer,* September 17, 2008.
314   "I'm an exhibitionist," from an unedited transcript of the McCaffery interview.
314   "I'll shine your shoes," from a letter to Richard Elman, May 1, 1986.
315   "The best thing," from a response to Marshall Boswell's questionnaire, May 18, 2002.
315   "sort of an artistic," from David Lipsky, *Although of Course,* at 61.
315   "sort of a joyless," from Lipsky, *Although of Course,* at 142.
315   "A certain Uncle," from a letter to Gerry Howard, January 1, 1987.
315   "turns the mouth," from a letter to Jonathan Franzen, May 2, 1989.
315   "not working under," from a letter to Jonathan Franzen, May 1, 1990.
315   "Title imposed by editor," from a letter to Brad Morrow, March 18, 1988.
315   "a seventeen-page," from Lipsky, *Although of Course,* at 34.
316   "a lot of hooha," from a letter to Christopher Hager, October 28, 1995.
316   "going to get dwarfed," from a letter to Brad Morrow, March 7, 1989.
316   "too Pynchonian," from a letter to Steven Moore, March 7, 1988.
316   "My nose could use," from a letter to Steven Moore, March 7, 1988.
316   "grows erect, and comes," from Thomas Pynchon, *Gravity's Rainbow* (New York: Penguin, 1995) at 20.
316   "some real personal," from a letter to Jonathan Franzen, August 13/14, 1989.
317   "I mean, I got very assertive," from Lipsky, *Although of Course,* at 138.
317   "The mere falling," from Paul de Man, *Blindness and Insight: Essays in the Rhetoric of Contemporary Criticism,* 2d ed. (Minneapolis: University of Minnesota Press, 1983) at 187.

317   "Seek out the artists," from a letter to Jonathan Franzen, May 21, 1990.

317   "absence of emotion" and "lack of clarity," from Mary Karr, "Against Decoration," *Parnassus*, Spring 1991.

318   "It doesn't work like that," from a response to Marshall Boswell's questionnaire, May 18, 2002.

318   "crazy and reject me," from a letter to Deb Larson, December 6, 1993.

319   "think[ing] out loud," from a letter to Sven Birkerts, November 14, 1993.

320   "The thing is," from the Scocca interview.

320   "You didn't get sober," from a letter to Evan Wright, October 17, 1999.

320   "I think he will fulfill," from an interoffice memorandum by Jay Jennings to Donna Doherty of *Tennis* magazine, June 20, 1995.

321   "preserve an oralish," from a fax to Joel Lovell of *Harper's*, circa 1998.

321   "by at least 25%," from a letter to Chris Hager, October 28, 1995.

321   "The resolution that reviewers," courtesy of Chris Hager.

321   "there is an ending," from an interview with WORD e-zine, May 17, 1996.

321   "a recovering smart aleck," from the Miller interview.

321   "I don't think he would have hated it," from Lipsky, *Although of Course*, at 231.

321   "Using skills... only Elizabeth has," from Lipsky, *Although of Course*, at 5.

322   "A grad student lent me some tapes," from a letter to Michael Schur, circa 1998.

322   "May the peace and blessing," from a letter to Don DeLillo, circa July 1999.

323   "We sort of 'cuddled and talked' instead," from a letter to Evan Wright, April 28, 1999.

324   "Huh? I've never been 'promiscuous,'" from a postcard to Nick Solomon, March 27, 2006.

324   "I know her, may have been," from a letter to Marie Mundaca dated January 27, 1998.

324   "I never gave Kenyon a transcript of it," from a letter to Christopher Hamacher, February 22, 2006.

325, 326   "What's tricky is just what you're asking" and "We all knew and know," from a letter to Becky Bradway, February 2007.

INDEX